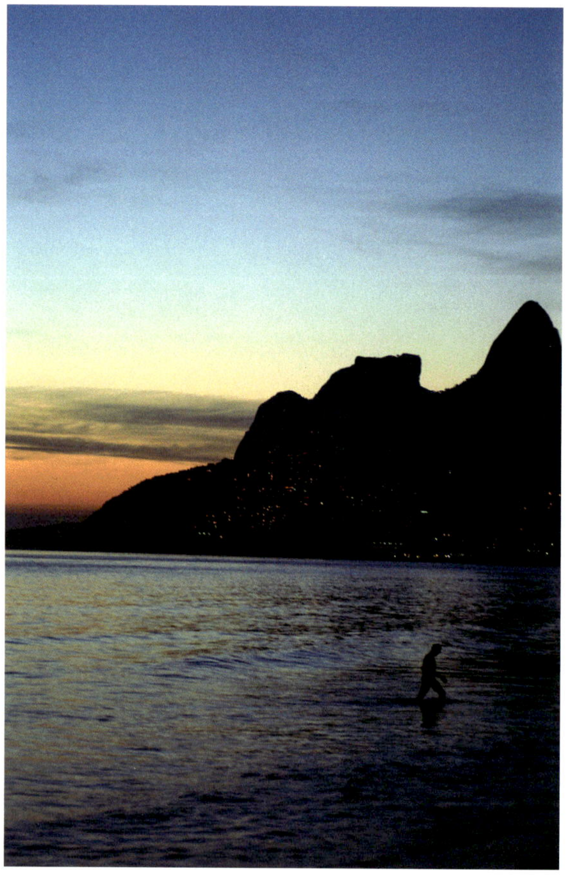

BRAZIL

As Origins Visuais da Cultura

Ralph Gibson

DAMIANI

DAMIANI

DAMIANI © 2005

DAMIANI EDITORE
Via Zanardi, 376
Tel. +39.051.6350805
Fax +39.051.6347188
40131 Bologna - Italy
www.damianieditore.it
info@damianieditore.it

Printed in Italy
Grafiche Damiani s.r.l.
www.grafichedamiani.it

Printed on
Ikono Silk 170gr.
distribuited by

antalis
antalis.com

Yemanjá has three sexes

BRAZIL

BRASIL is a place of many meanings. Many heartbeats occur simultaneously...this vast land is held in the eyes of hundreds of millions of humans who live there in the most amazing of all social experiments. If everything happens at the same time, then the reflected images of the place all become signs of what is happening, what will happen and what it means to be there. Is Brasil a sound or a smell or a woman? Is Brasil water or air or fever in the blood? A perfect example of Brasil is the most fundamental element...the purest water holding its own air and earth. Can the waters of the Rio Negro ever marry the Amazona in one coital embrace? Never together, never apart, never to die separated. Who loves this country loves the abstract and there is surely no Brasilian more abstract than Heitor Villa-Lobos. His 12 études for the guitar are a more visual portrait of the place than any words or images could dare to attempt.

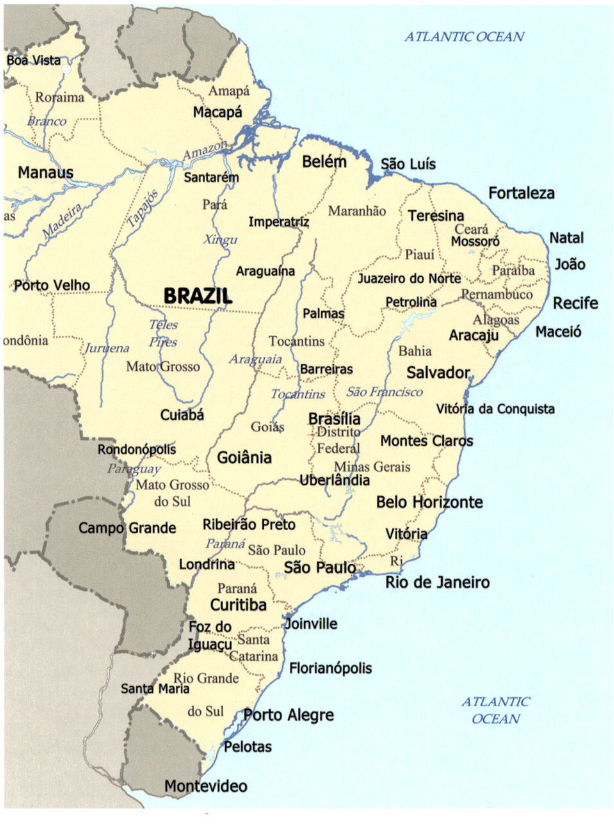

Il Brasile è un luogo dai molti significati. Innumerevoli emozioni emergono simultaneamente. Questa terra incommensurabile è contenuta negli occhi di centinaia di milioni di esseri umani che vivono immersi nel più incredibile degli esperimenti sociali. Se ogni cosa accade nello stesso momento, tutte le immagini riflesse del luogo diventano segni di ciò che sta accadendo, di ciò che accadrà e di ciò che significhi trovarsi qui. Il Brasile è un suono, un odore, o una donna? Il Brasile è acqua, aria o febbre nel sangue? Un esempio perfetto del Brasile è l'elemento essenziale... l'acqua purissima che abbraccia la propria aria e la propria terra. Potranno le acque del Rio Negro mai unirsi a quelle del Rio delle Amazzoni in un unico amplesso? Mai uniti, mai lontani, mai separati nella morte. Chi ama questo paese ama l'astratto, e non esiste indubbiamente brasiliano più astratto di Heitor Villa-Lobos. I suoi 12 studi per chitarra costituiscono una rappresentazione più efficace di quanto qualsiasi parola o immagine possa tentare di creare.

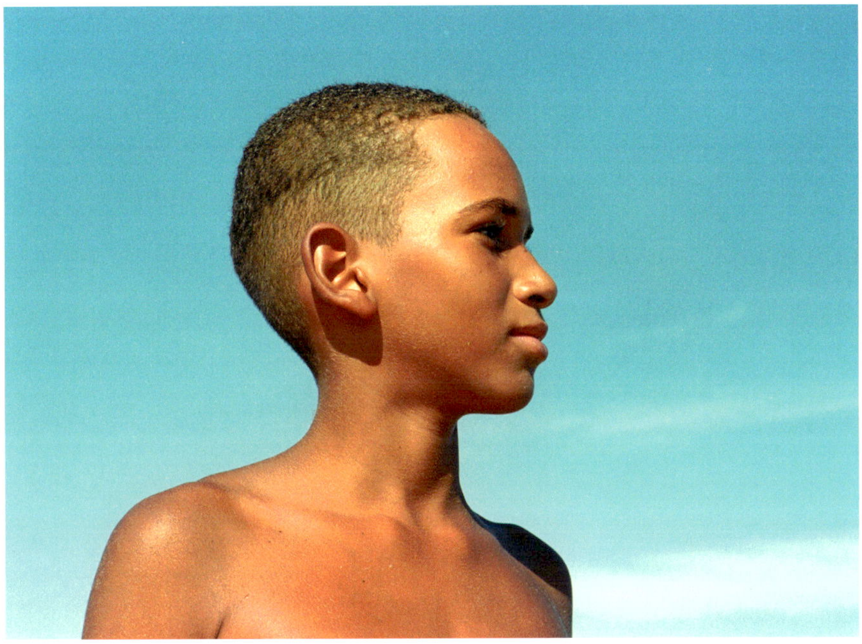

The arch angel Nestor flew to the moon. The clouds parted and the space rushed towards him. He was the first deep space navigator. He flew directly into mythology. Once there he realized that his purpose was complete. Returning to earth the only familiar signs were in the water. Different colors of blue and green guided him, indicating by tidal surges whre he should fly. Eventully he landed but had difficulty focusing his eyes. For a few days he followed water by smell and feel, going deeper into the jungle. There he met a woman who restored the purity of his vision. Her name is Amazona. Nestor asked Amazona what they should call their son. She sighed and replied:" Mameluke".

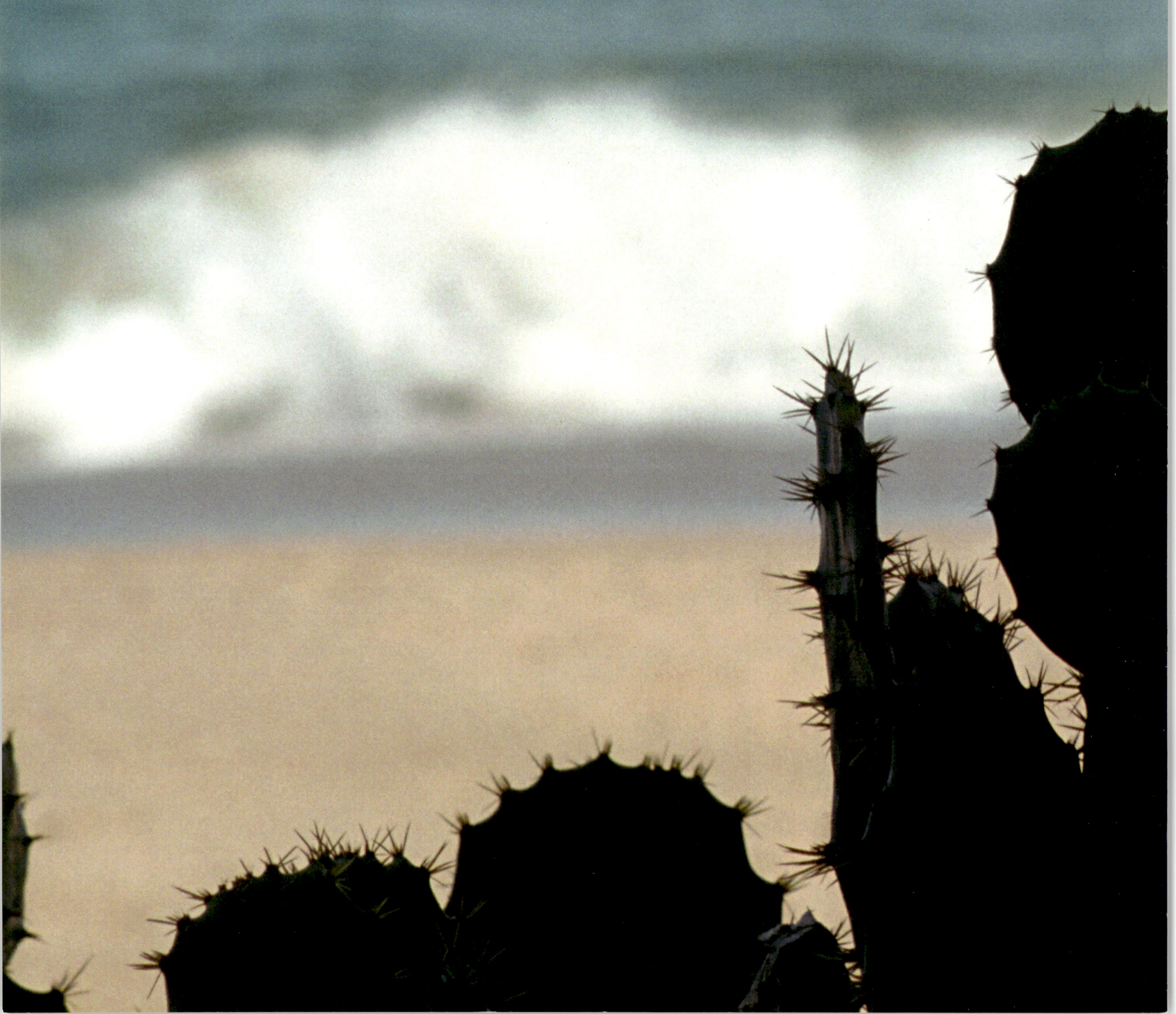

L'arcangelo Nestore volò verso la luna. Le nuvole si divisero e lo spazio si precipitò verso di lui. Era il primo navigatore dello spazio profondo. Volò direttamente dentro la mitologia. Una volta arrivato si rese conto di aver raggiunto il suo obiettivo. Tornando verso terra, gli unici segnali familiari si rivelarono nell'acqua. Diverse tonalità di blu e di verde lo guidarono, indicandogli con improvvise ondate la direzione in cui volare. Infine atterrò, ma trovò difficile mettere a fuoco ciò che vedeva. Per alcuni giorni seguì odori e sensazioni, inoltrandosi progressivamente nella giungla. Lì incontro una donna che restituì purezza alla sua visione. Il suo nome era Amazona. Nestore chiese ad Amazona come avrebbero dovuto chiamare loro figlio. Lei Sospirò e rispose: “Mameluke”.

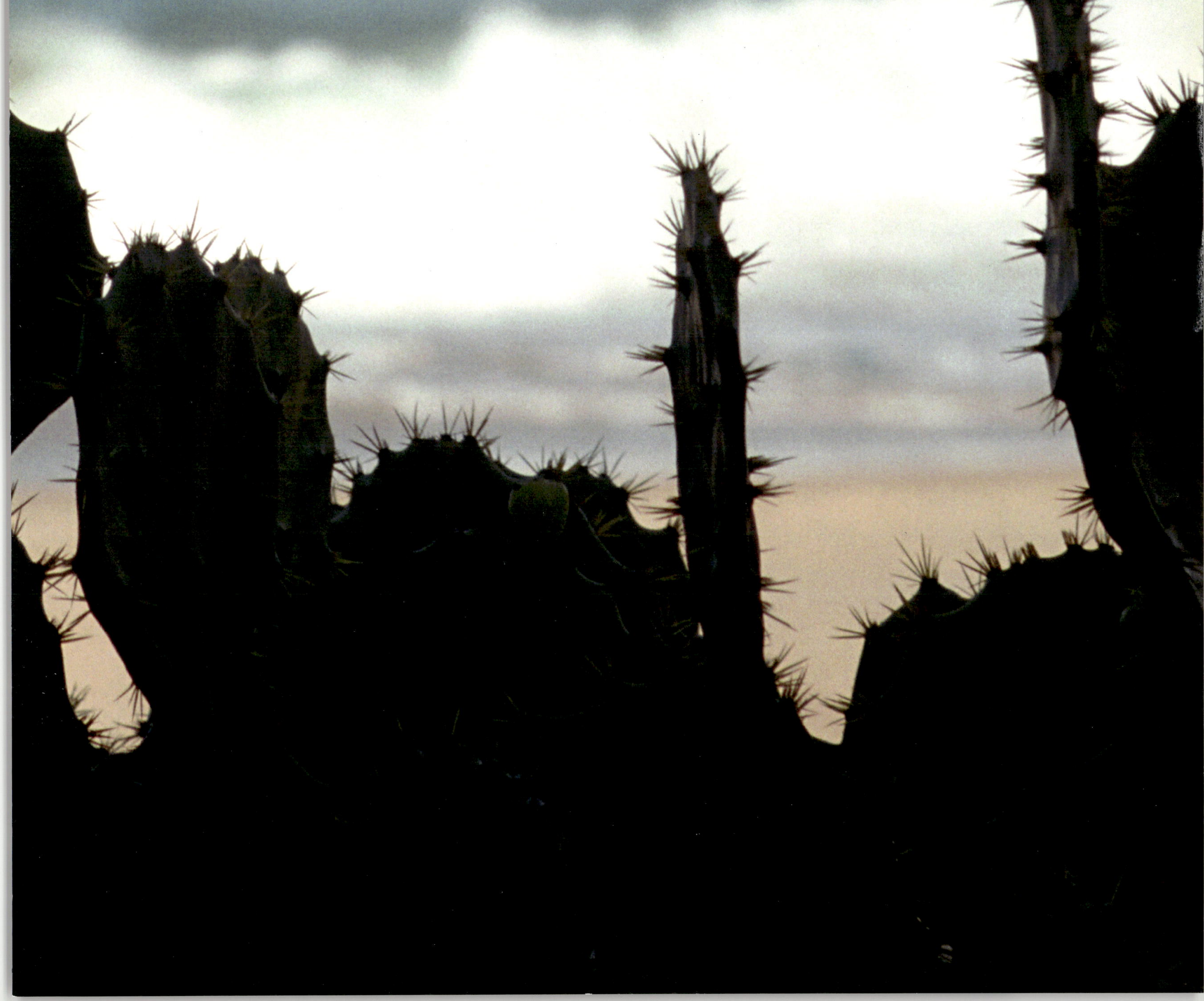

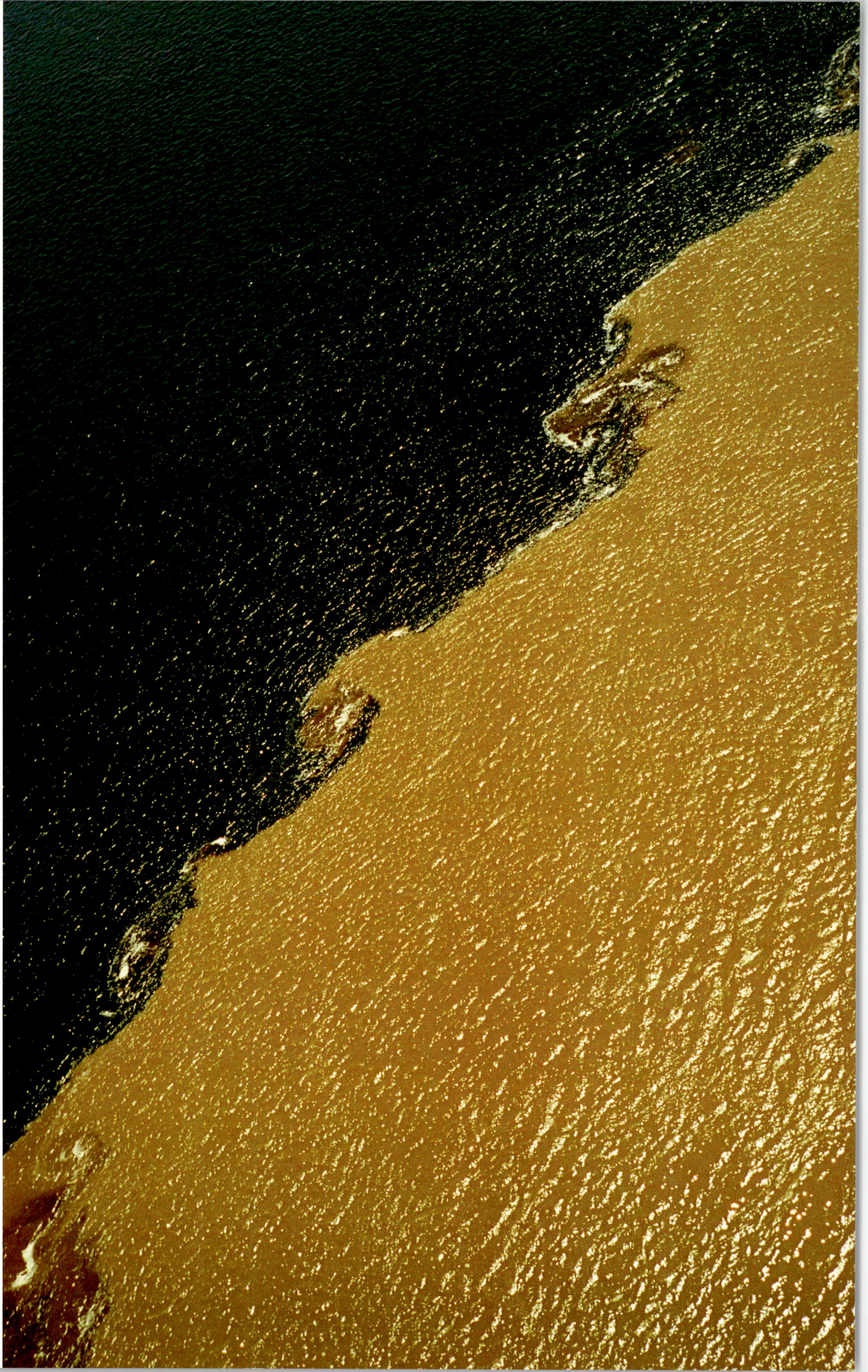

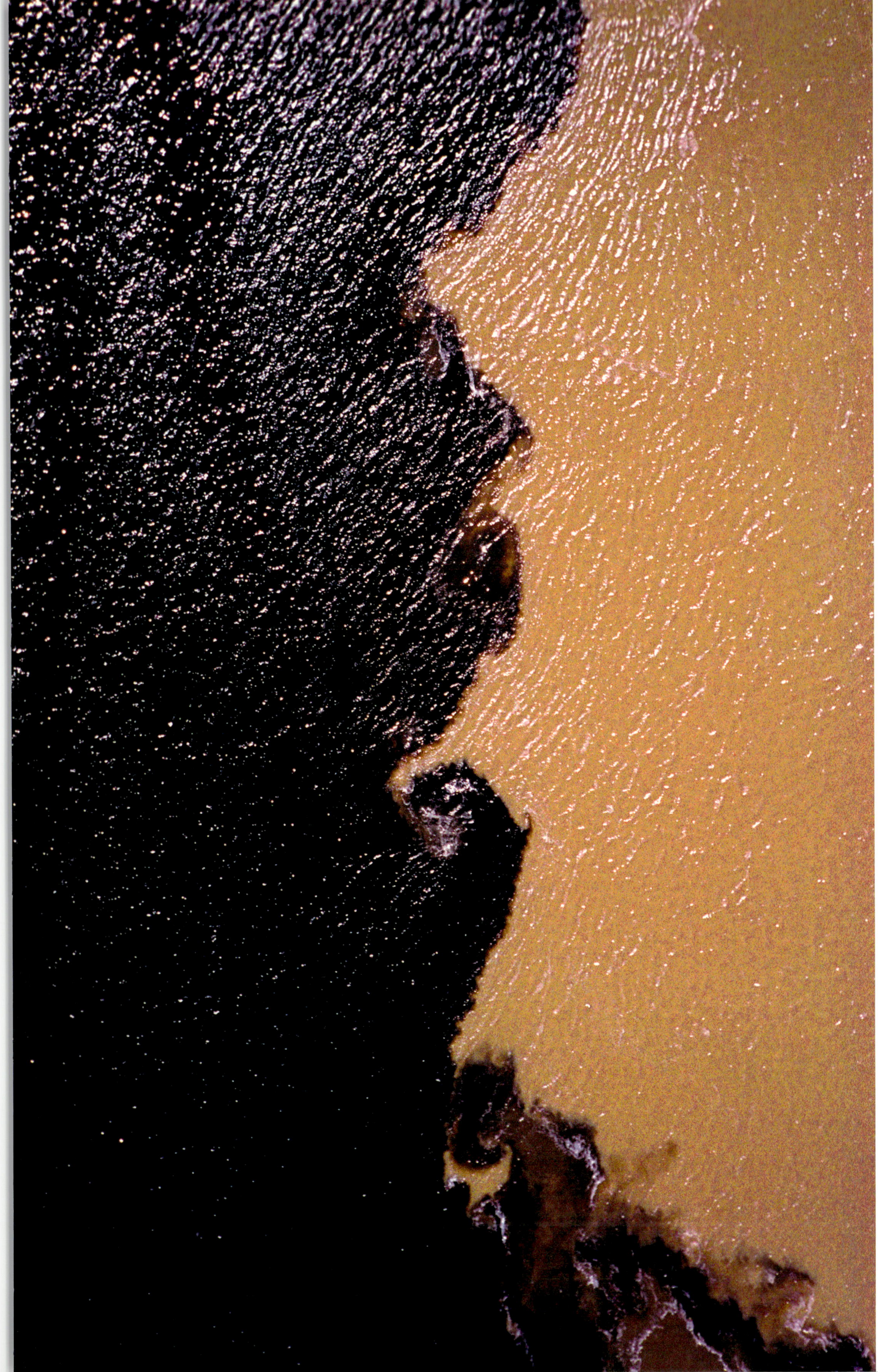

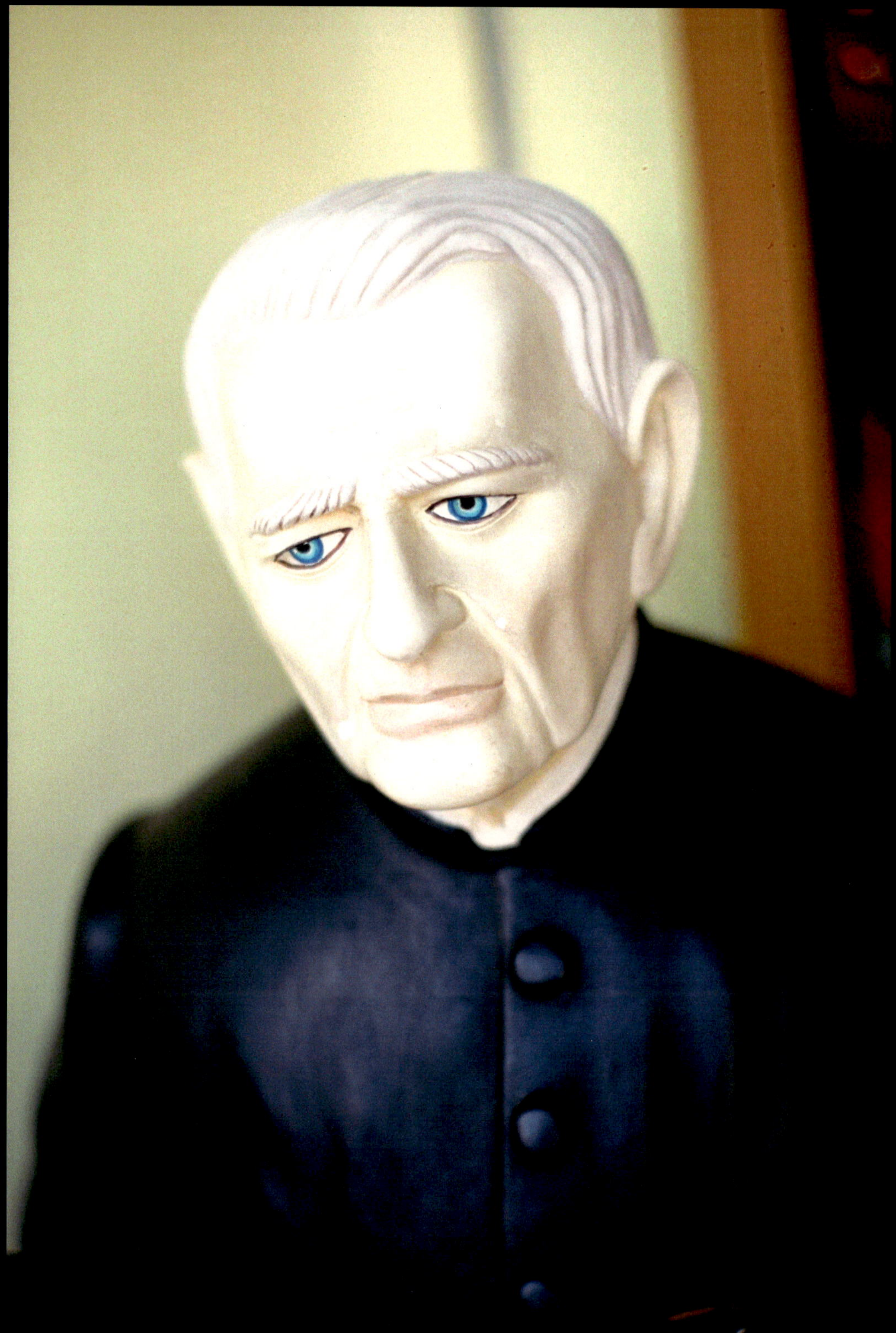

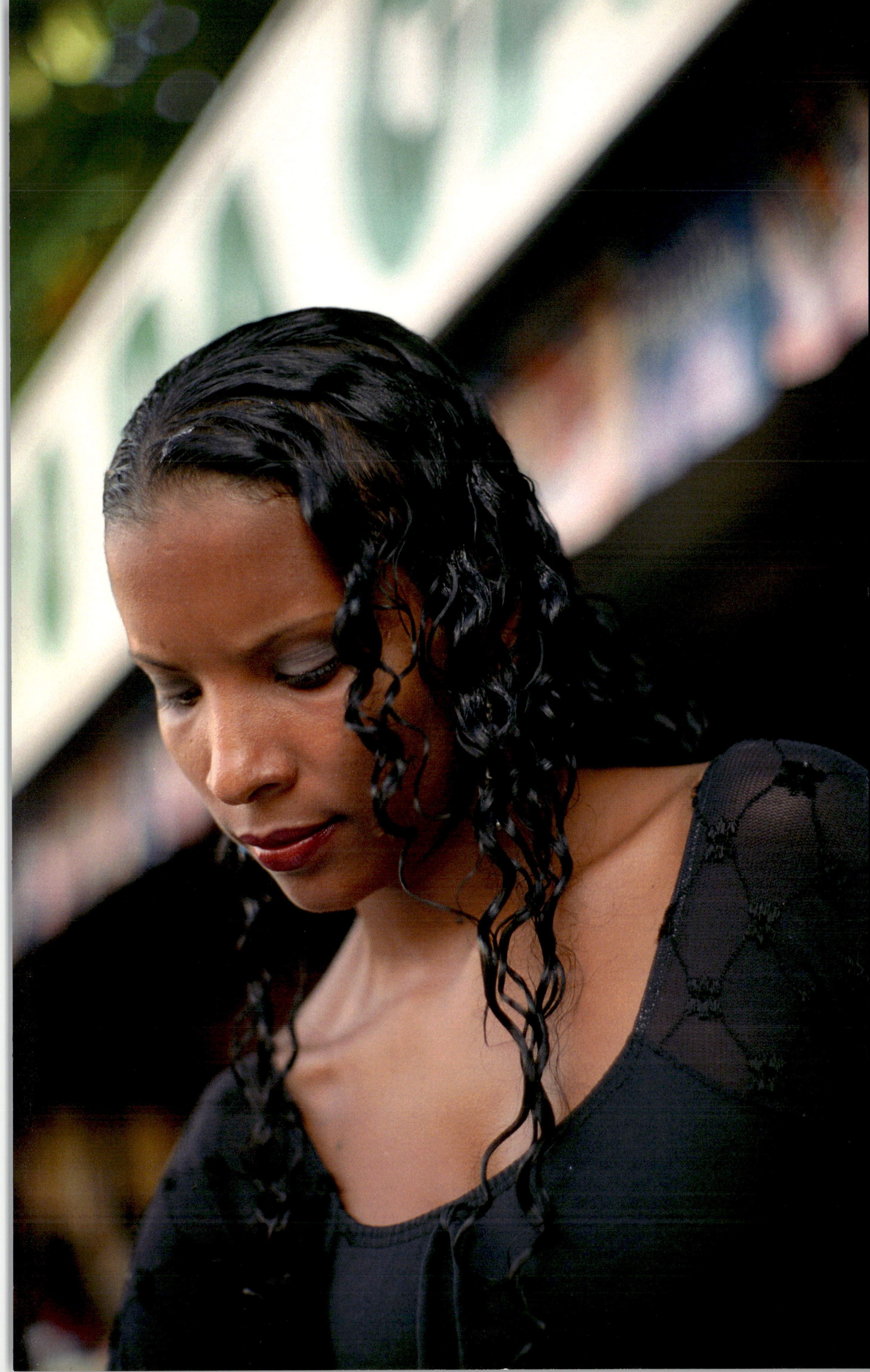

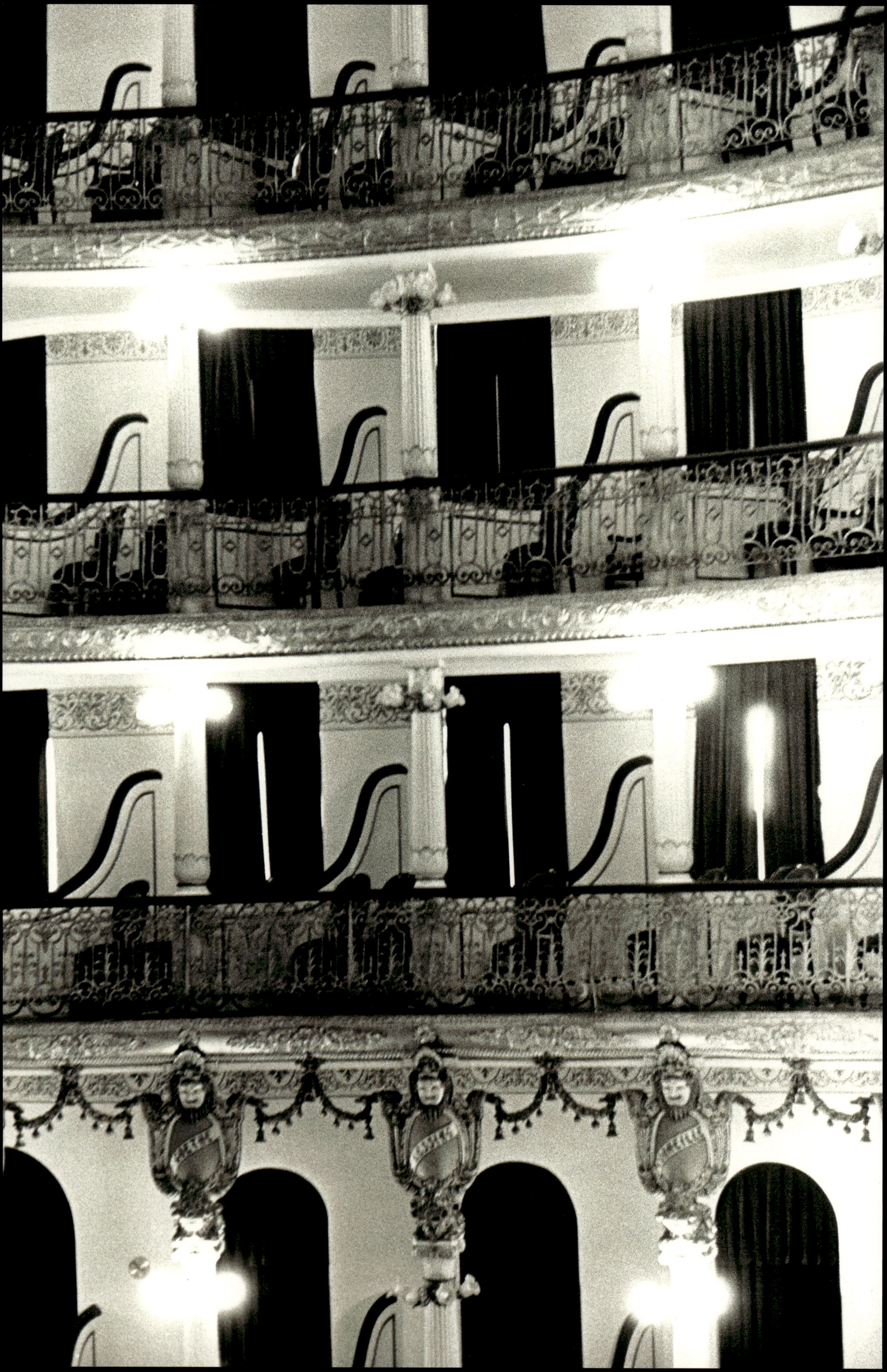

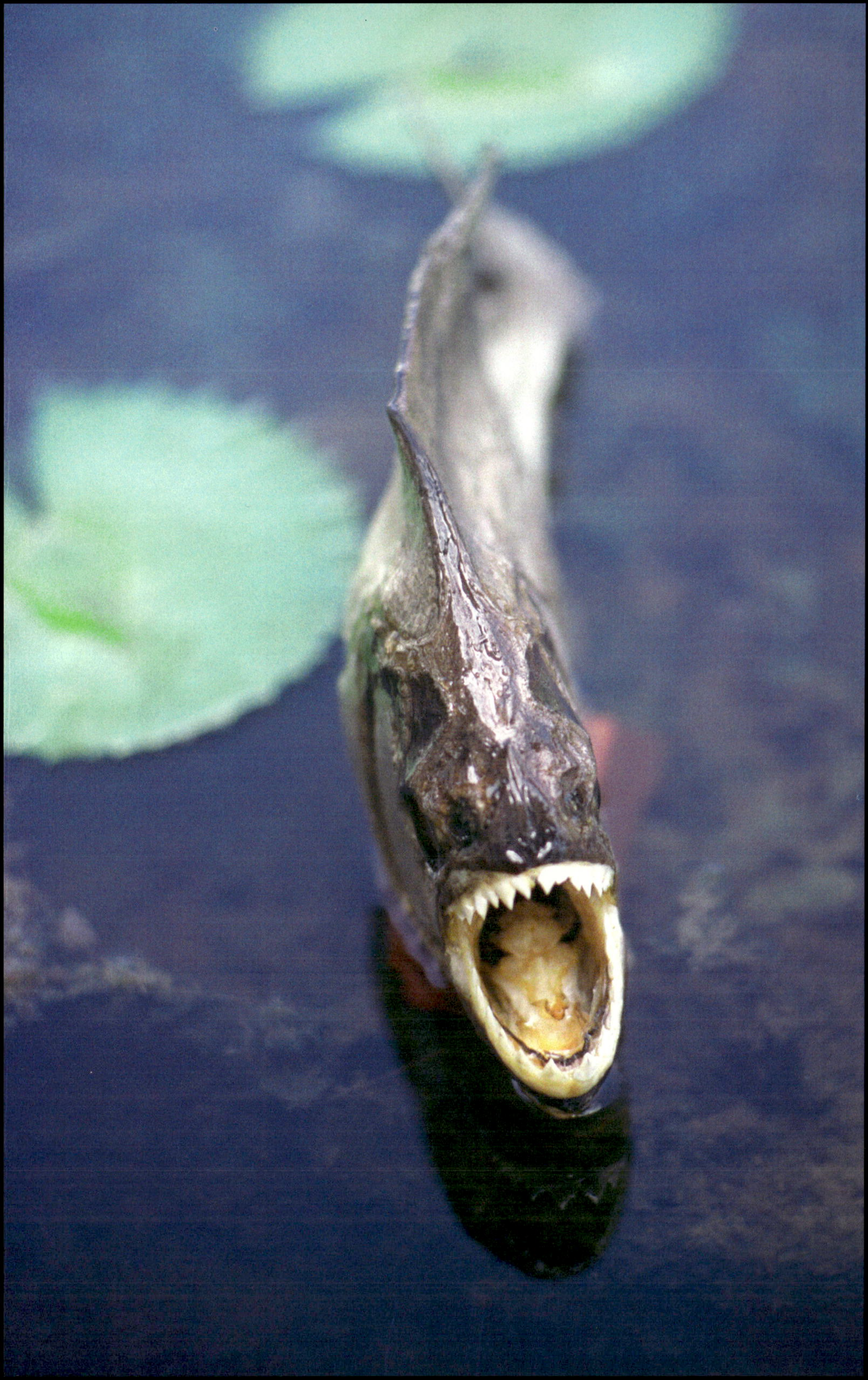

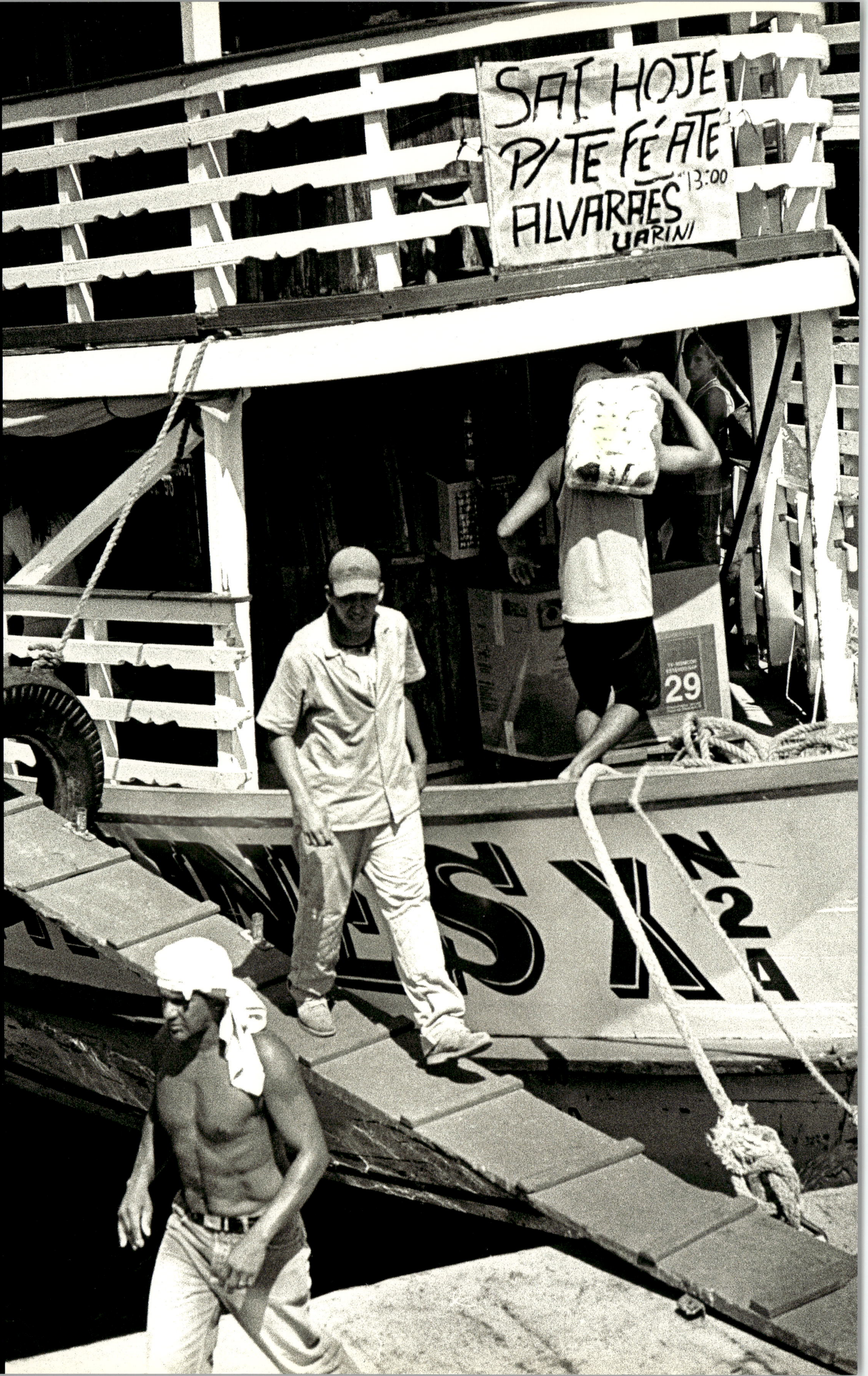
SAI HOJE
P/ TEFÉ ATE
13:00
ALVARÃES
UARINI
29

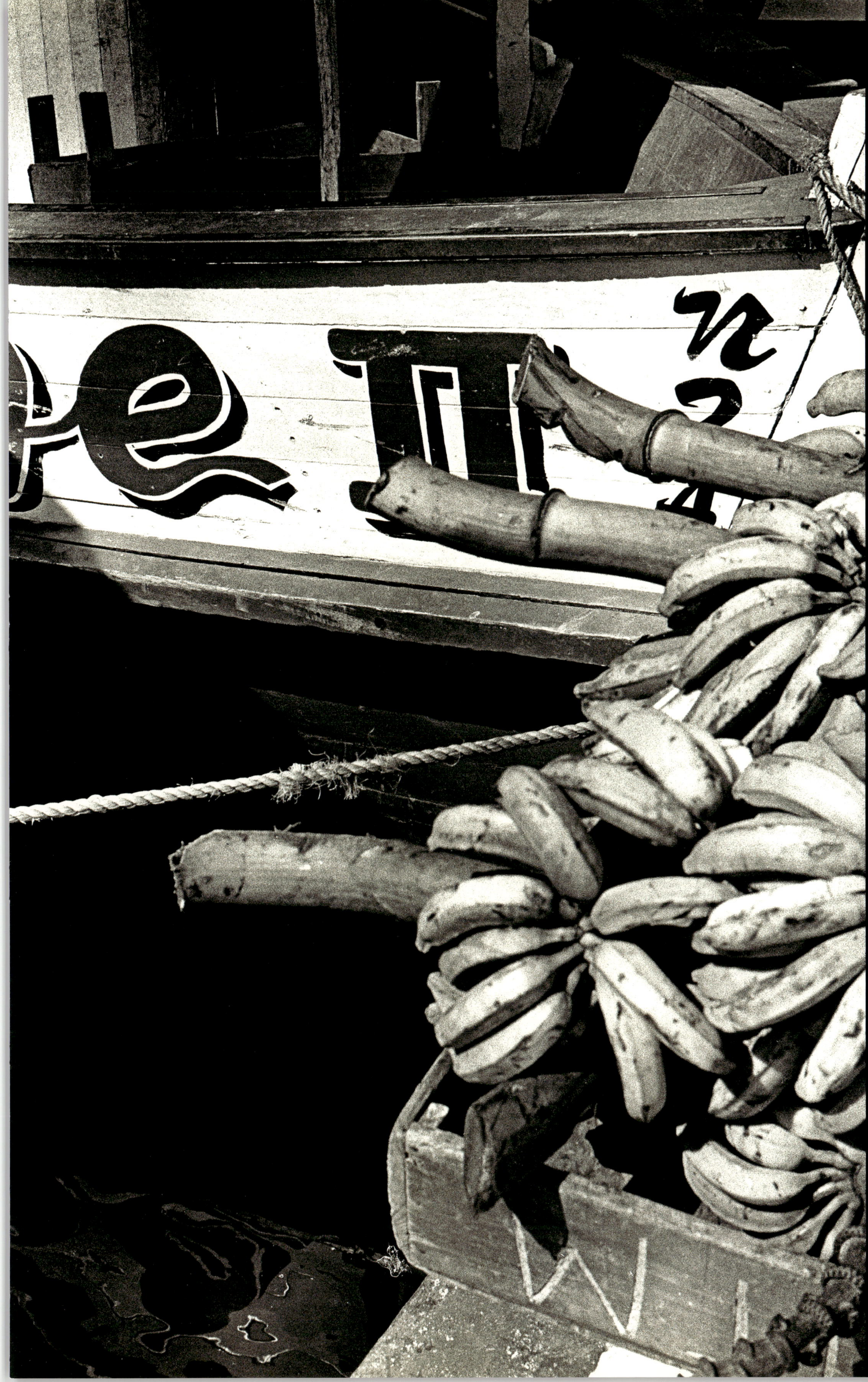

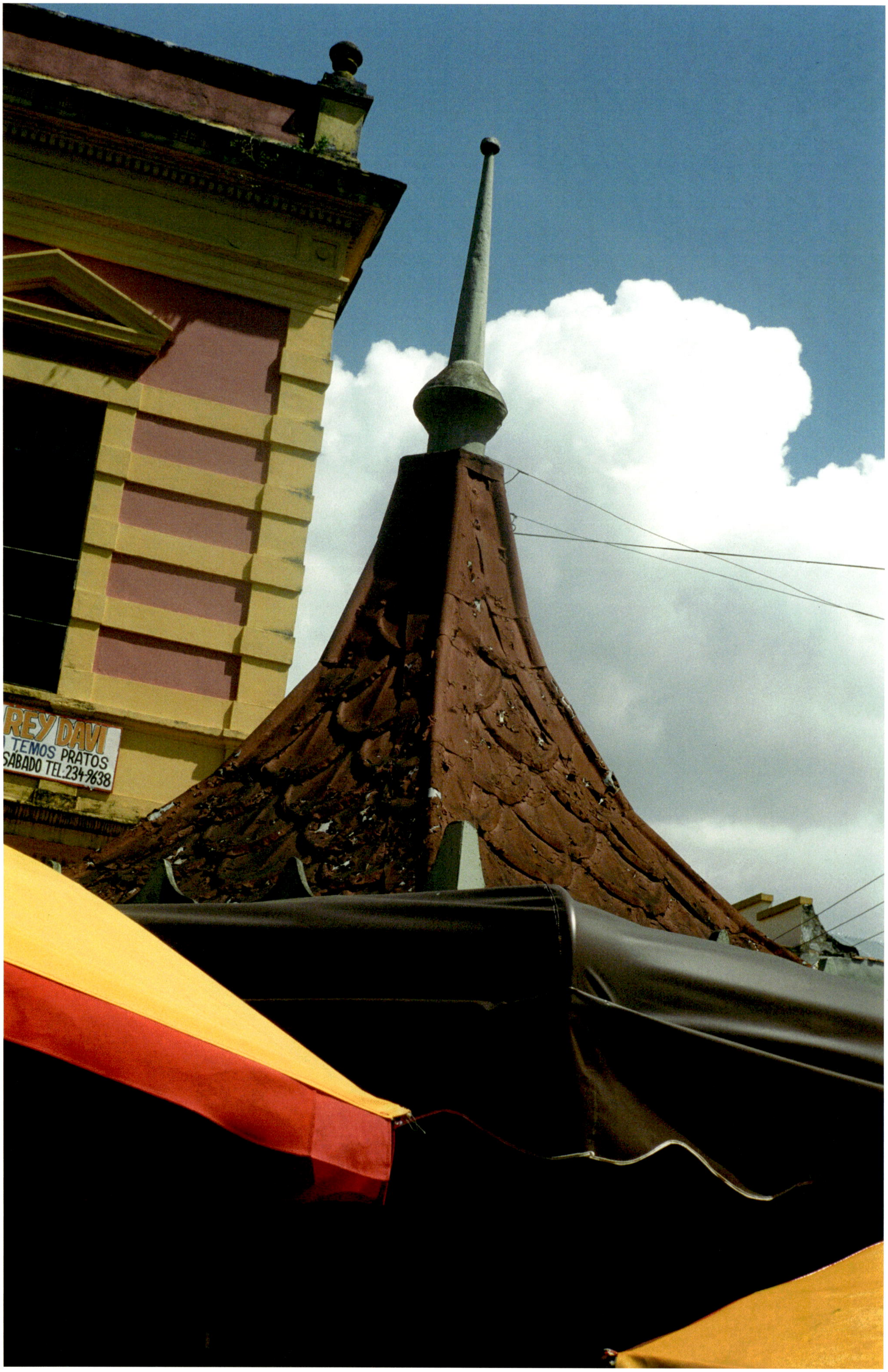
REY DAVI
TEMOS PRATOS
SÁBADO TEL:234-9638

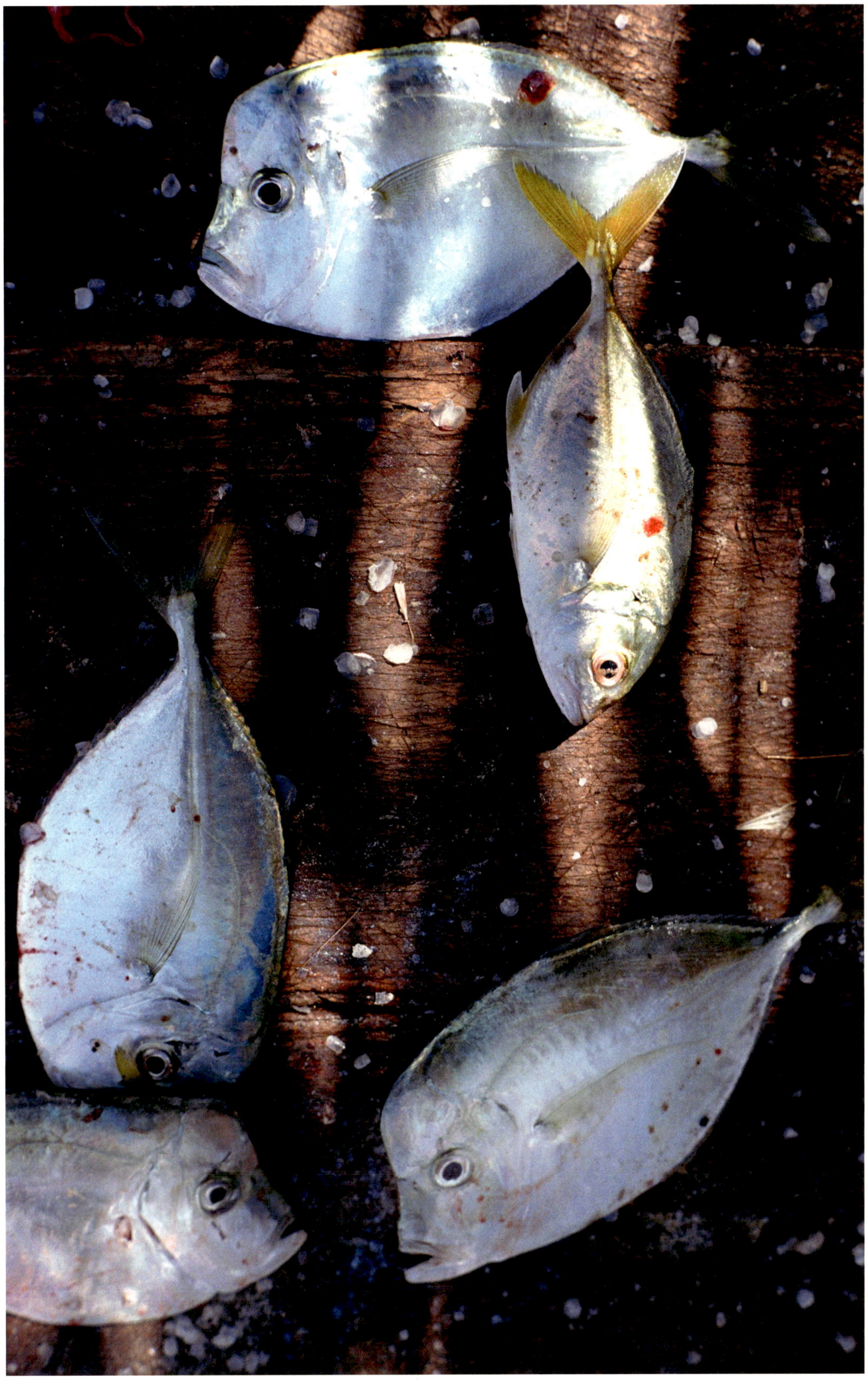

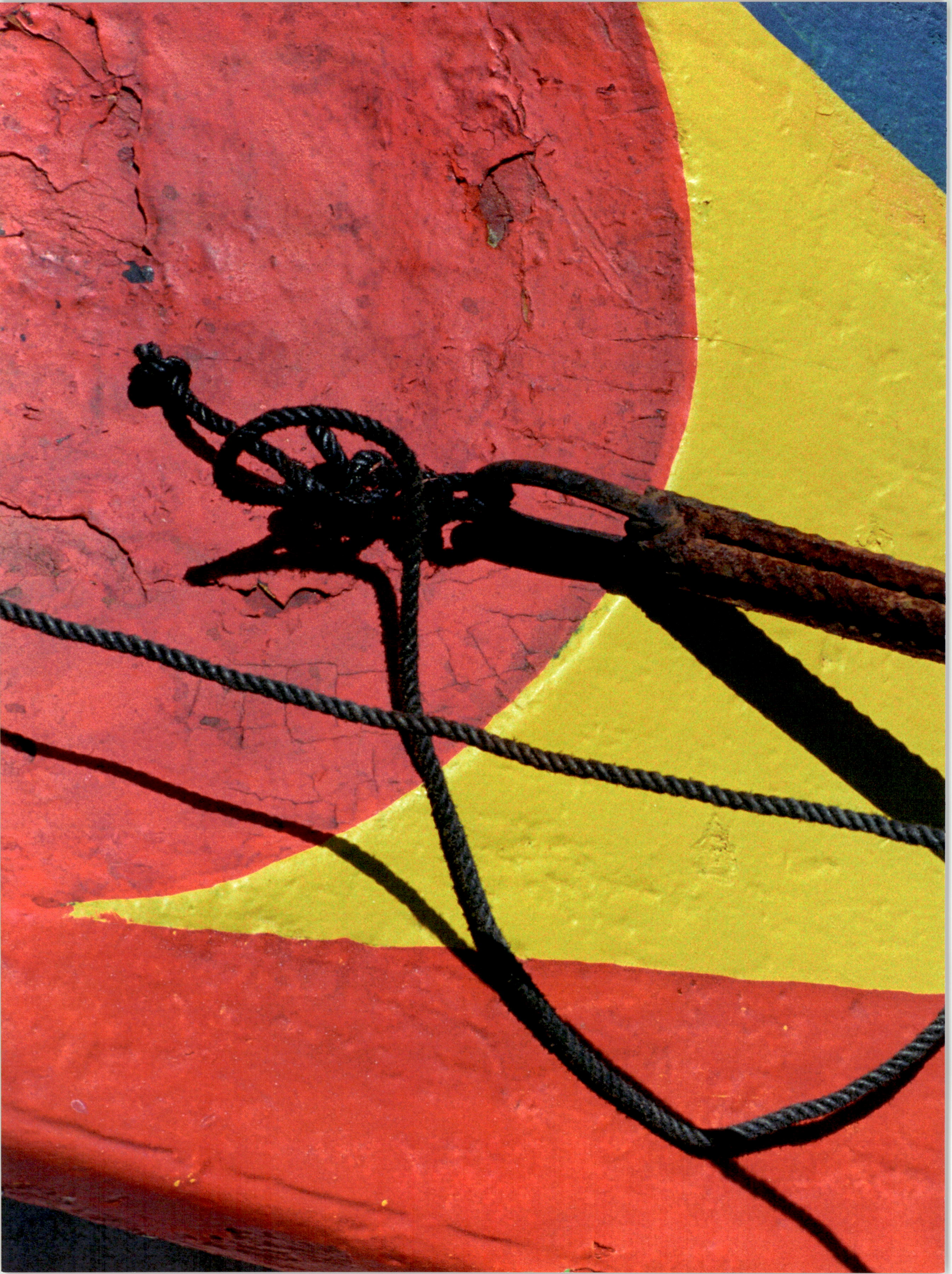

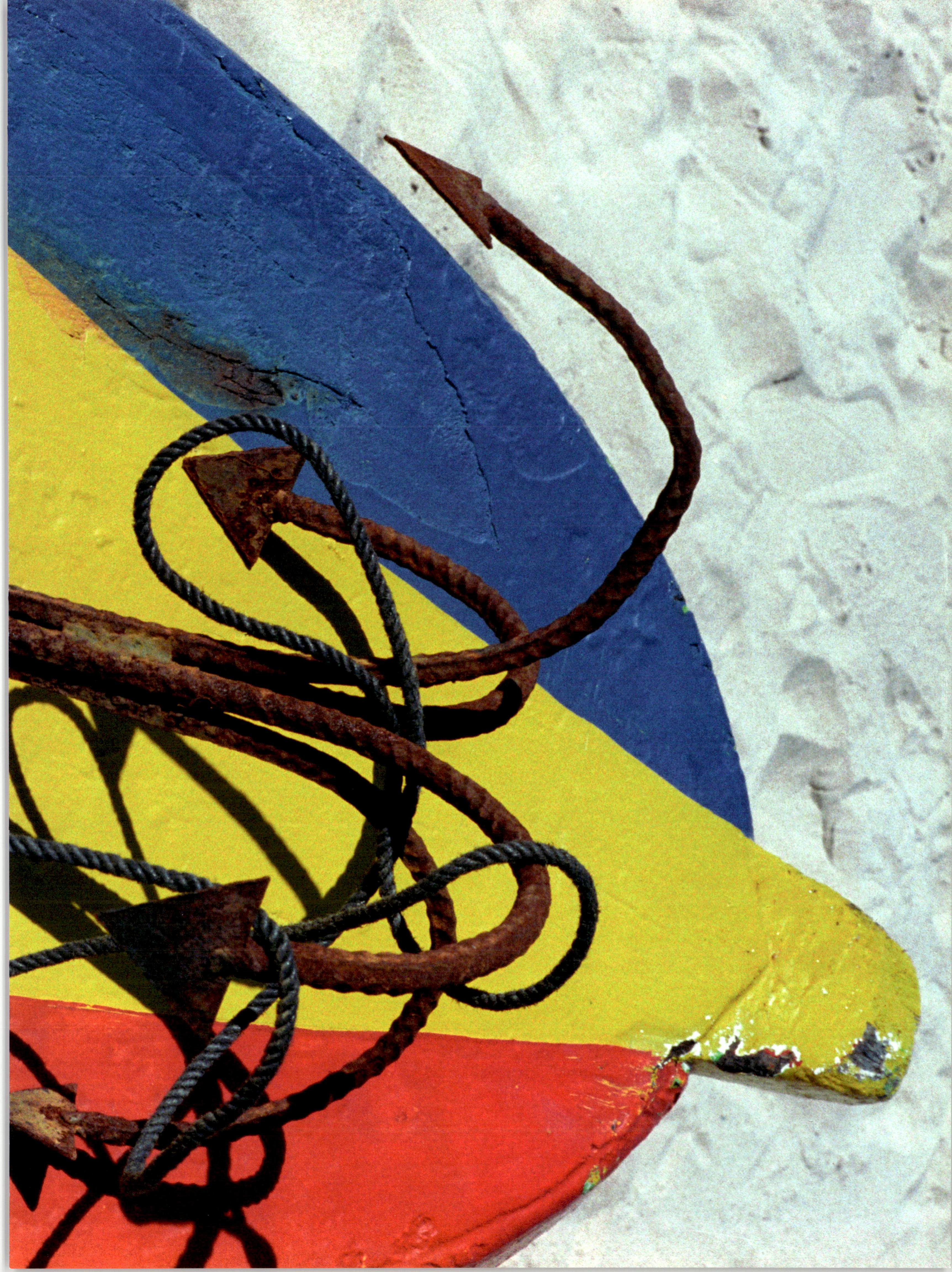

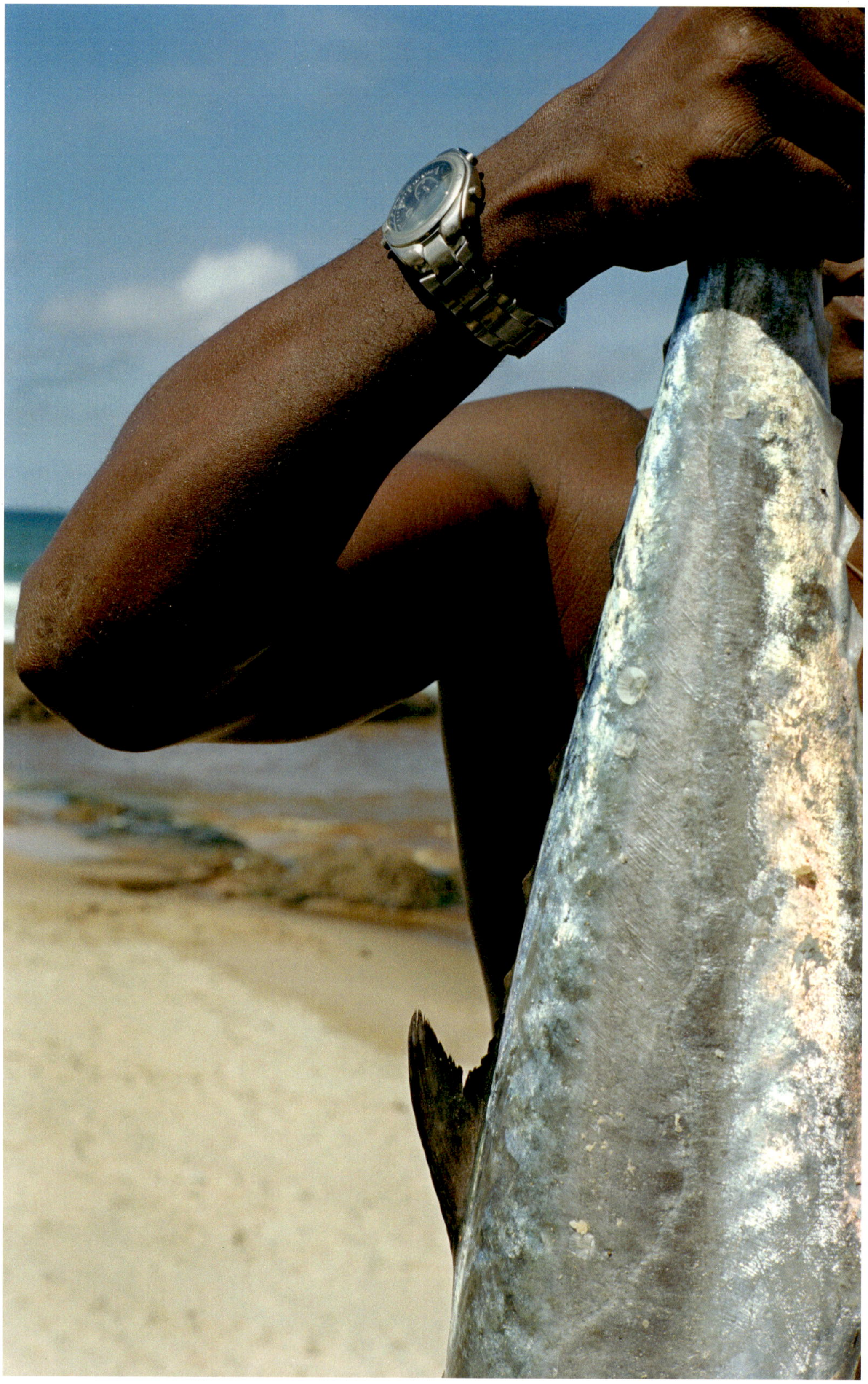

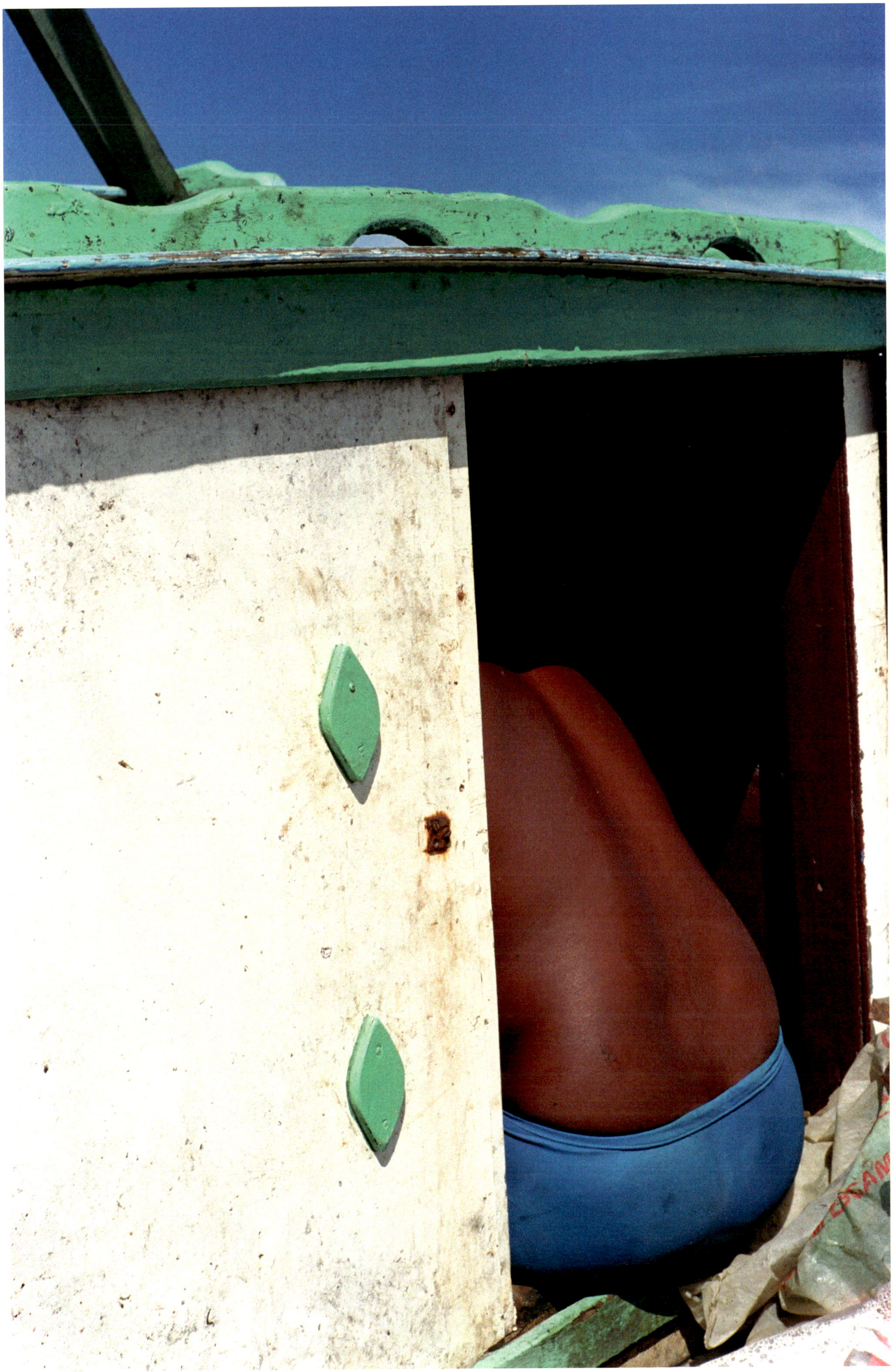

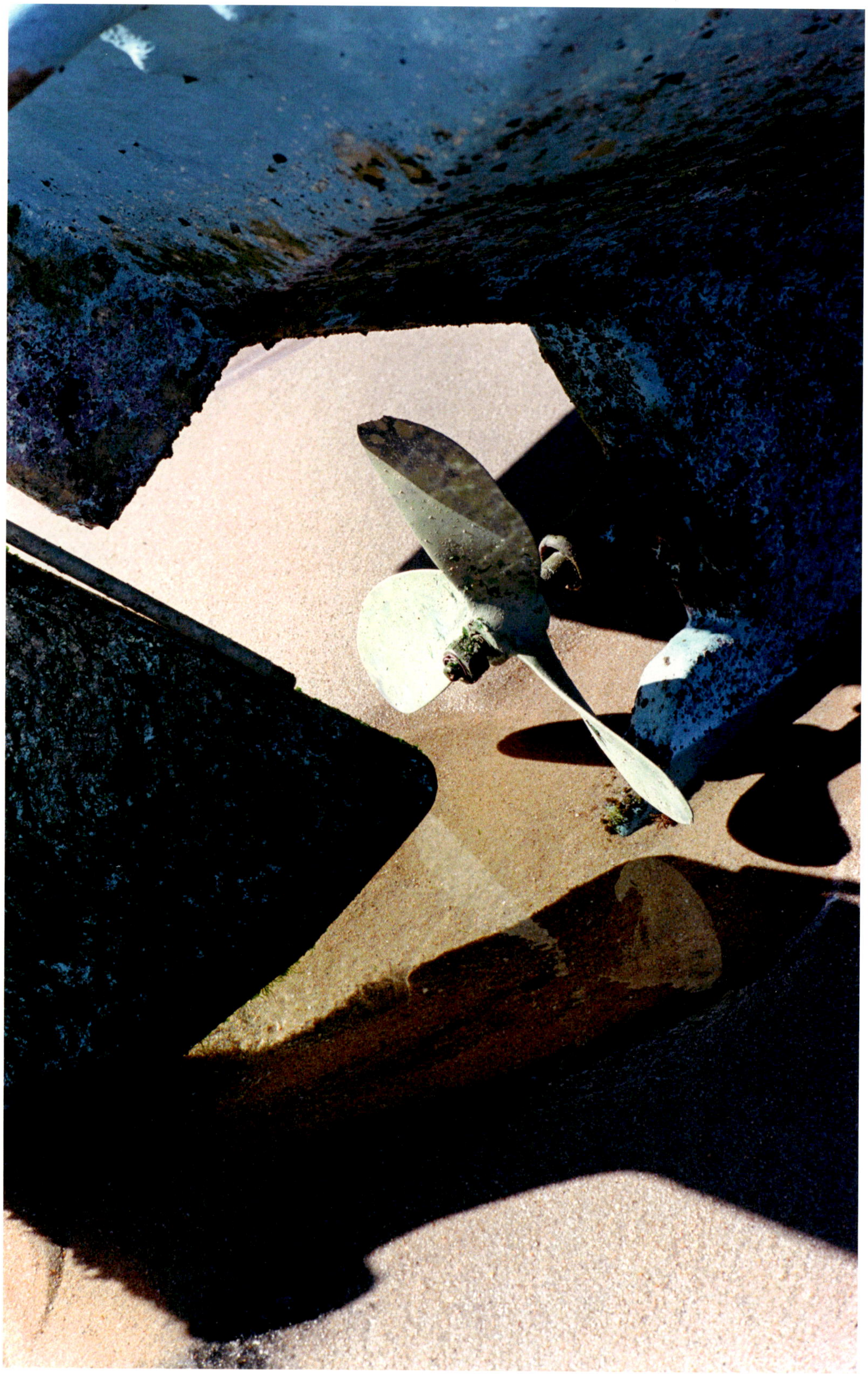

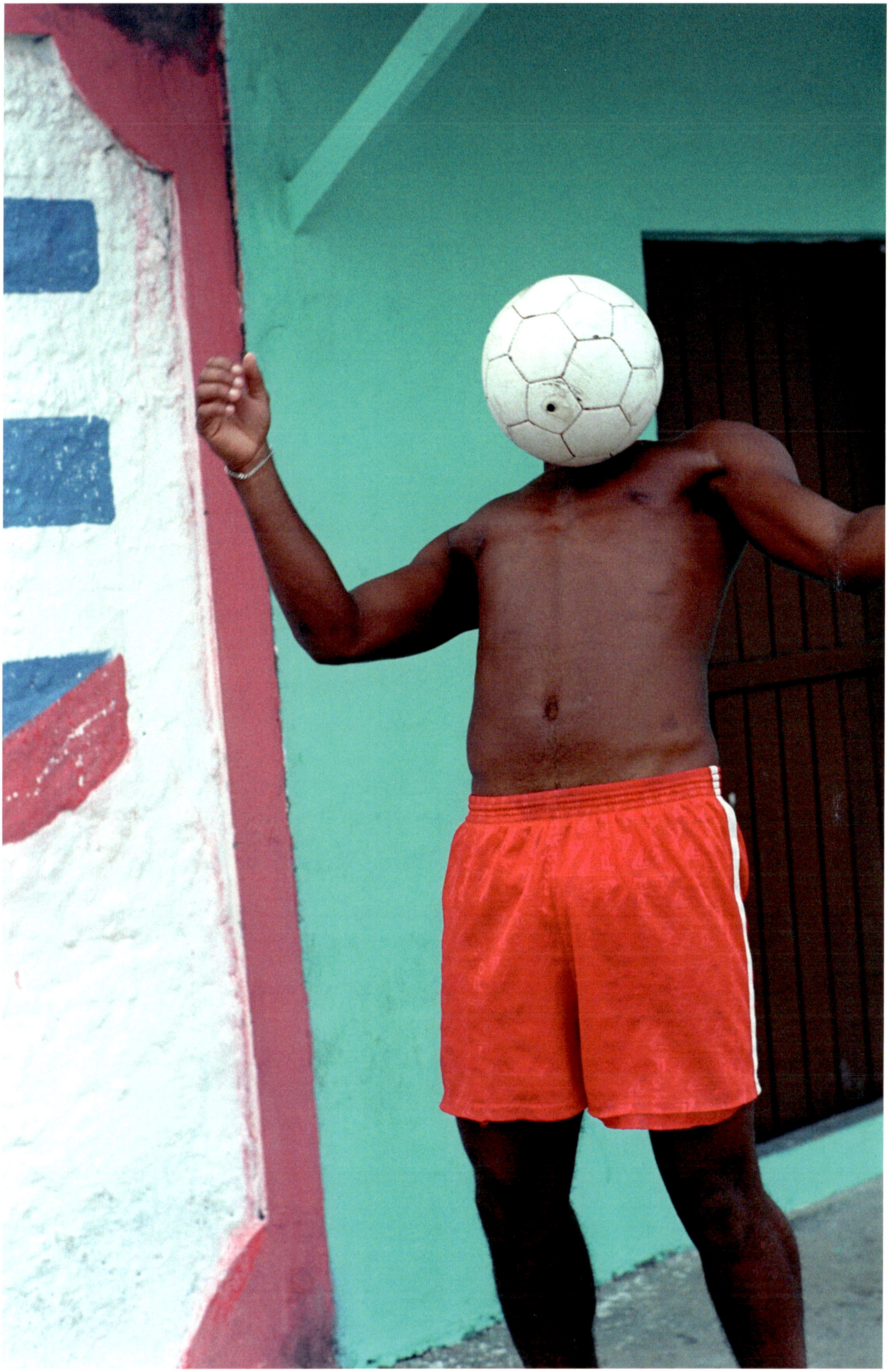

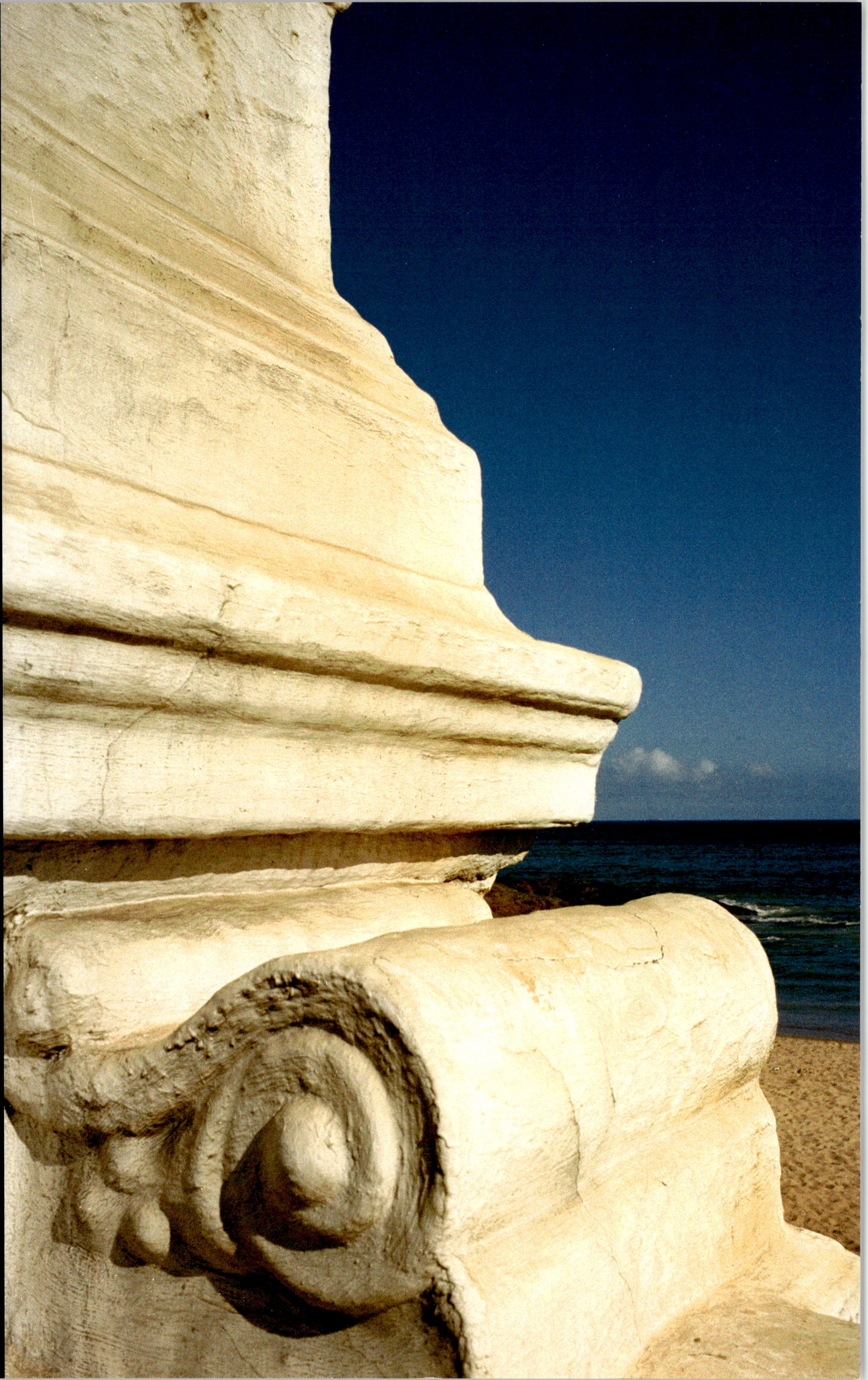

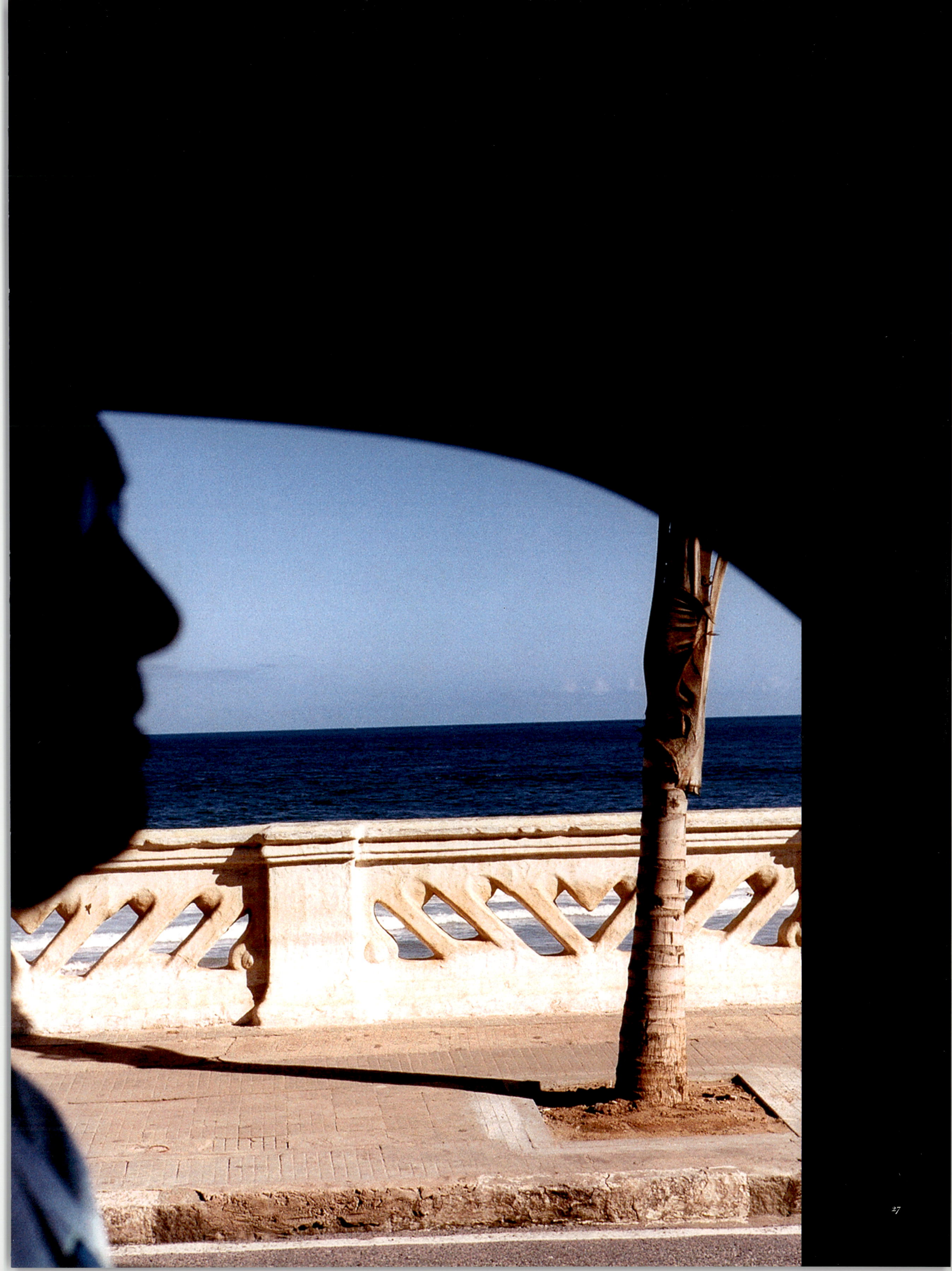

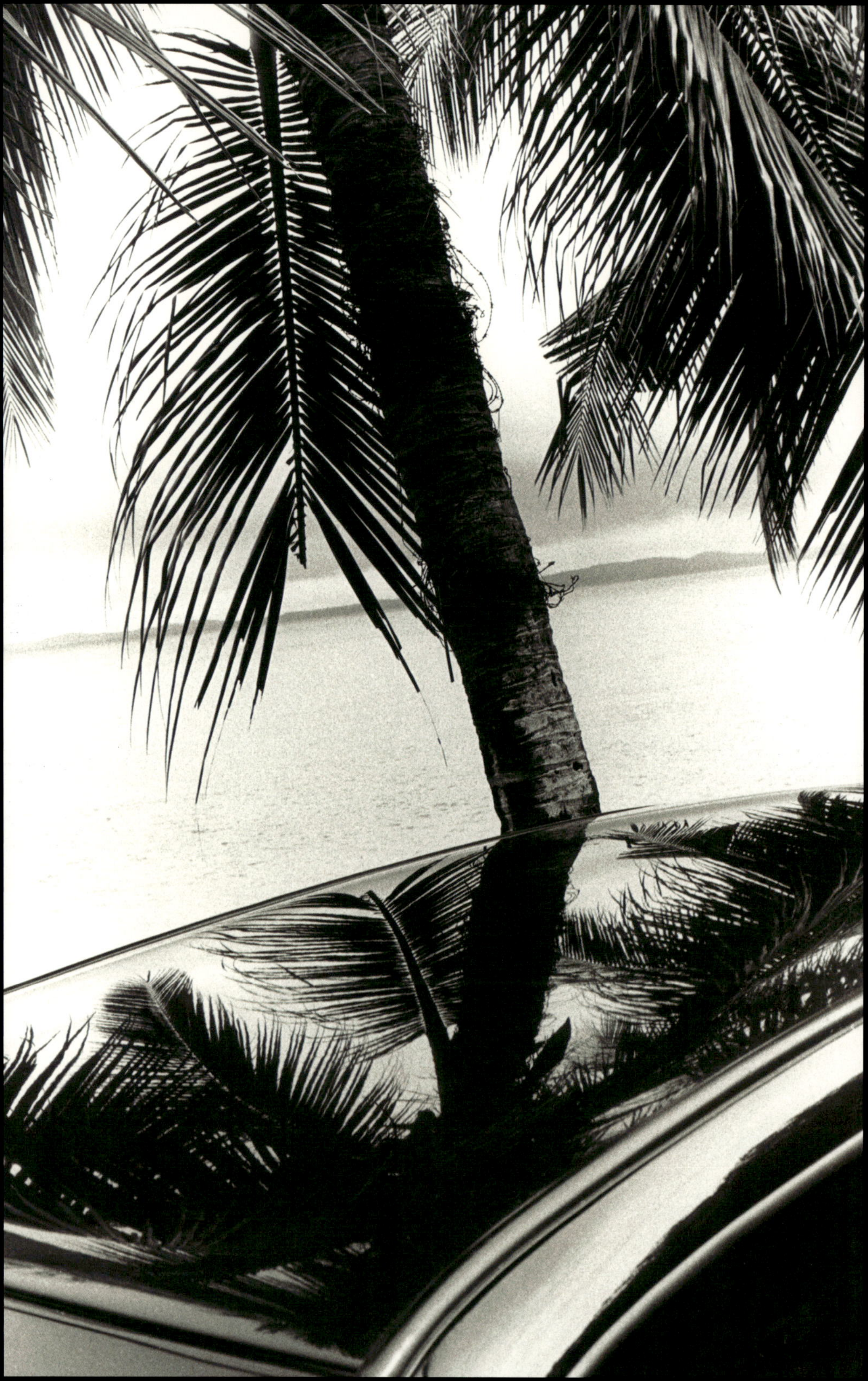

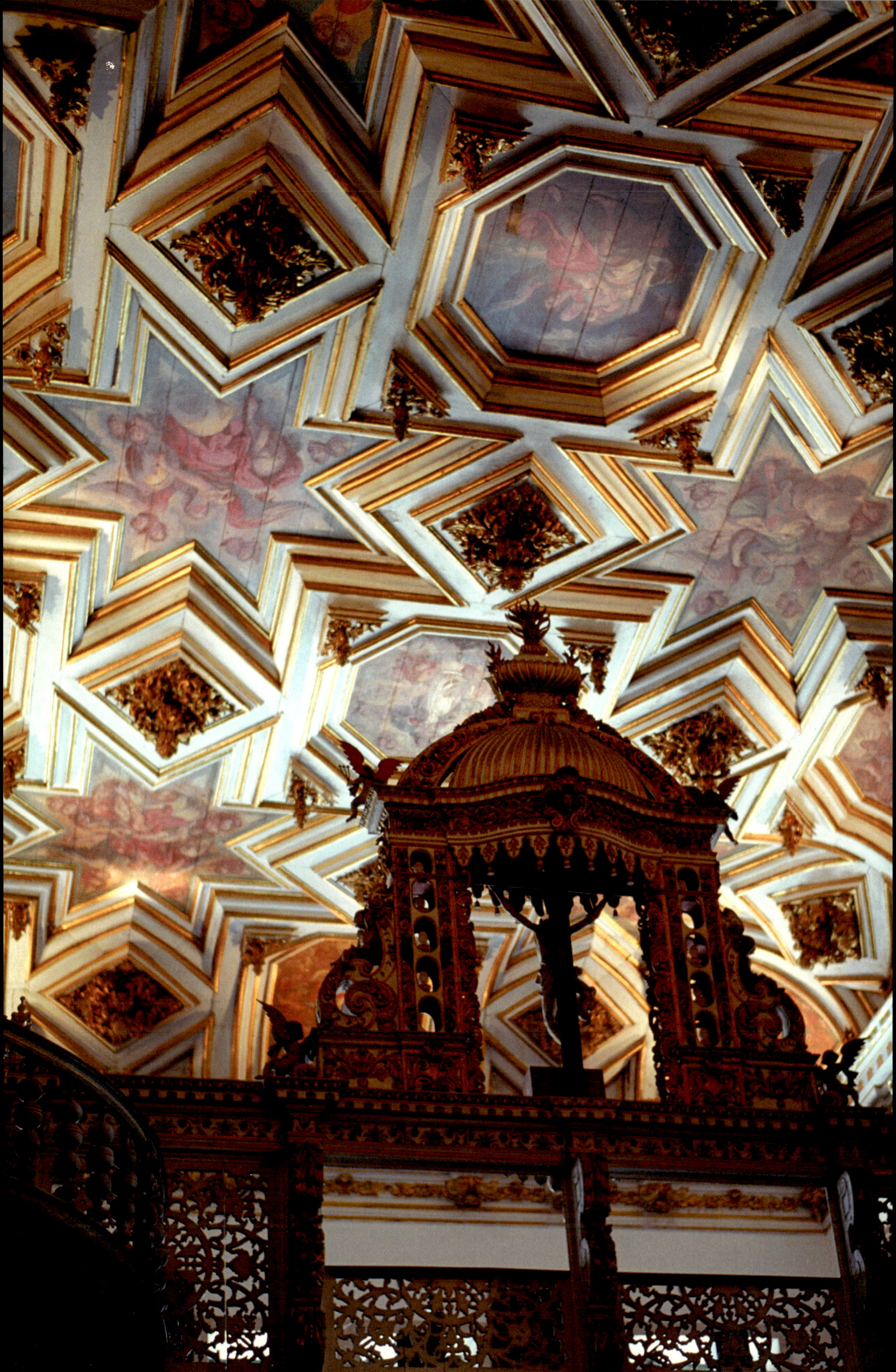

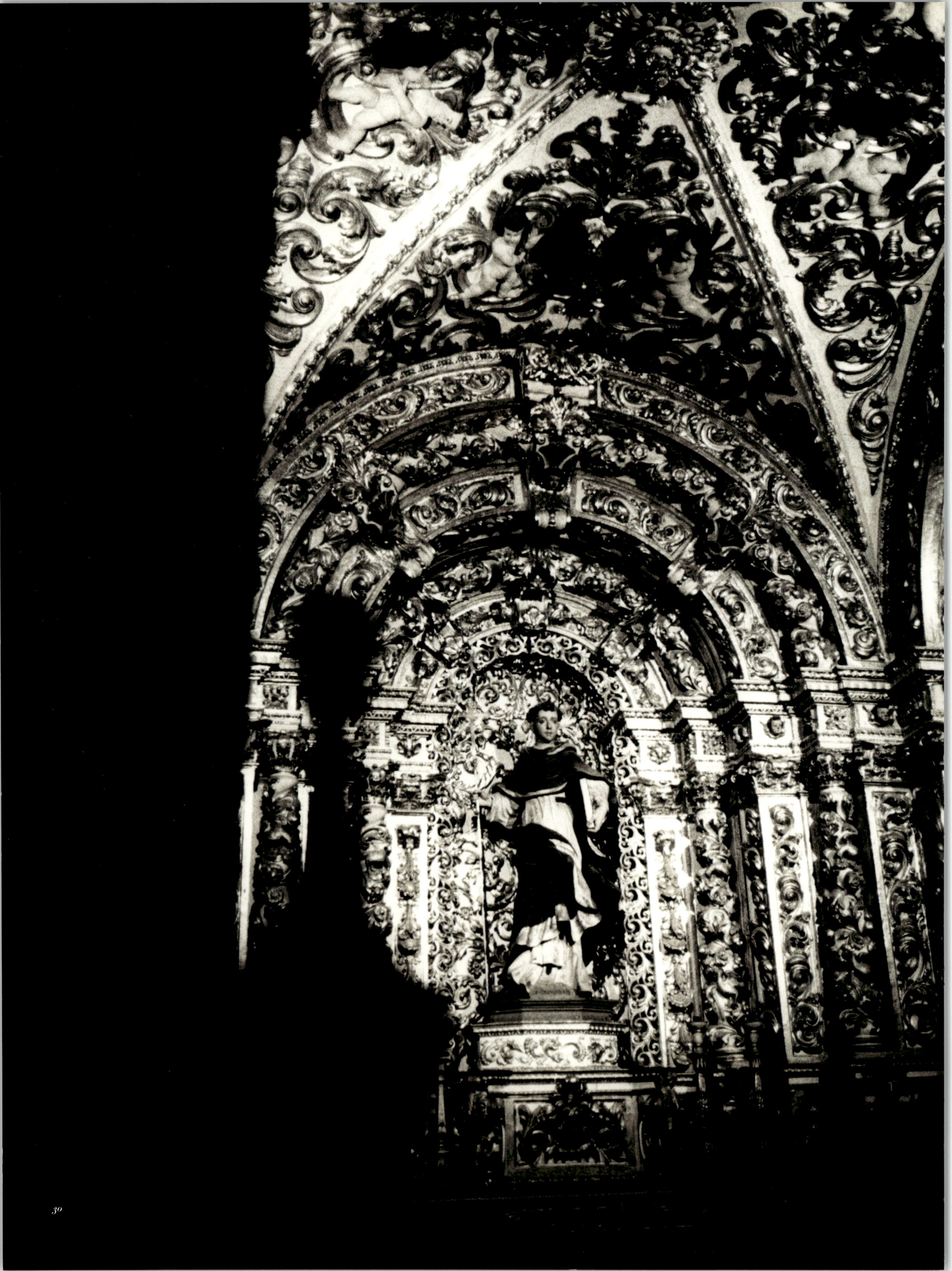

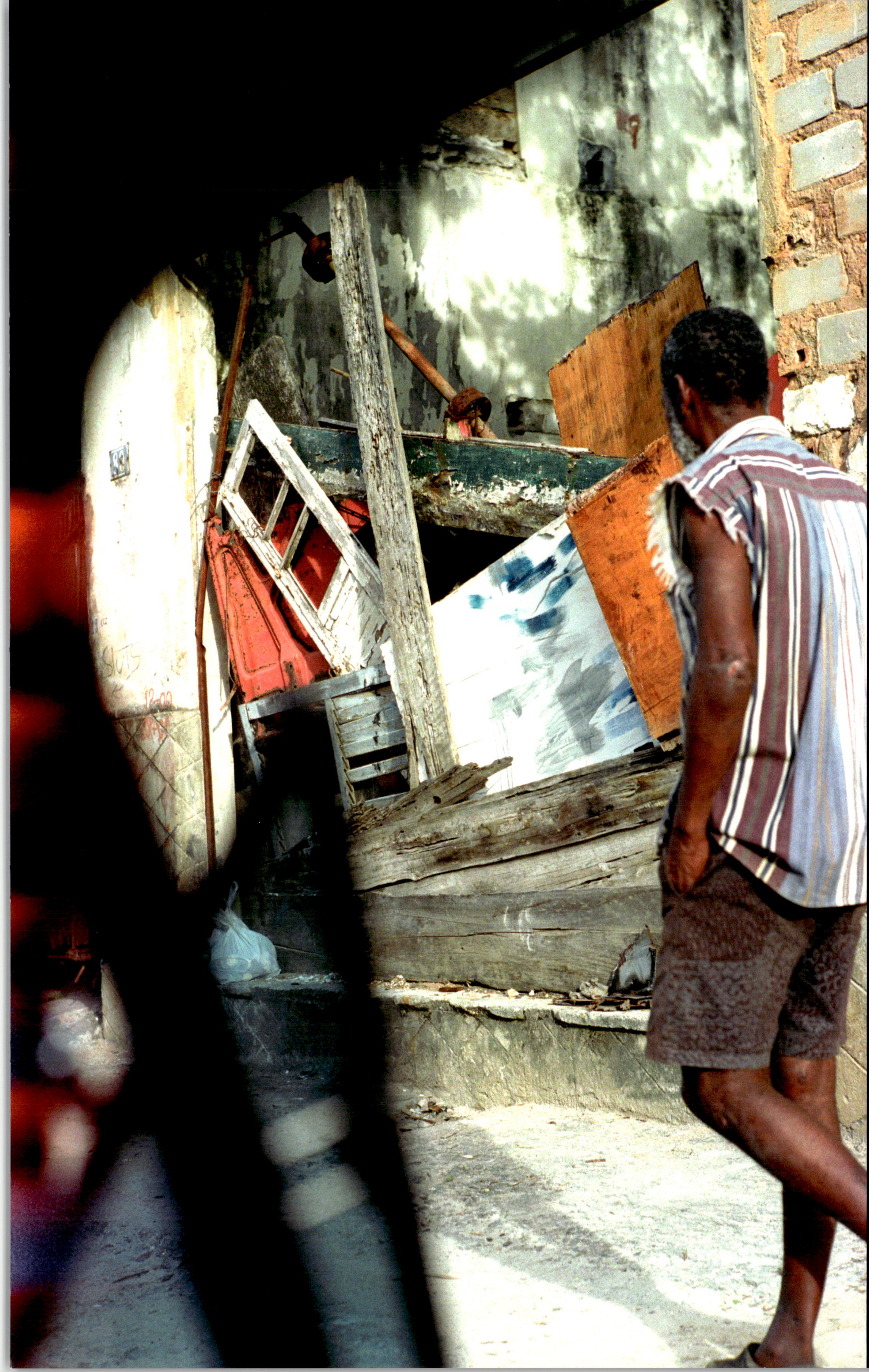

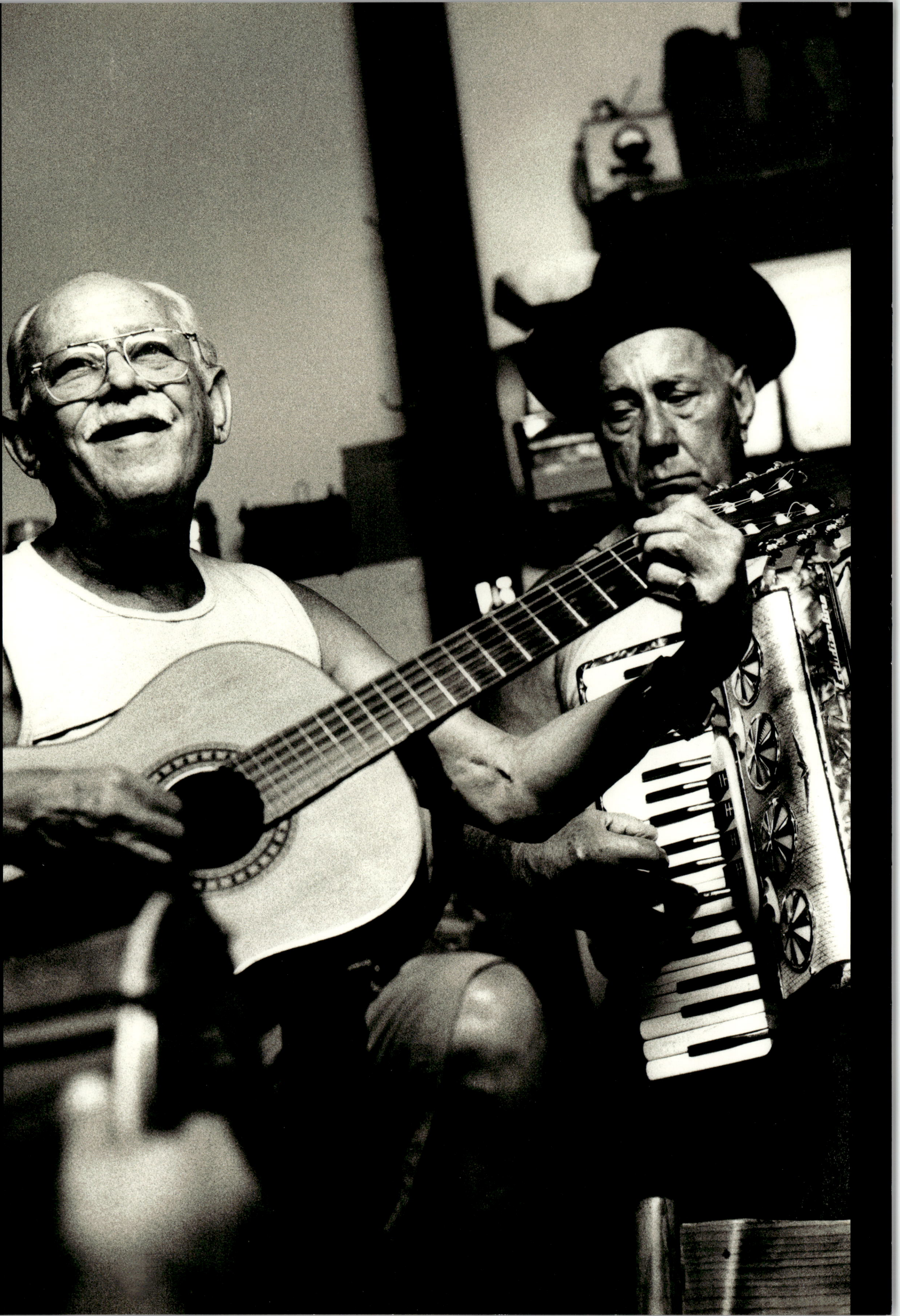

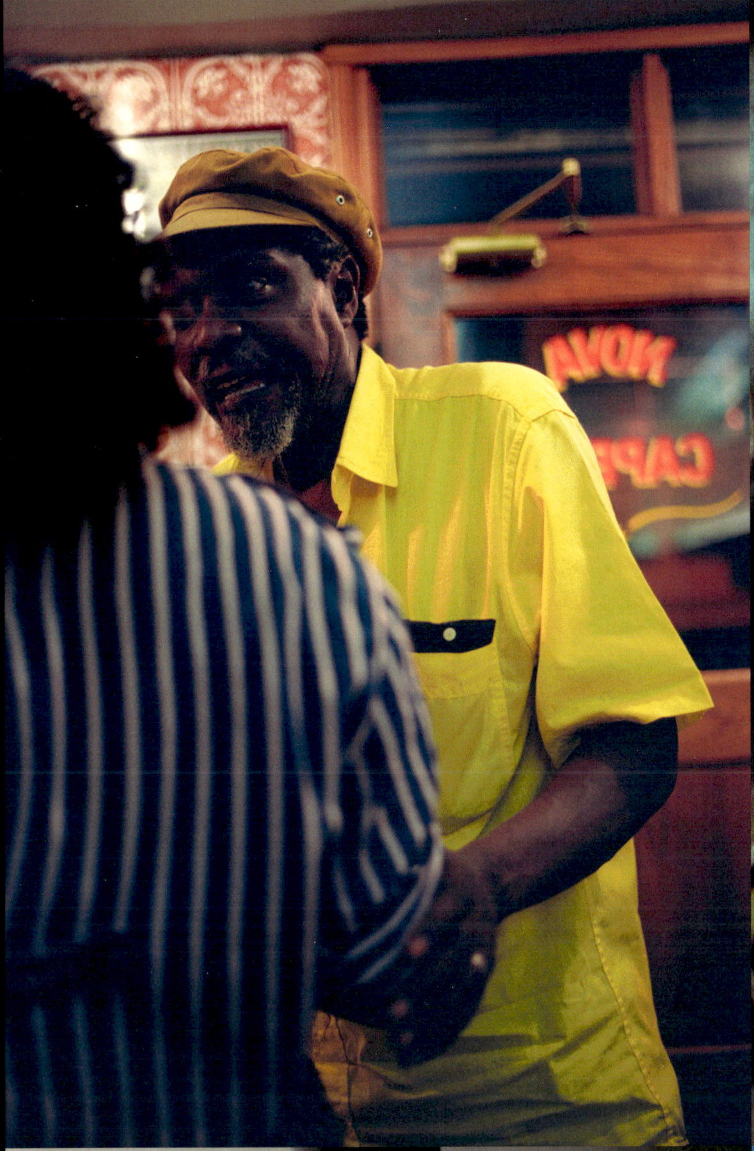
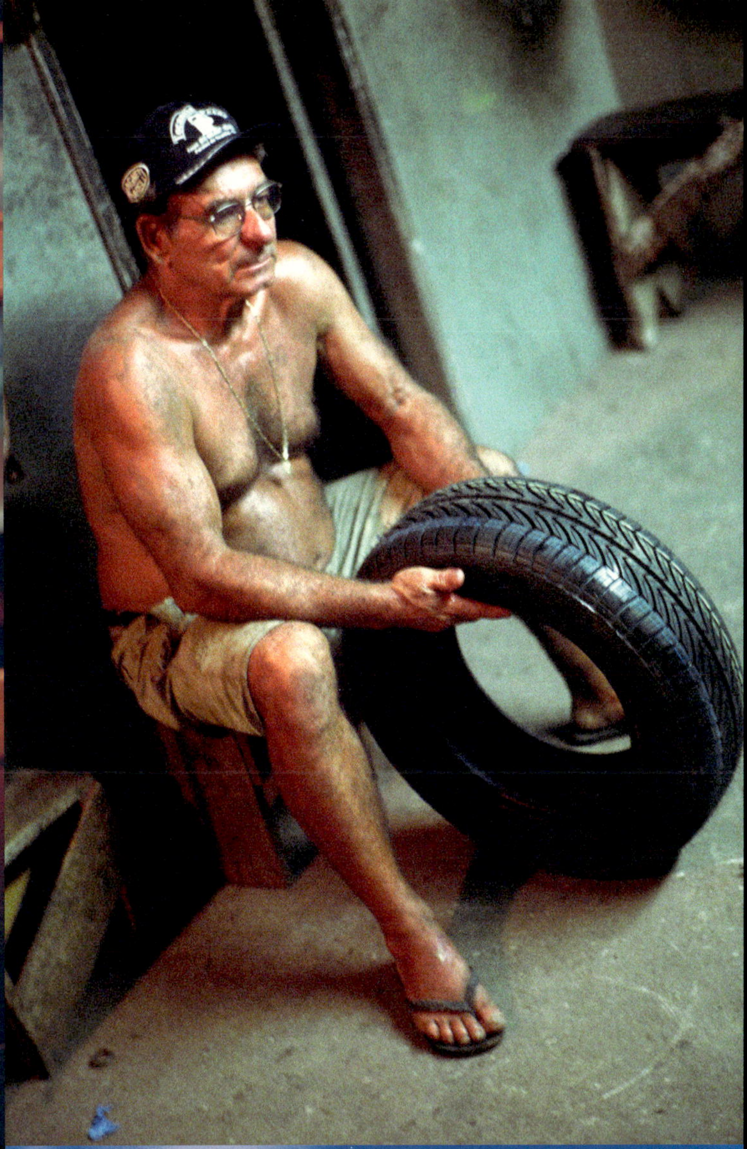
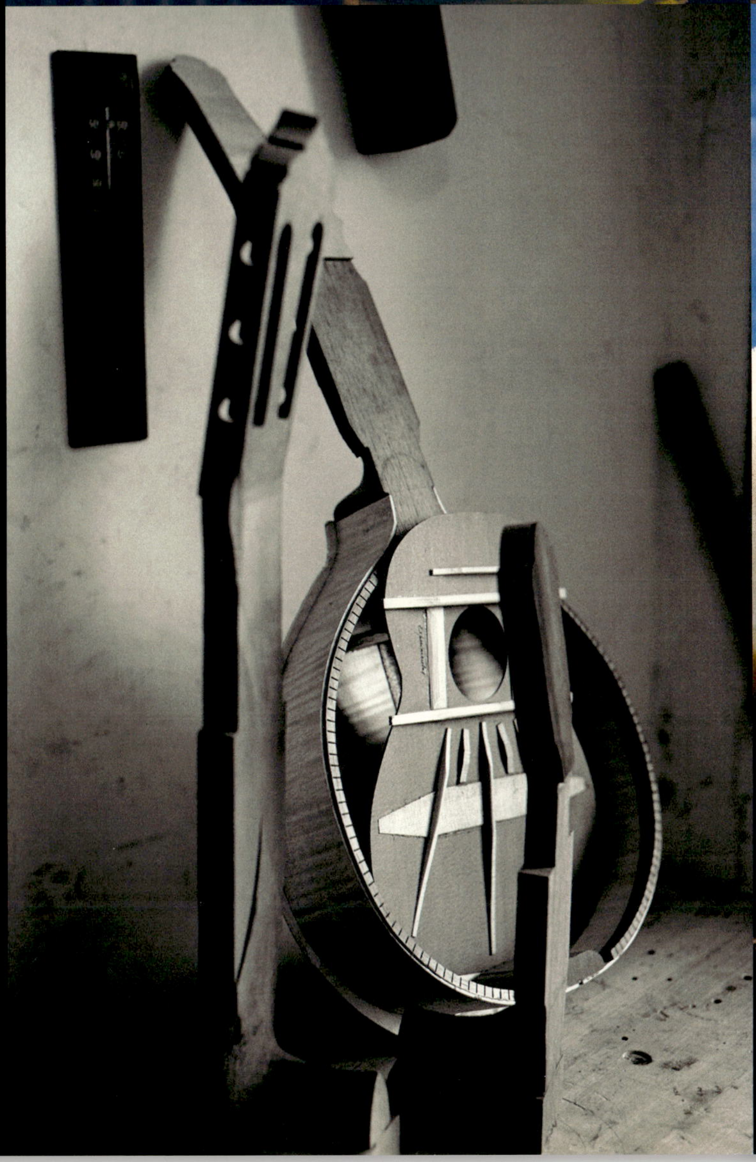
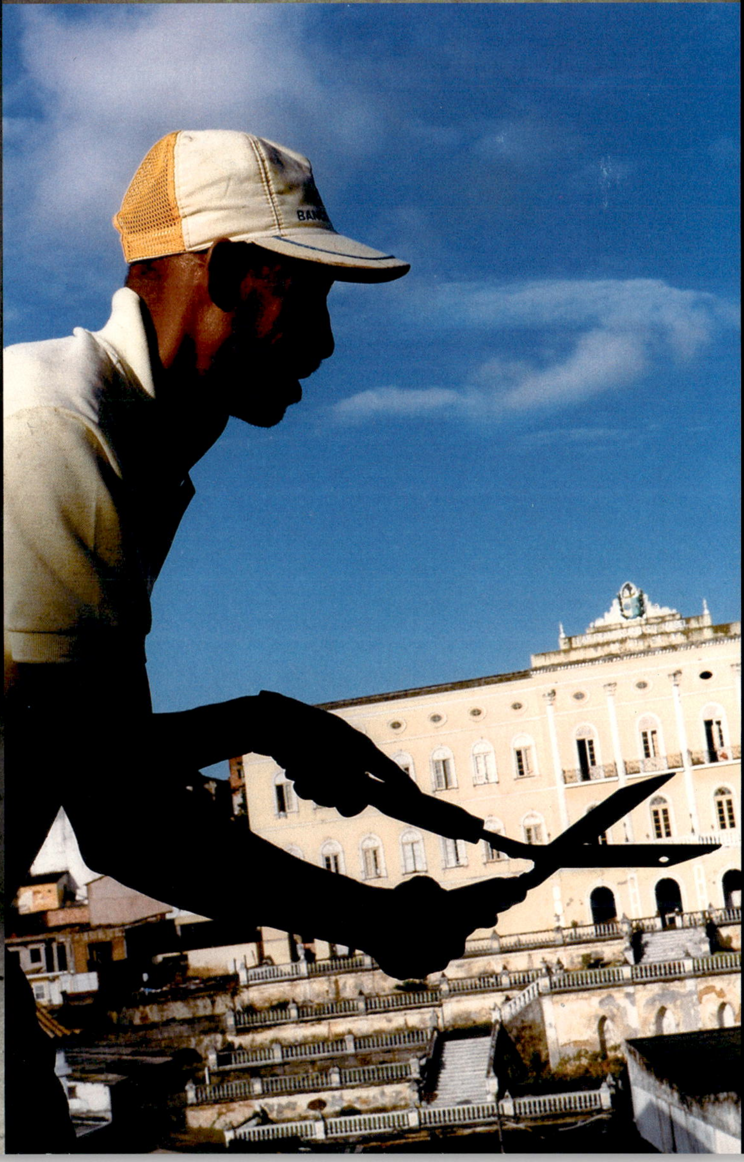

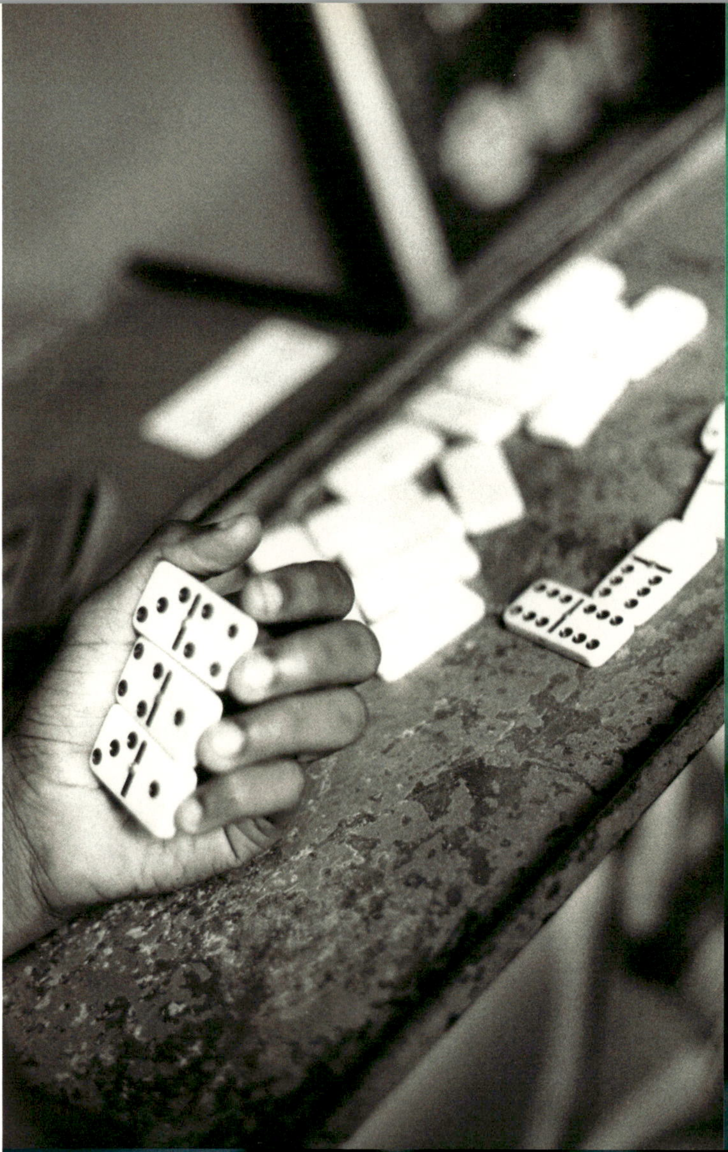

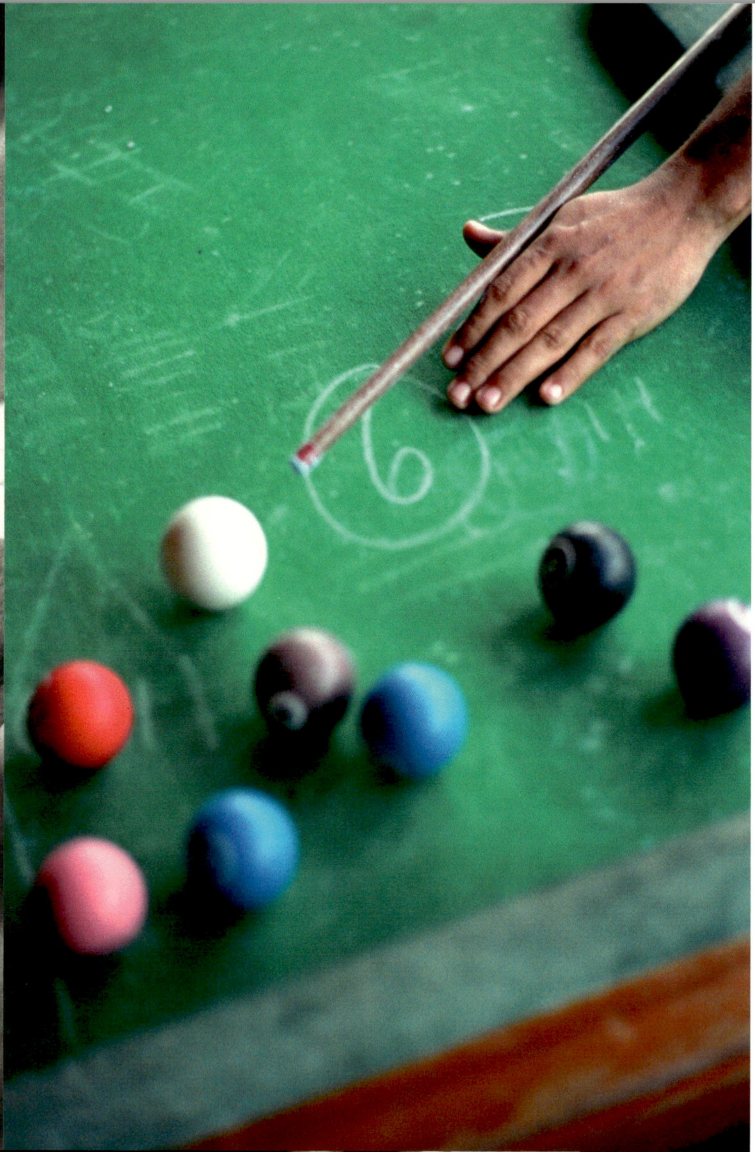

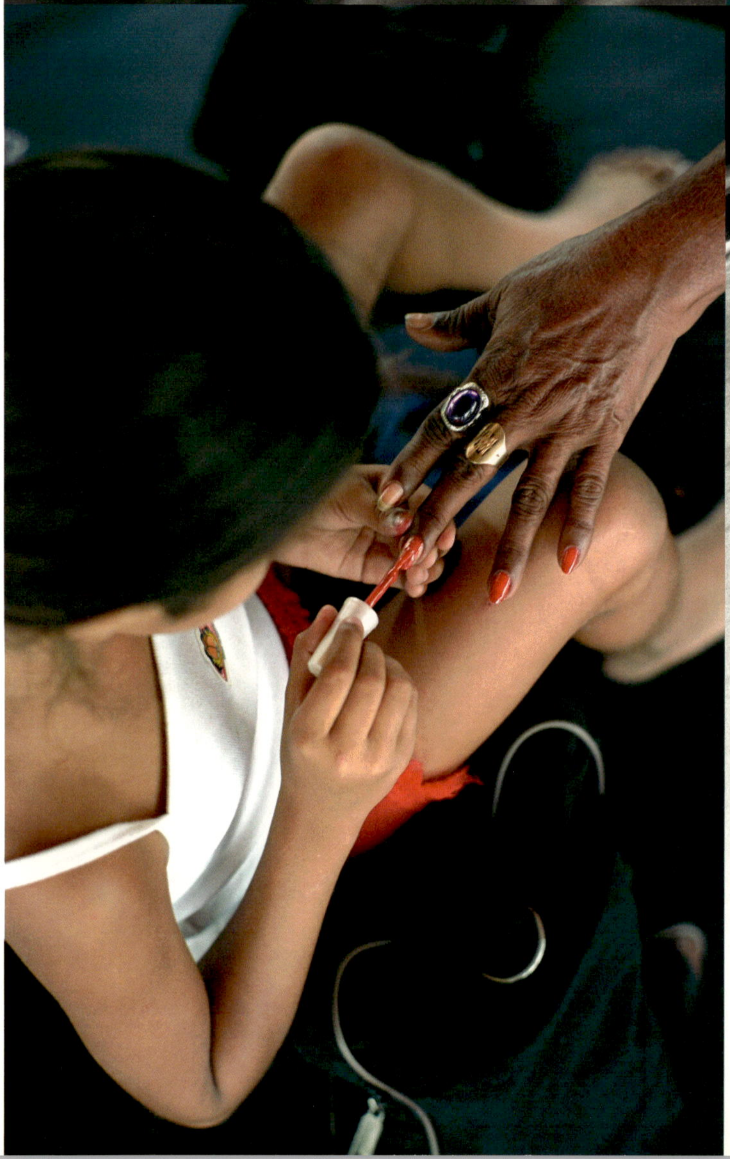

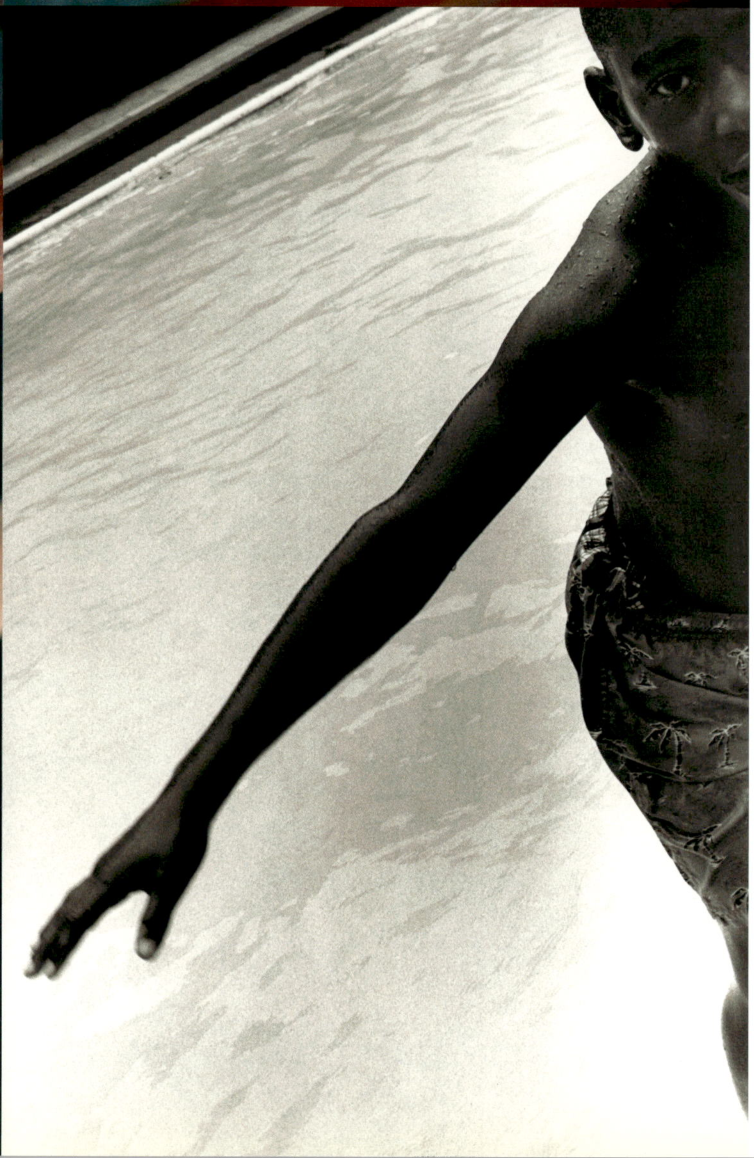

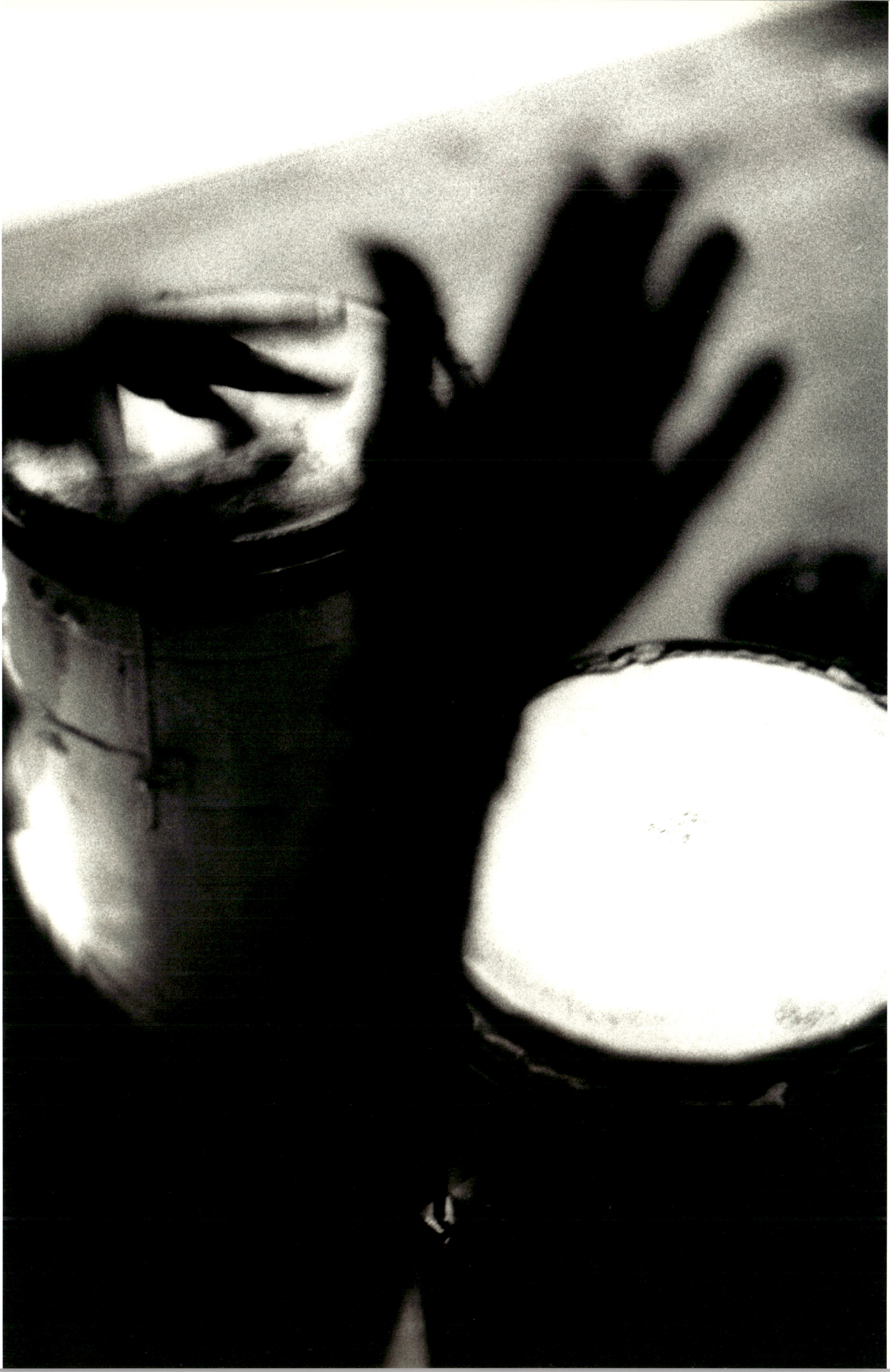

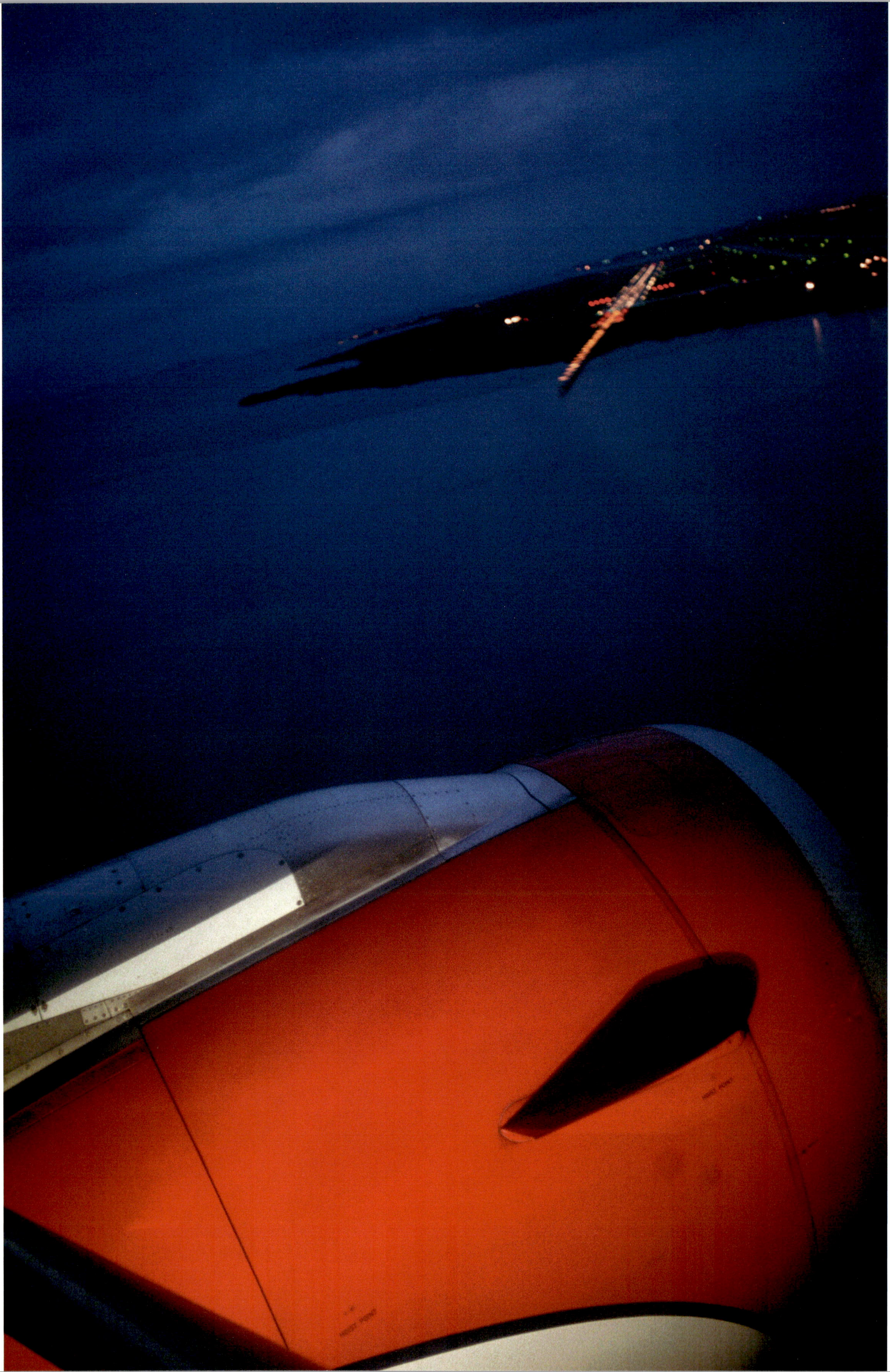

Even before the plane landed I knew, looking out the porthole, that Rio would be my new favorite city. And within the first few hours I realized that this place would fascinate me for a long time. How do citizens define the urban experience when it is immediately flattened up against nature? As if to ask, what is more beautiful, the city or the sea; the people or the architecture? These thoughts stimulate a desire to penetrate the core of the thing, to enter the place itself. It seems that if other cities are sensual in their timbre, Rio is overtly sexual. A smile from a Carioca on the beach will echo for an entire day. Music pours out of every doorway. Life is fully celebrated. The aura of Brasil floats above the throngs and smells and sounds and the visitor is taken away without choice into the whirlpool of experience.

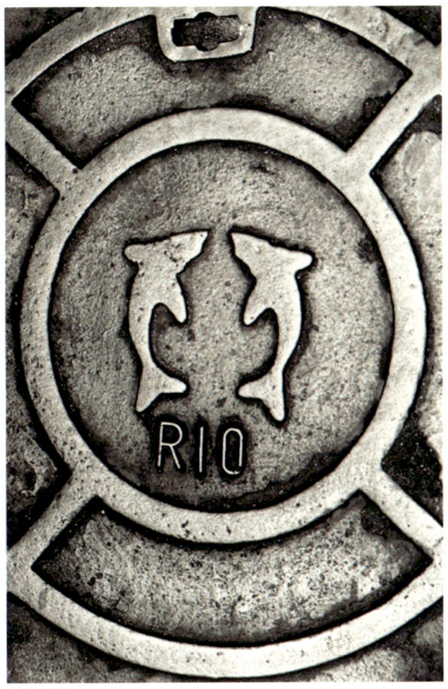

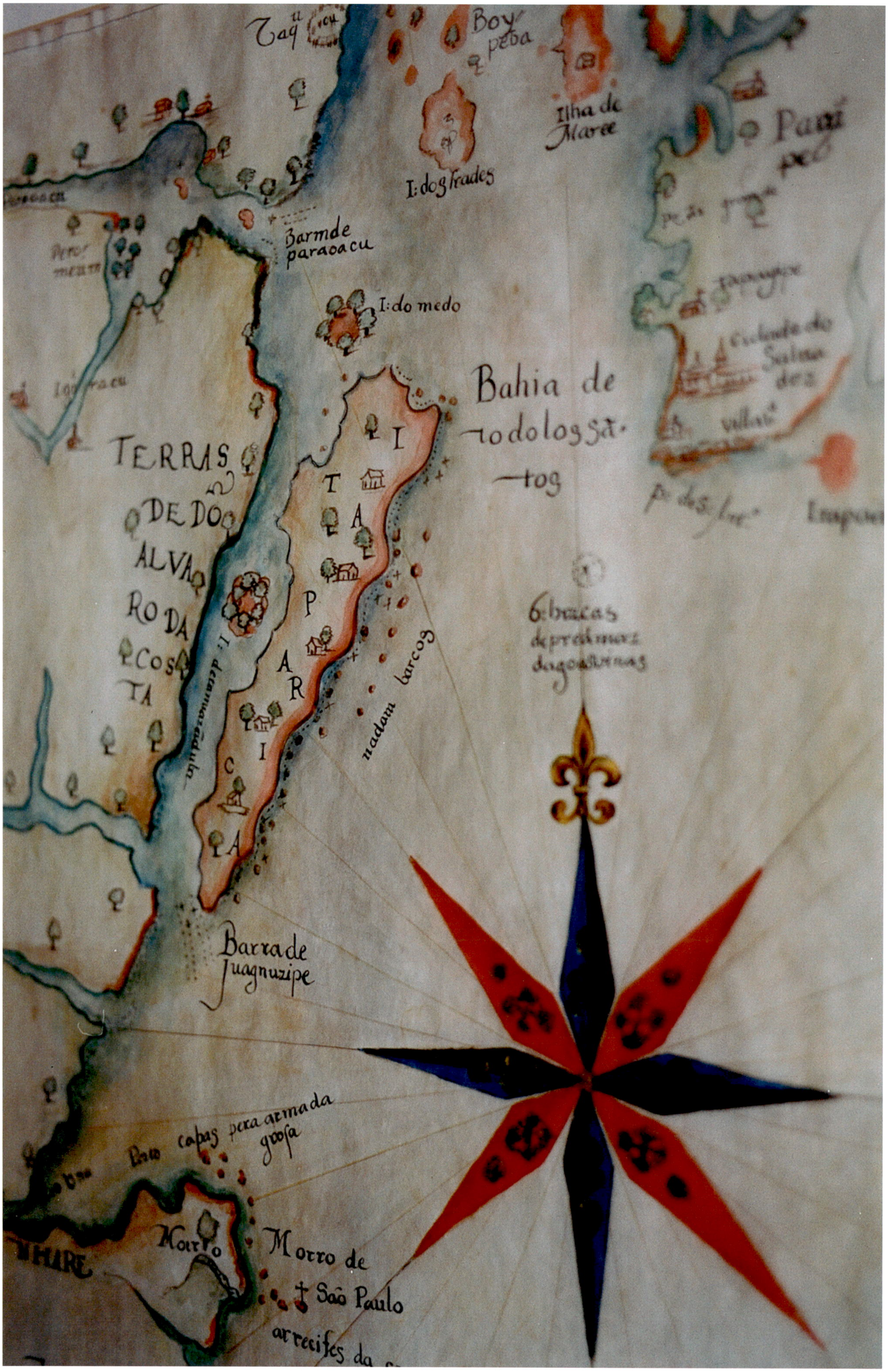
Boy peba
Ilha de Maree
I: dos frades
Barmde paraoacu
I: do medo
Bahia de todolos sã tos
TERRAS DE DO ALVA RO DA COS TA
I T A P A R I C A
nadam barcos
Barra de Juagnuzipe
capas pera armada grosa
Morro
Morro de São Paulo
arrecifes da

Ancor prima di atterrare sapevo, guardando dall'oblò, che Rio sarebbe diventata la mia nuova città preferita. E nell'arco di poche ore mi resi conto che questo posto mi avrebbe incantato per lungo tempo. In che modo i cittadini definiscono l'esperienza urbana quando questa è irrimediabilmente appiattita contro la natura? Come a chiedere se sia più bella la città o il mare; la gente o l'architettura. Tali riflessioni stimolano il desiderio di penetrare l'essenza delle cose, di addentrarsi nel luogo stesso. Se altre città sono dotate di carattere sensuale, Rio sembra essere esplicitamente sessuale. Il sorriso di un Carioca sulla spiaggia risuonerà per un'intera giornata. La musica sgorga da ogni uscio. La vita è al culmine della sua celebrazione. L'aura del Brasile galleggia al di sopra delle masse, degli odori e dei suoni, mentre il viaggiatore è catturato senza scampo nel vortice dell'esperienza.

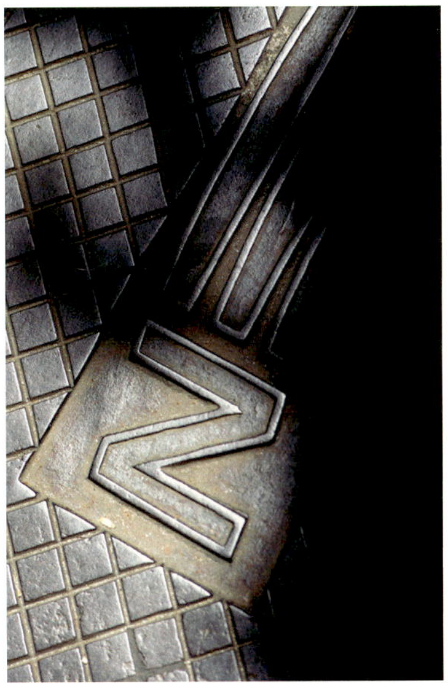

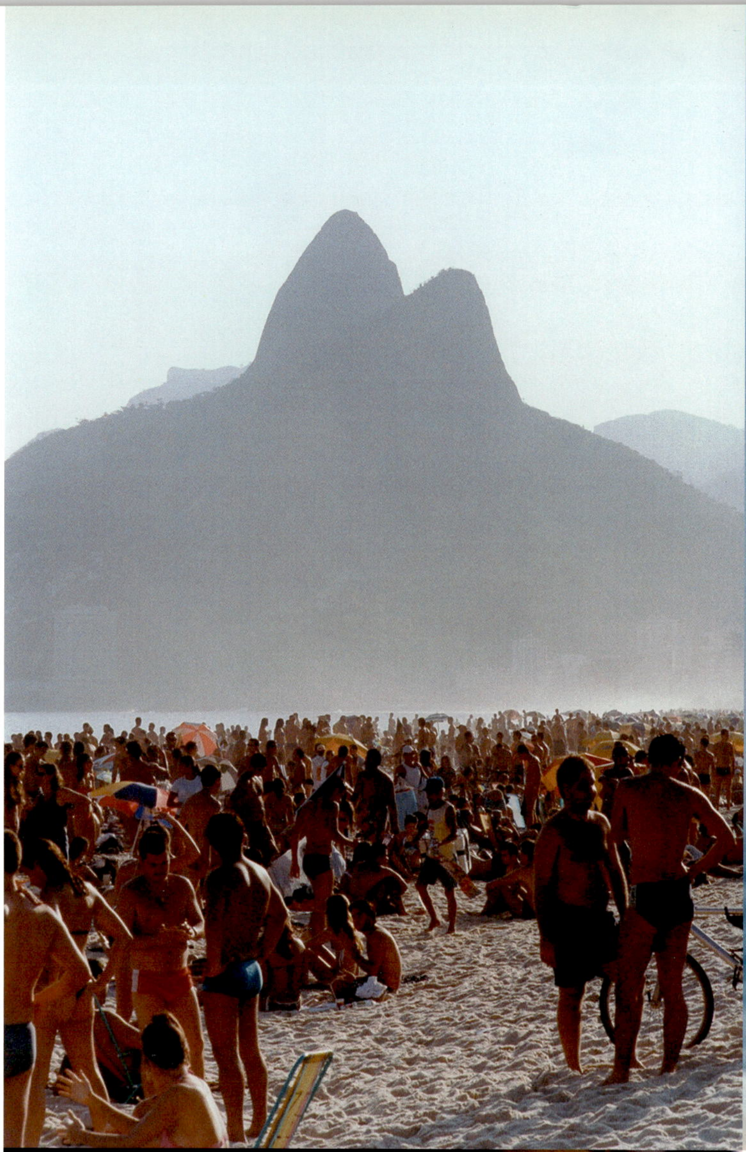

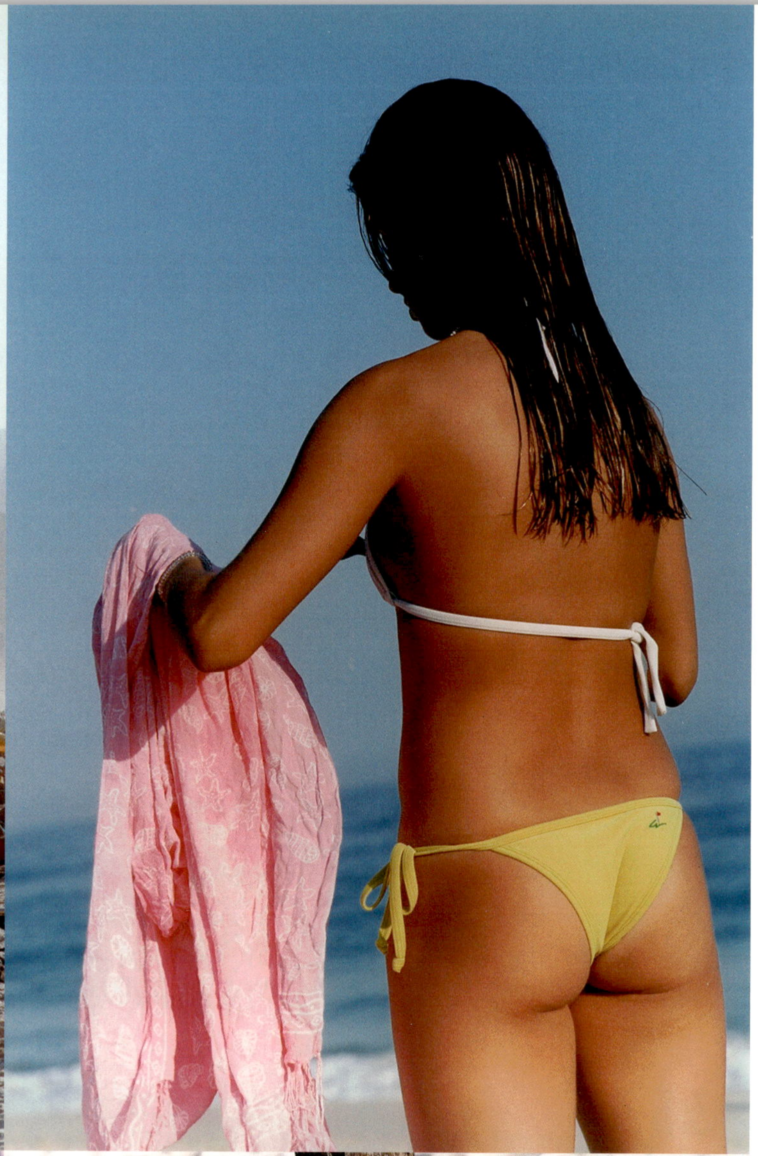

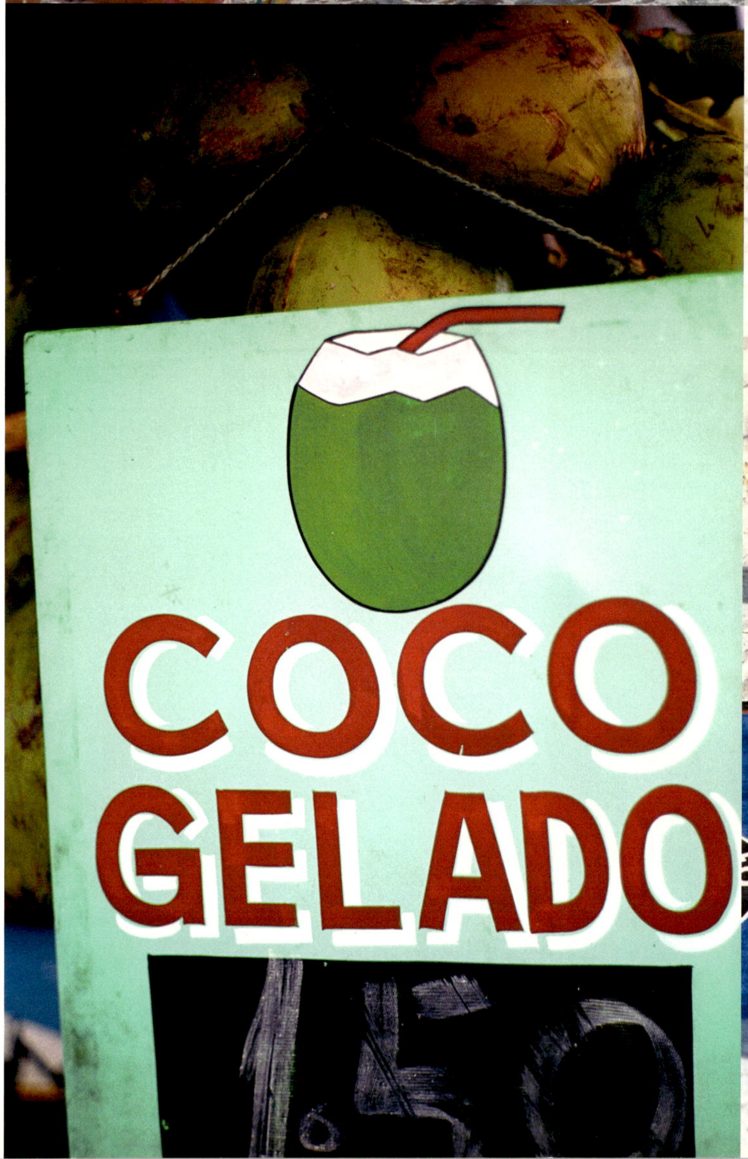
COCO
GELADO

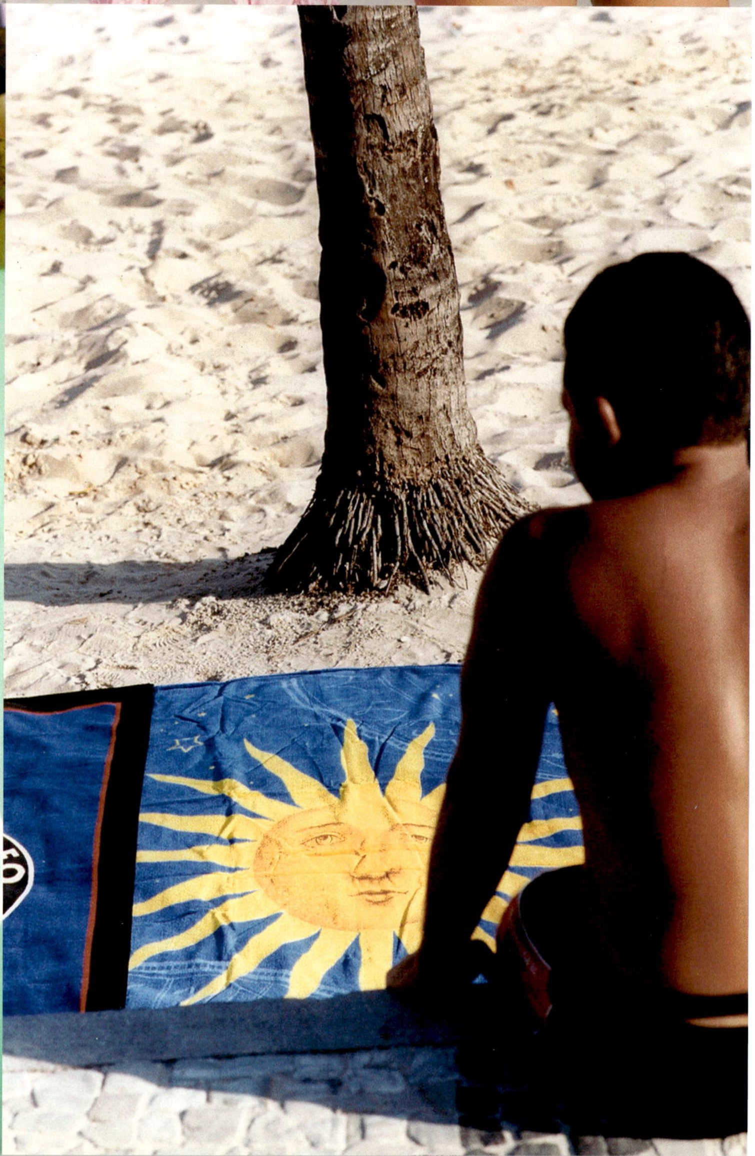

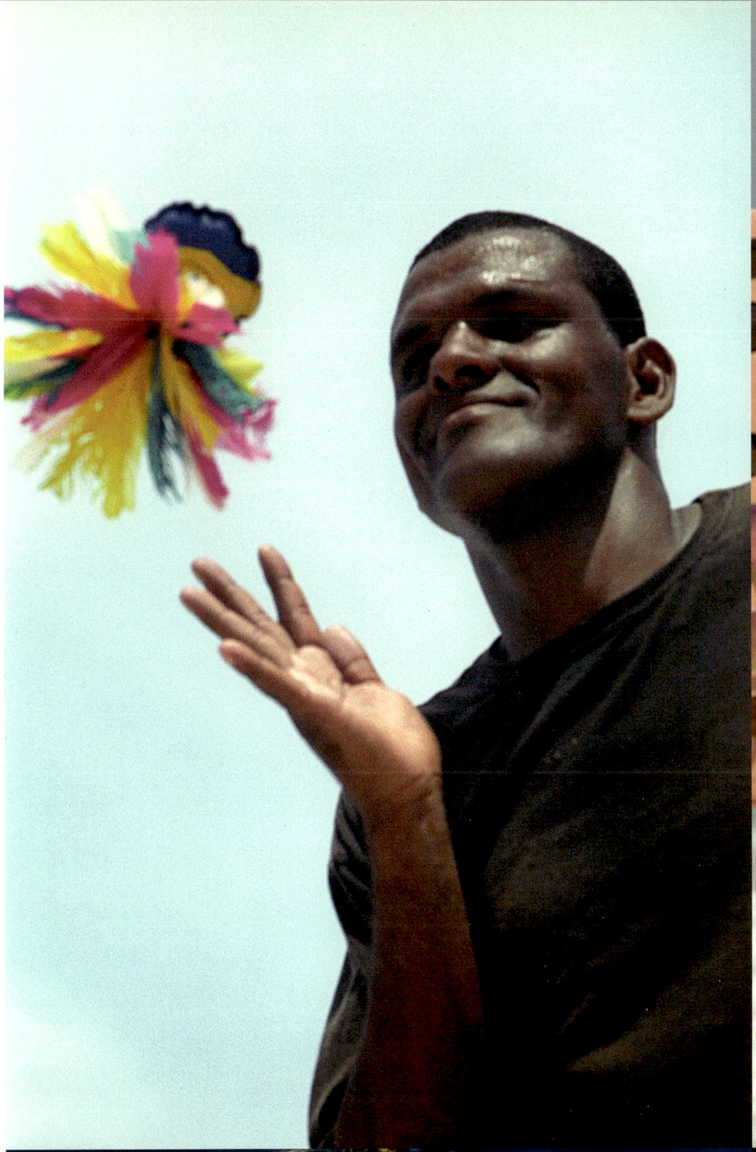
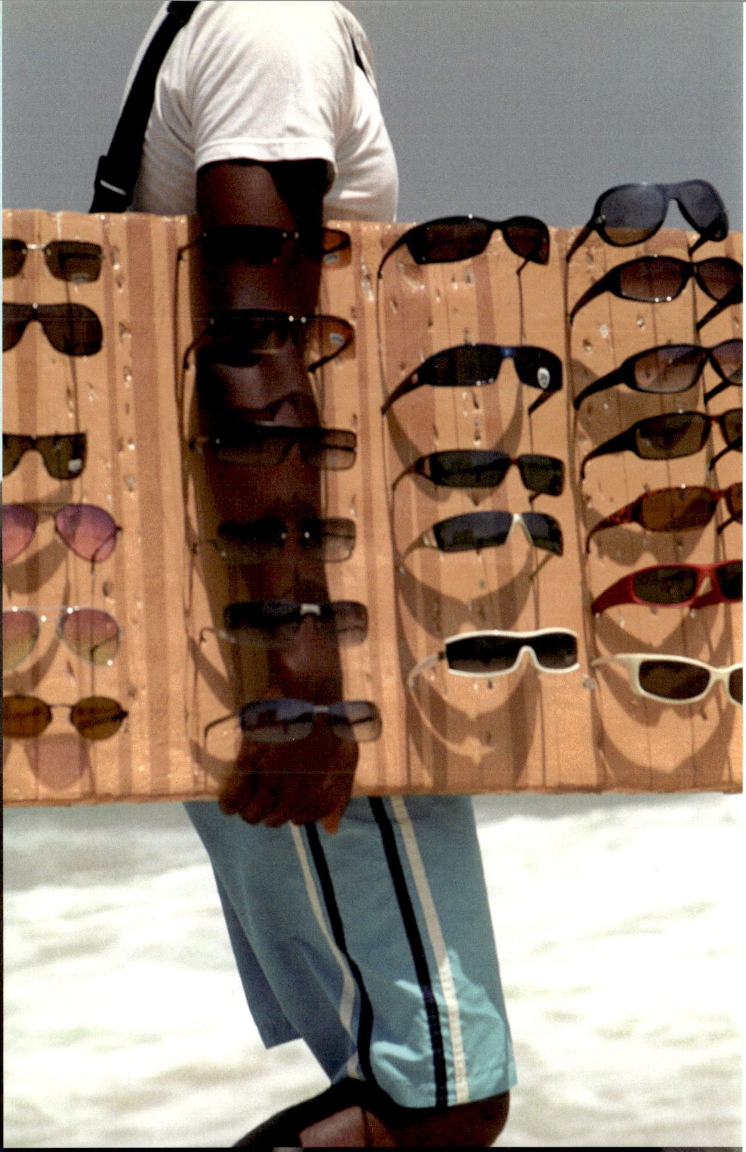
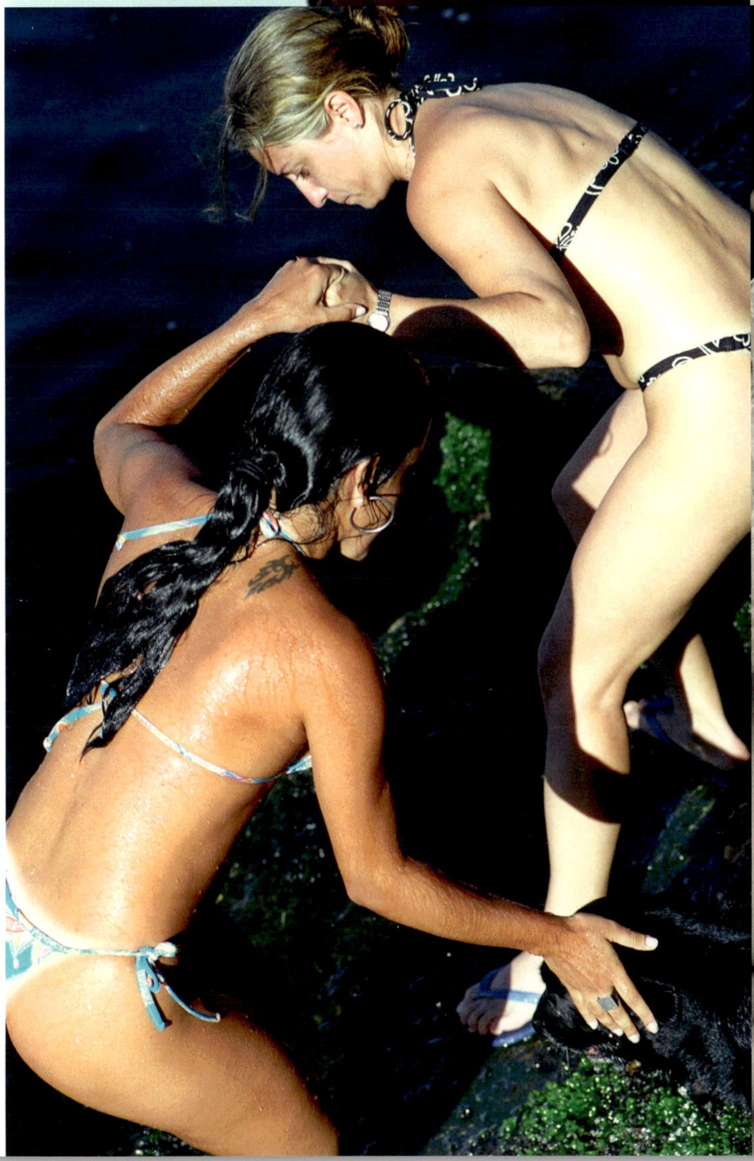
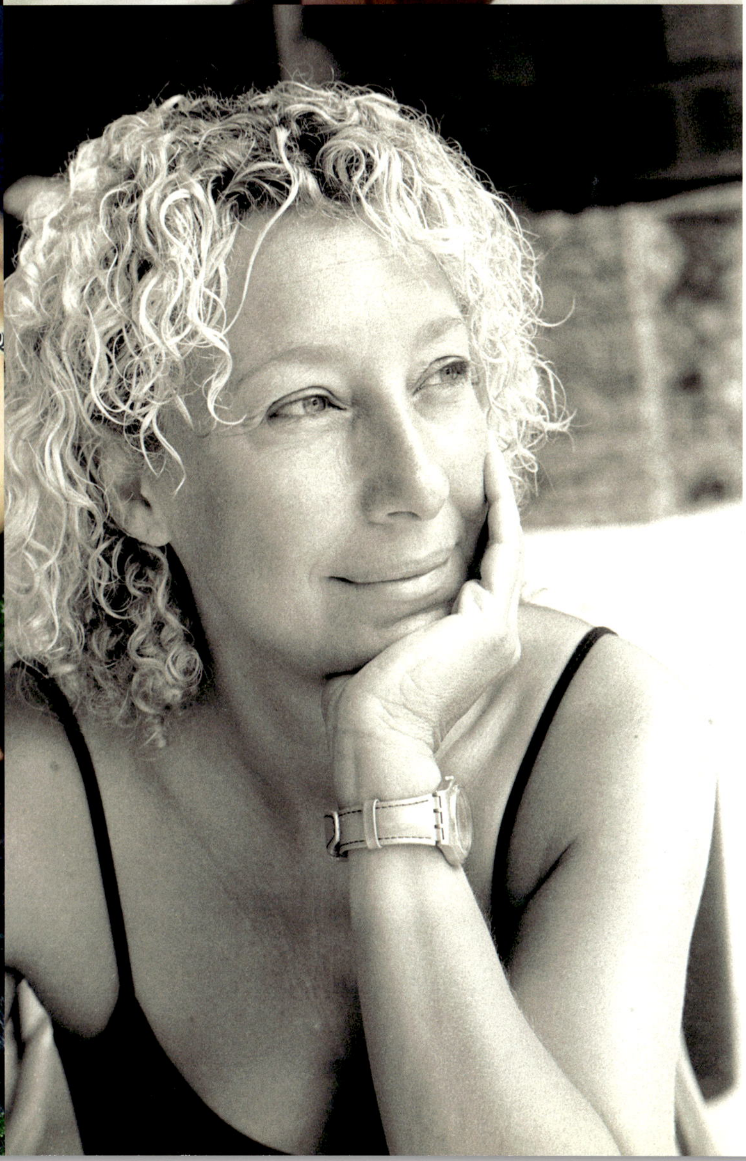

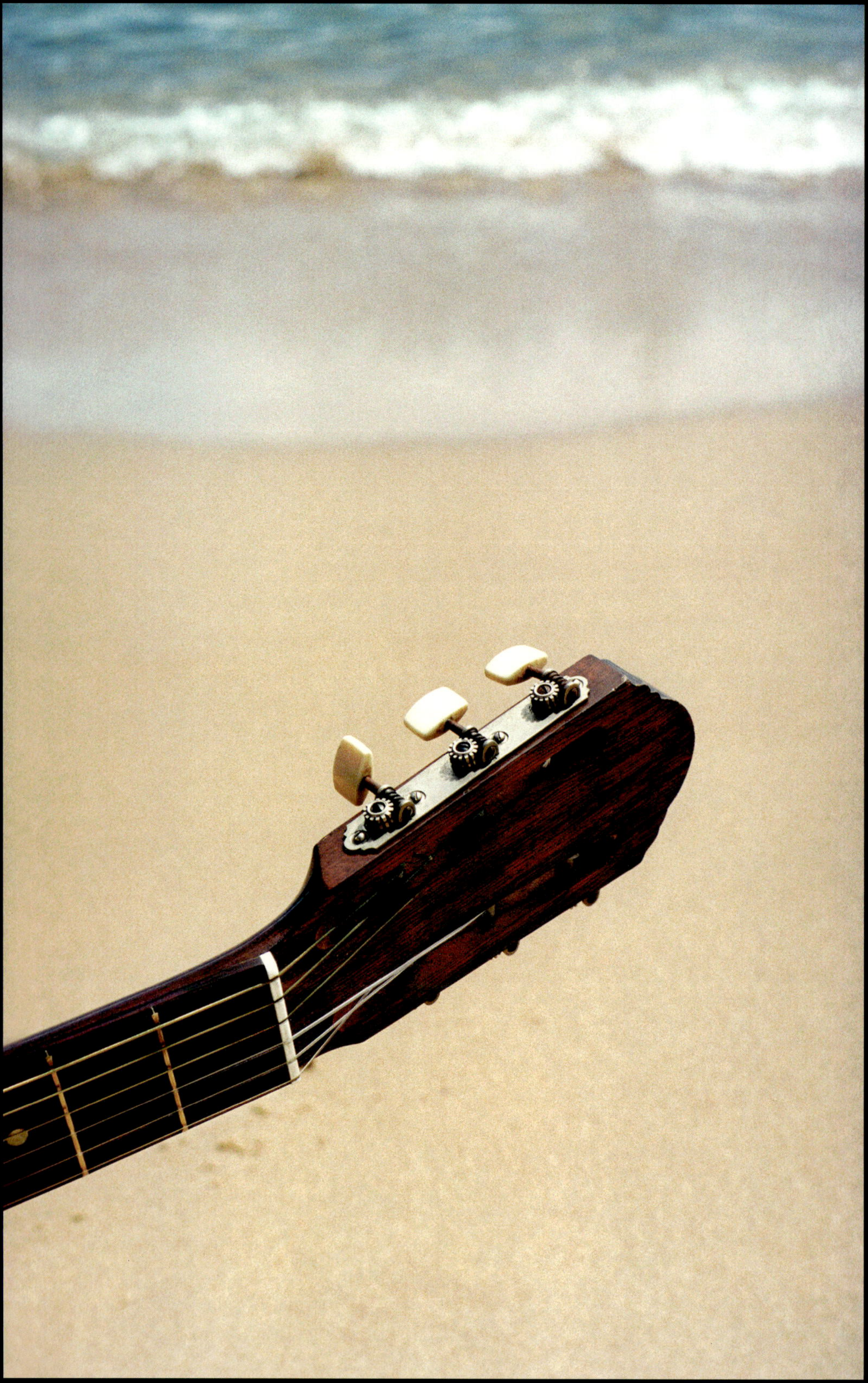

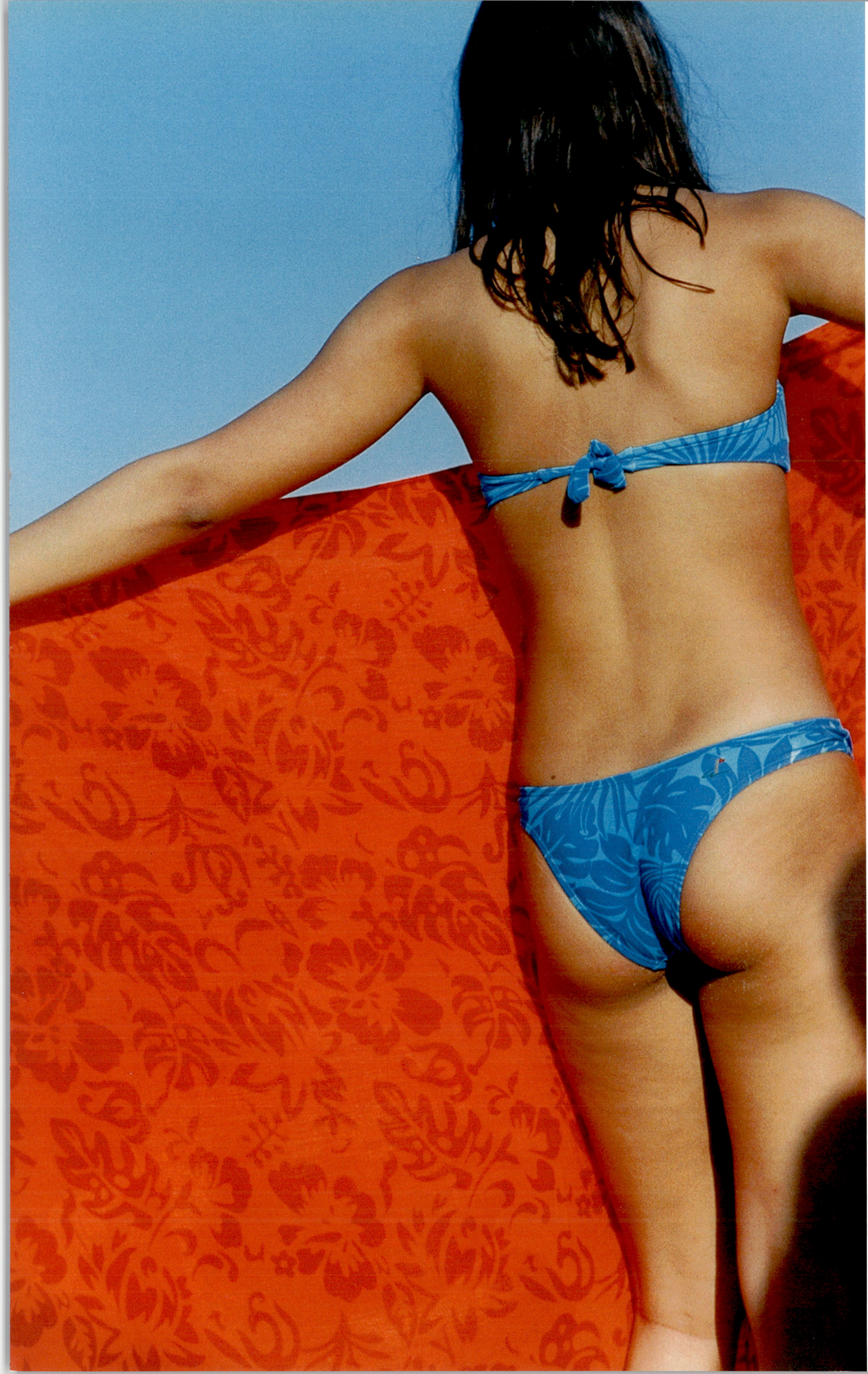

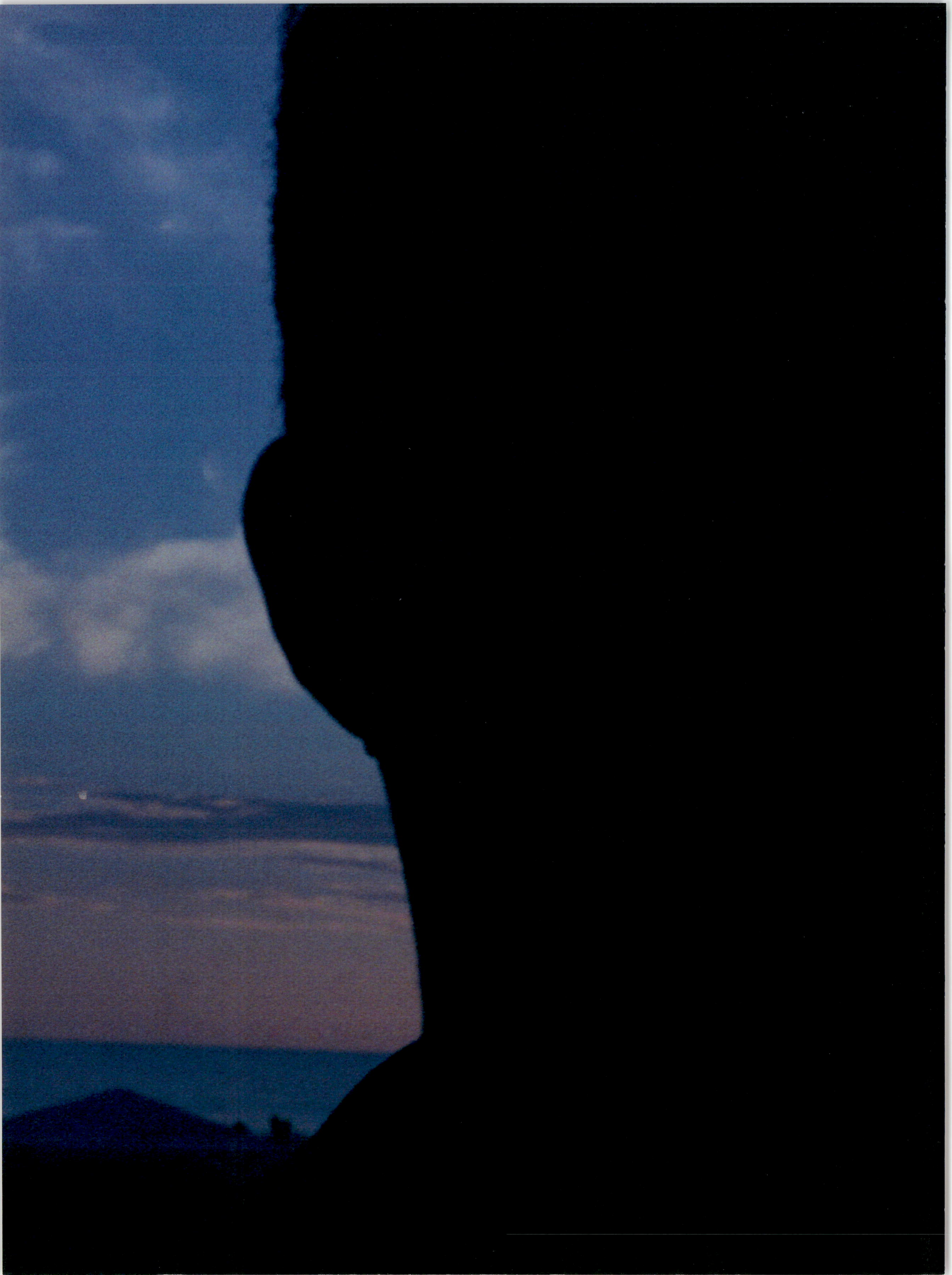

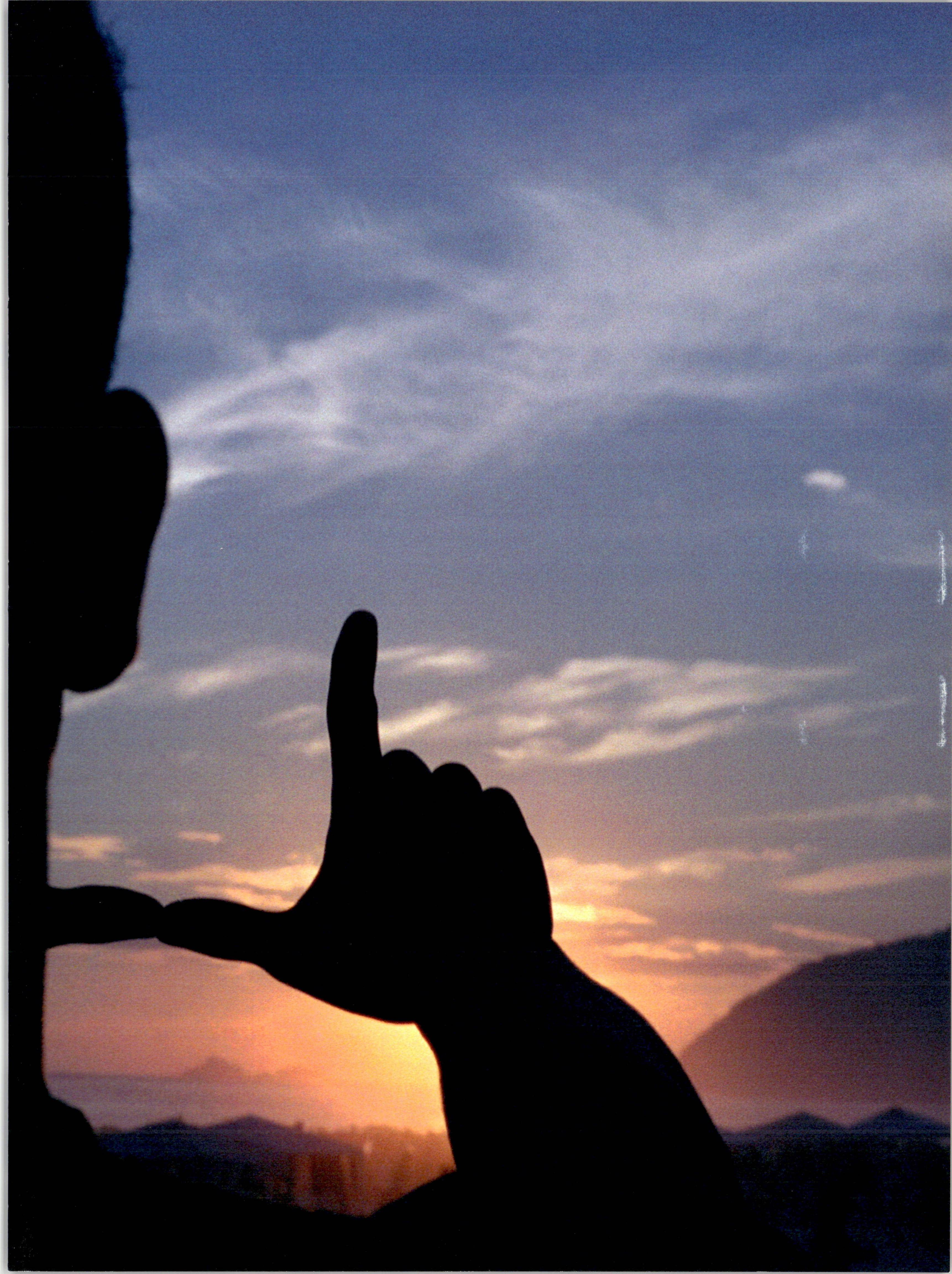

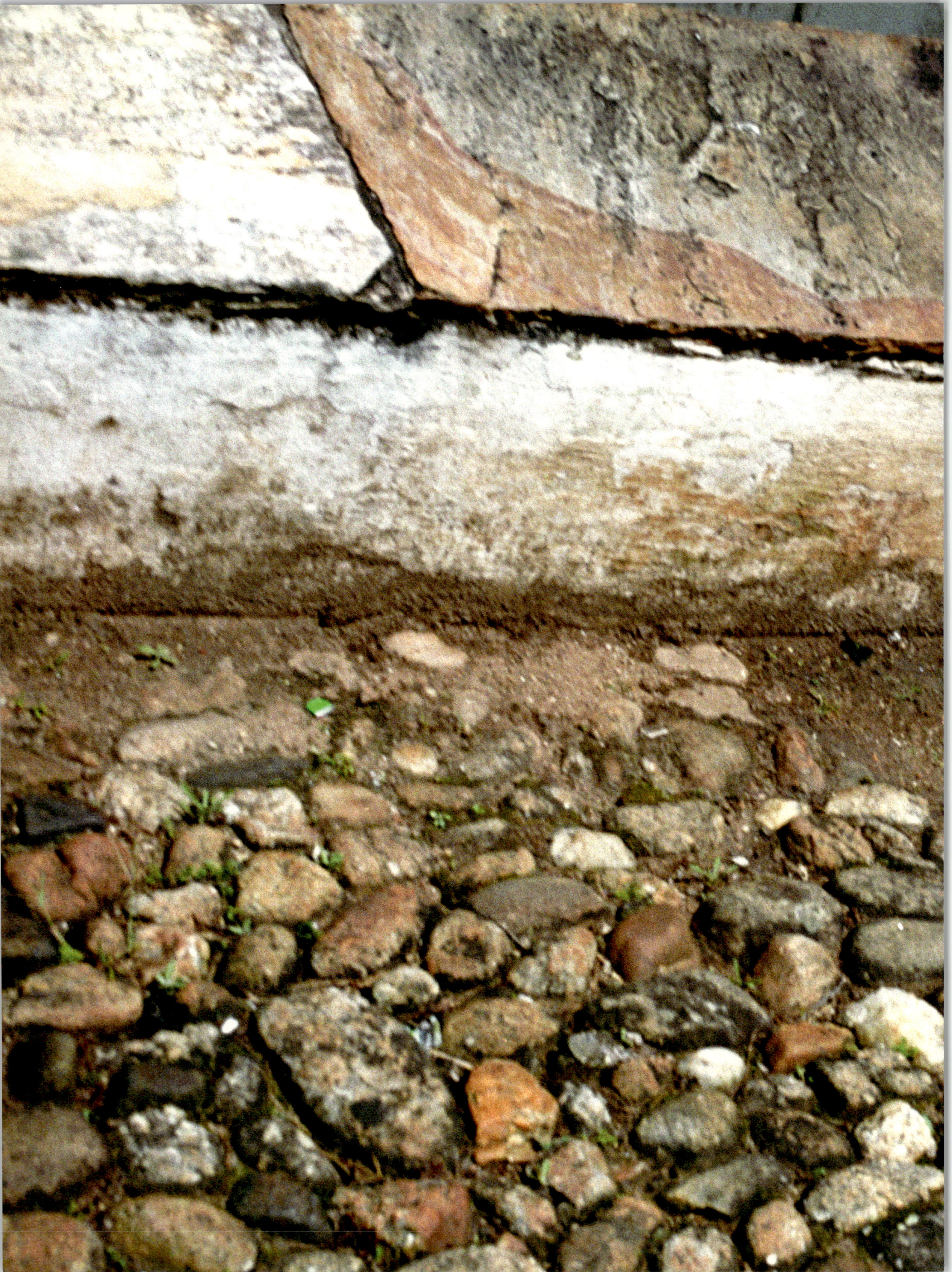

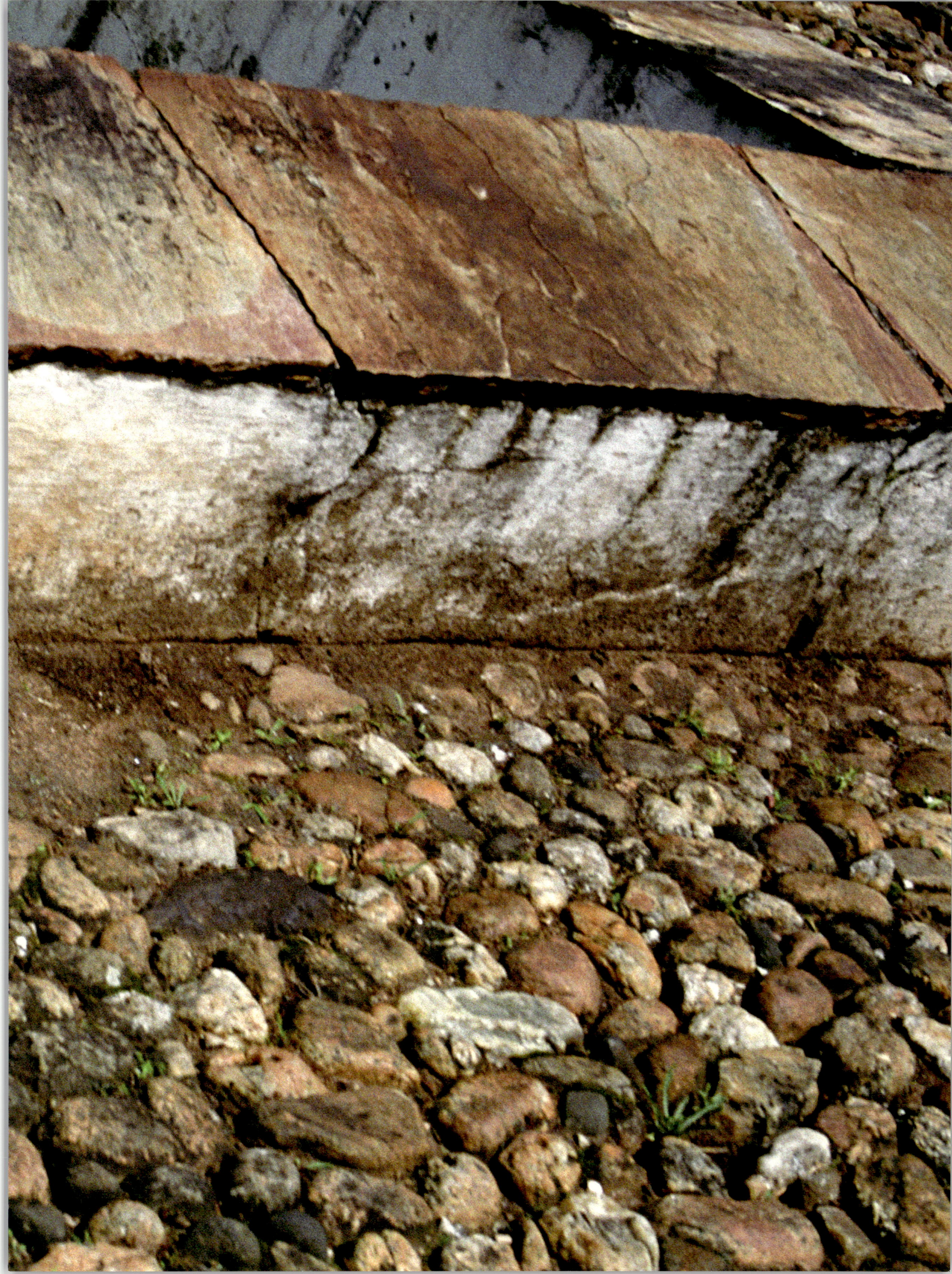

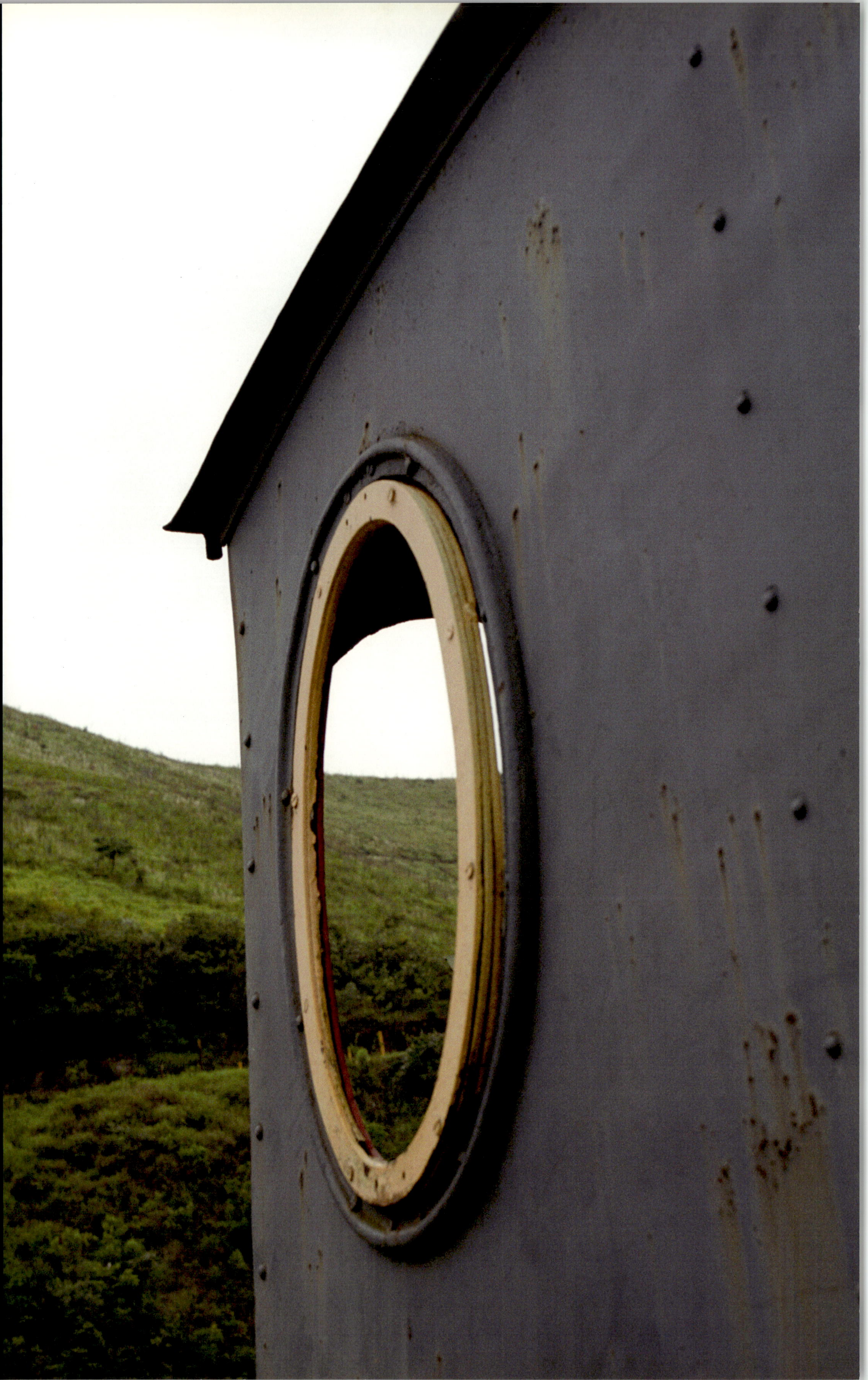

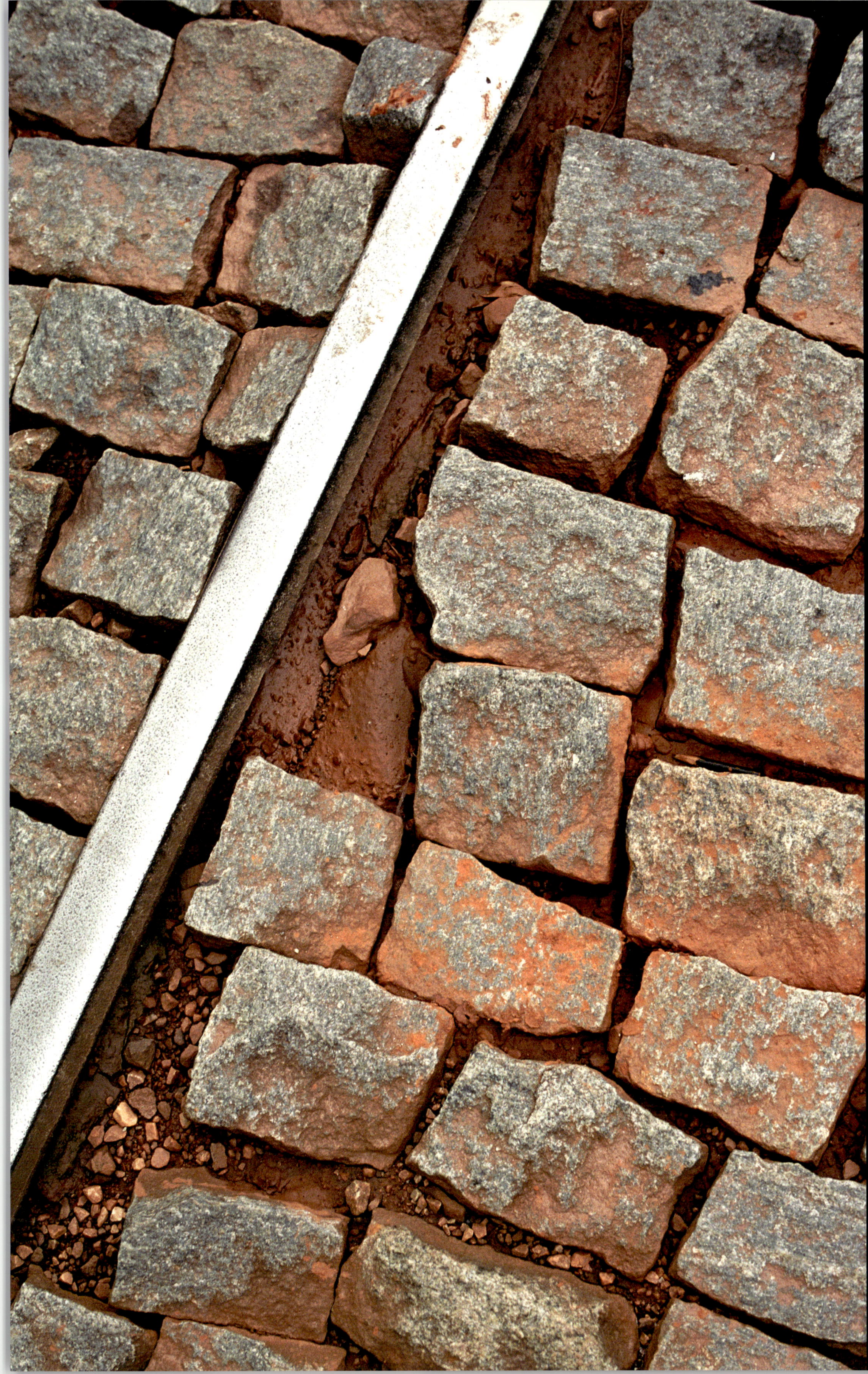

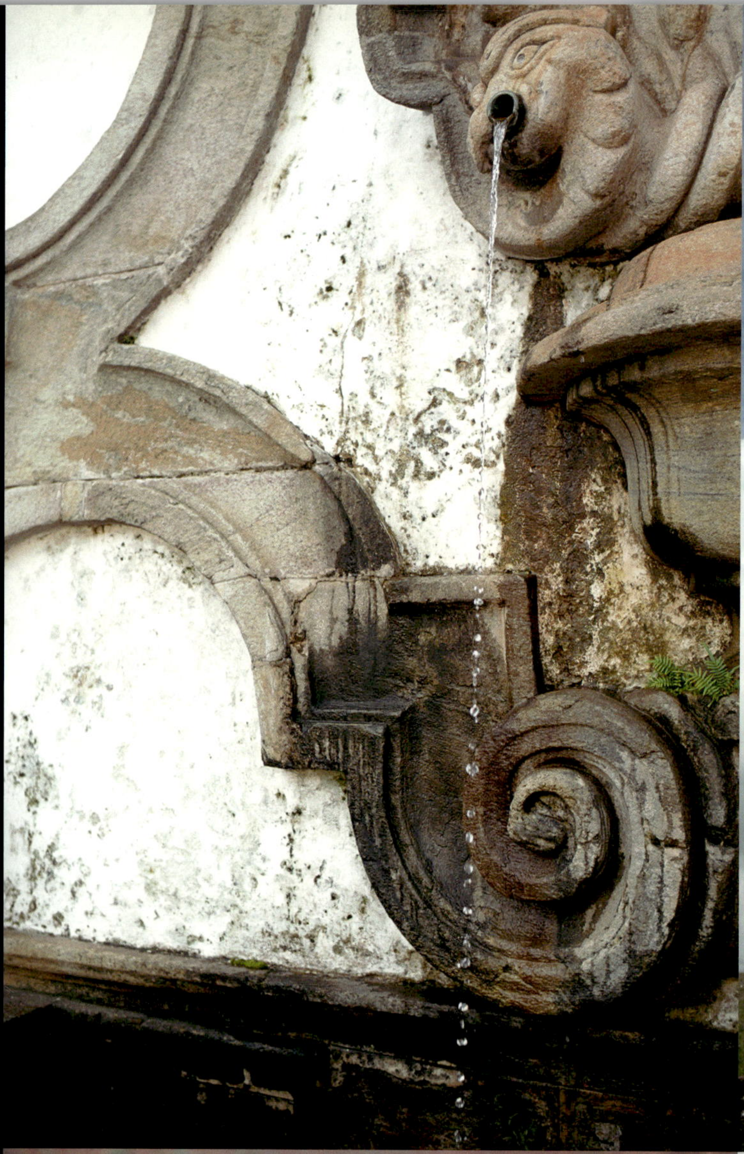
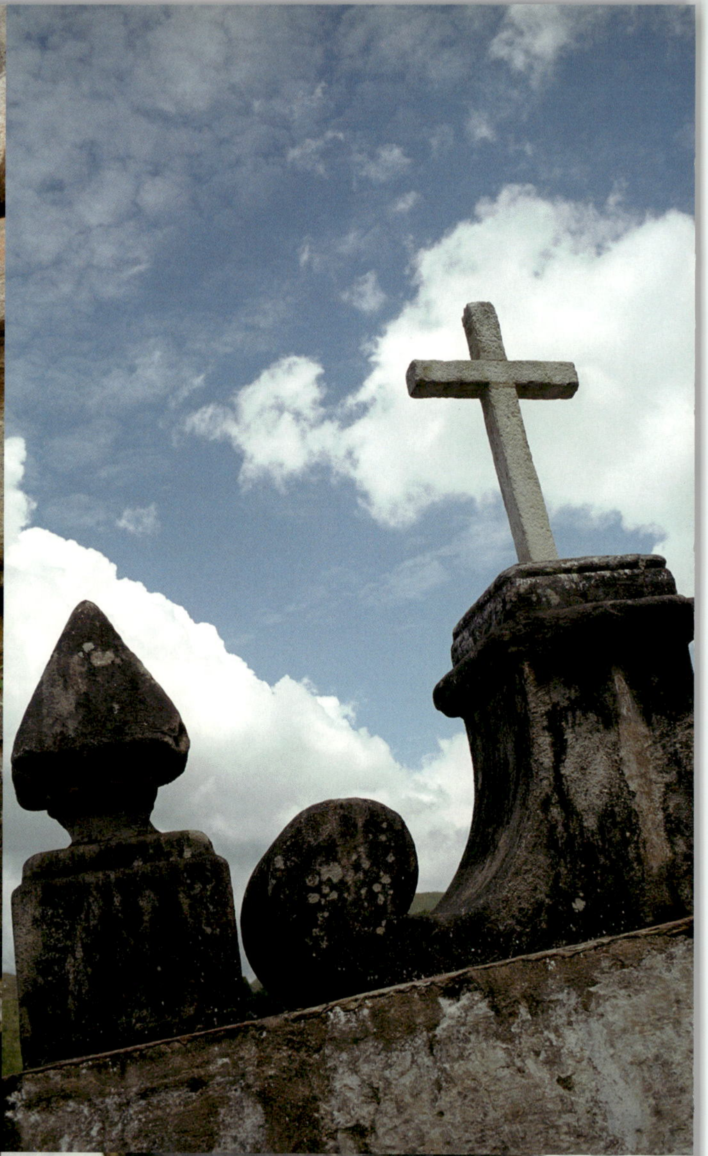
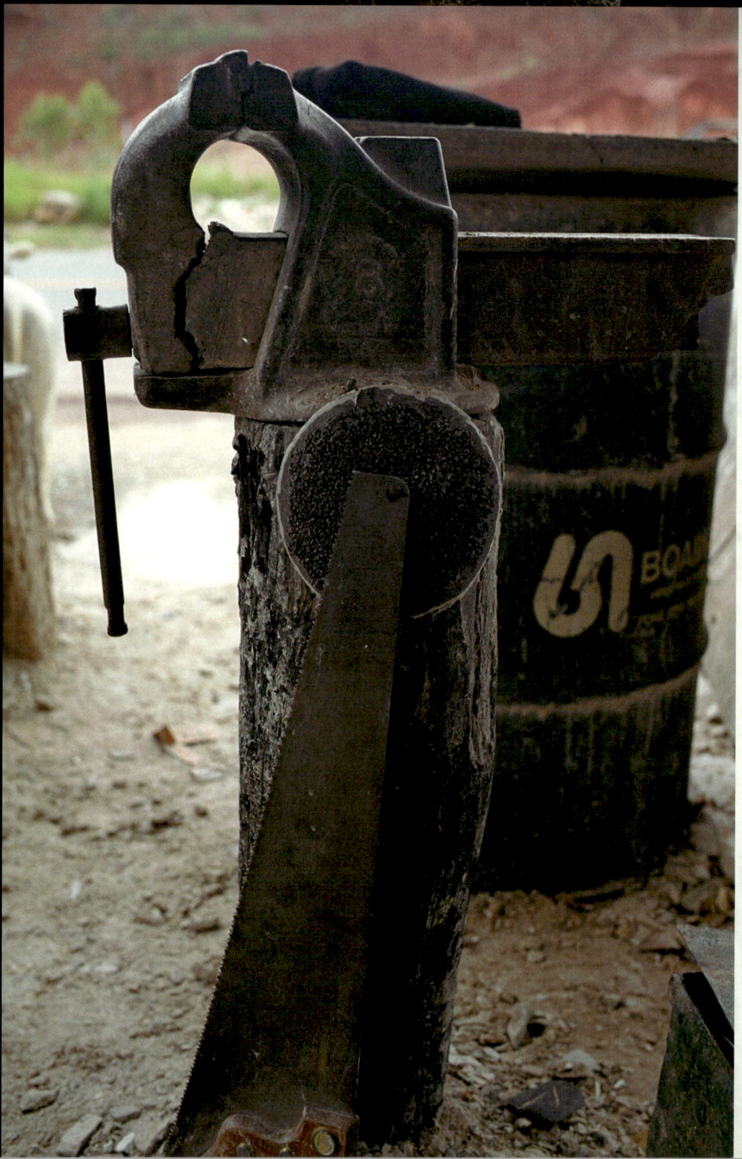
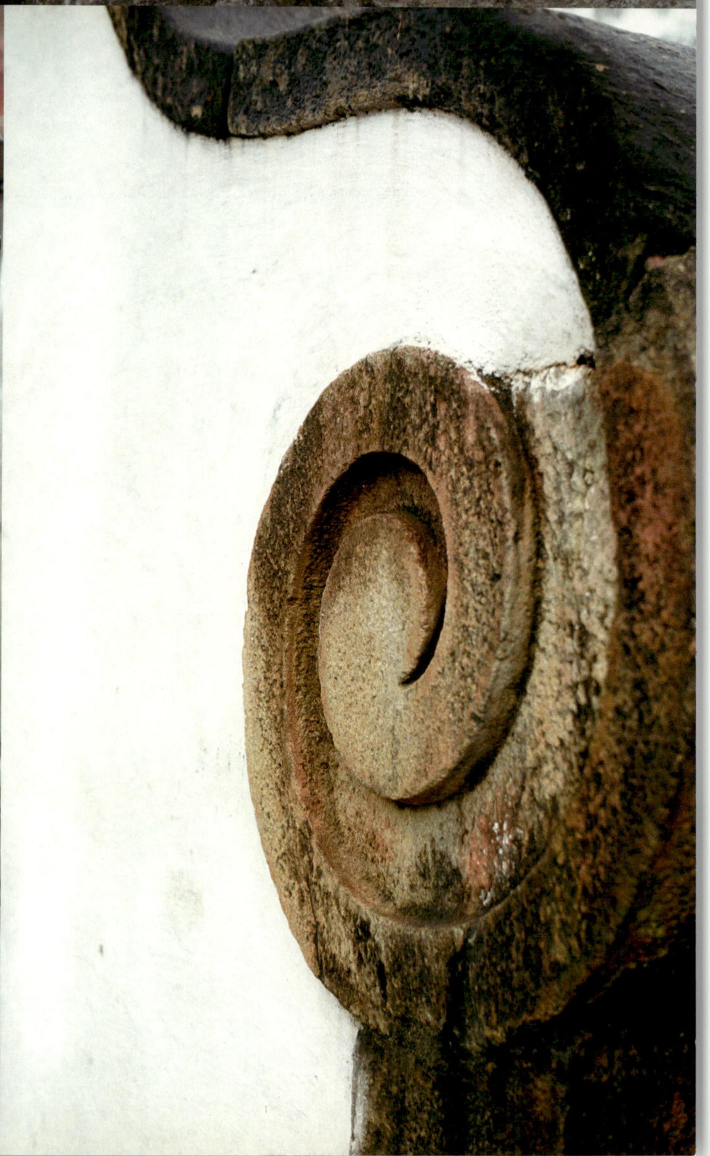

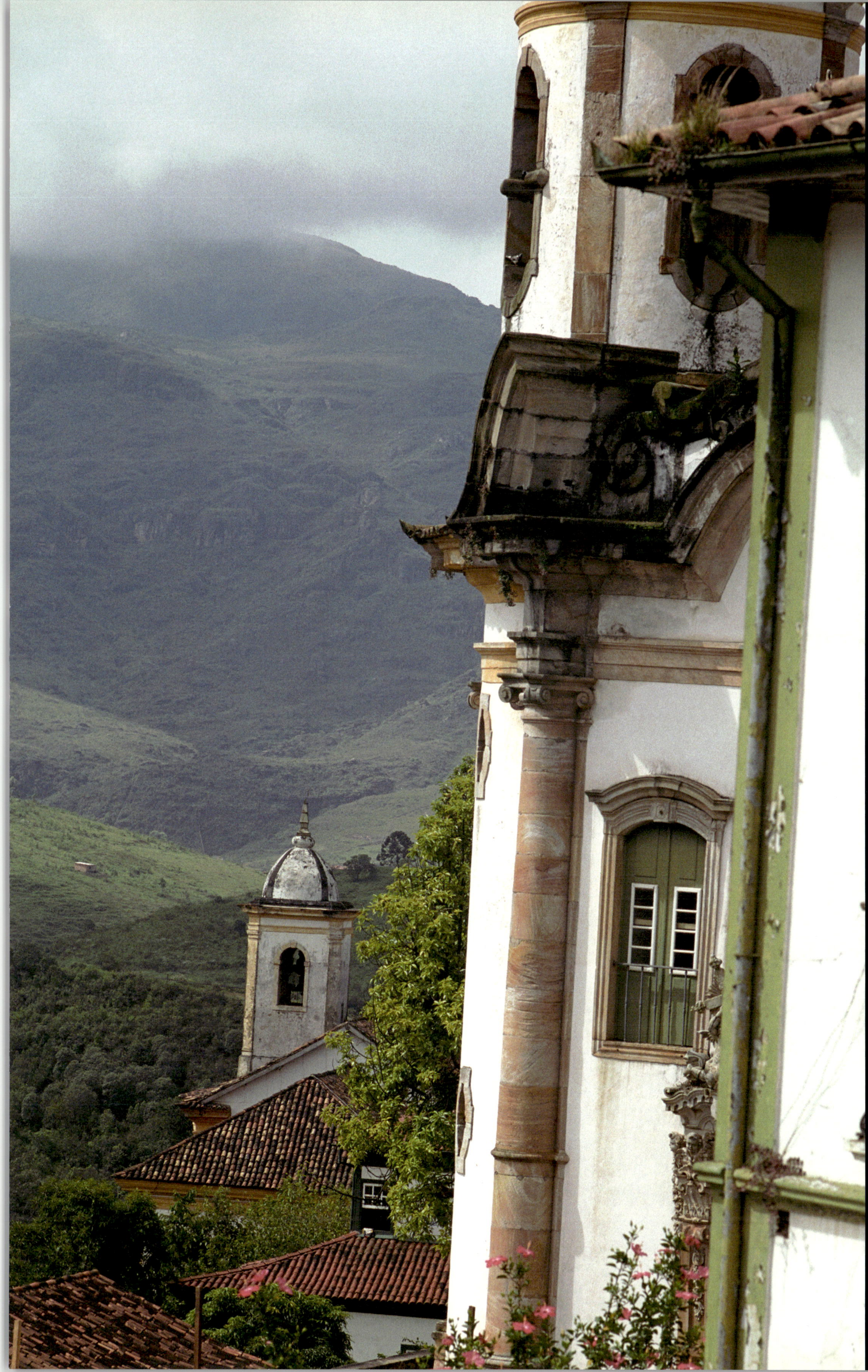

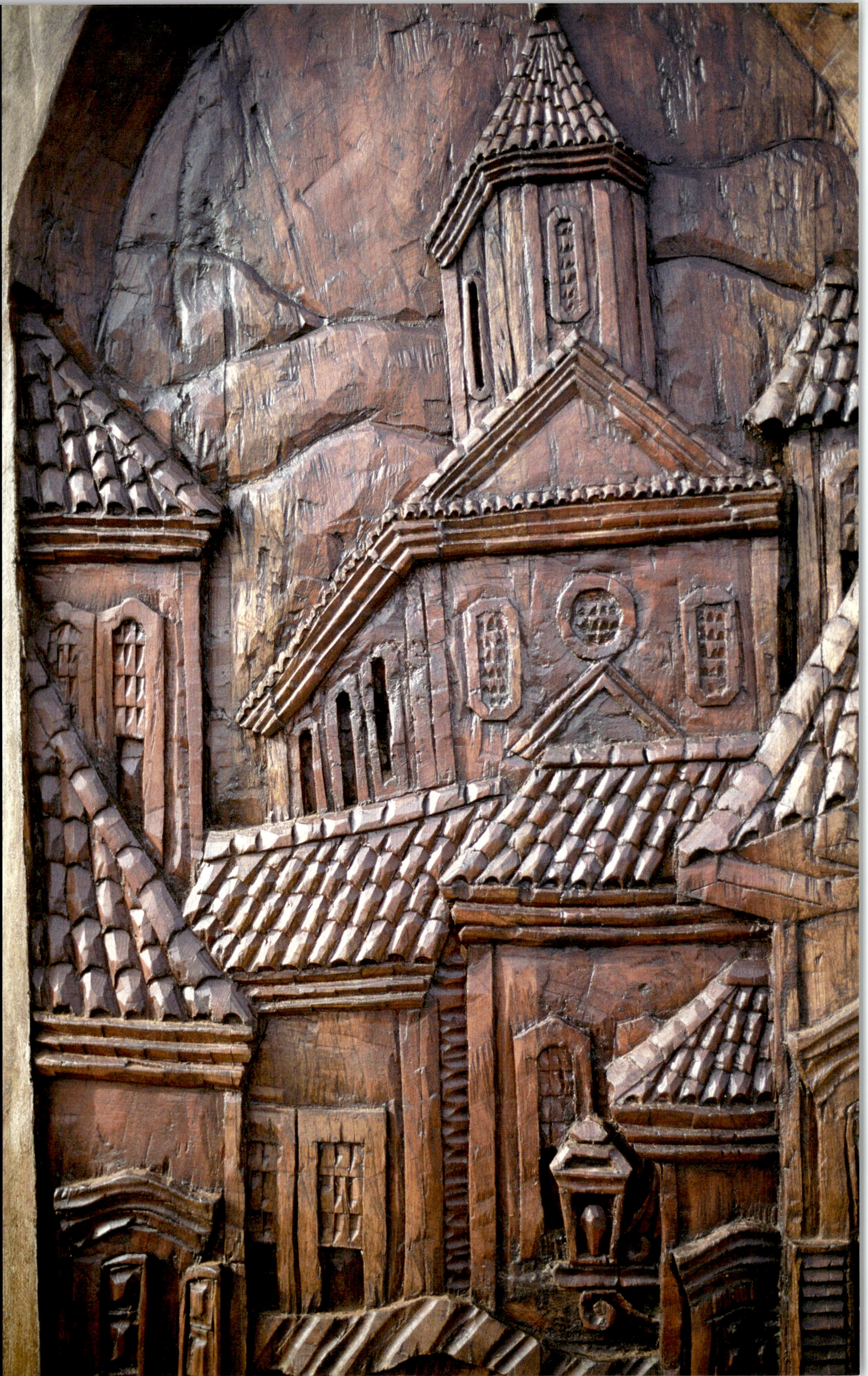

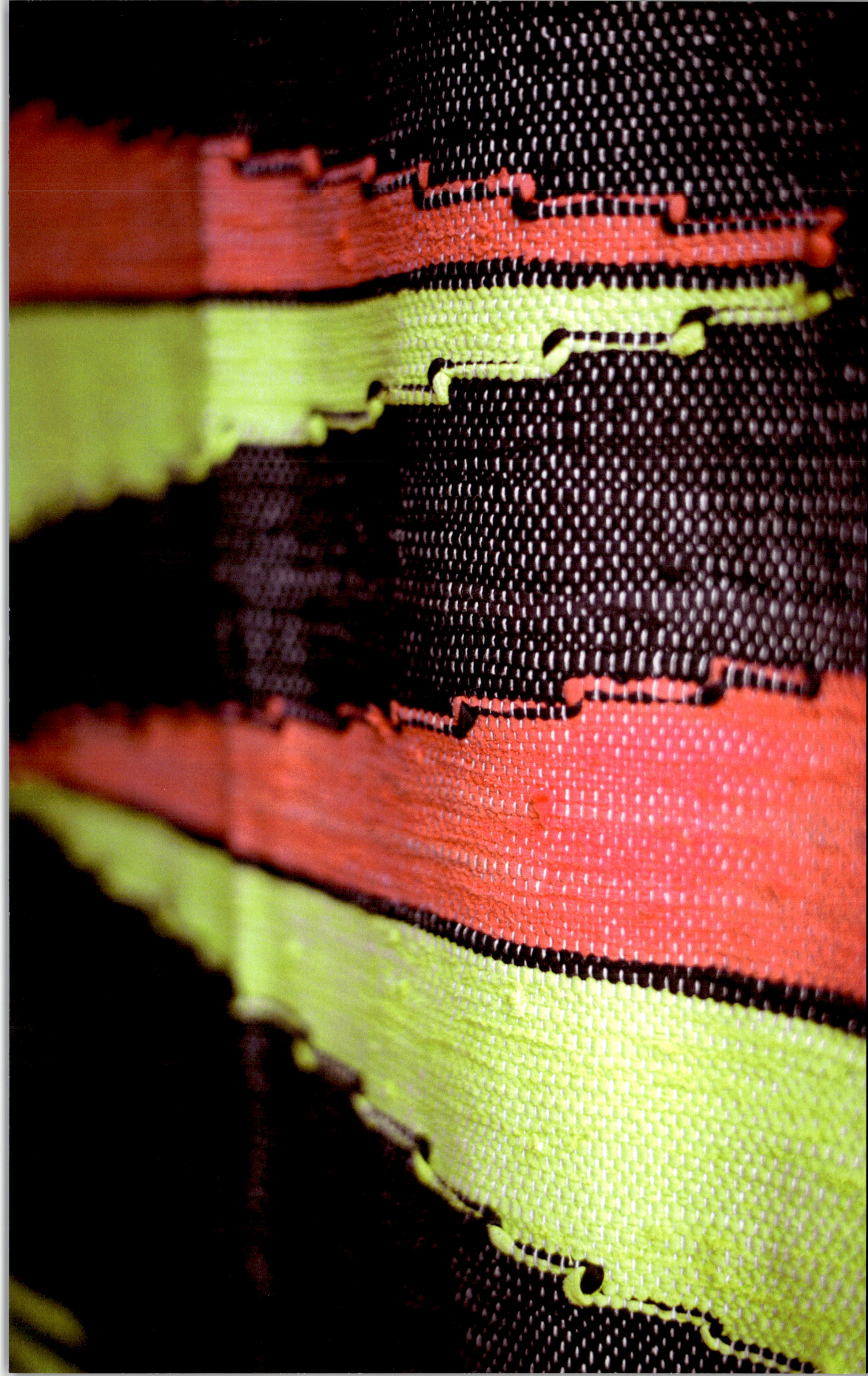

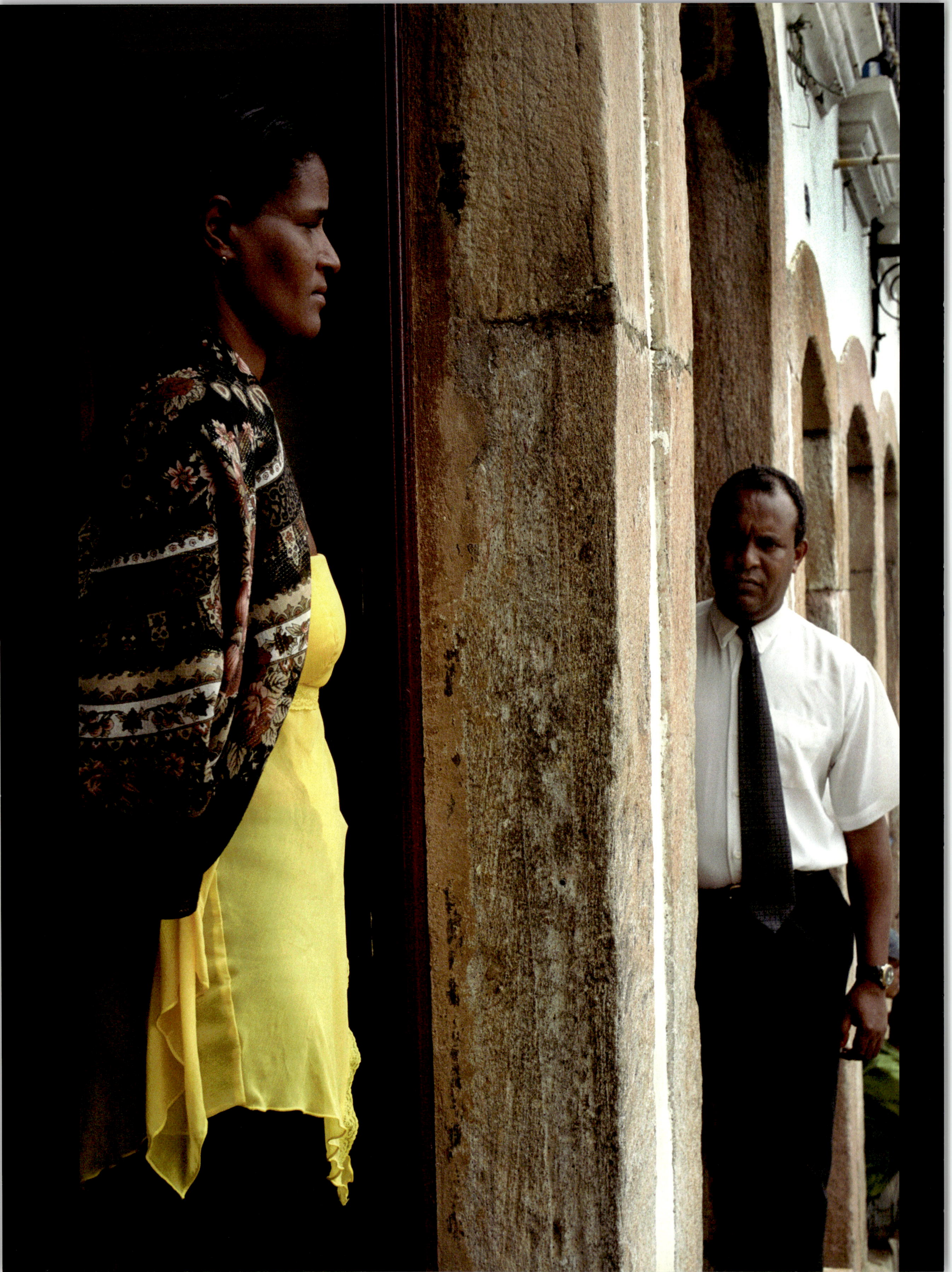

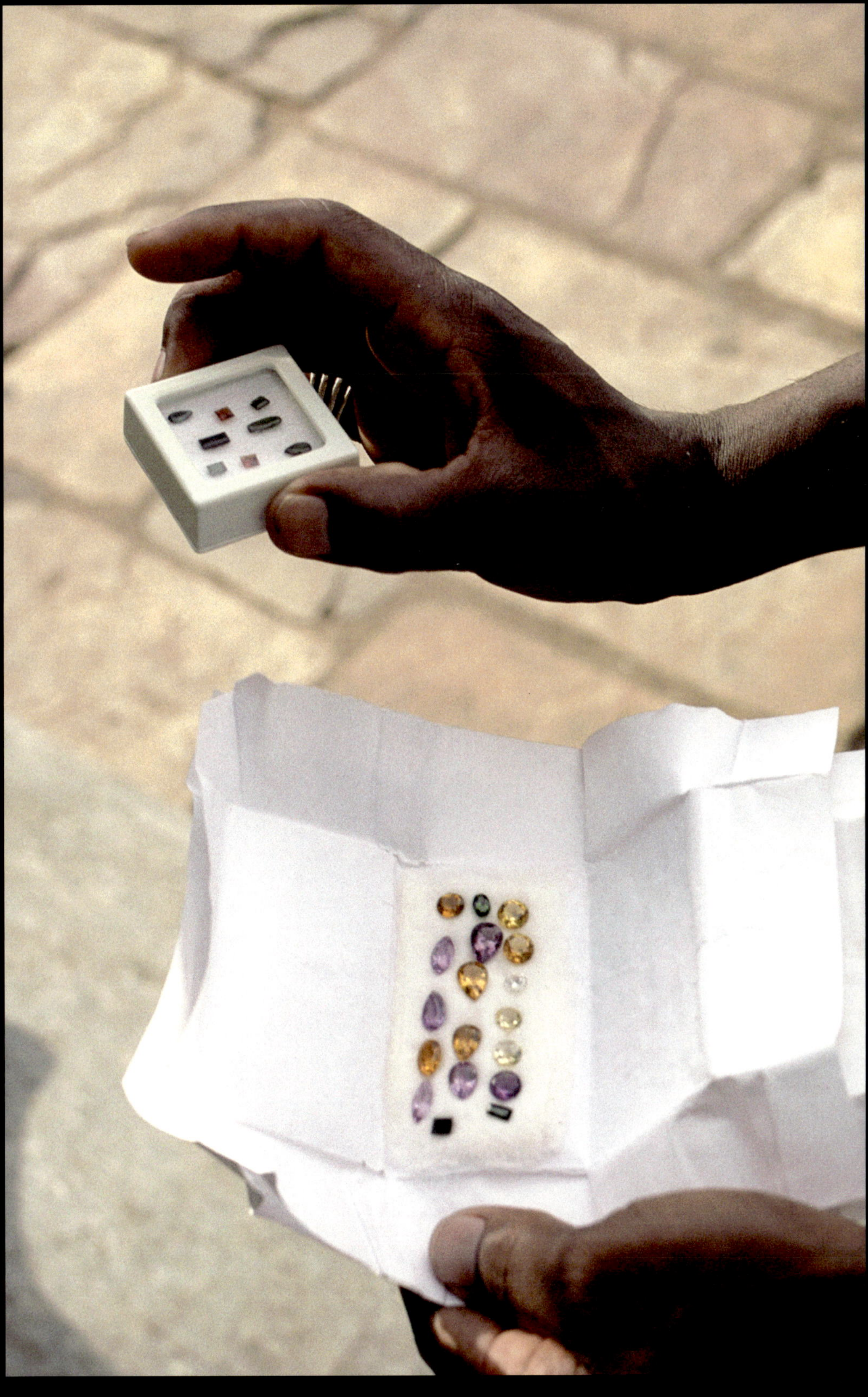

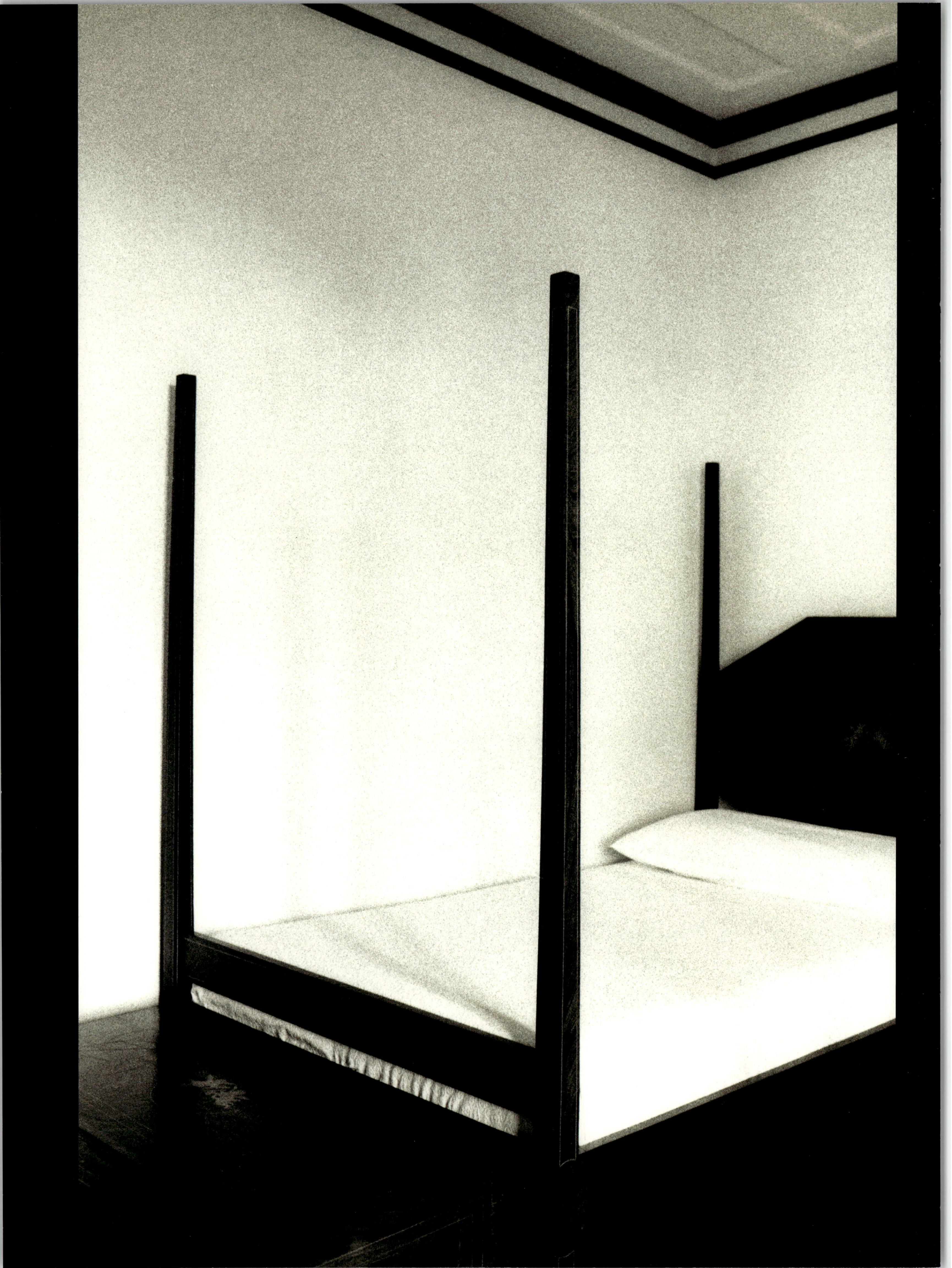

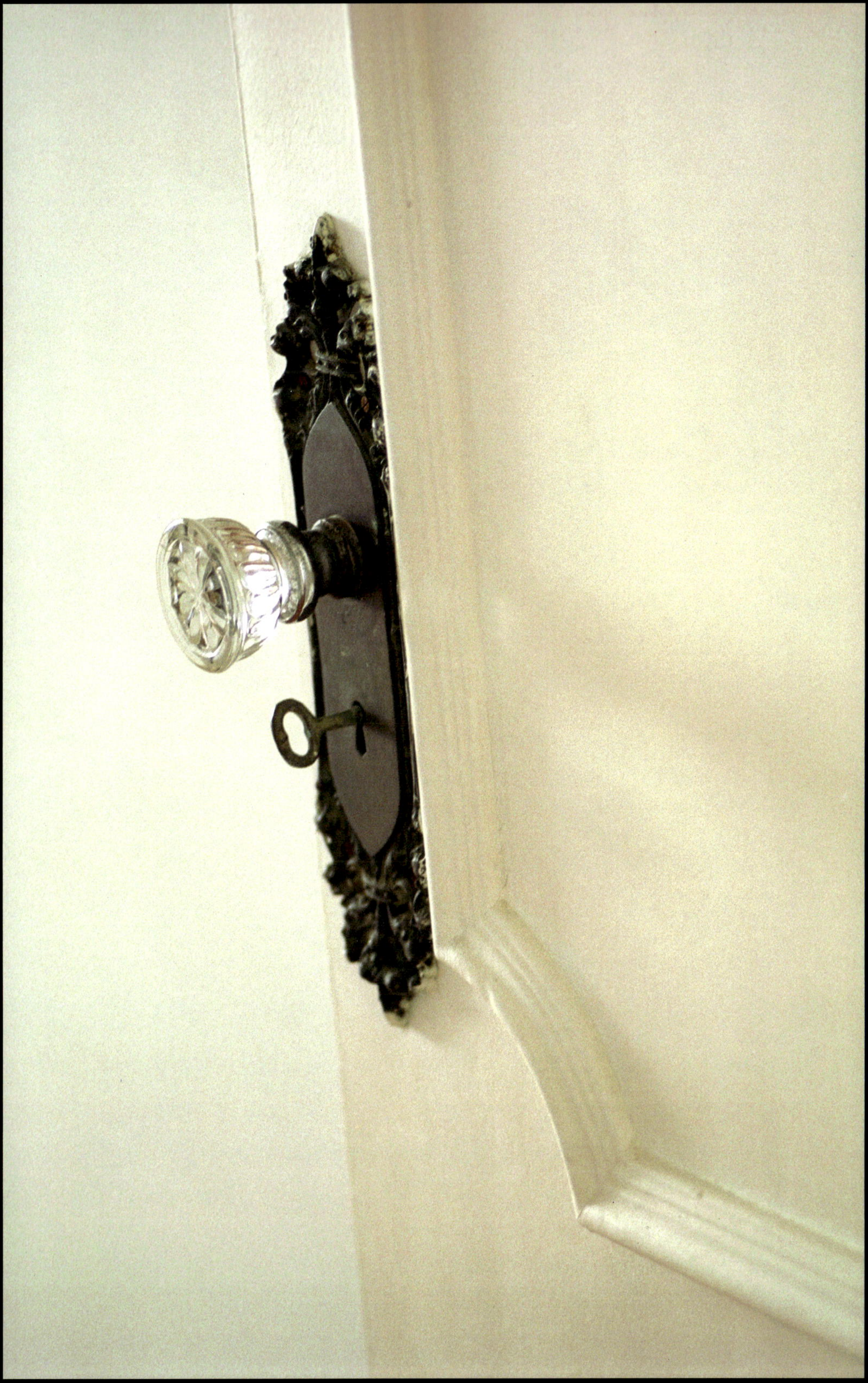

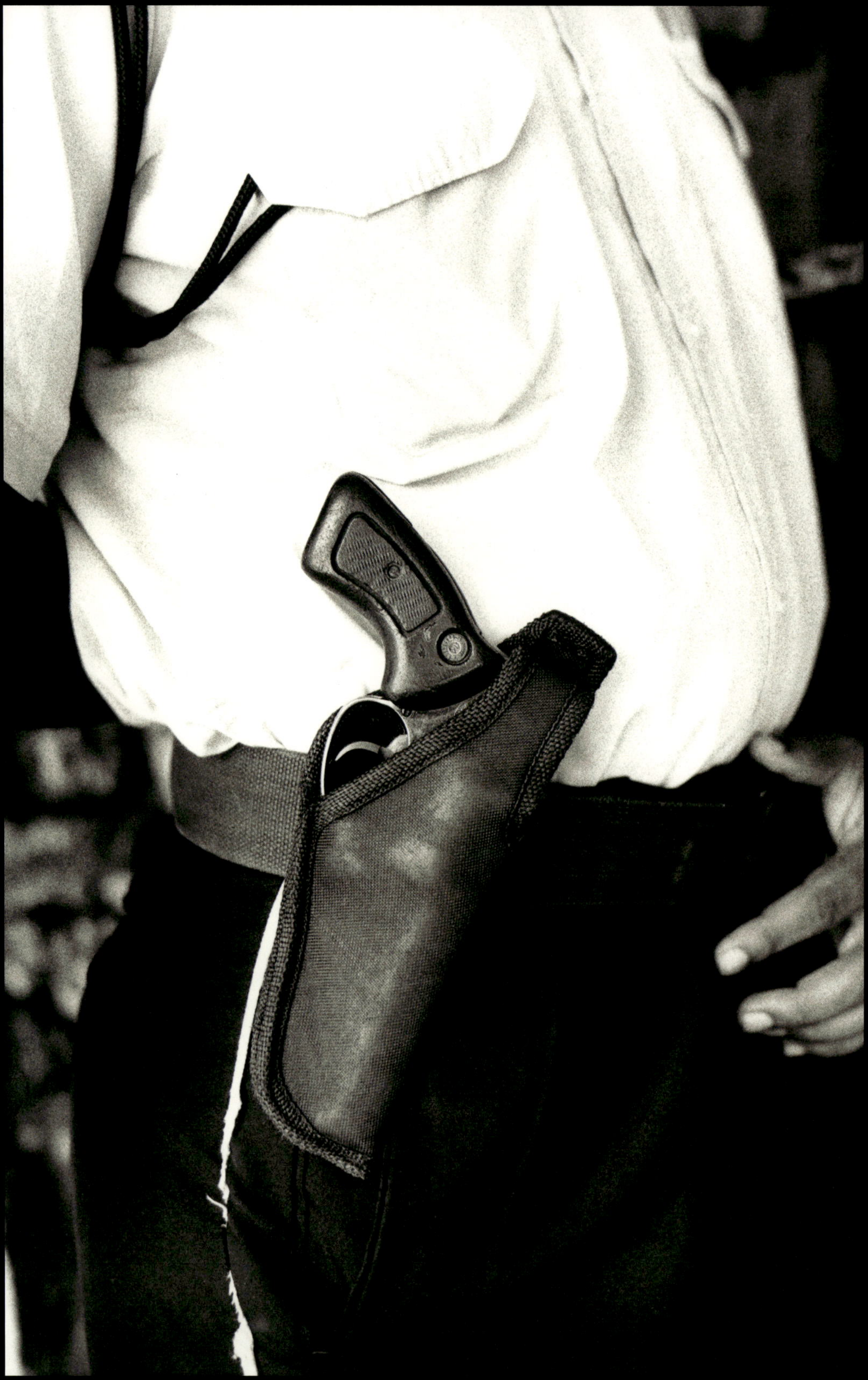

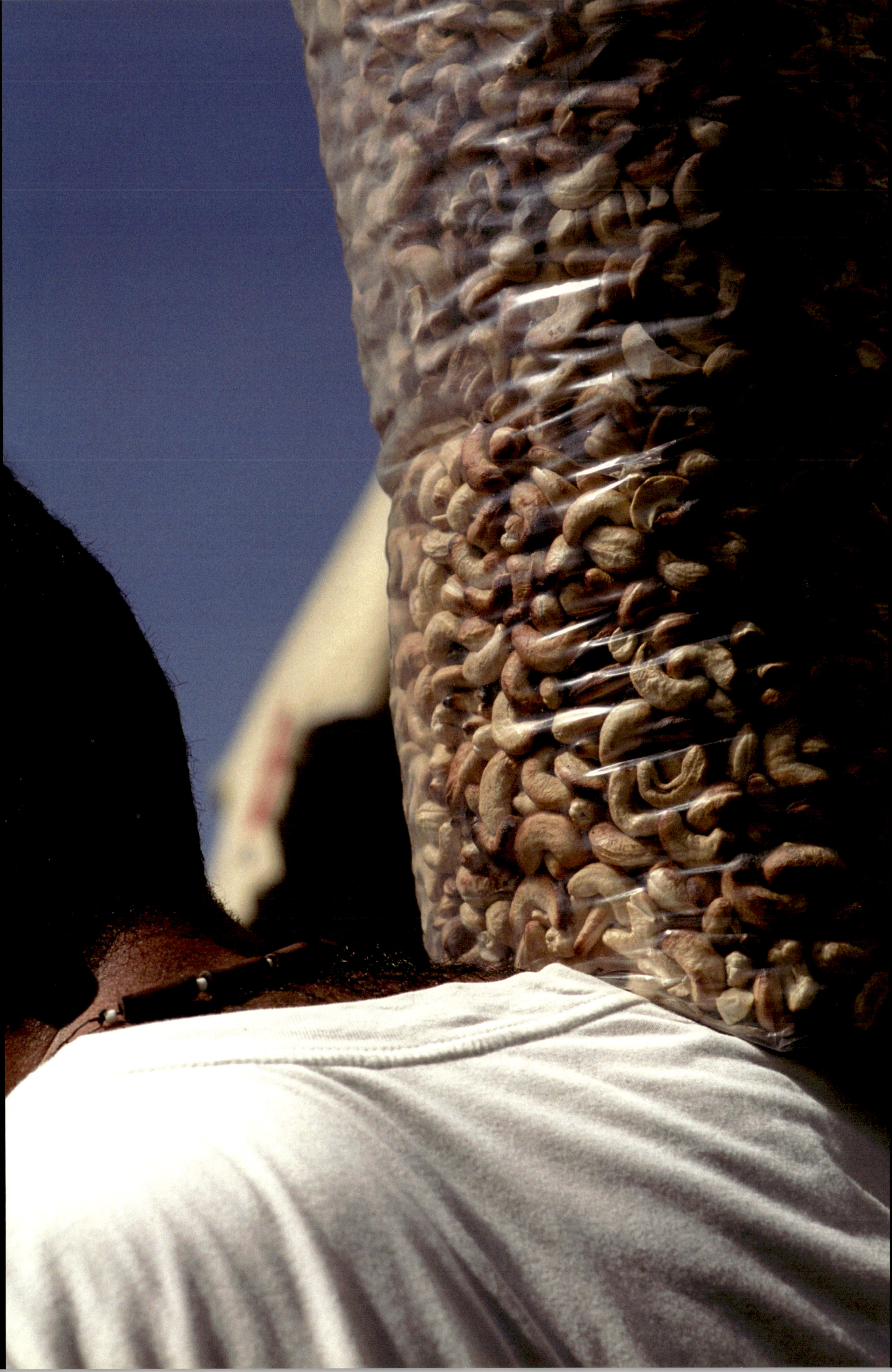

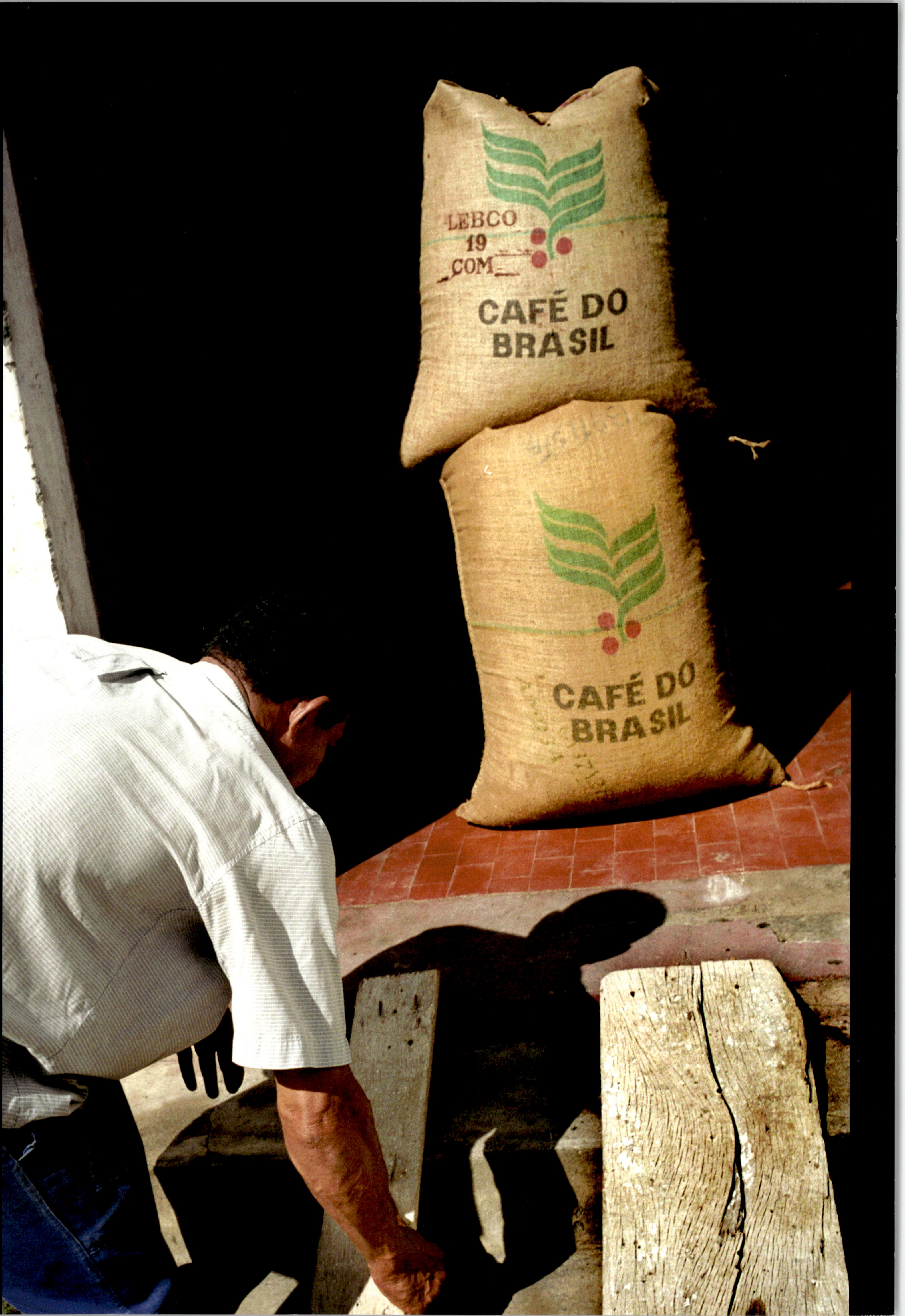
LEBCO
19
COM
CAFÉ DO
BRASIL
CAFÉ DO
BRASIL

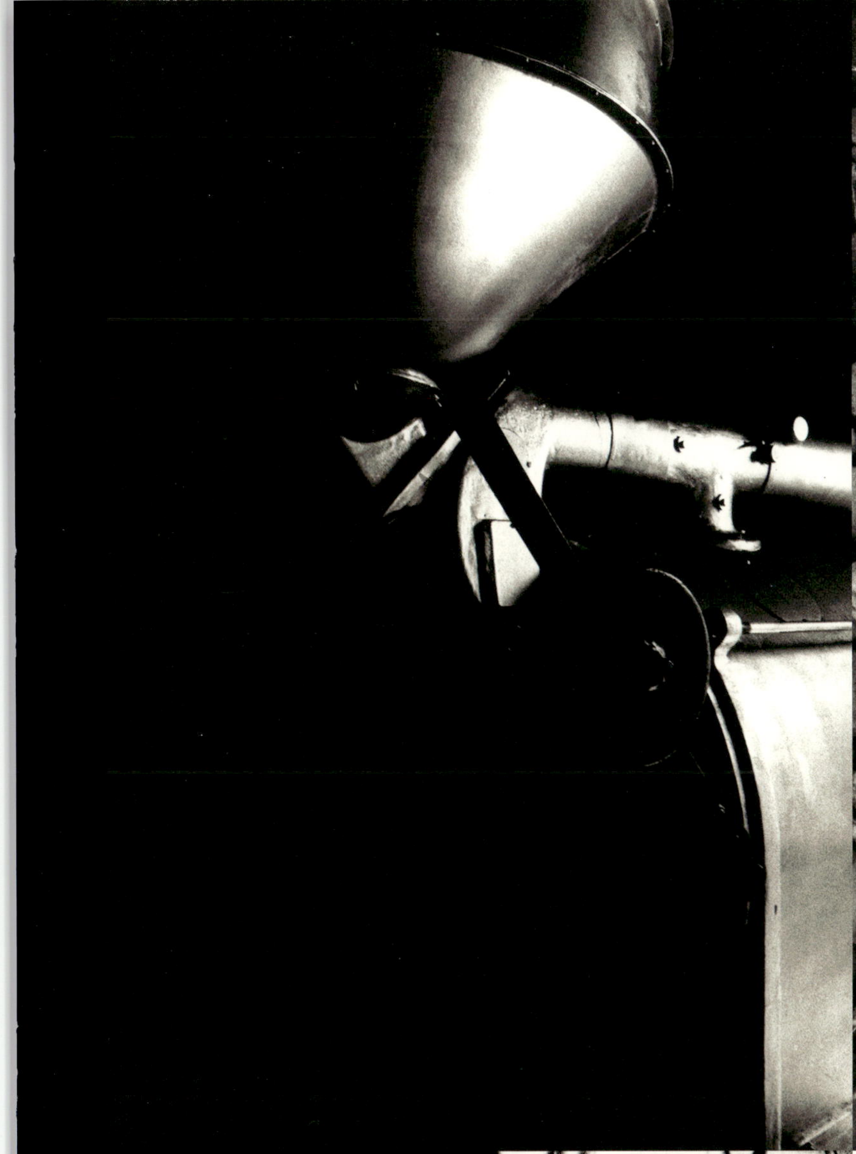
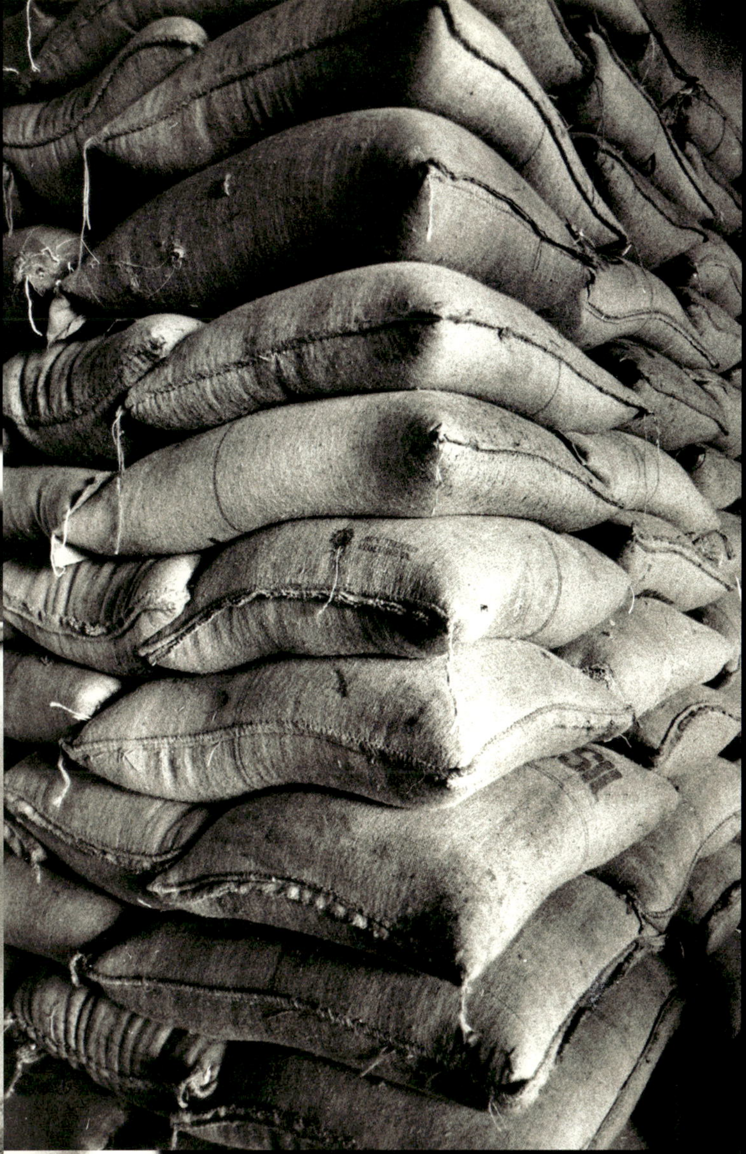
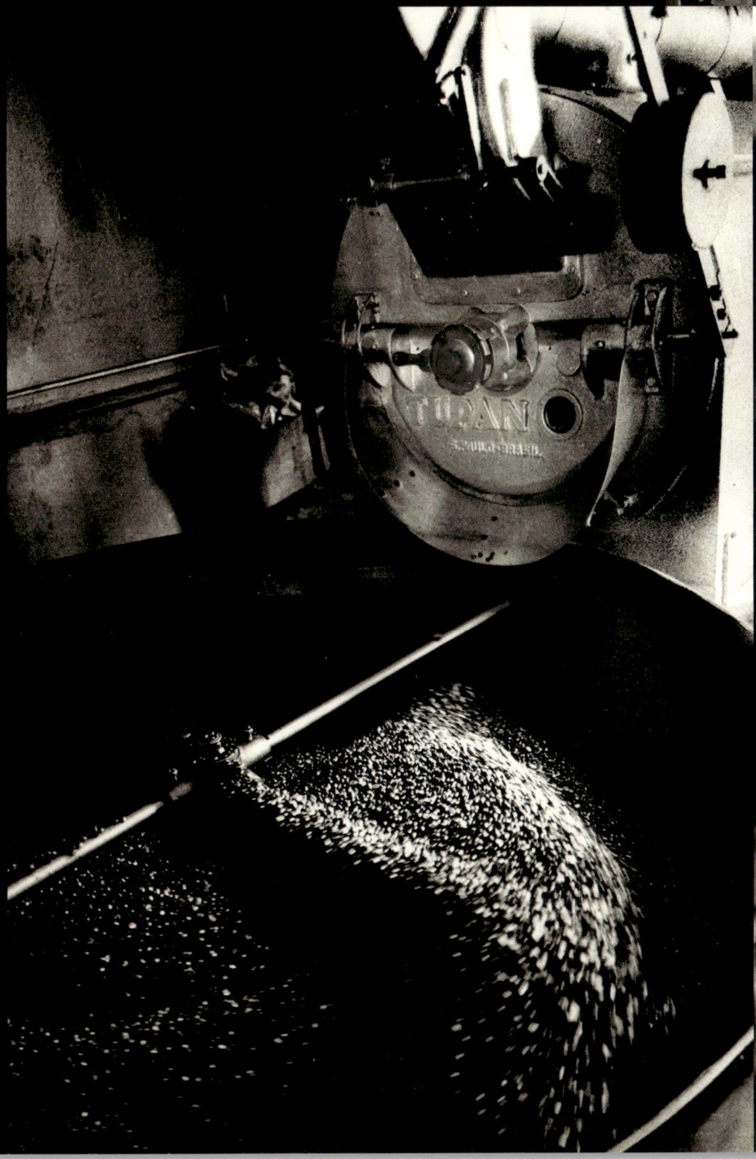
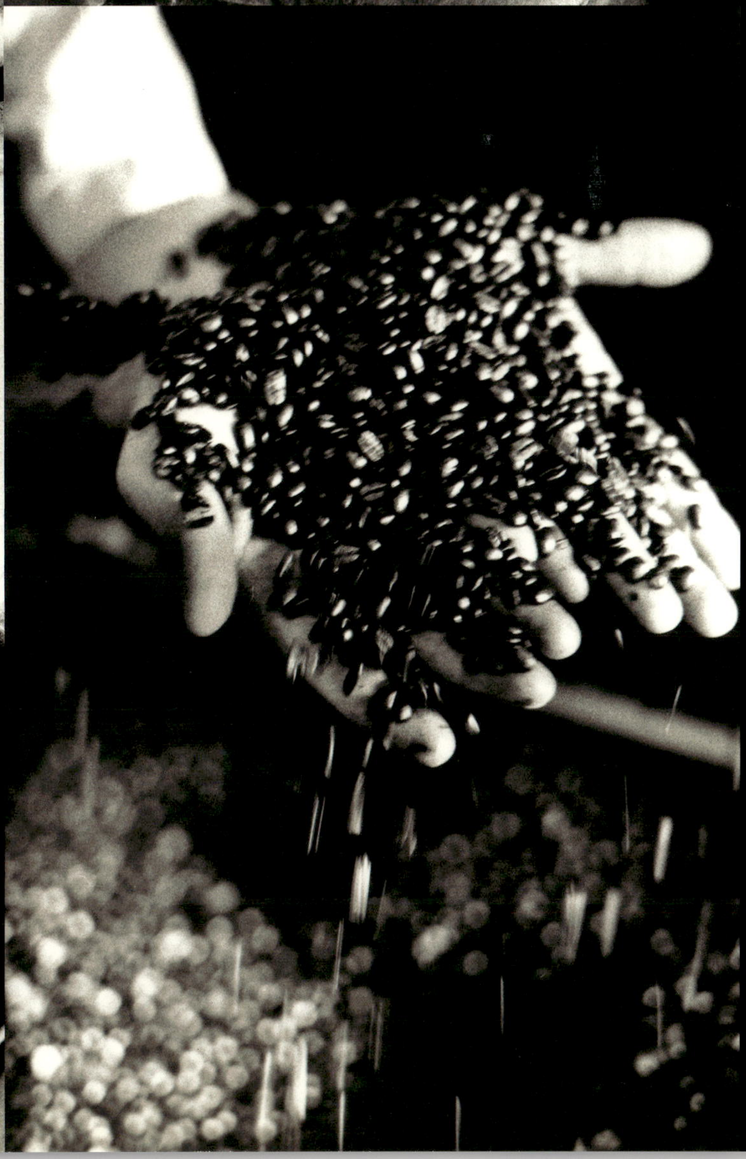

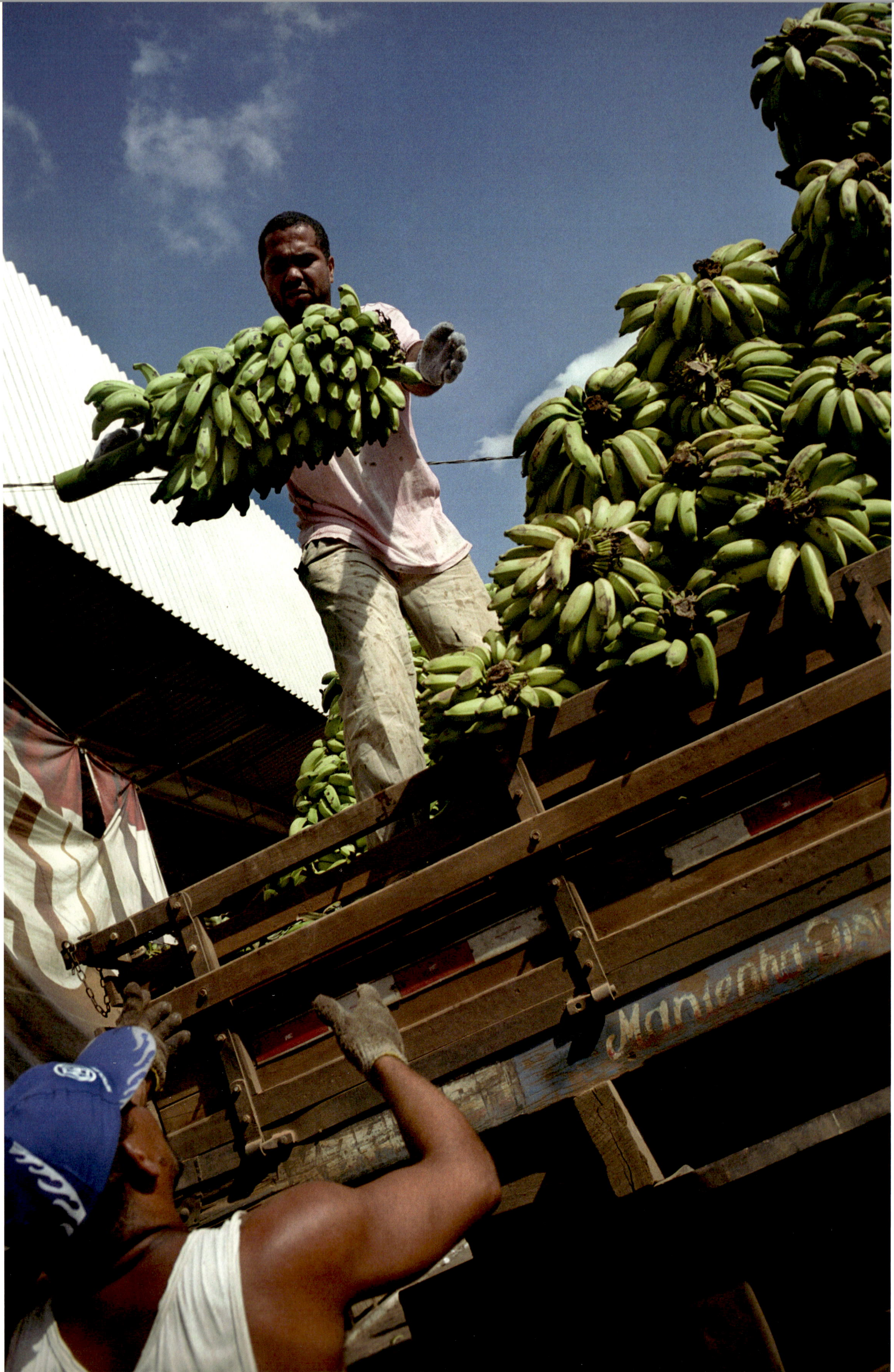
Mantenha

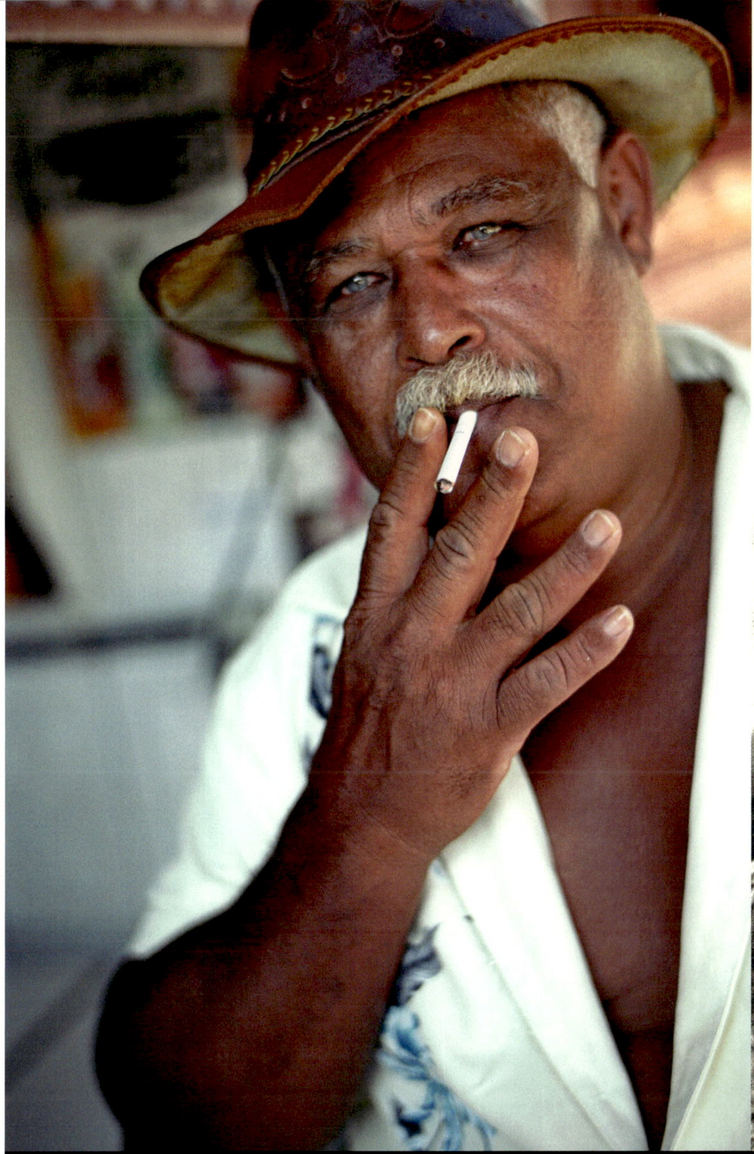
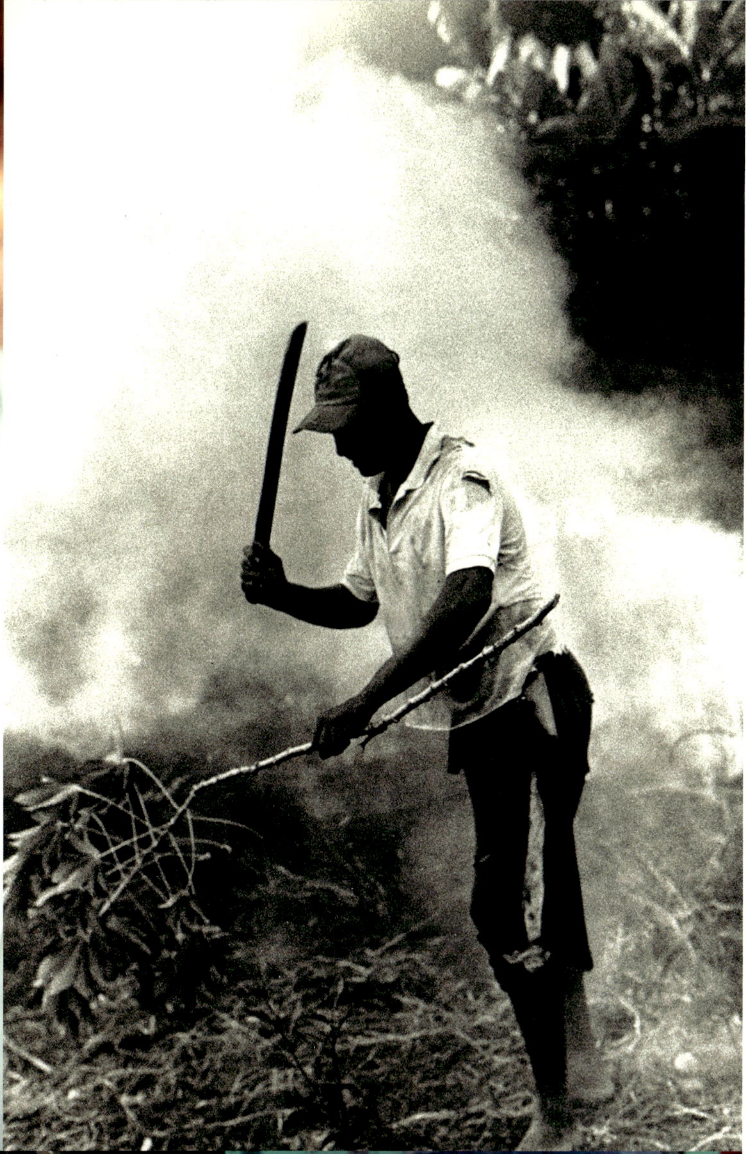
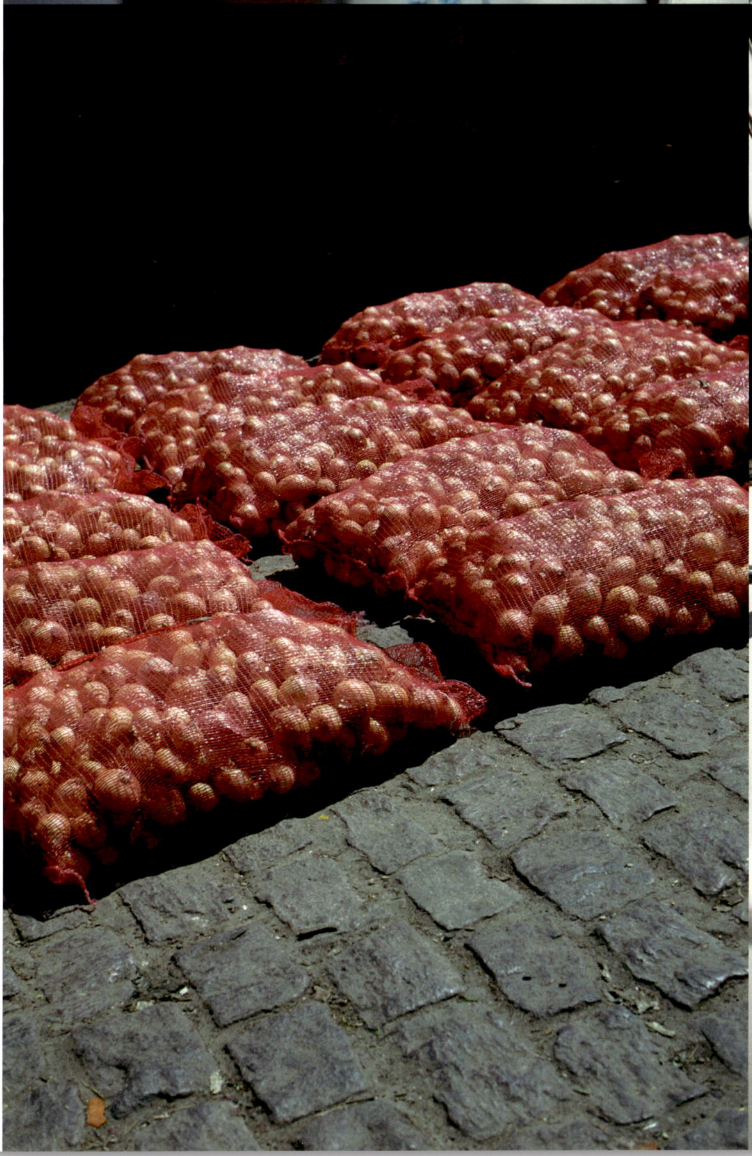
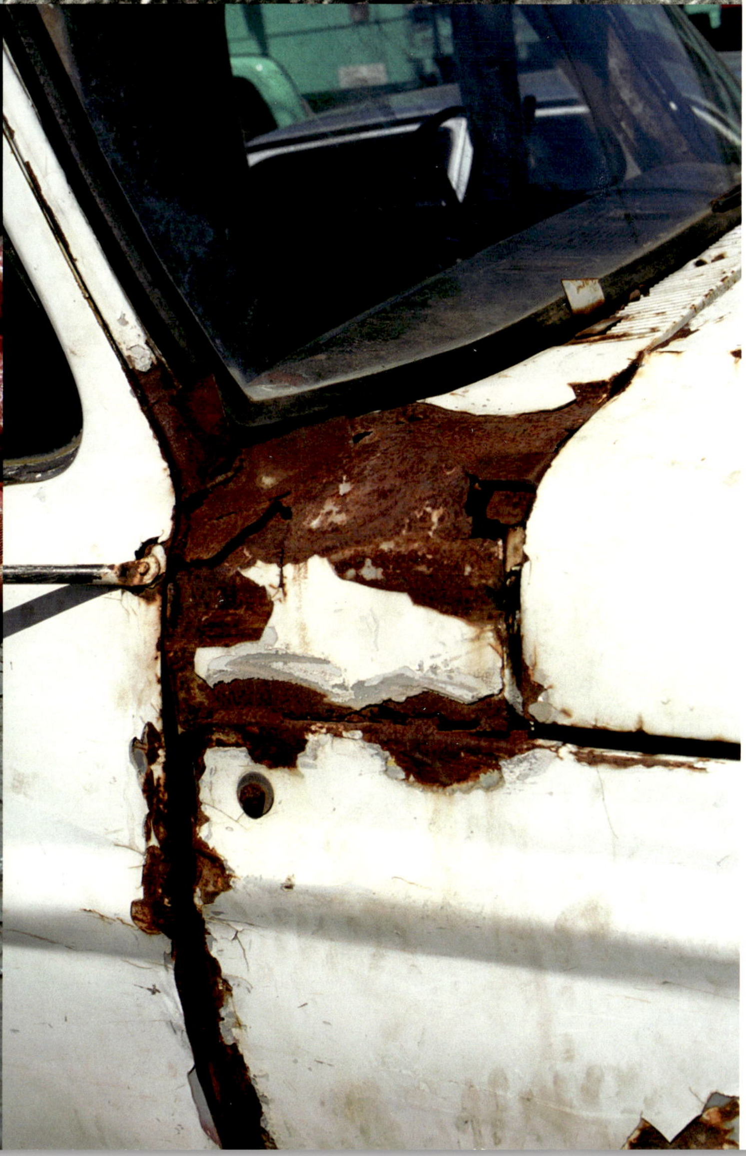

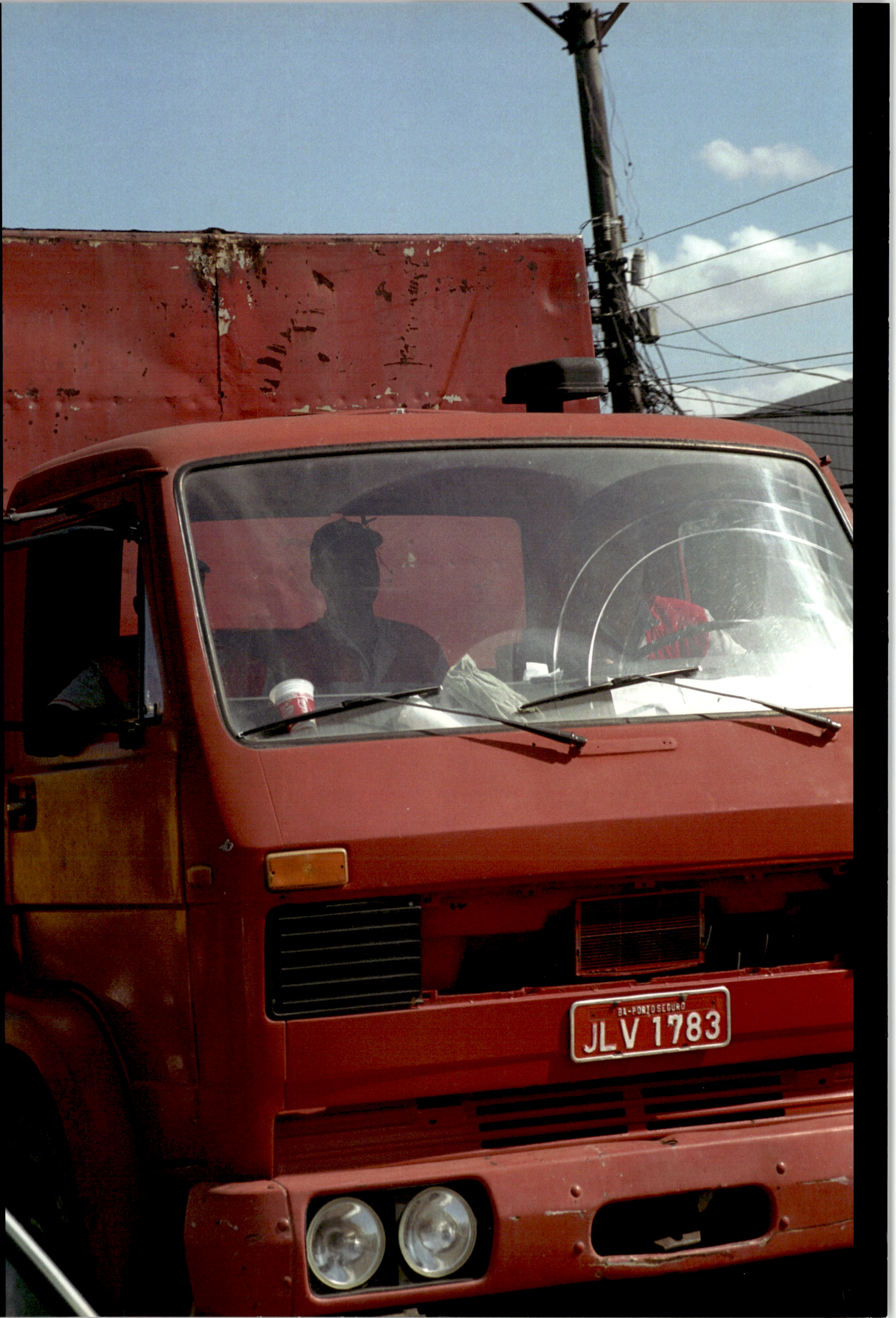
BA-PORTO SEGURO
JLV 1783

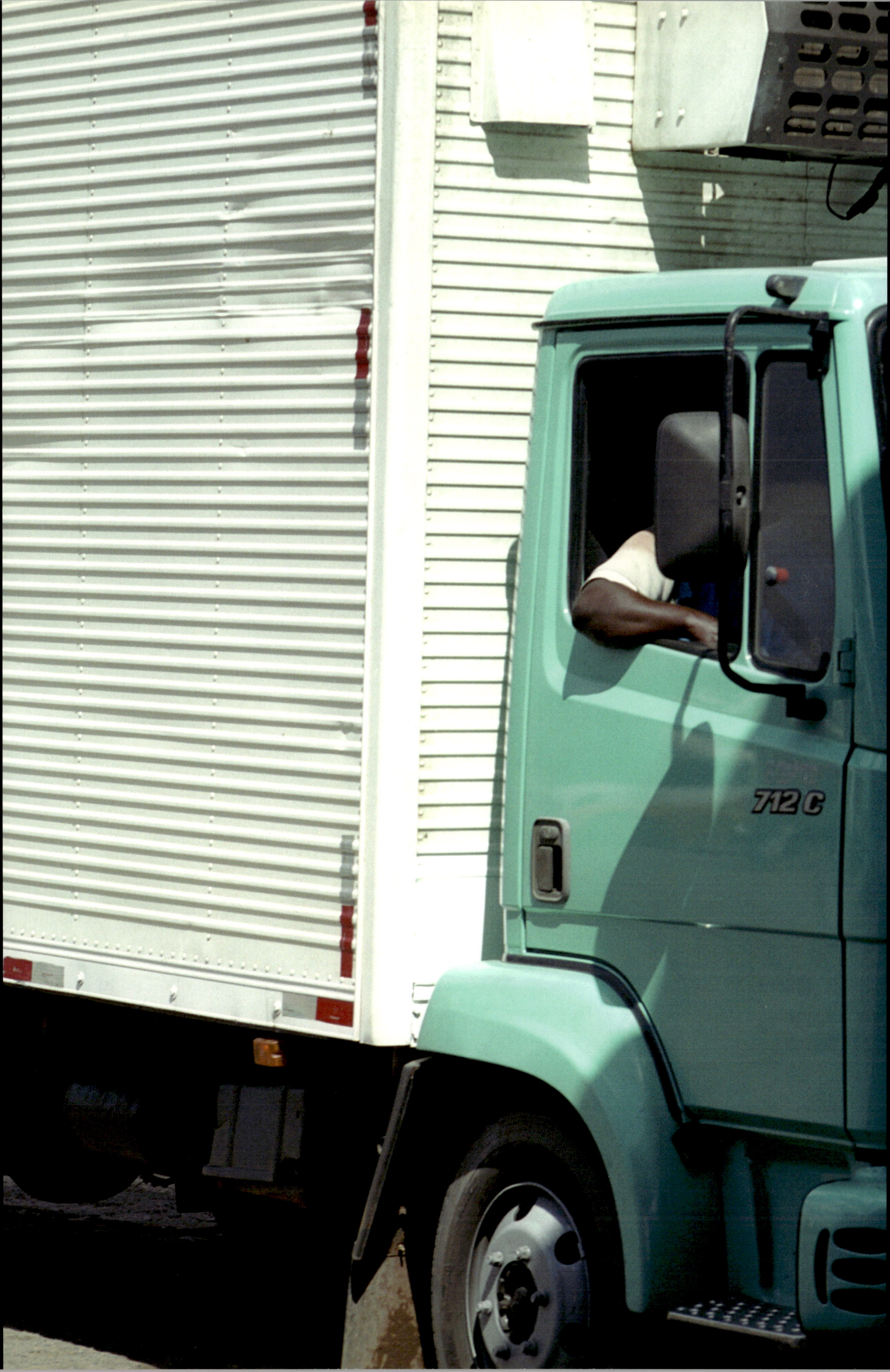
712 C

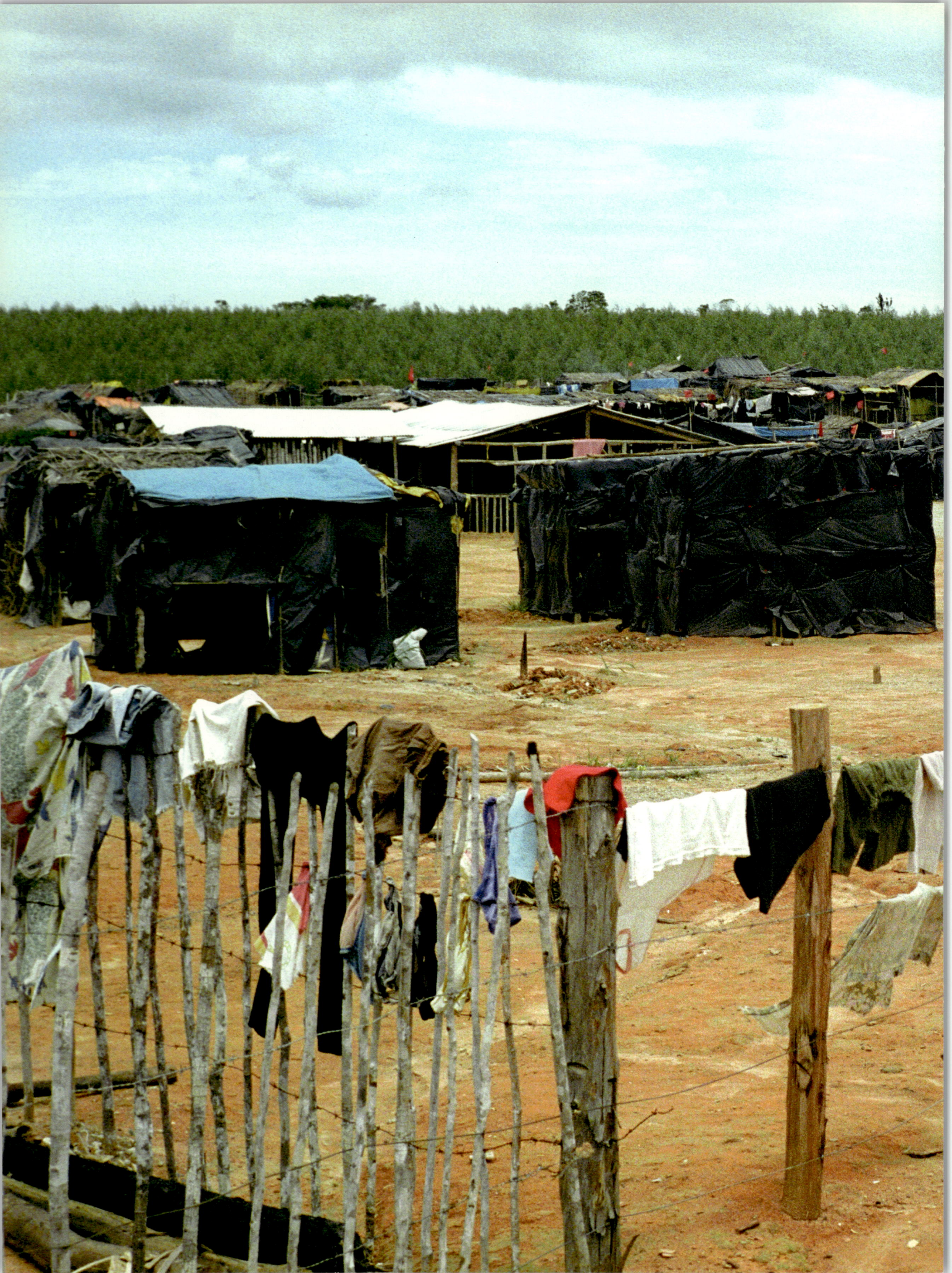

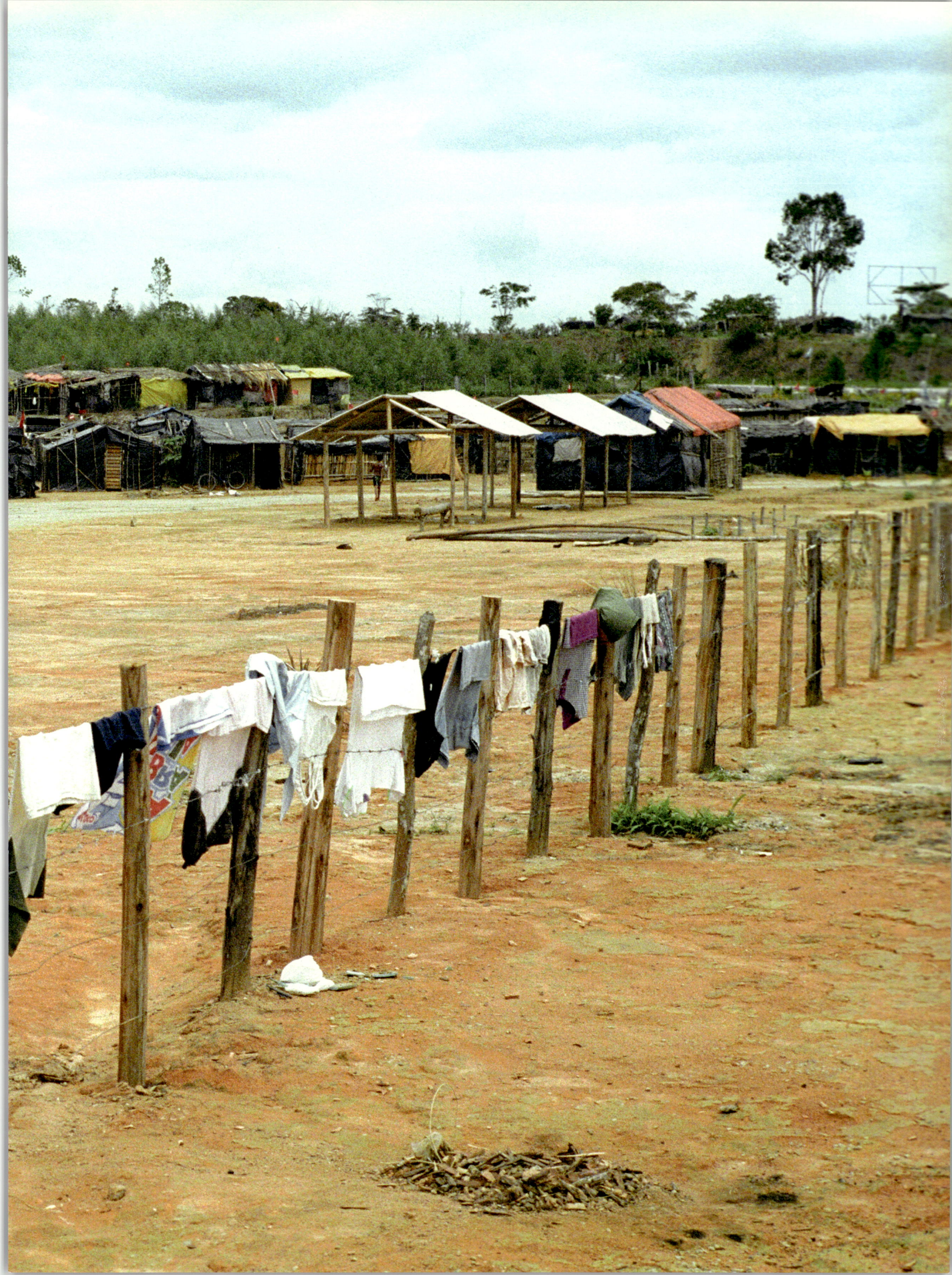

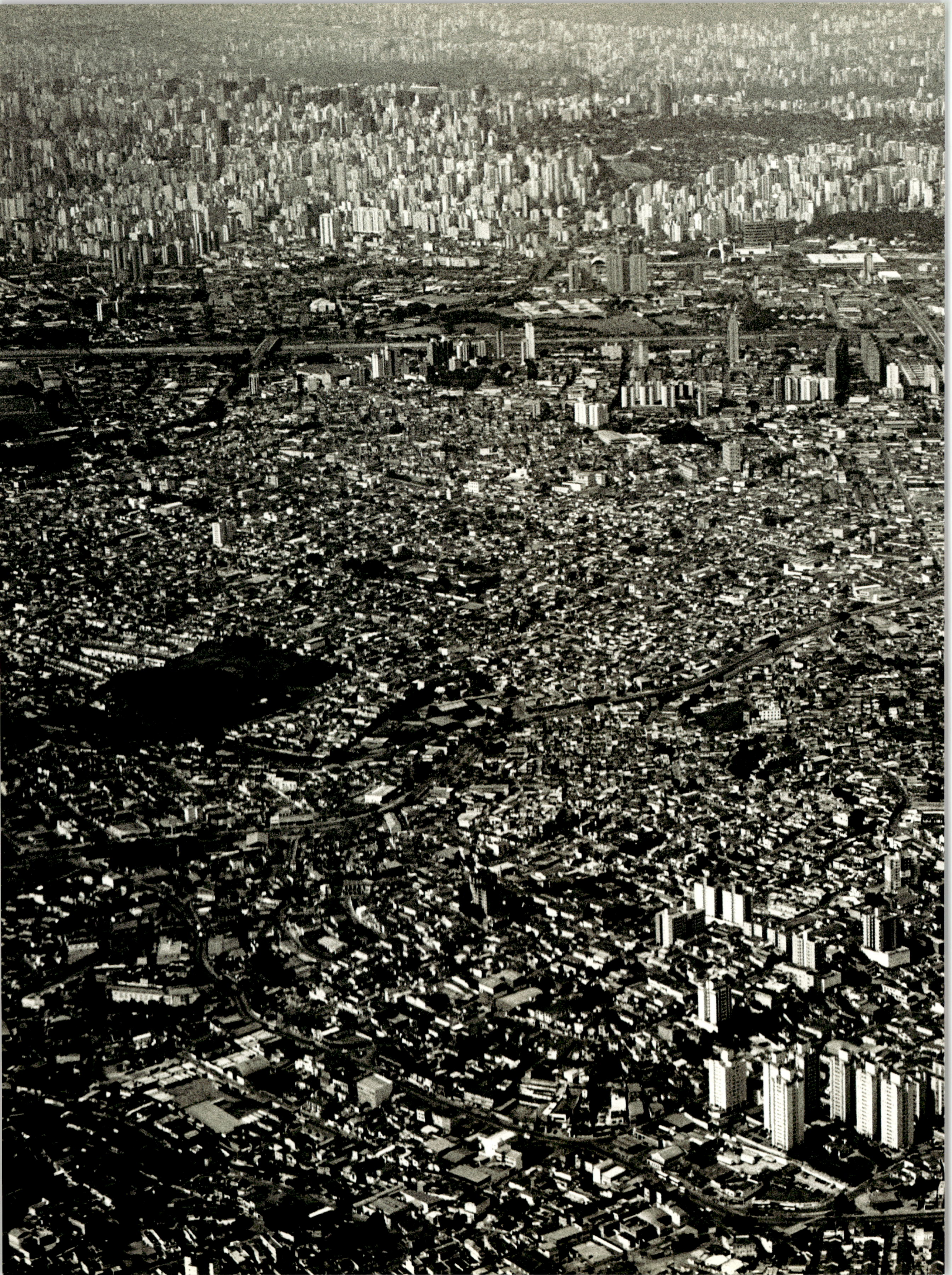

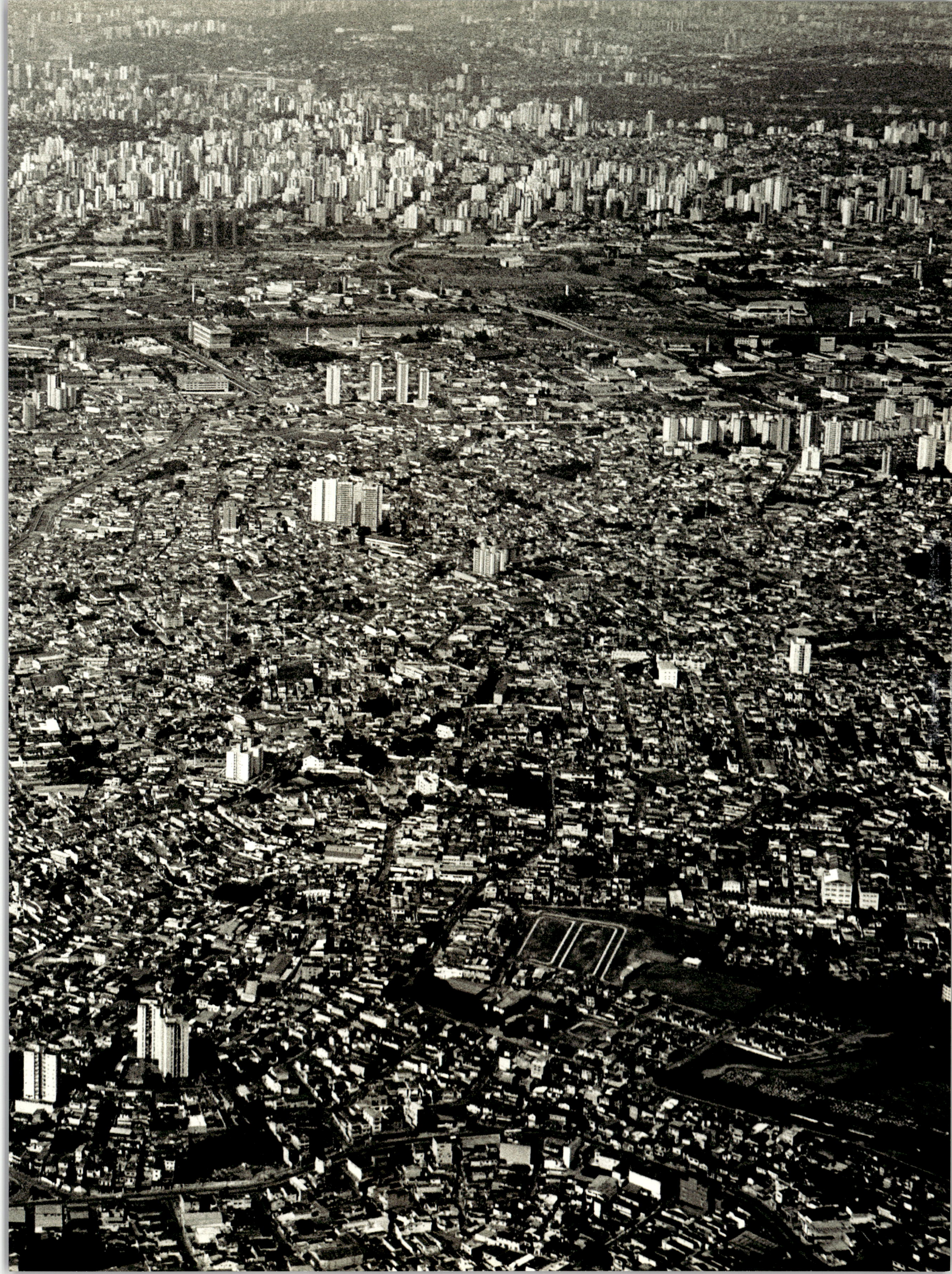

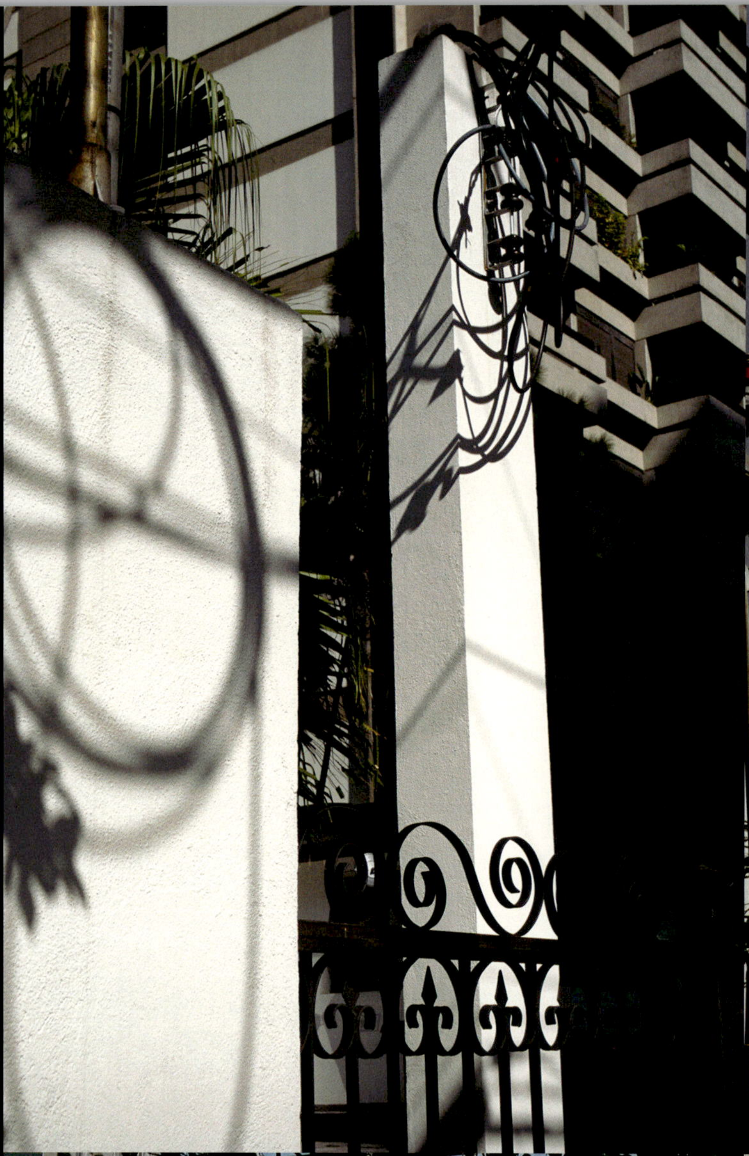

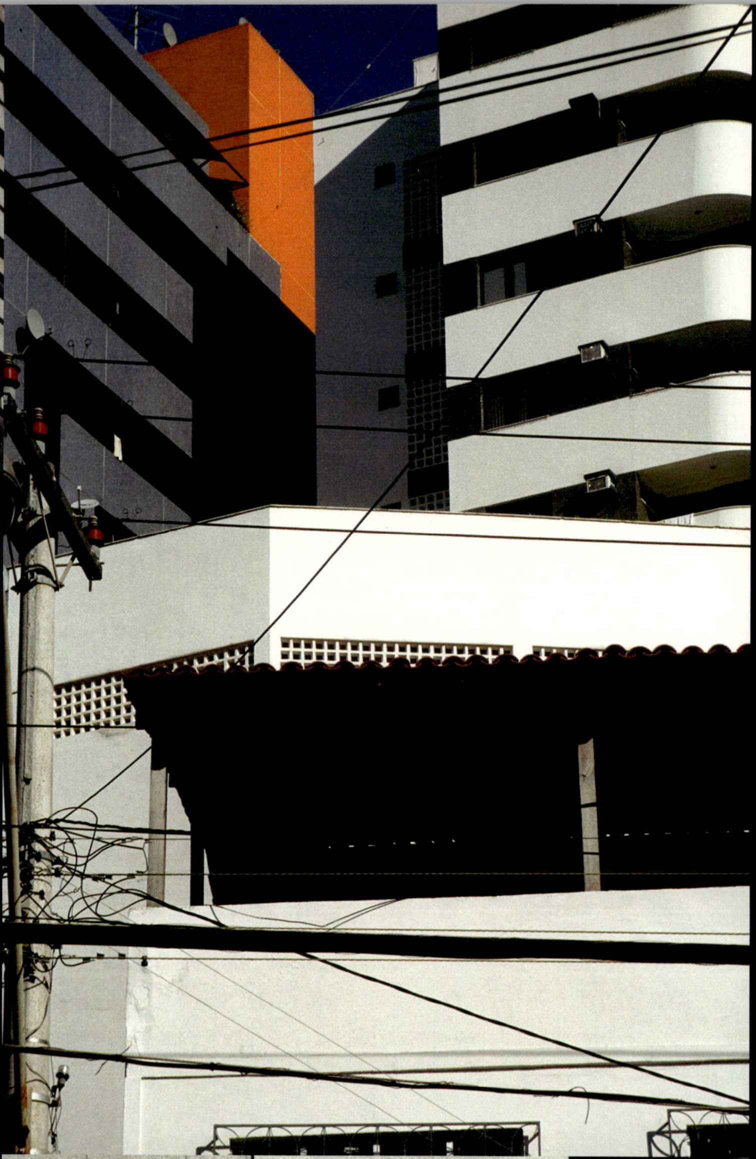

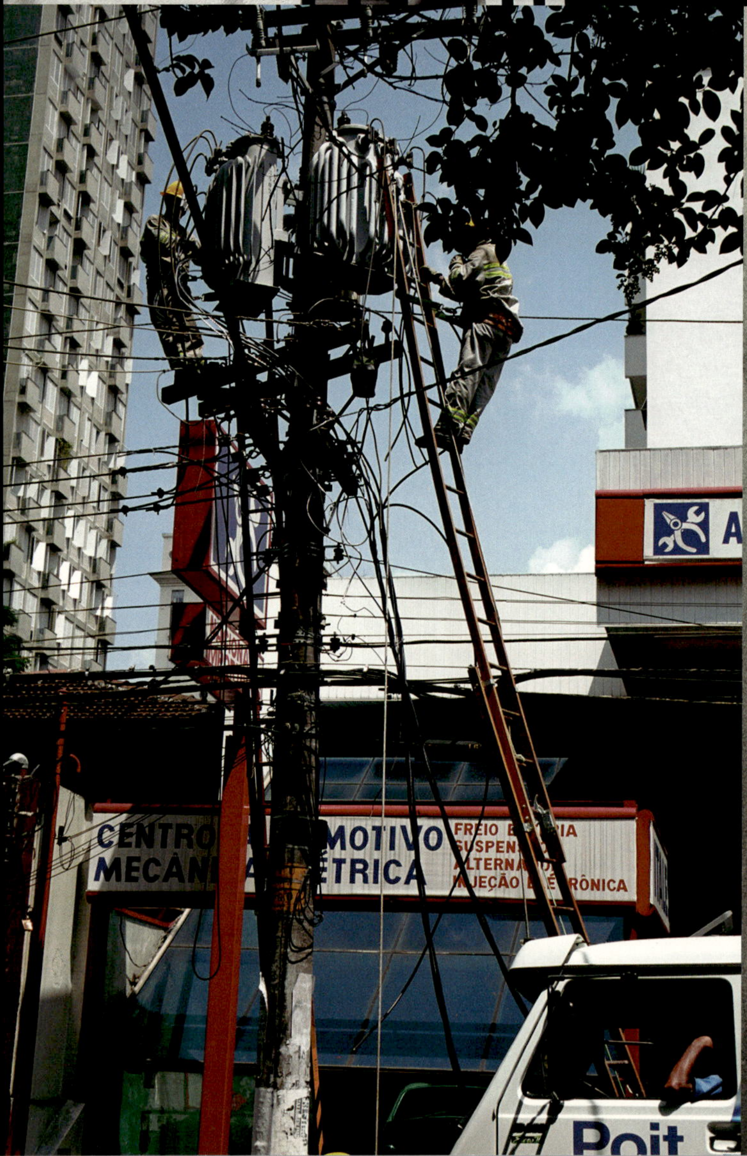
CENTRO
FREIO

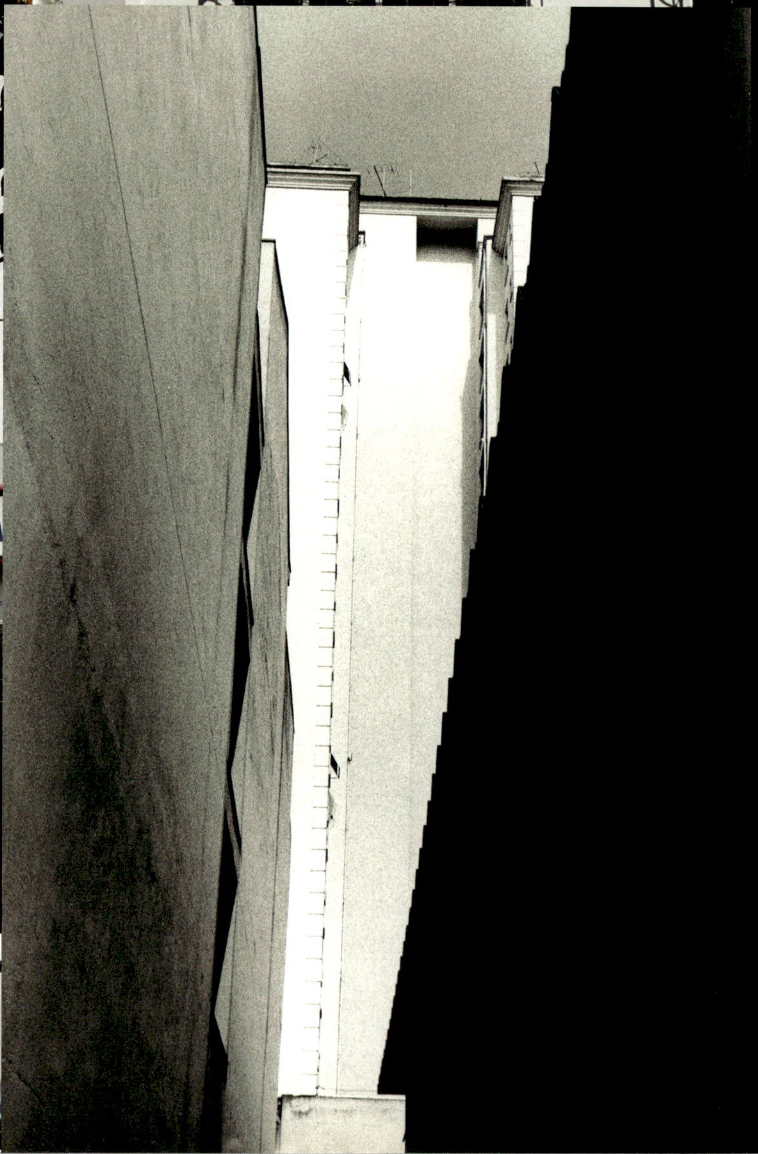

Sao Paulo is an urban experience that defies comprehension. The place cannot be rationally explained. Random groups of disparate ideas collide across all barriers. Texture turns to color, motion becomes noise. Steel rots and crumbling stone soars skyward certain to last yet another century. New buildings remain unfinished and abandoned by an economy that crushes hundreds of thousands of people into non-spaces clinging to mountain walls. Infrastructure endures in spite of the absence of infrastructure. Signage is its own language, shaped by the vernacular of the people.

In Sao Paulo architecture must be believed in order to be seen. Otherwise it doesn't exist. There is no True North here, the place has been built with a bent compass needle. The Favelas of Brasil remain the most beautifully proportioned to human scale and ingenuity.

San Paolo è un'esperienza urbana che sfida la comprensione. Un luogo che non può essere spiegato razionalmente. Fasci disordinati di idee si scontrano da un capo all'altro di ogni barriera. La consistenza diventa colore, il movimento diventa rumore. L'acciaio imputridisce e la pietra fatiscente si innalza al cielo, certa di sopravvivere ancora un altro secolo. Le nuove costruzioni rimangono incompiute e abbandonate da un'economia che costringe centinaia di migliaia di persone in non-luoghi a ridosso delle pareti montuose. Le infrastrutture resistono nonostante l'assenza di infrastrutture. La segnaletica è l'unico linguaggio, modellato dal dialetto della popolazione.

Per essere vista, a San Paolo l'architettura deve essere immaginata. Altrimenti non esiste. Qui non esiste un Nord Geografico, questo luogo è stato costruito con una bussola dall'ago piegato. Le favelas brasiliane rimangono quelle più armoniosamente proporzionate alla dimensione umana ed alla sua creatività.

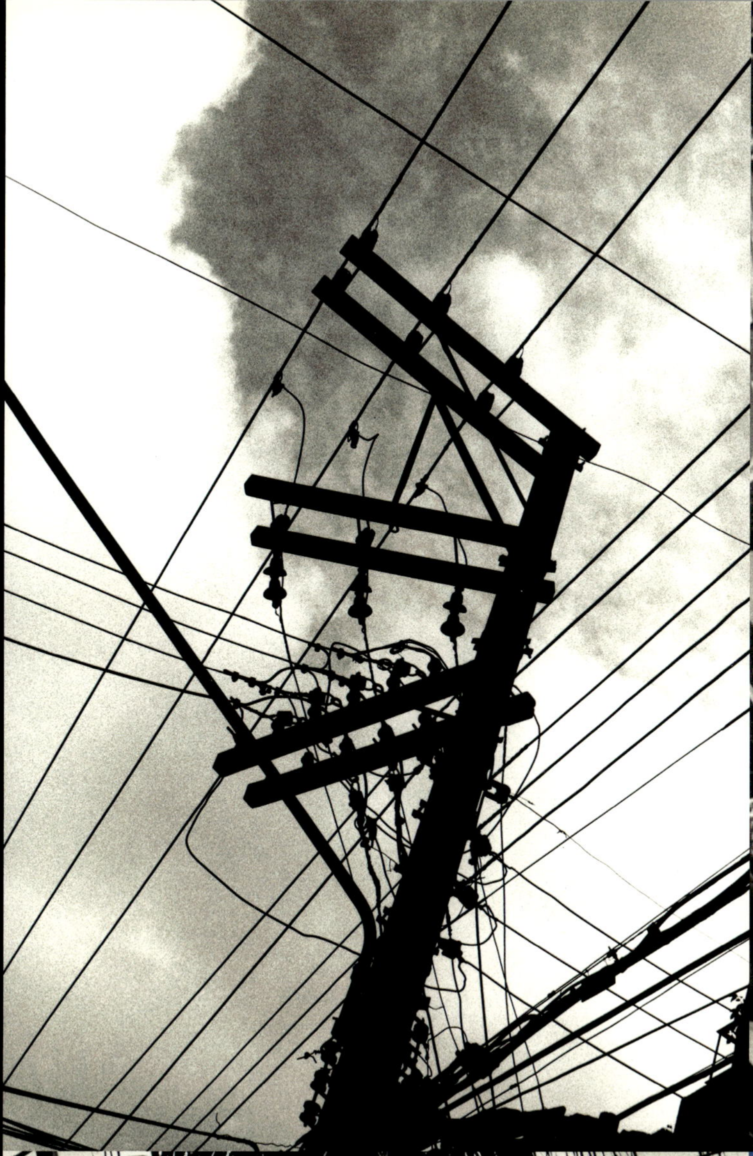
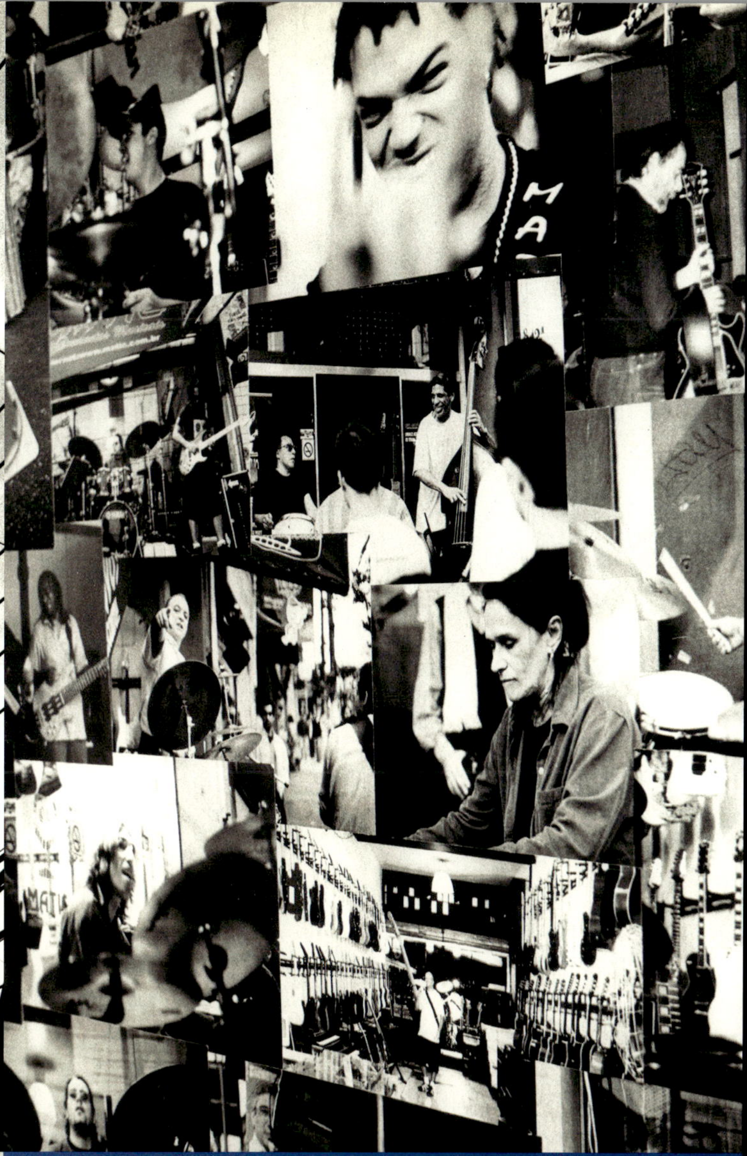
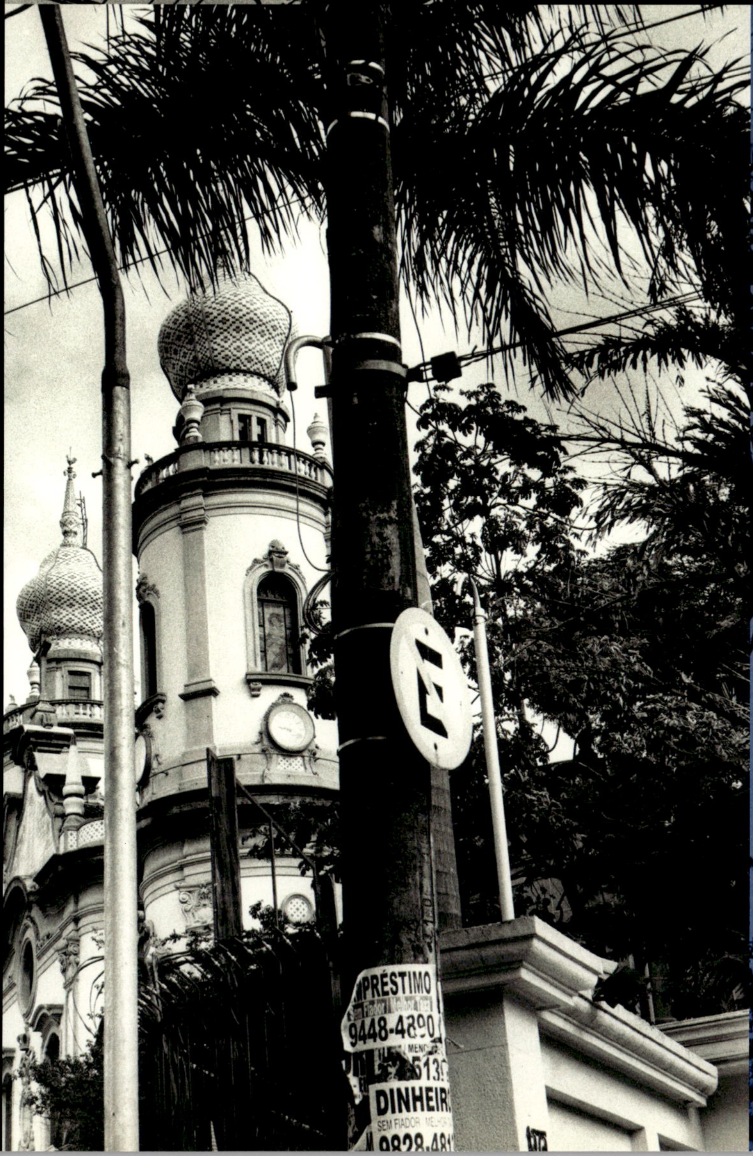
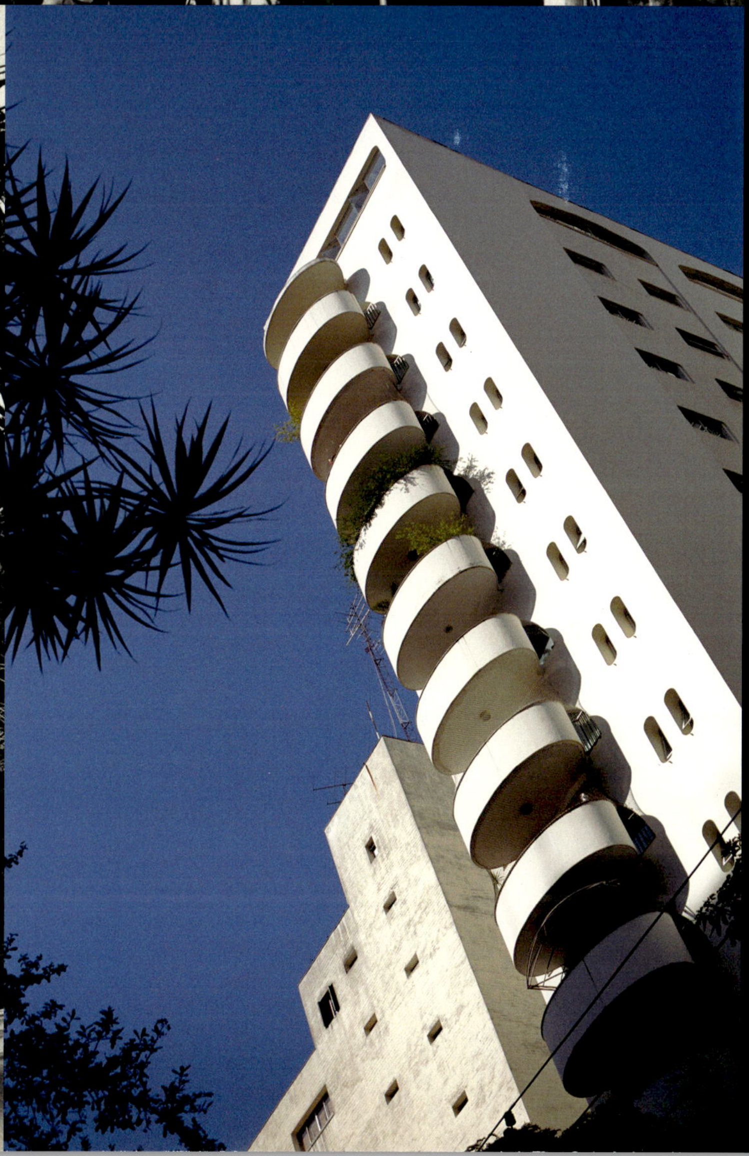

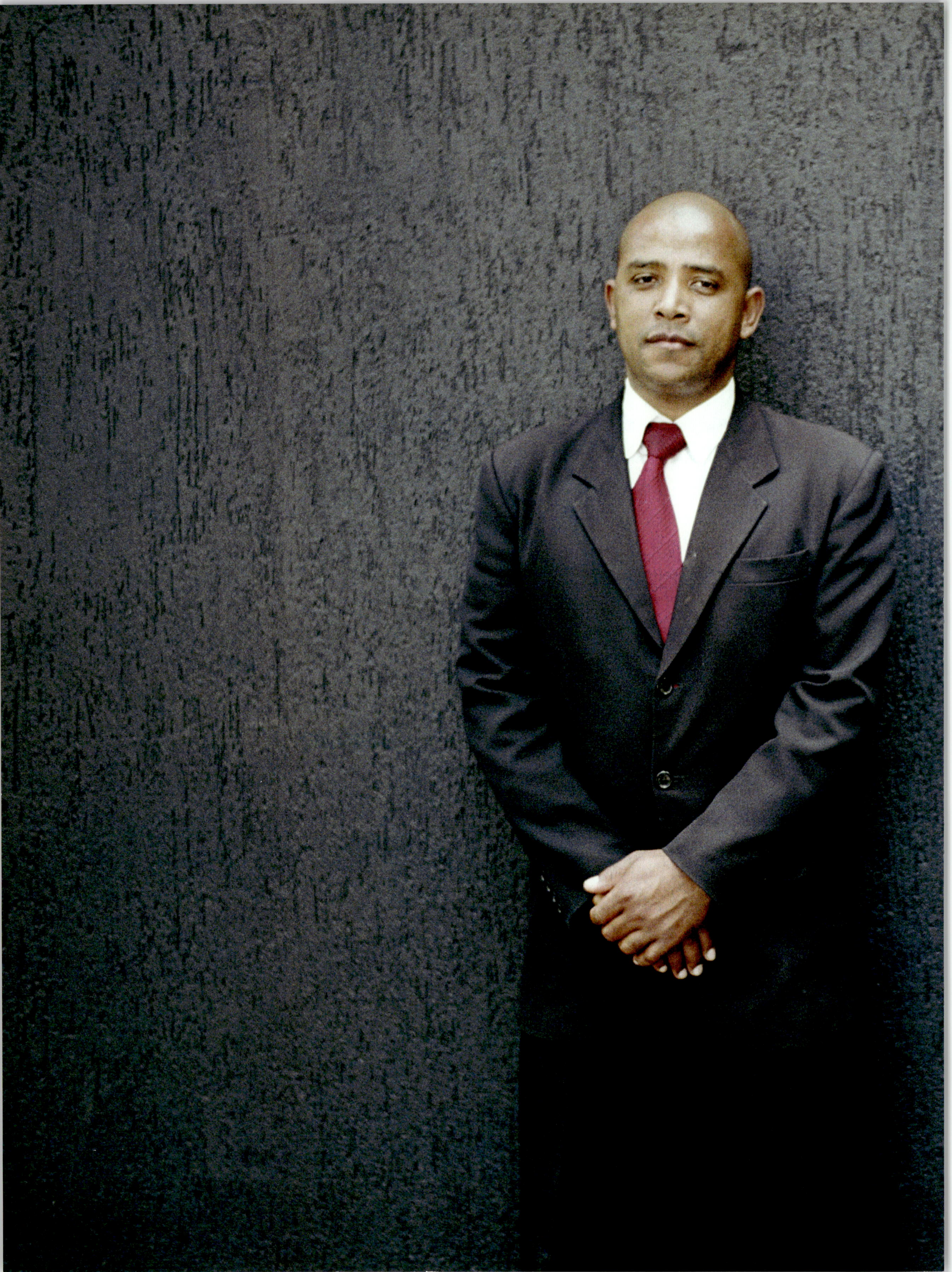

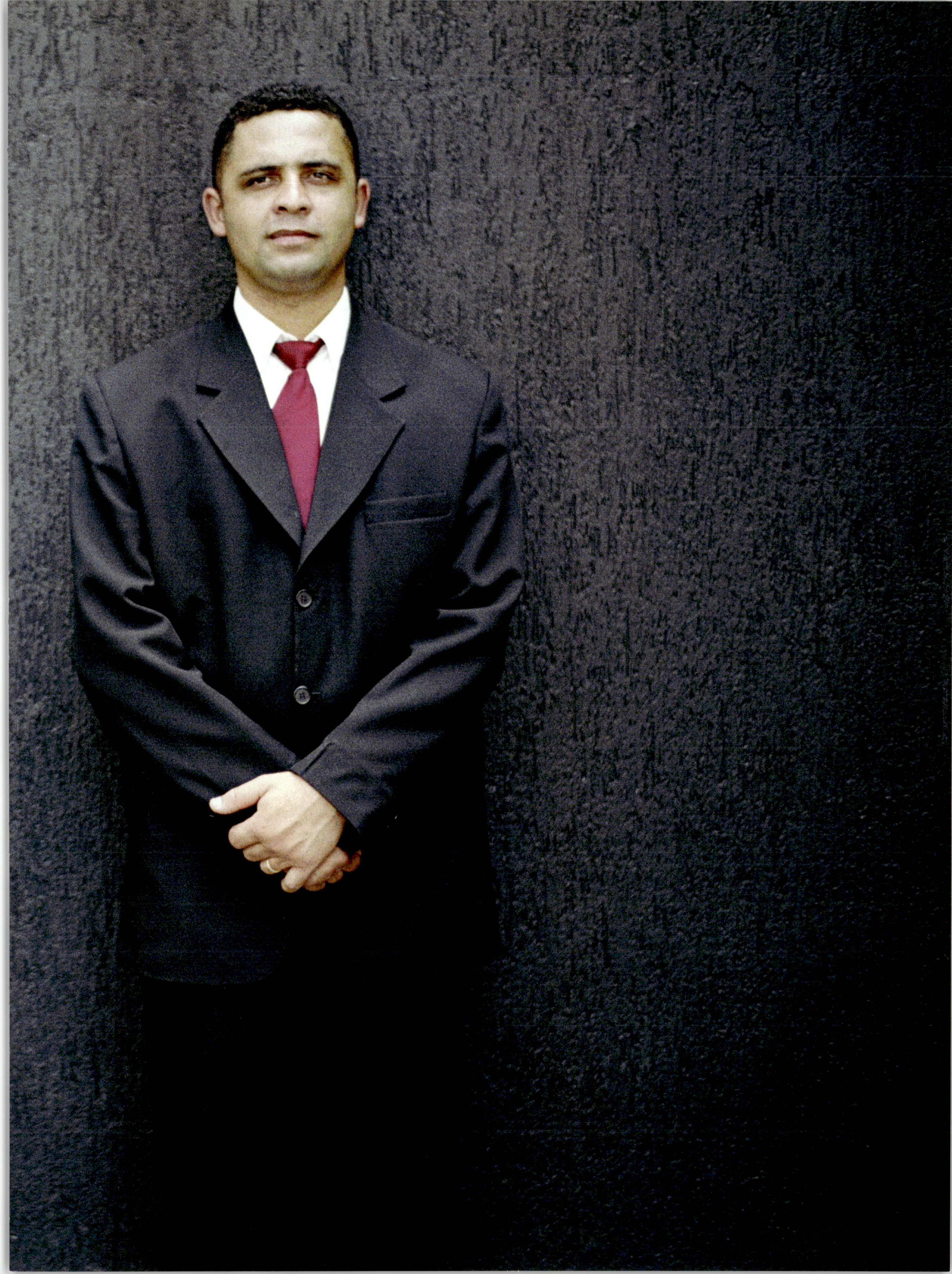

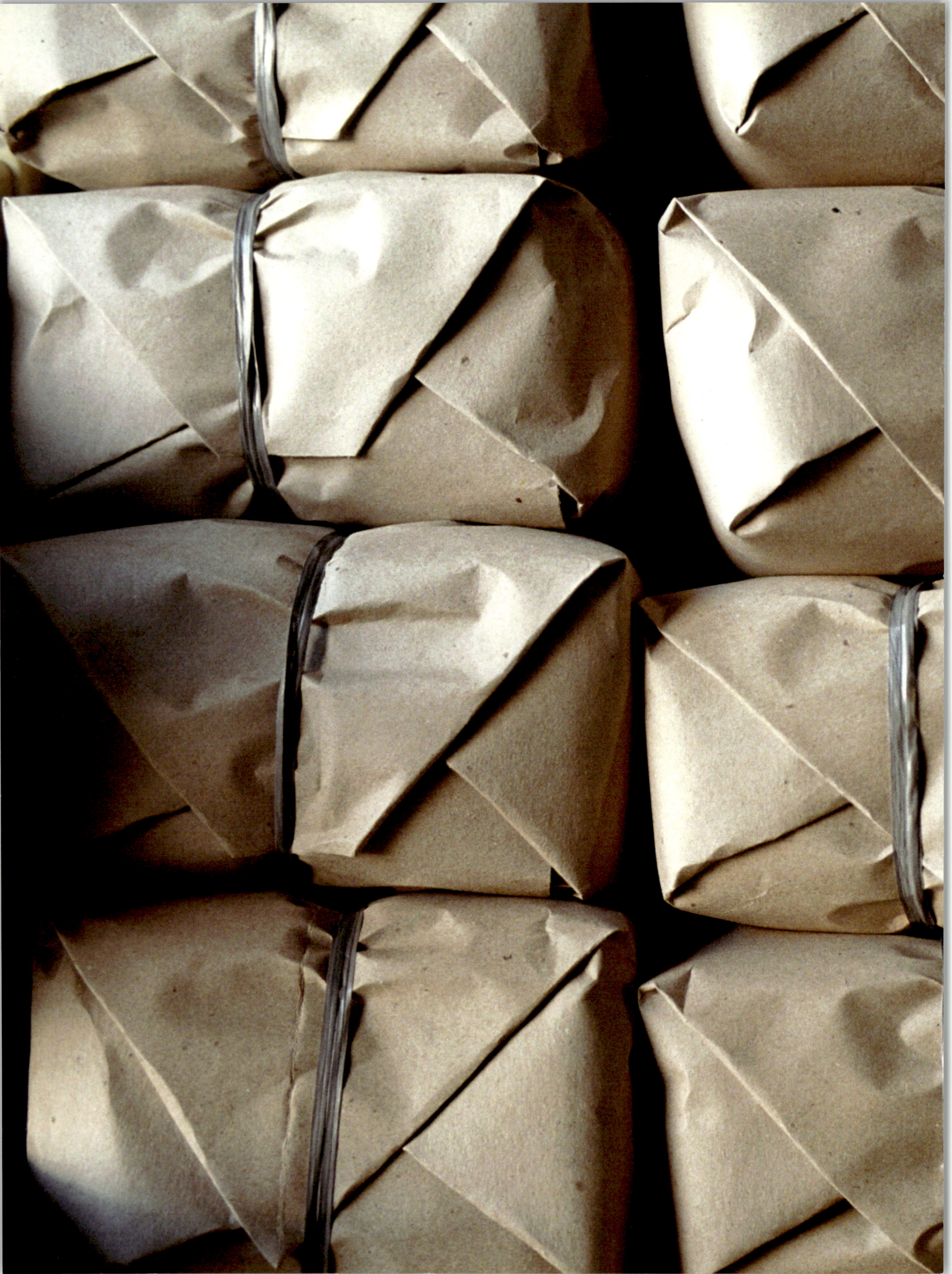

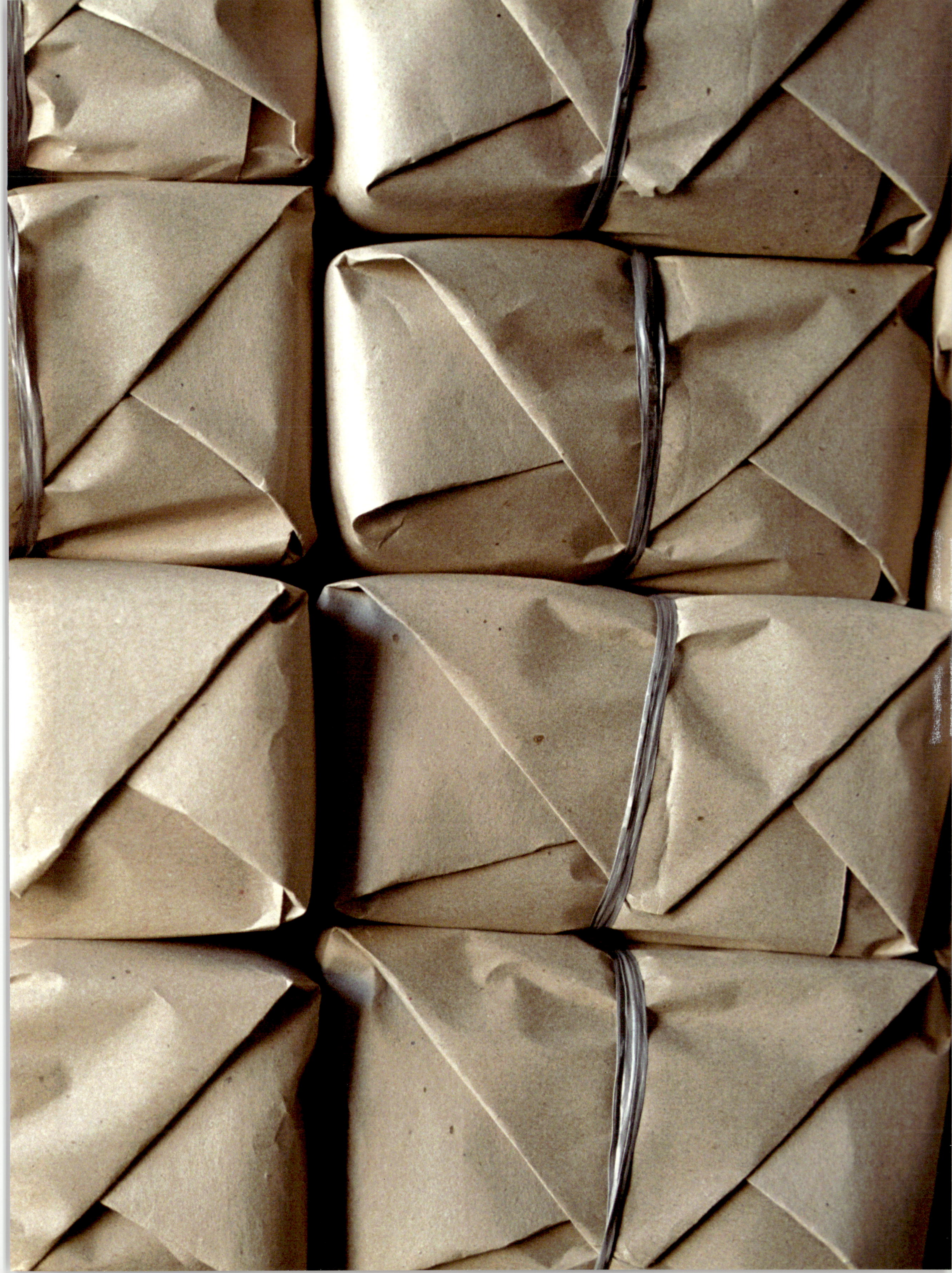

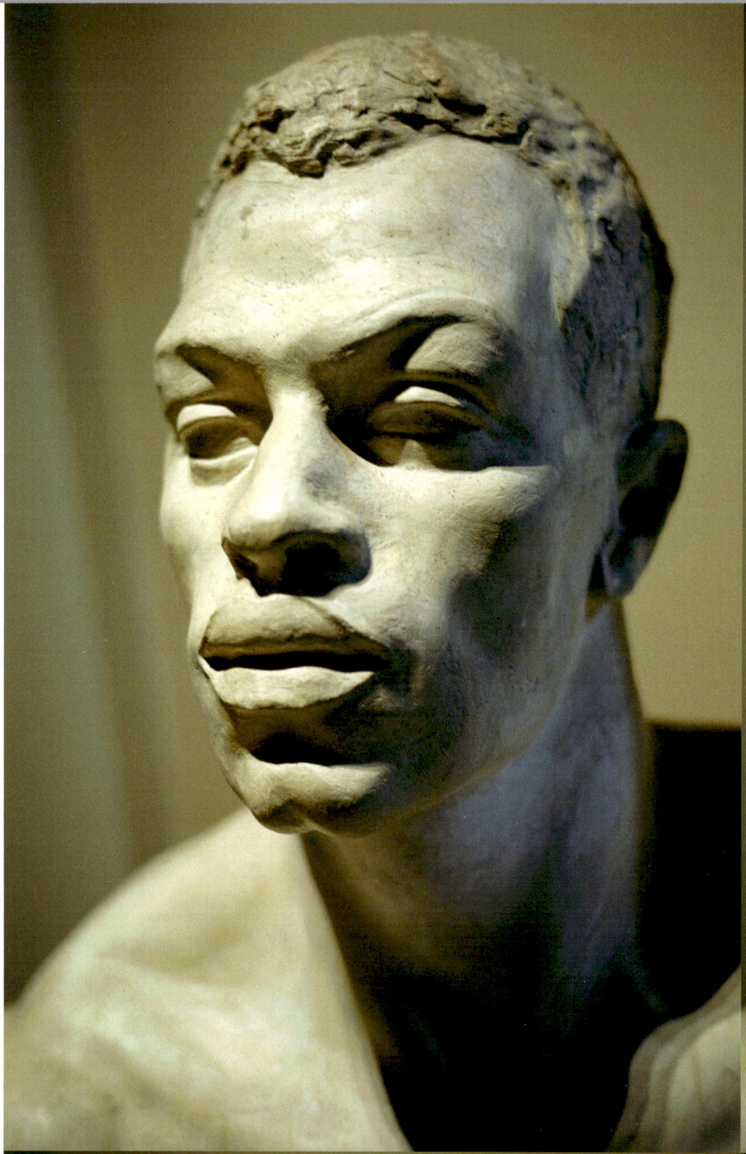
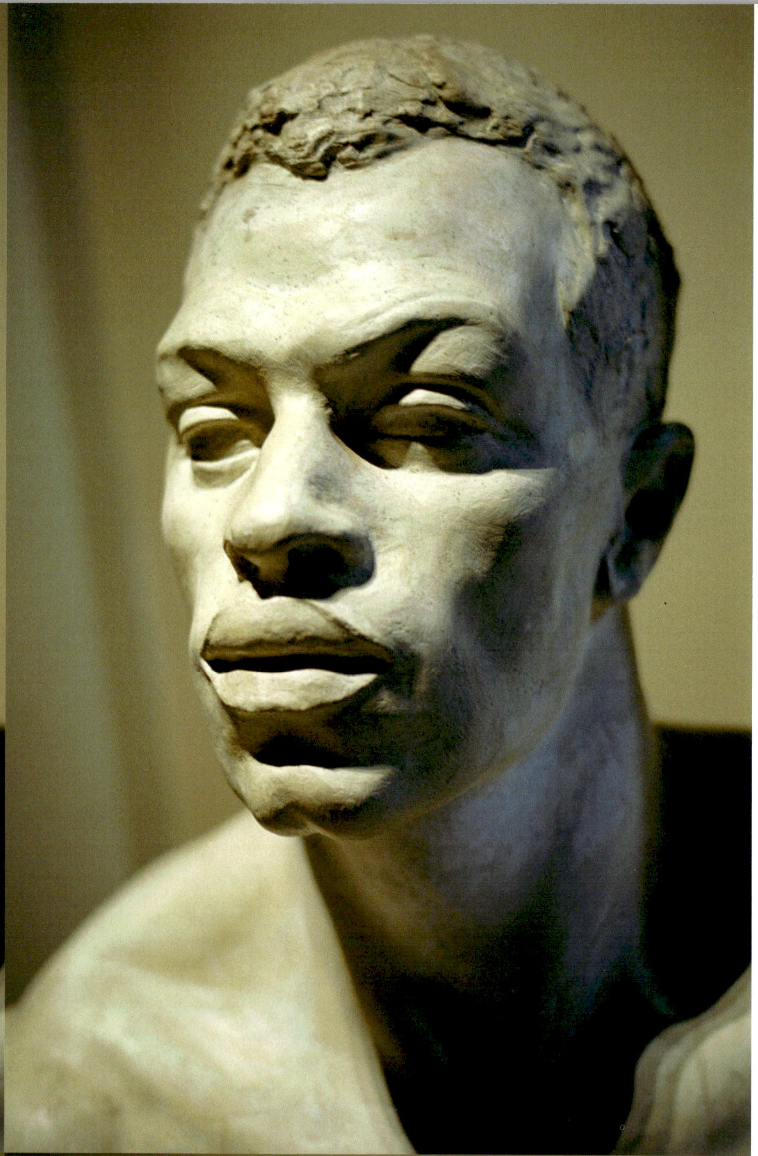
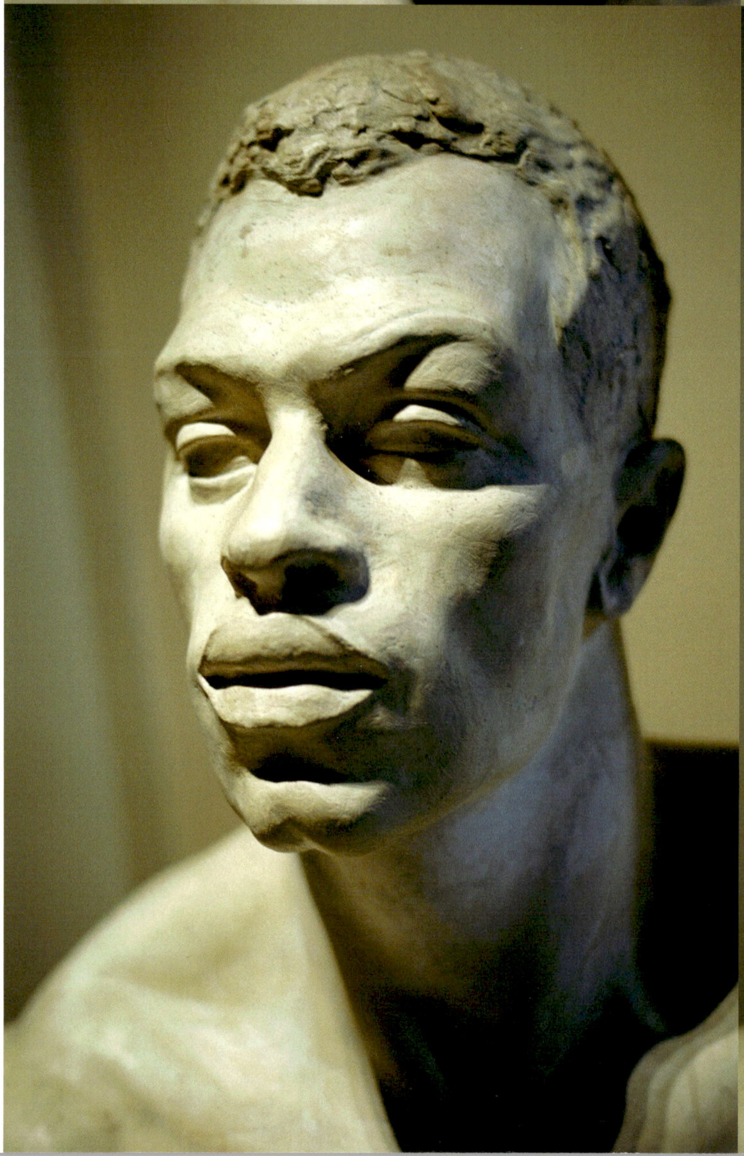
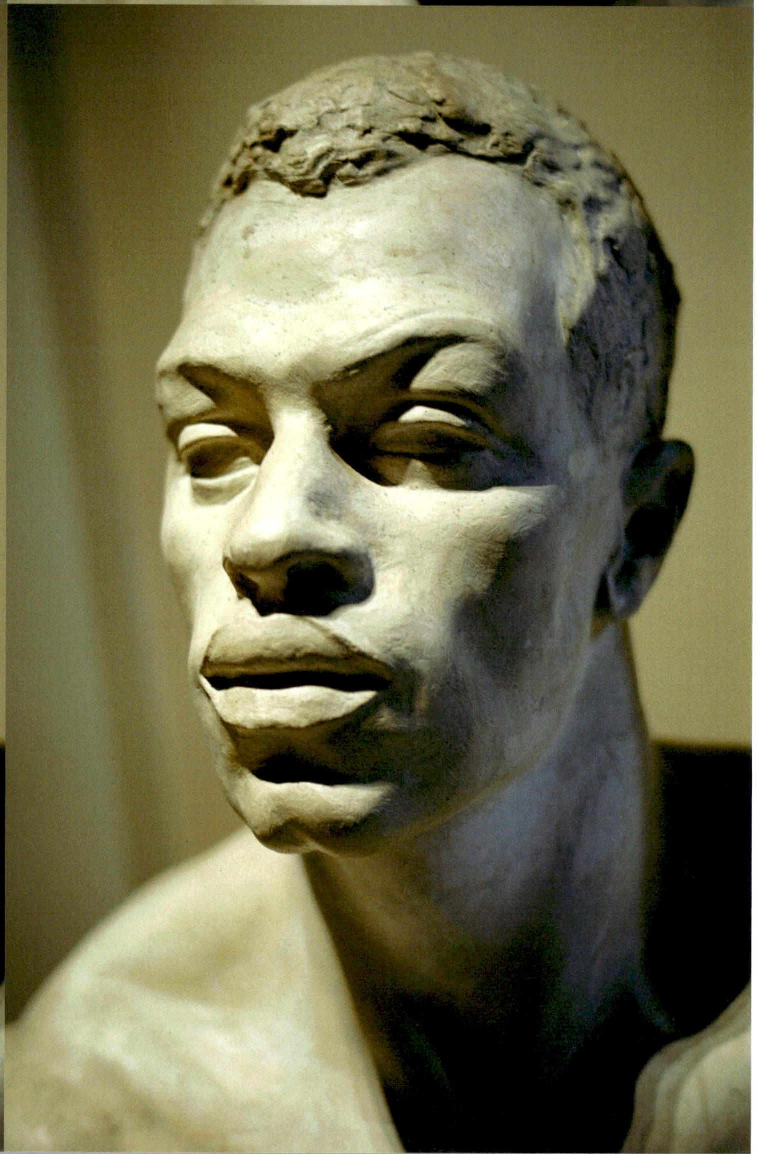

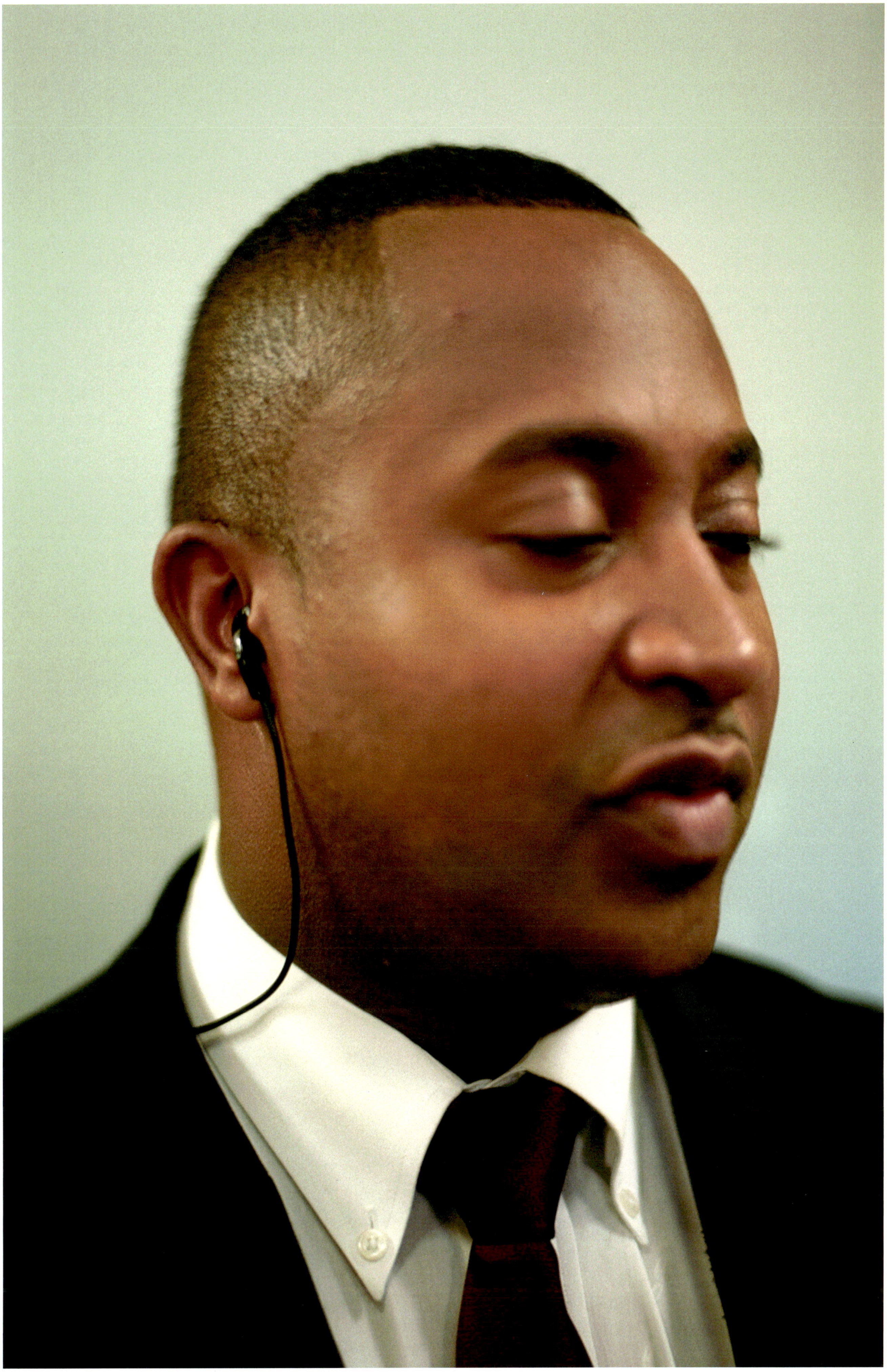

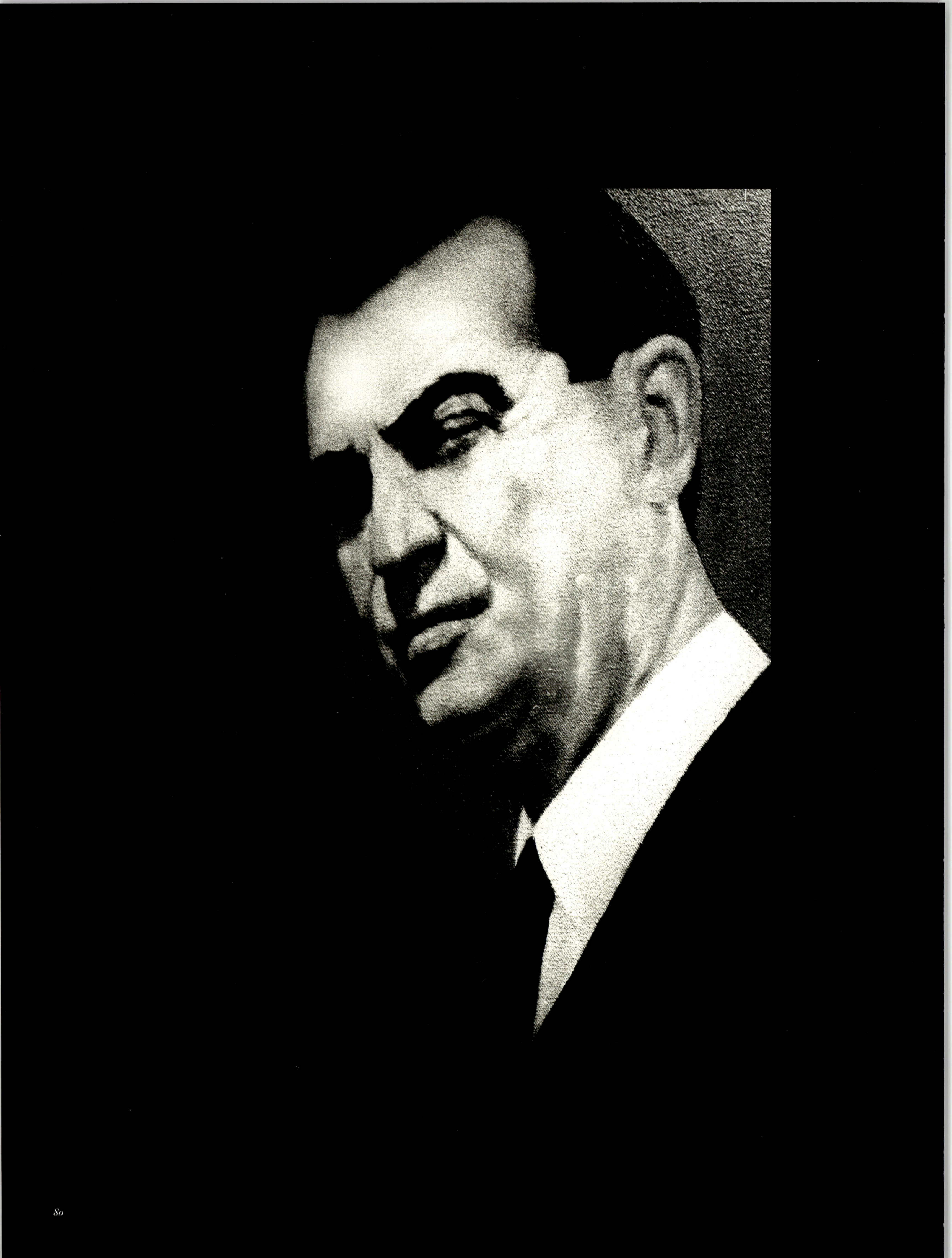

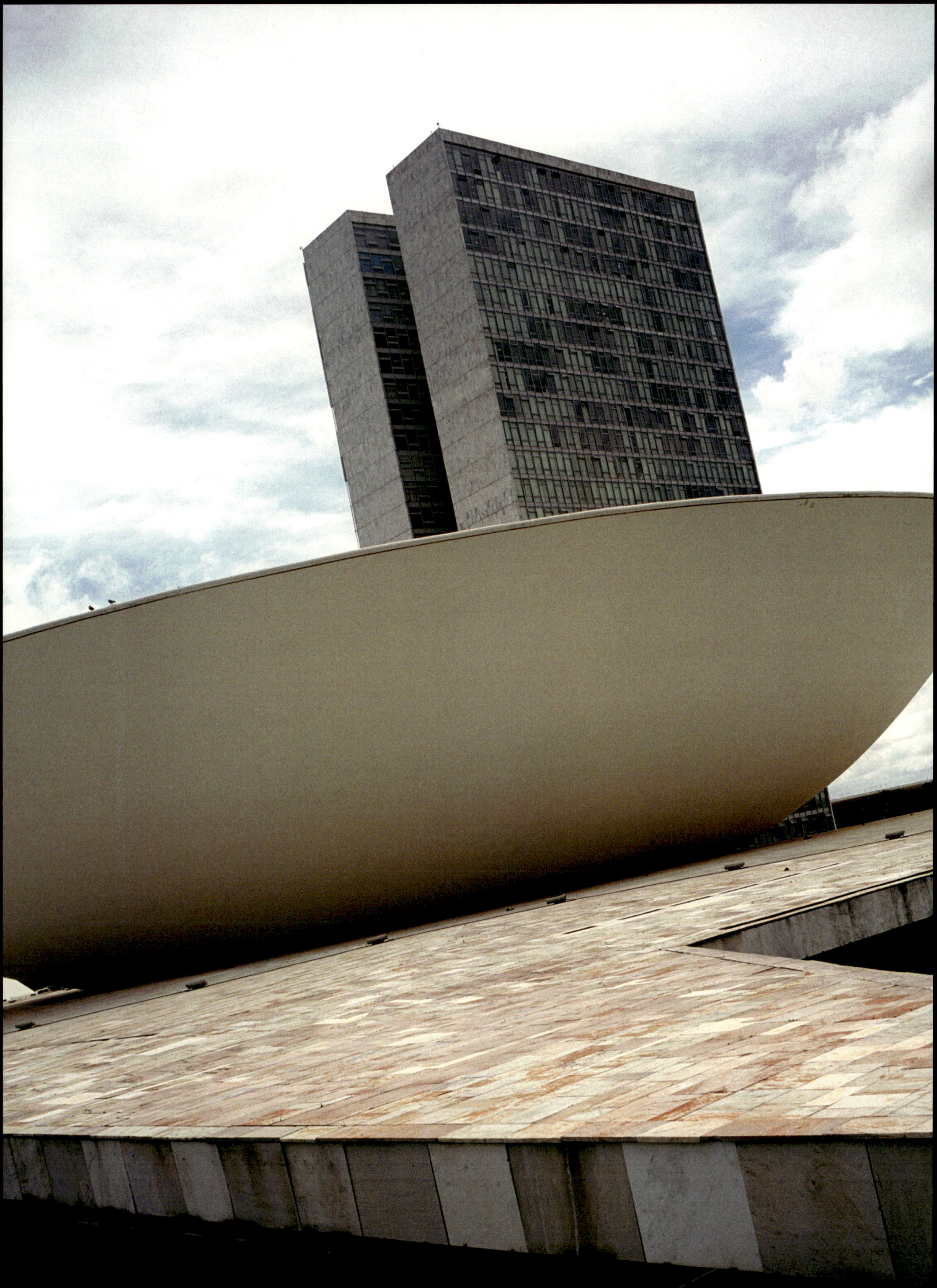

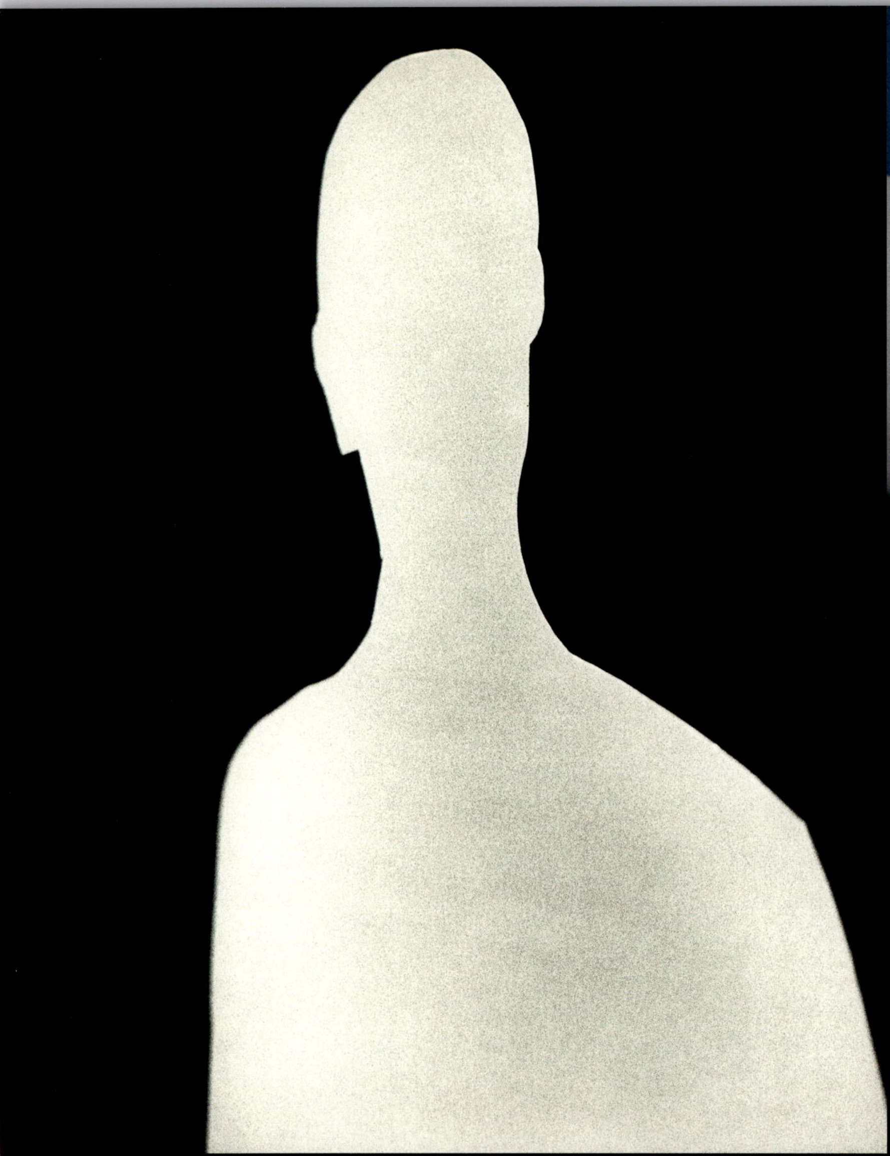

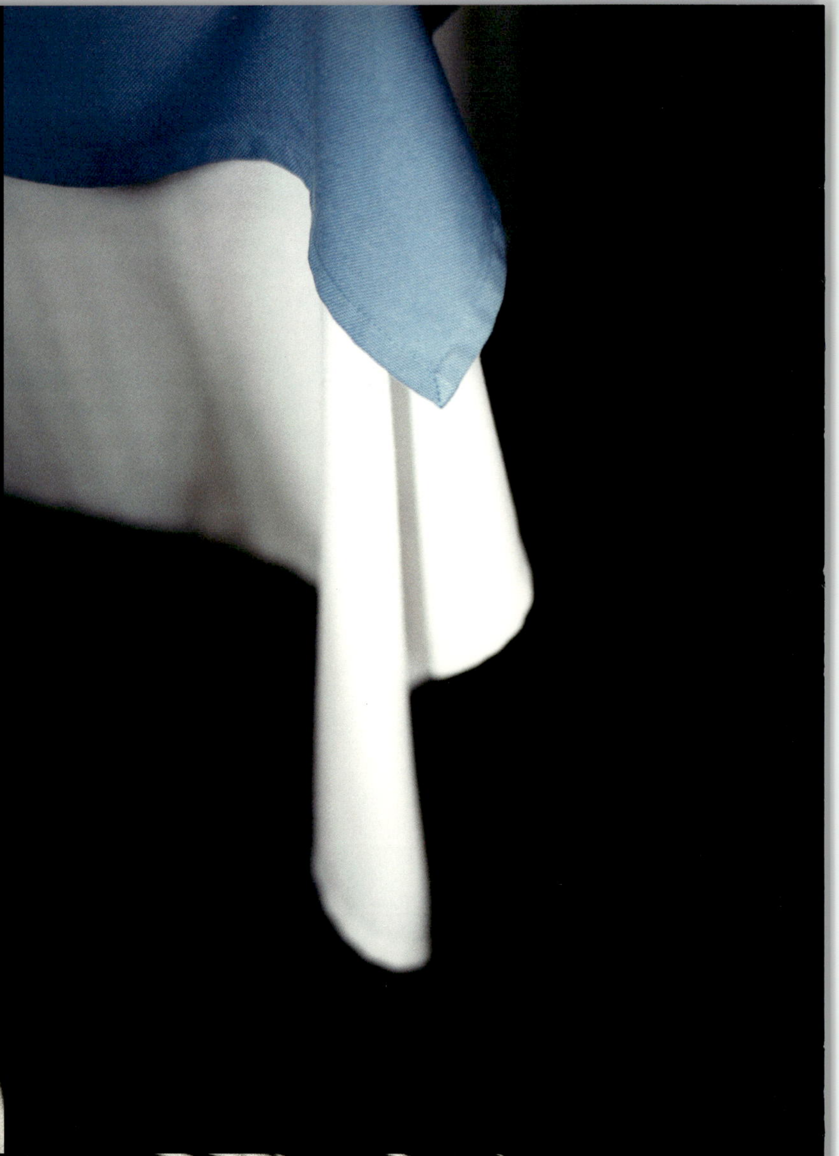

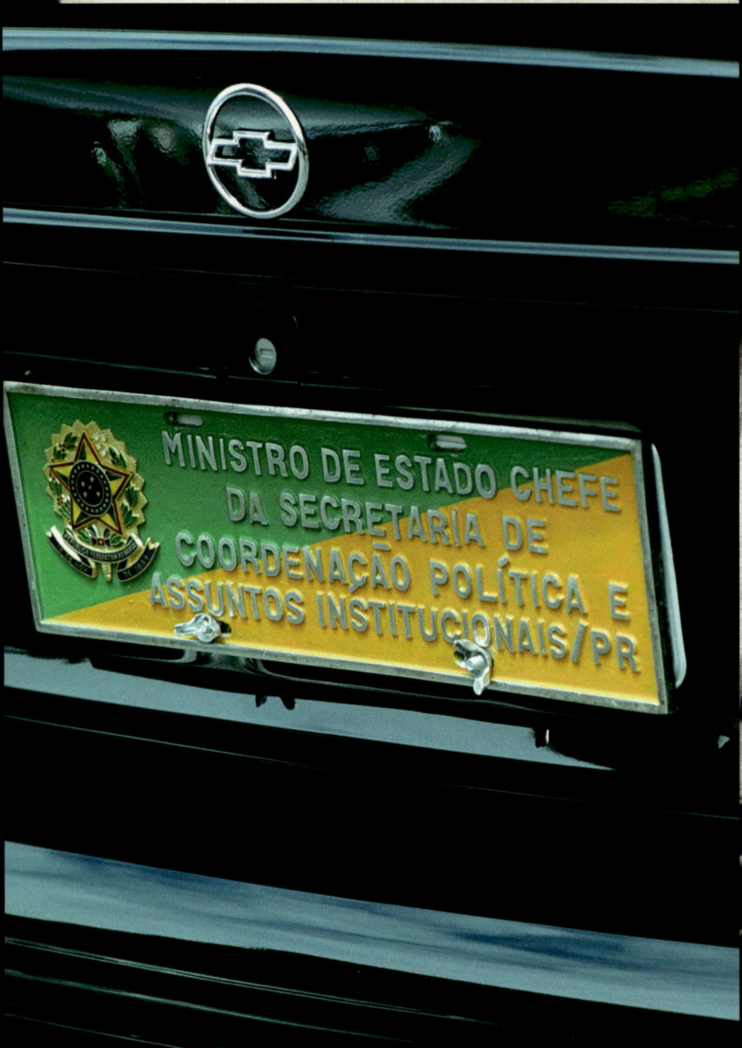

MINISTRO DE ESTADO CHEFE
DA SECRETARIA DE
COORDENAÇÃO POLÍTICA E
ASSUNTOS INSTITUCIONAIS/PR

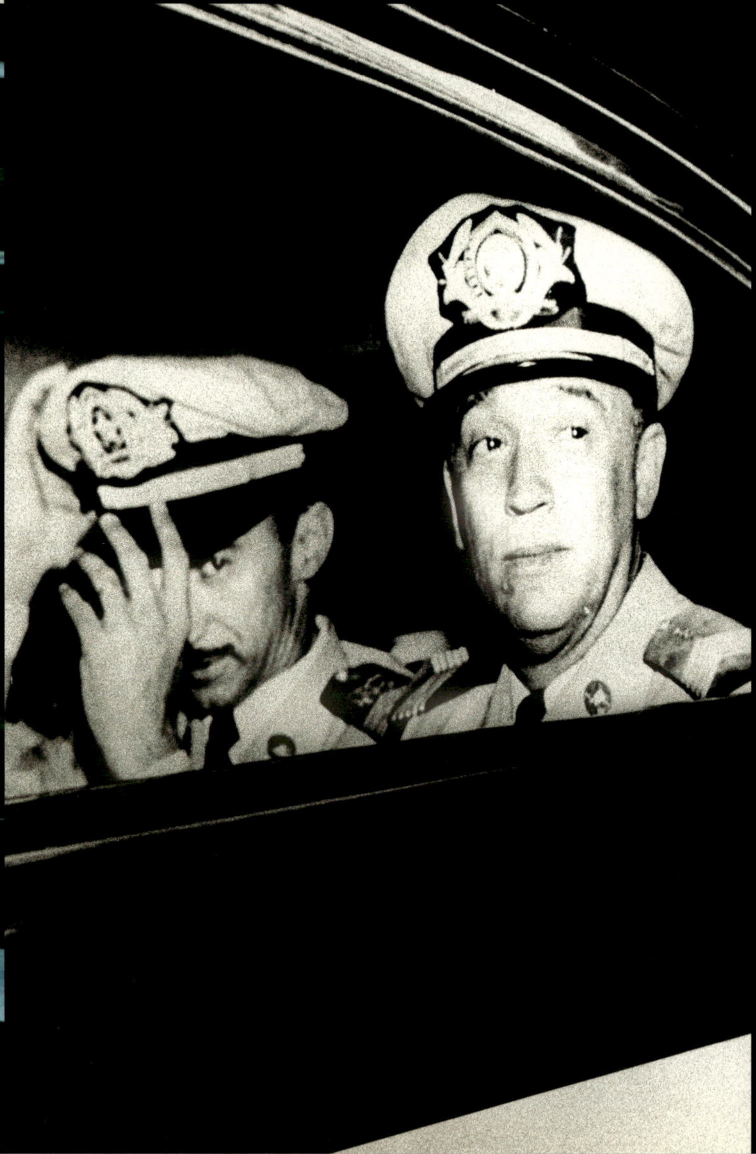

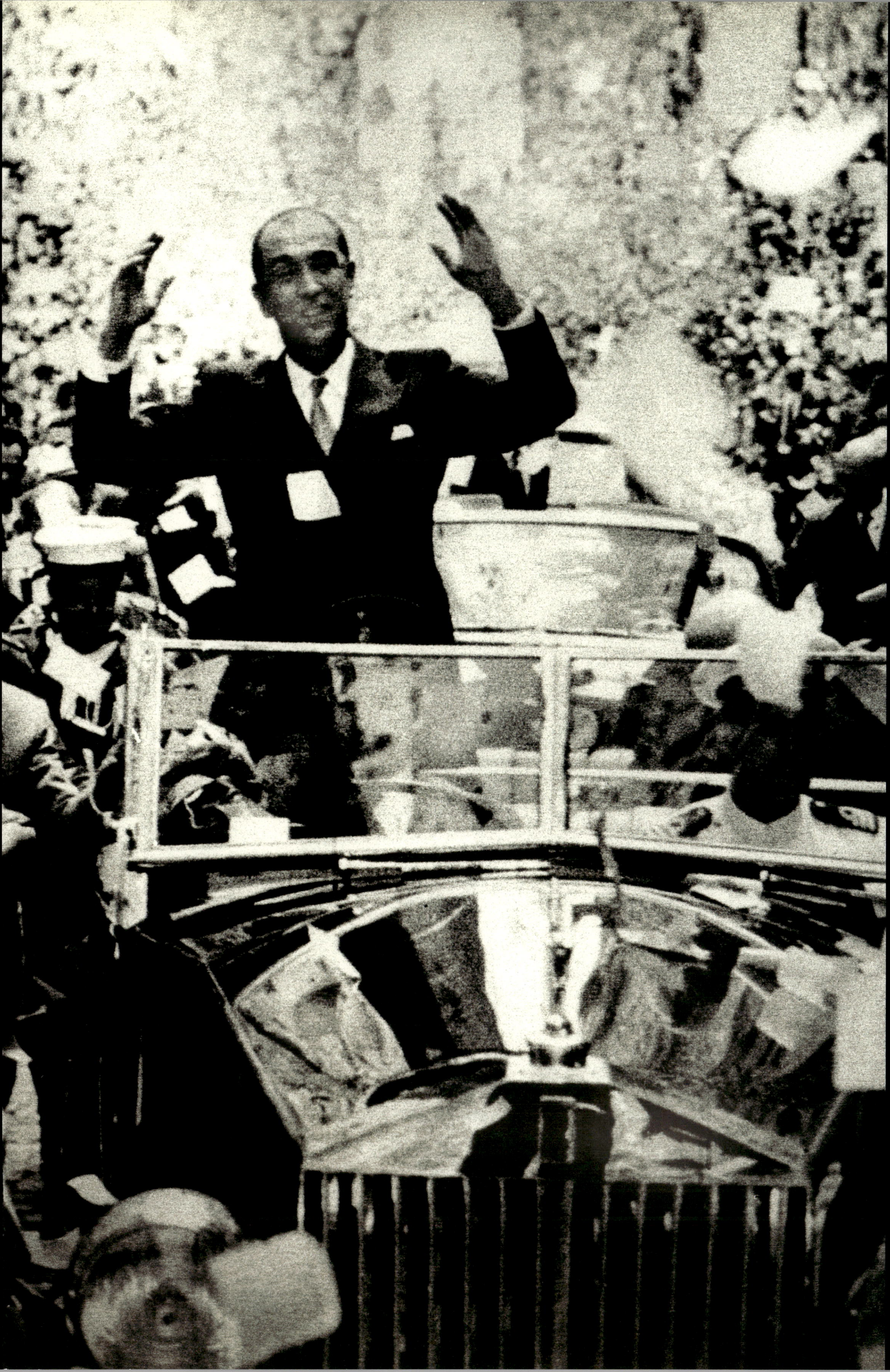

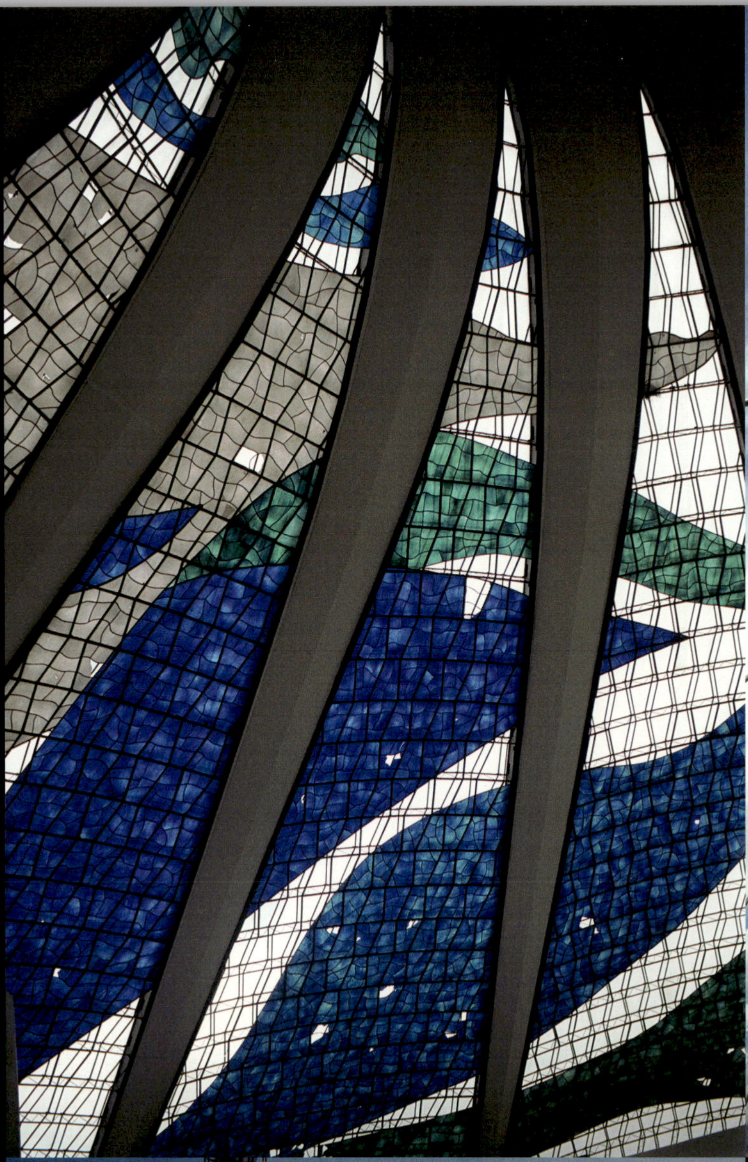
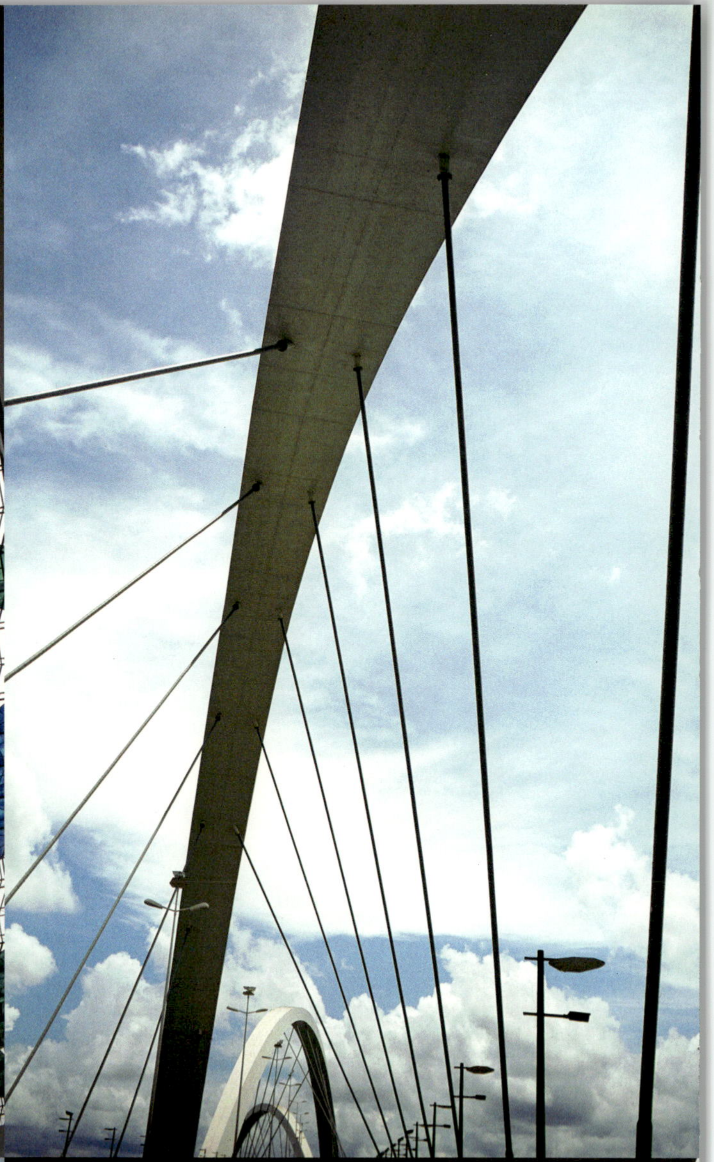
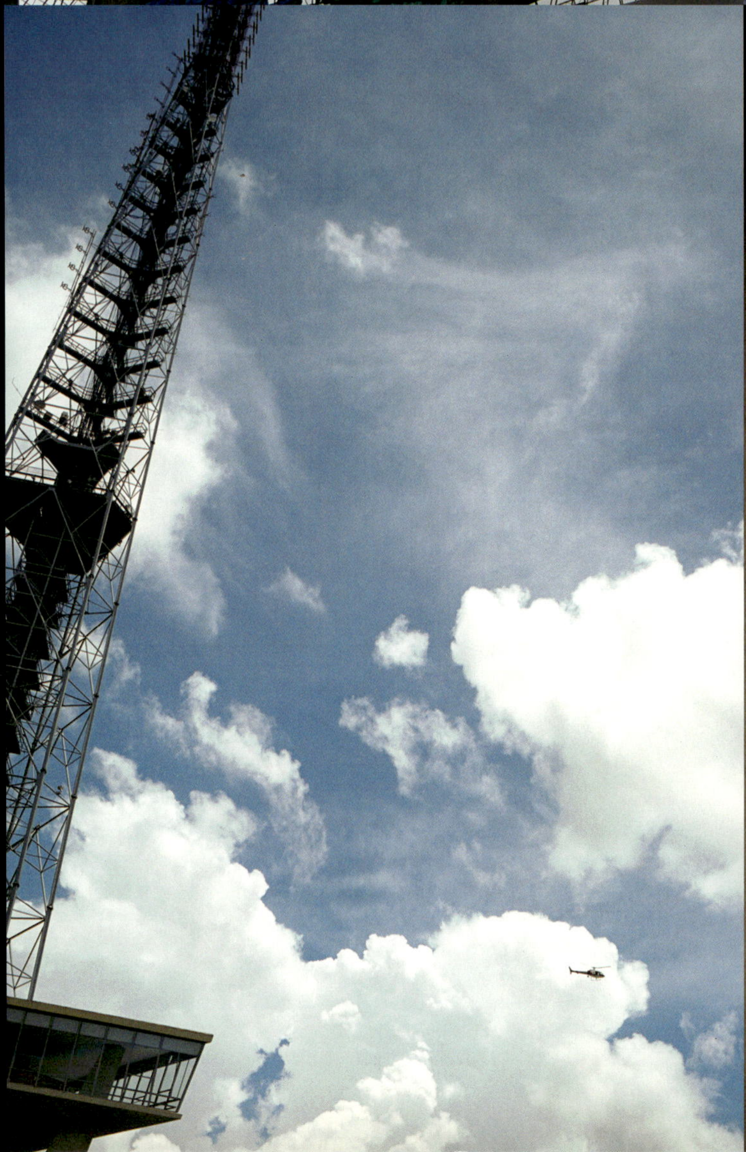
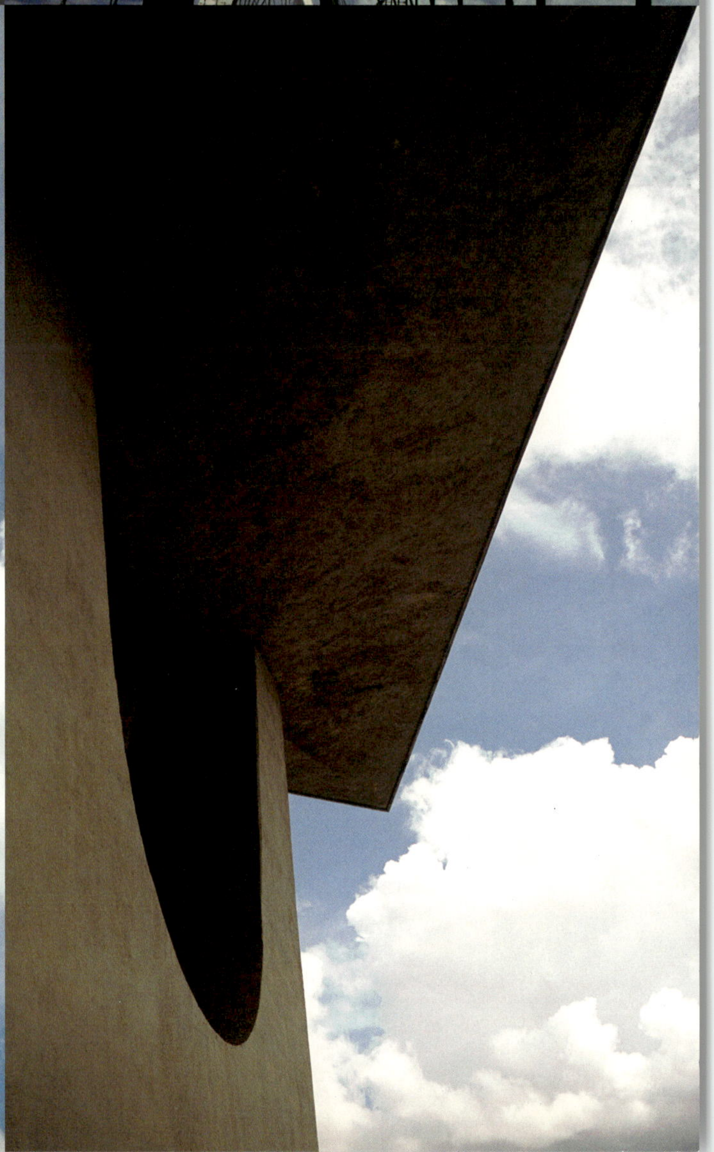

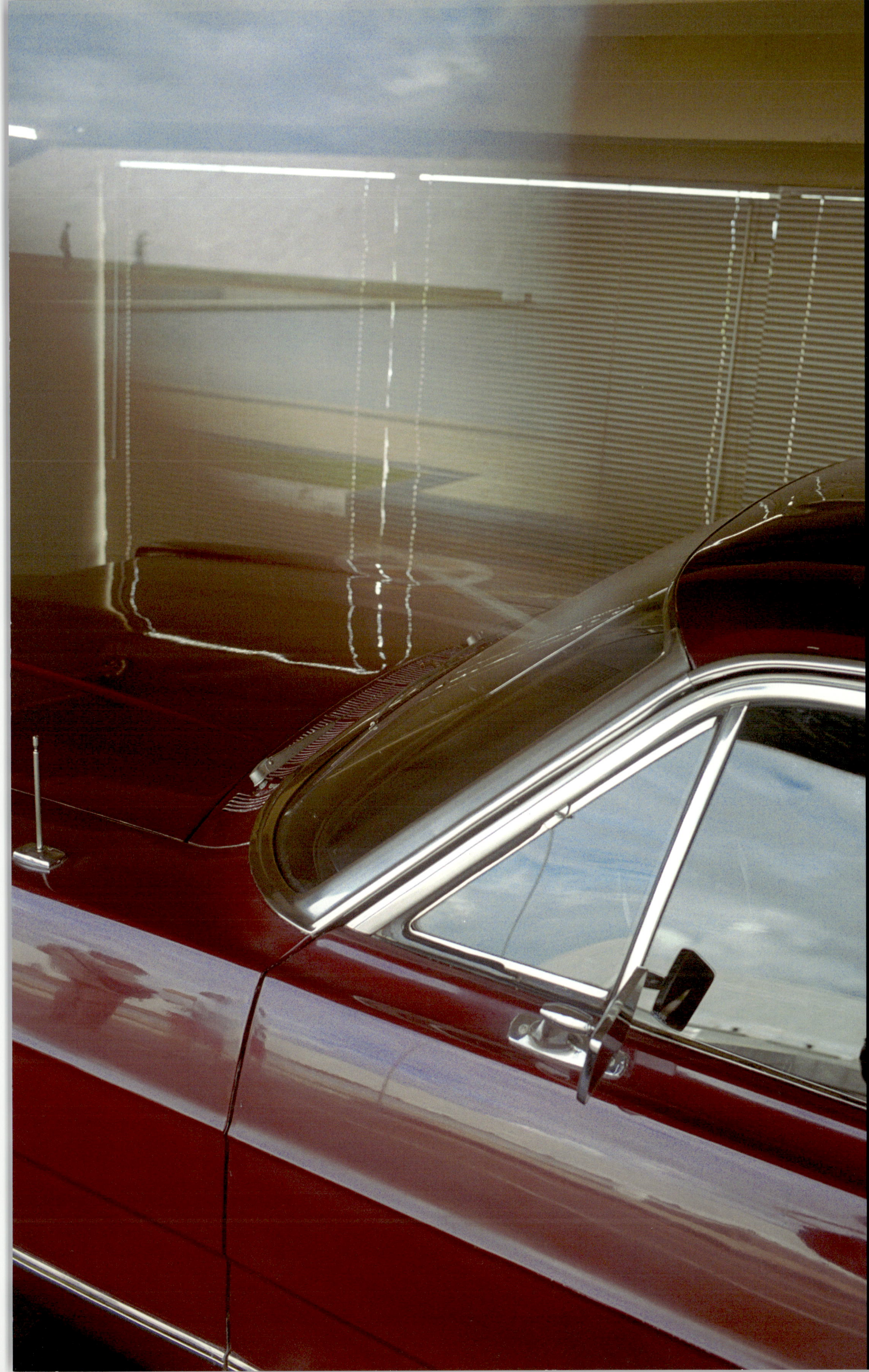

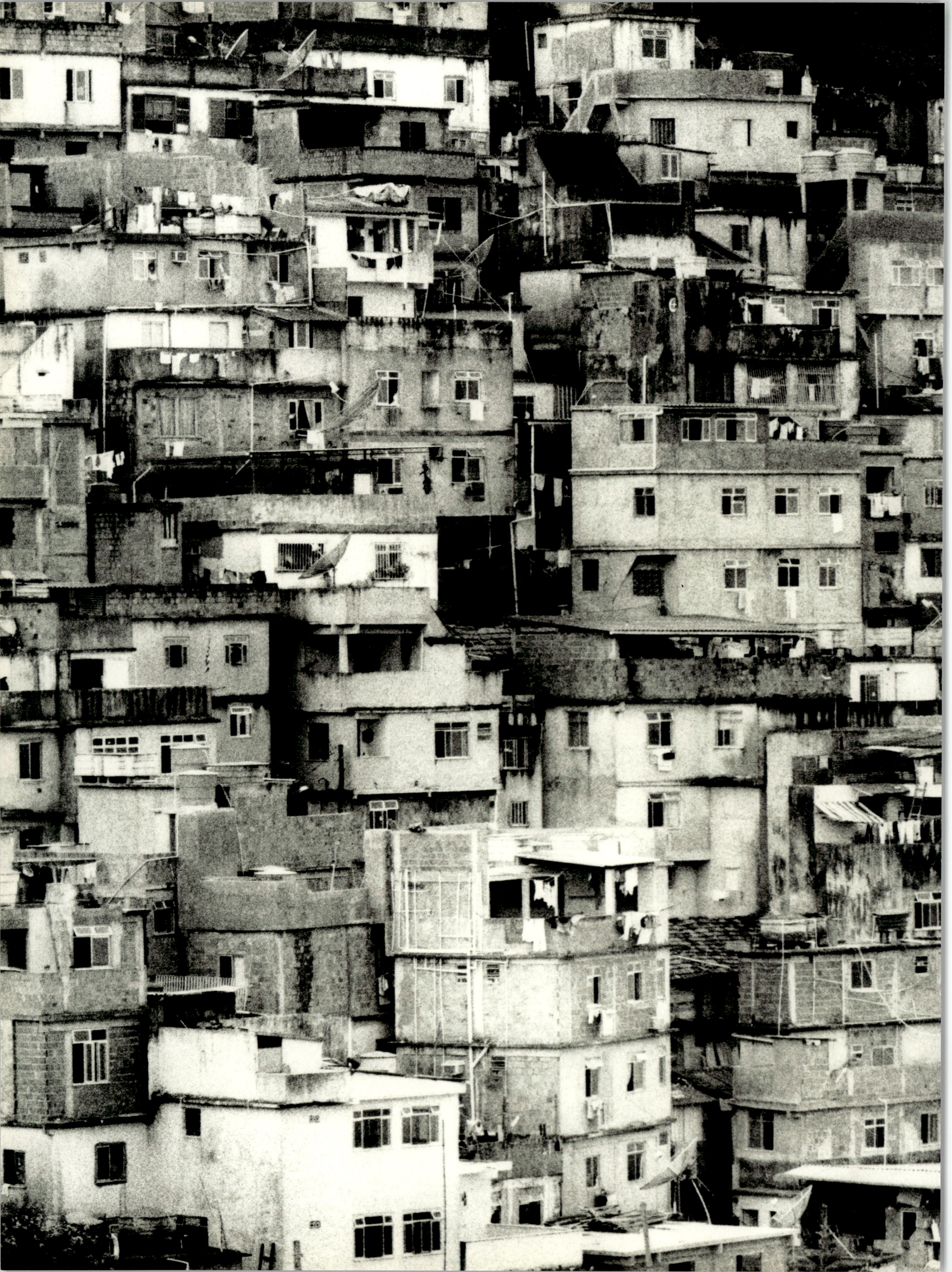

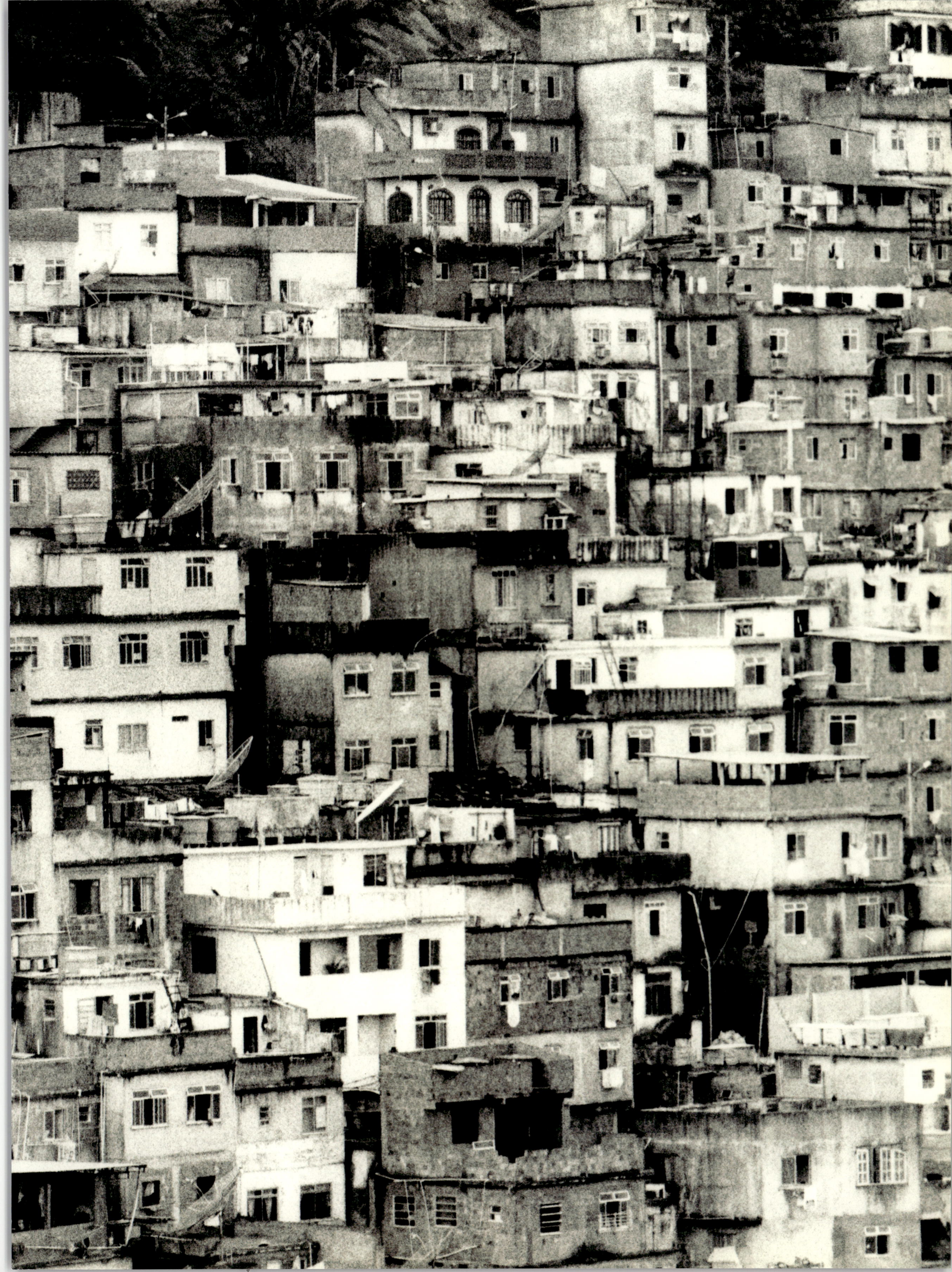

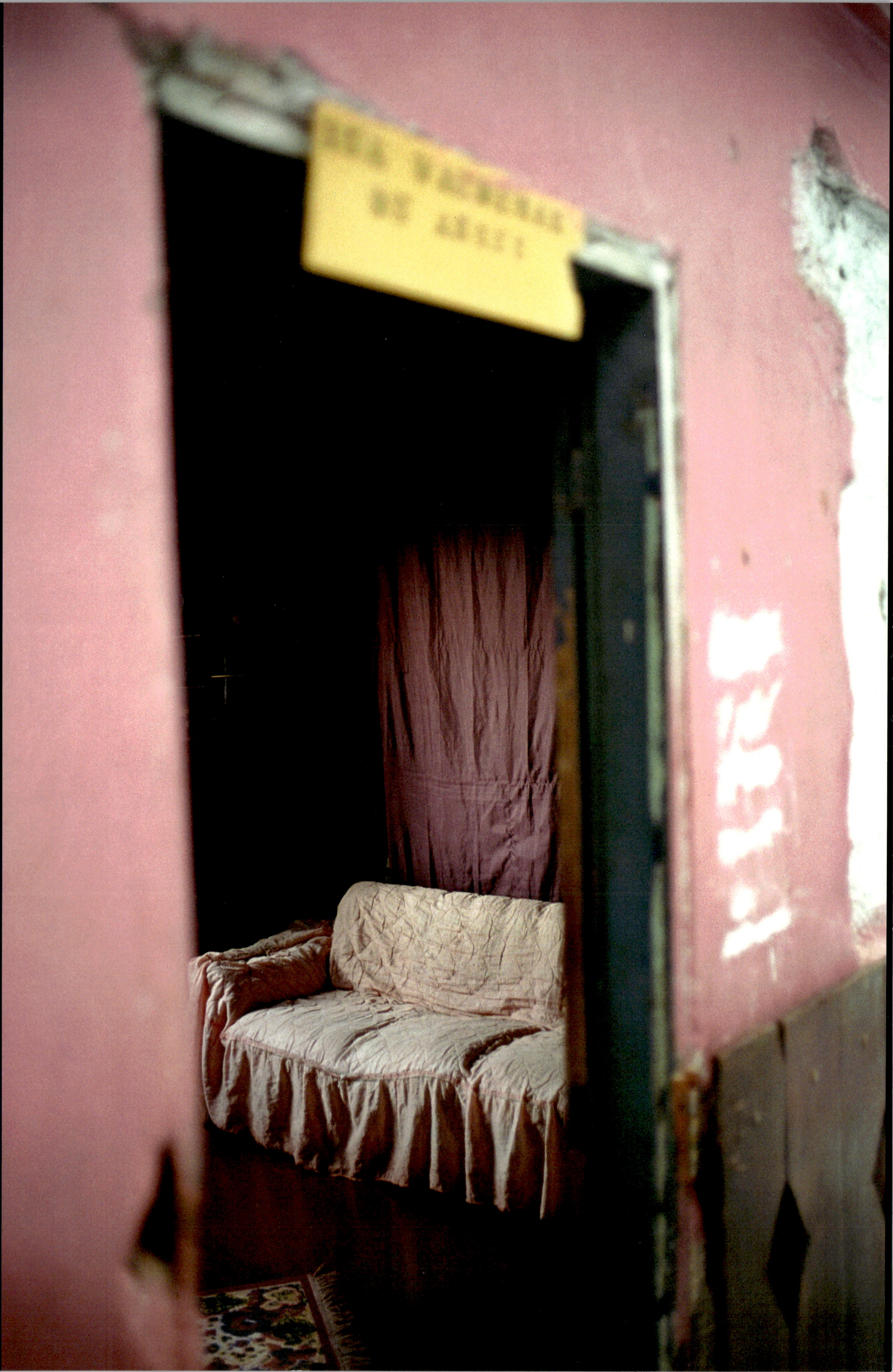

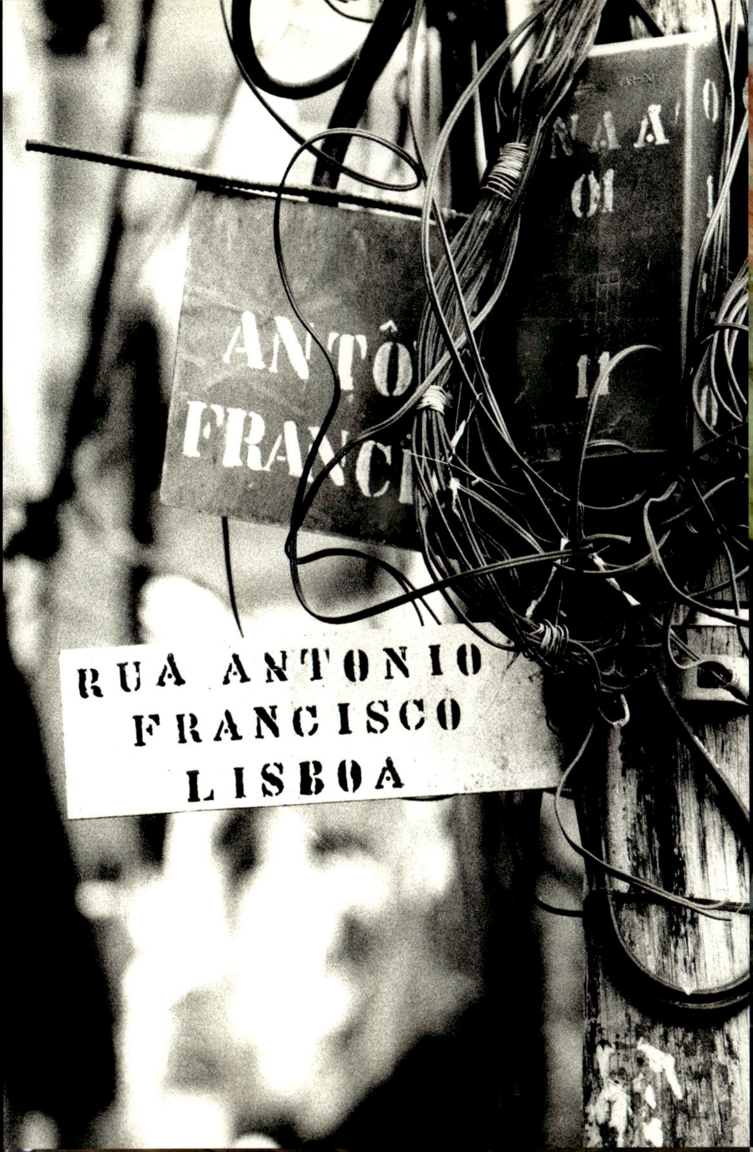
RUA ANTONIO
FRANCISCO
LISBOA
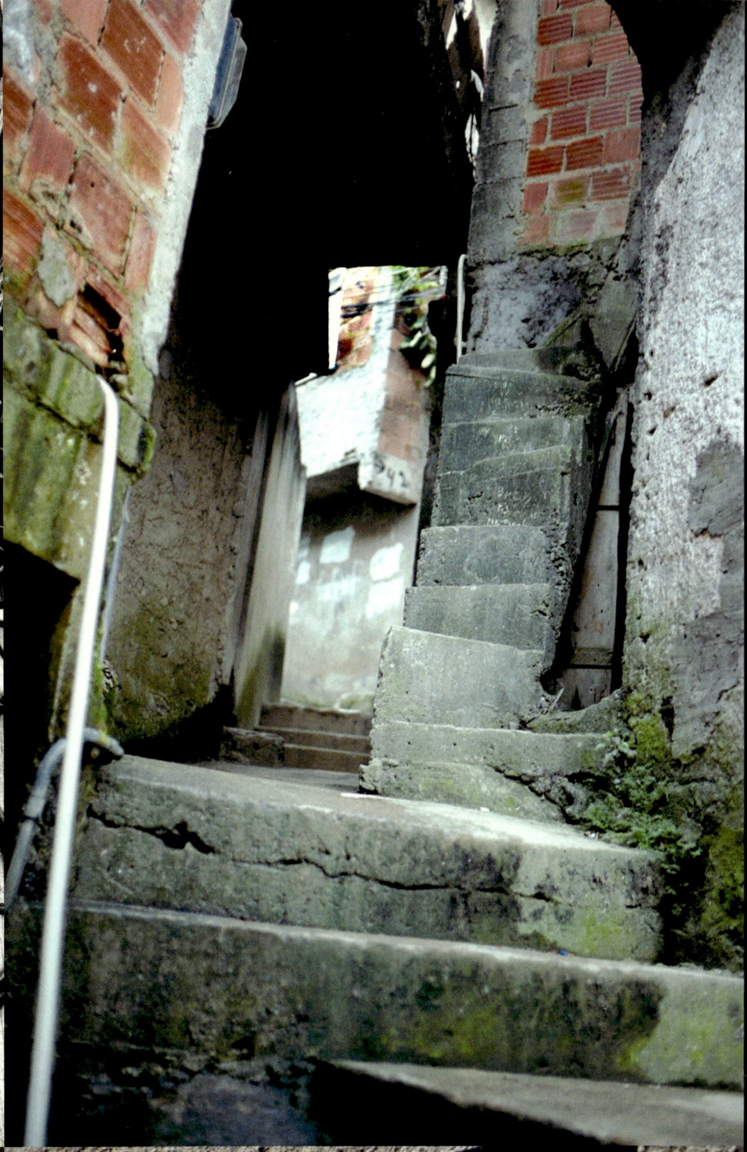
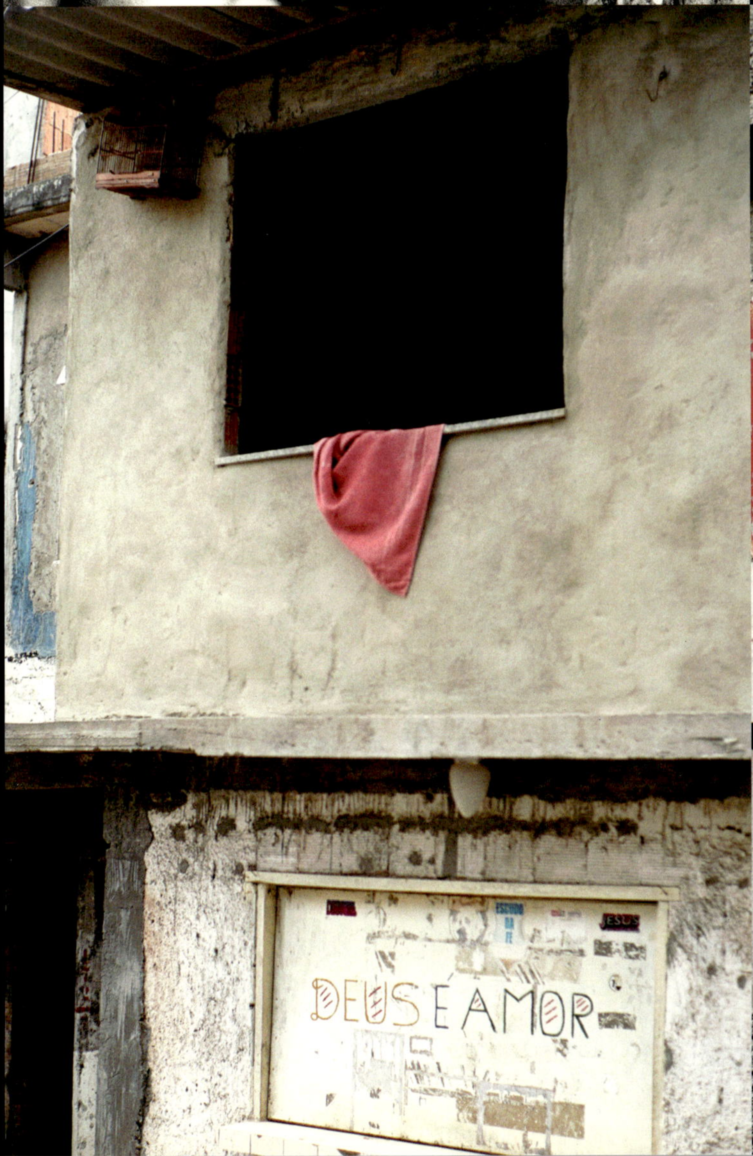
DEUS É AMOR
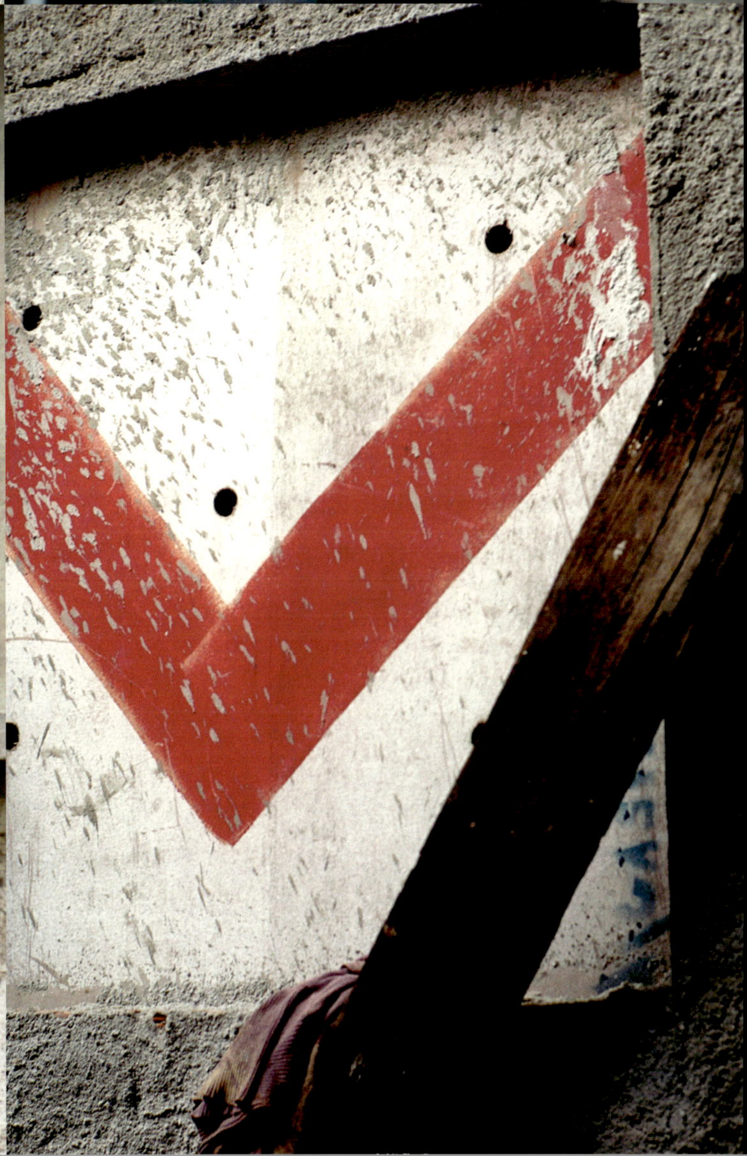

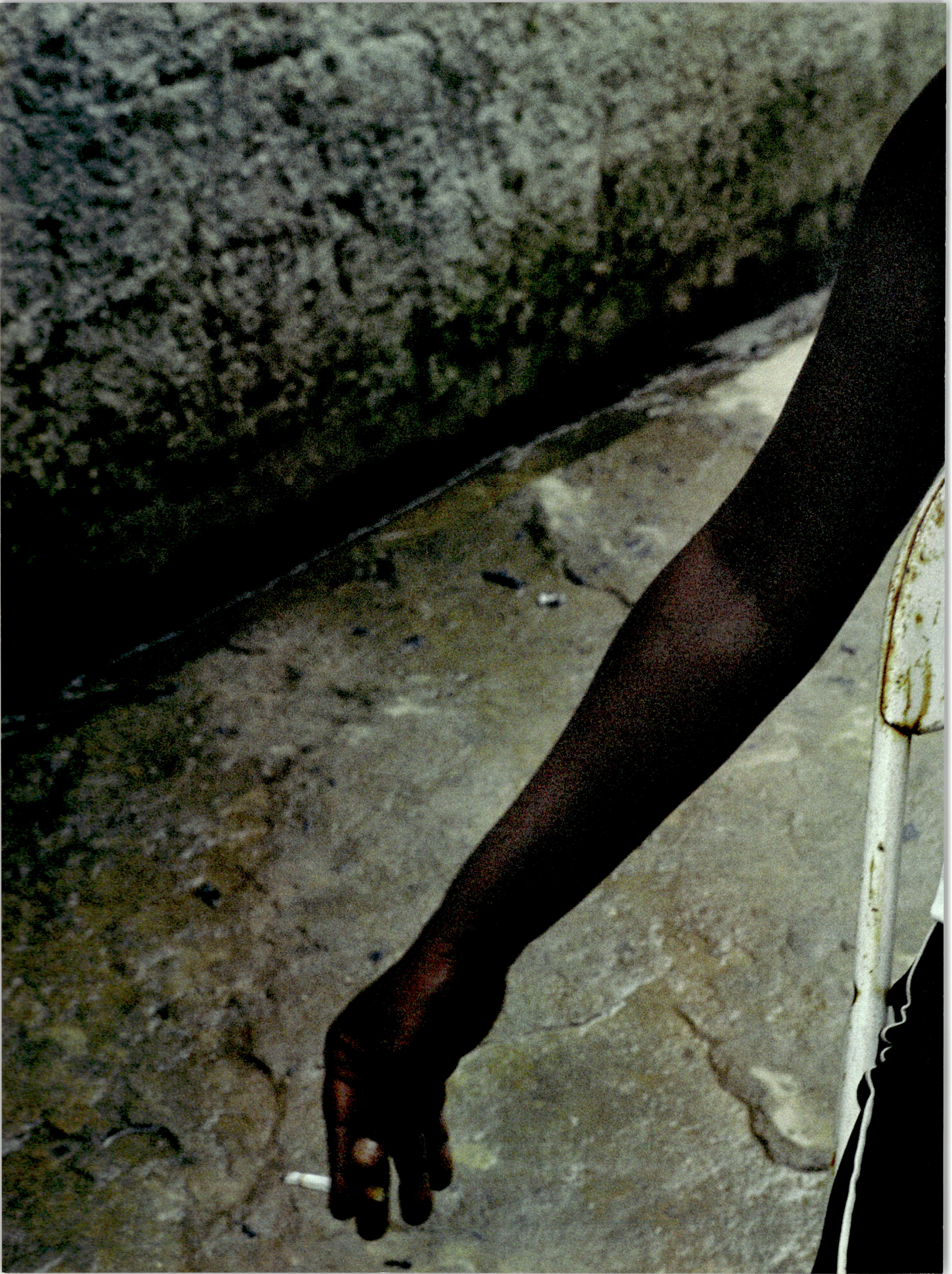

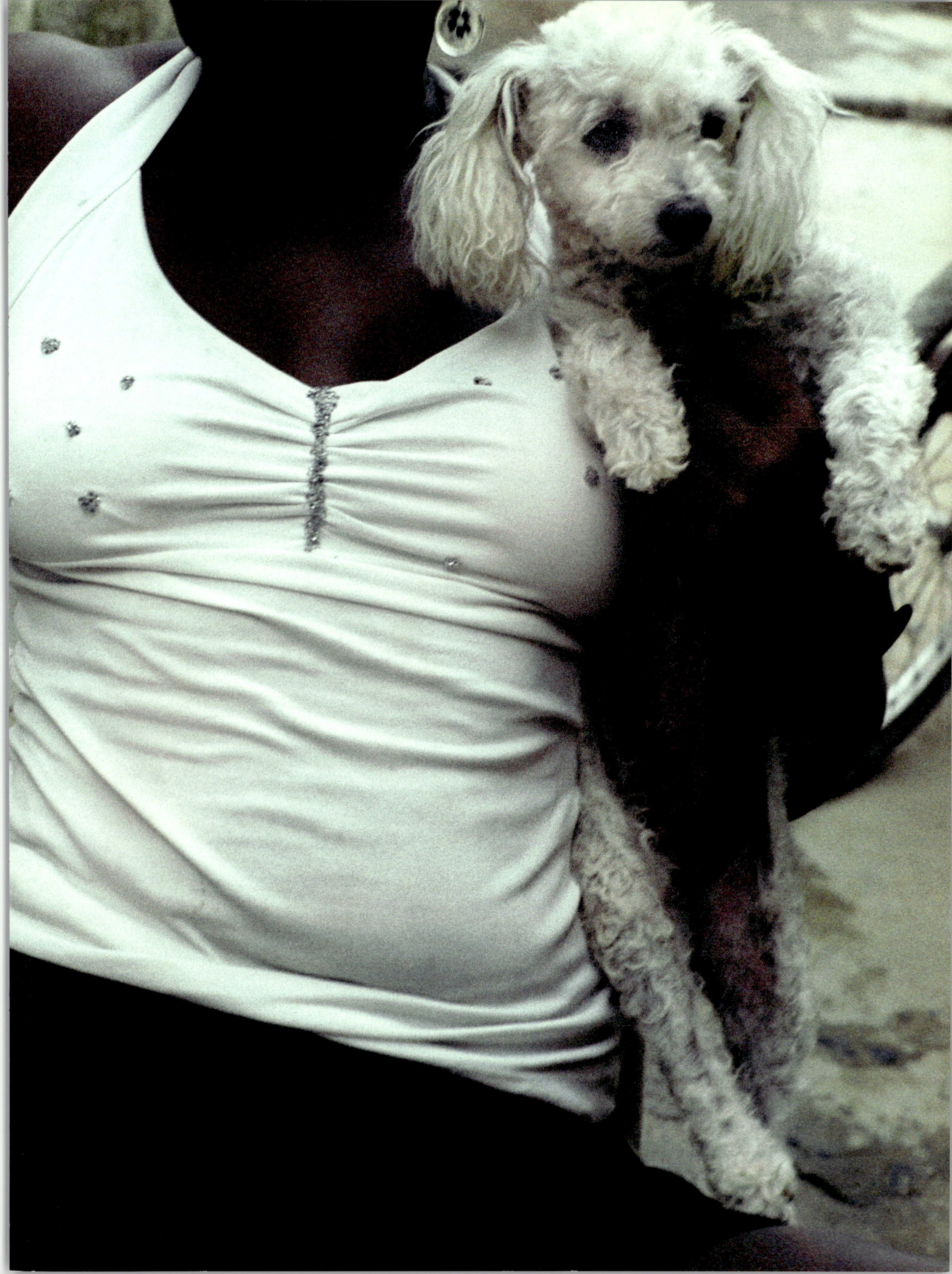

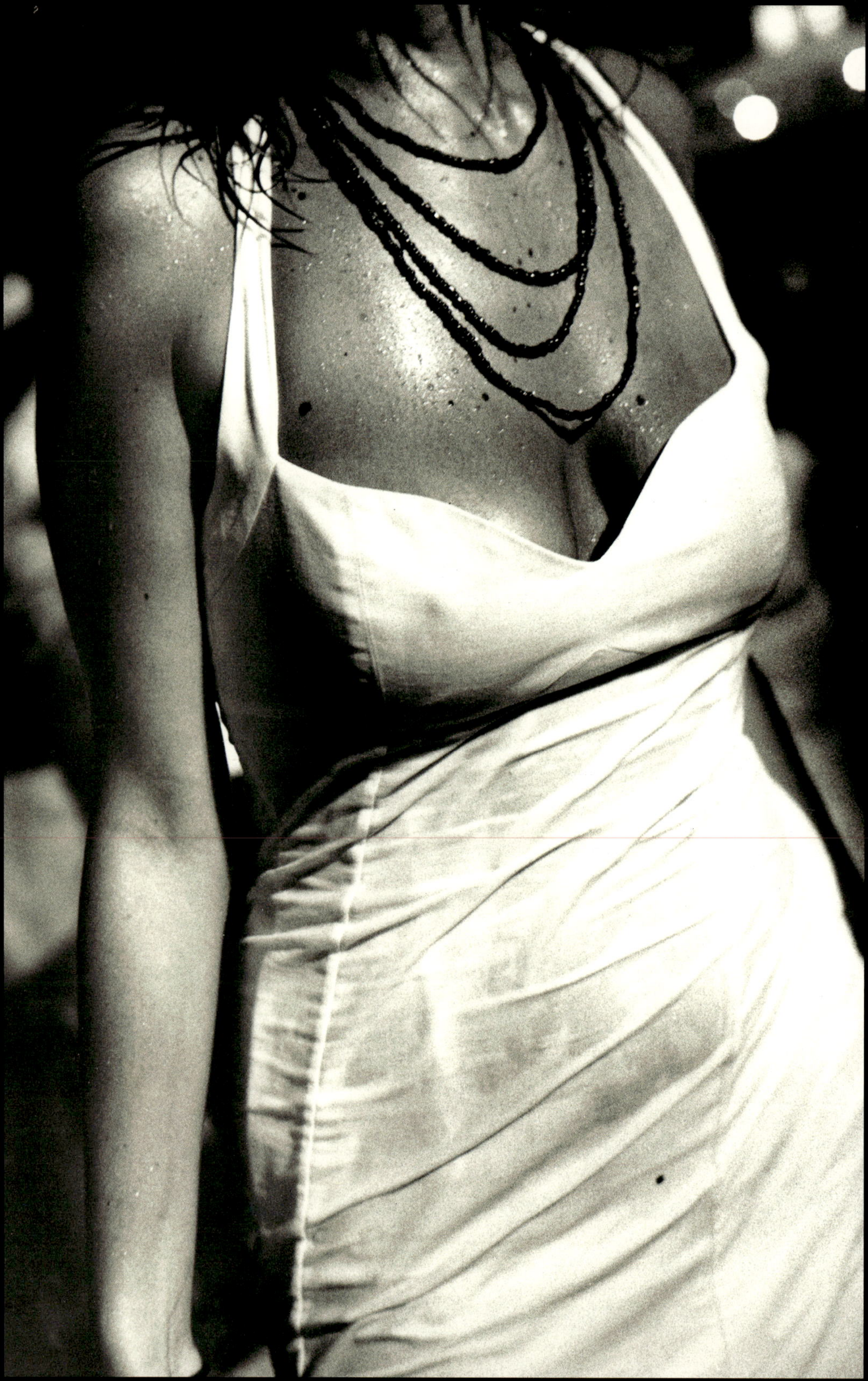

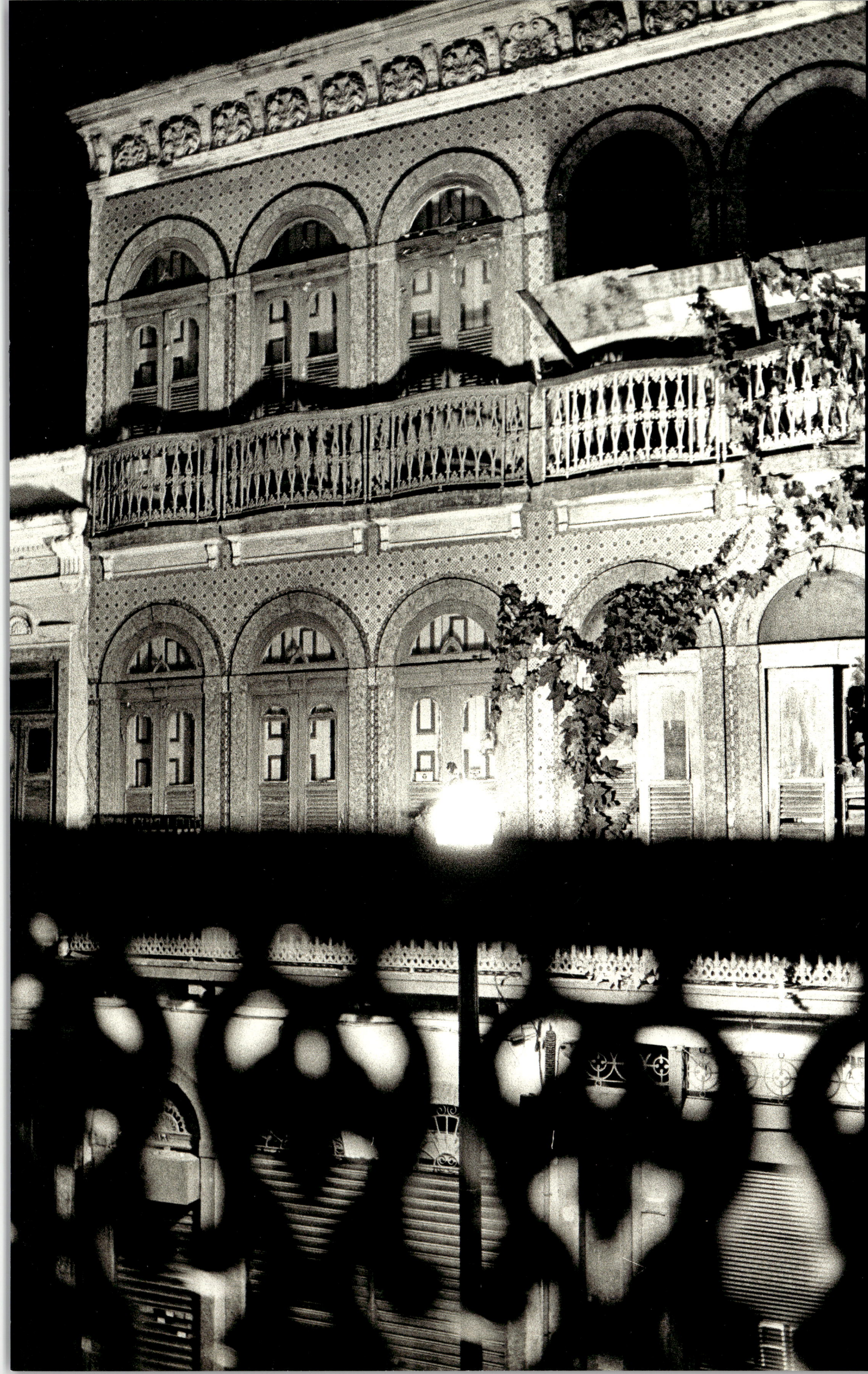

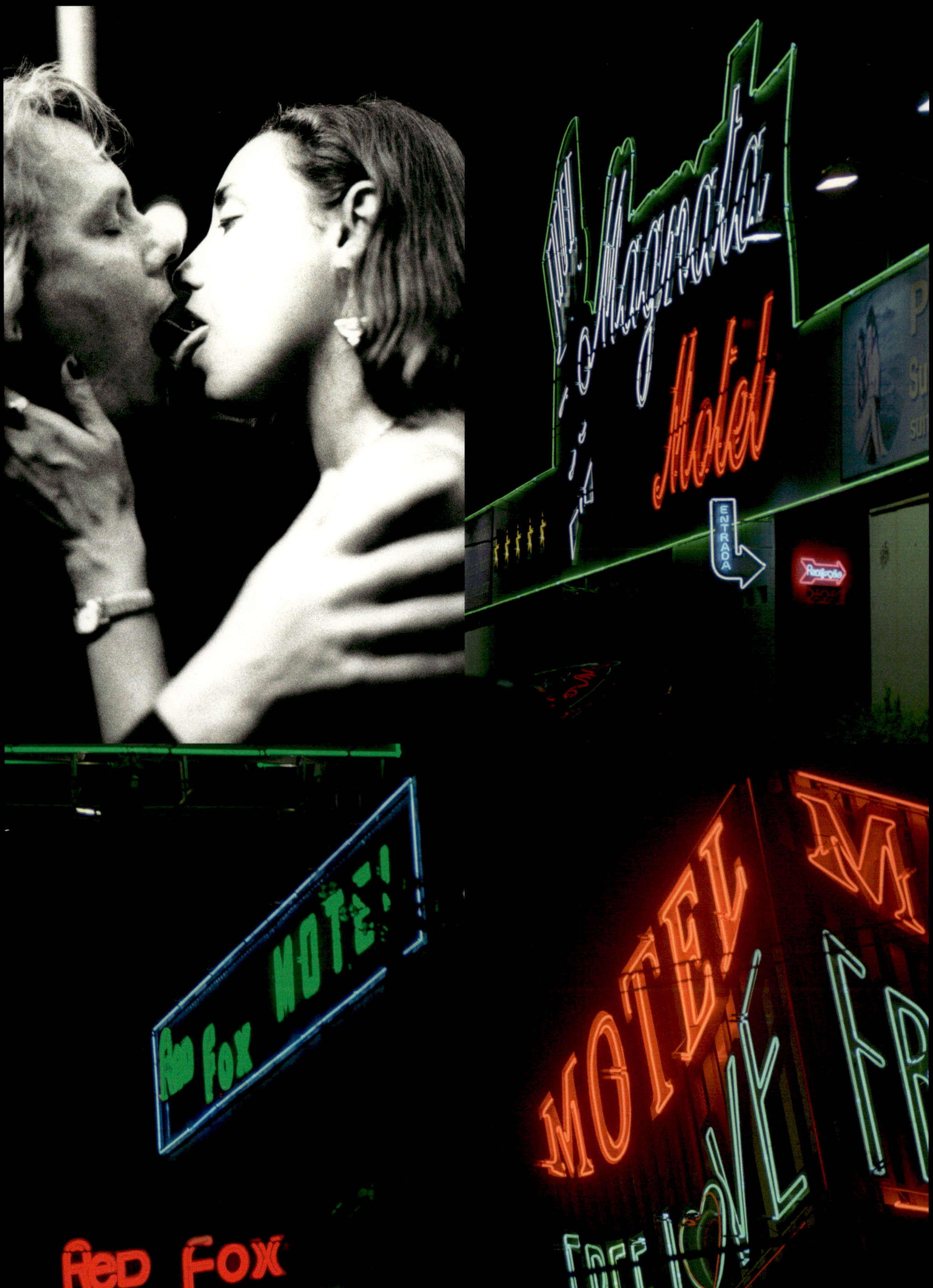
Magnata
Motel
ENTRADA
Red Fox MOTEL
MOTEL
FREE LOVE
Red Fox
MOTEL

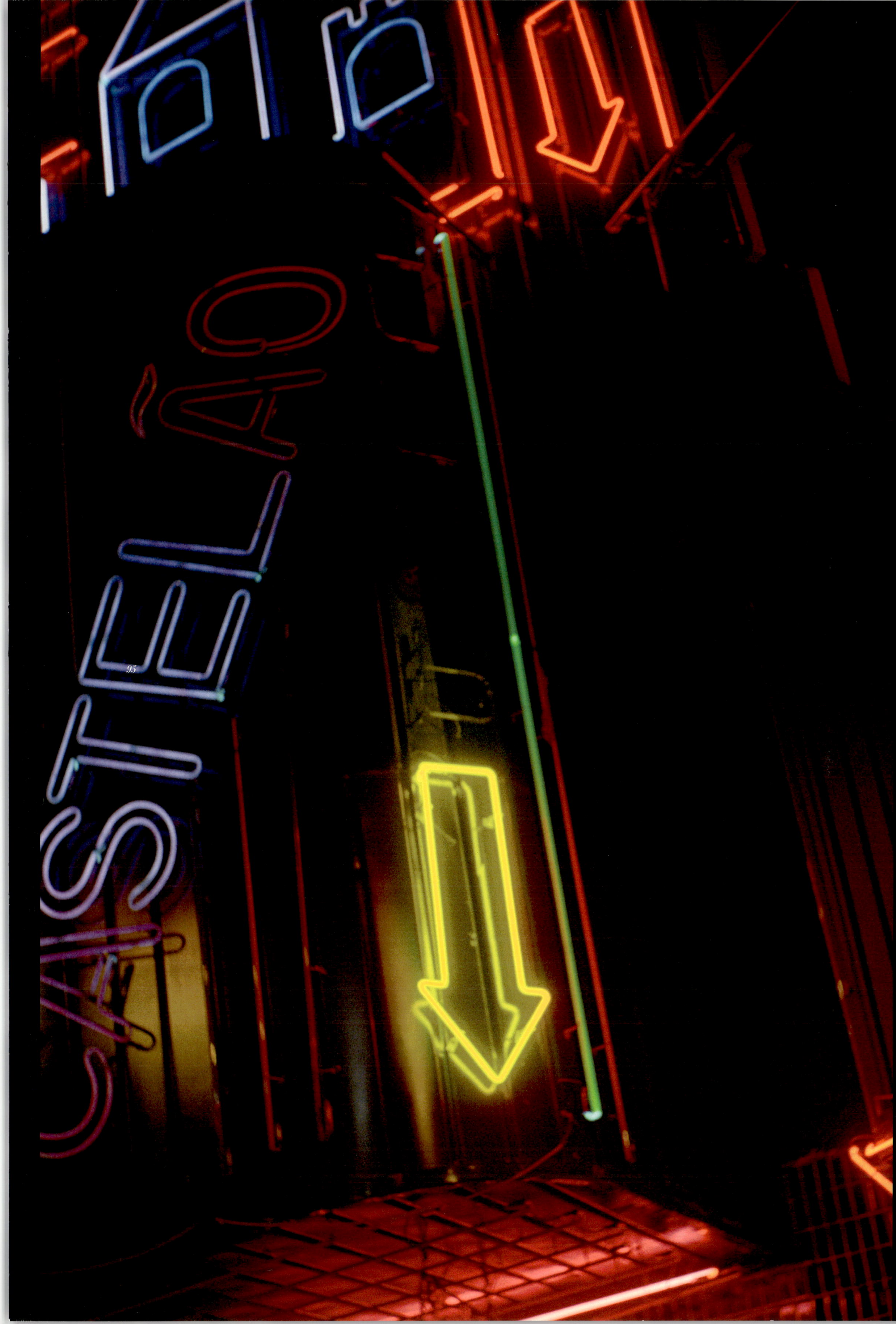

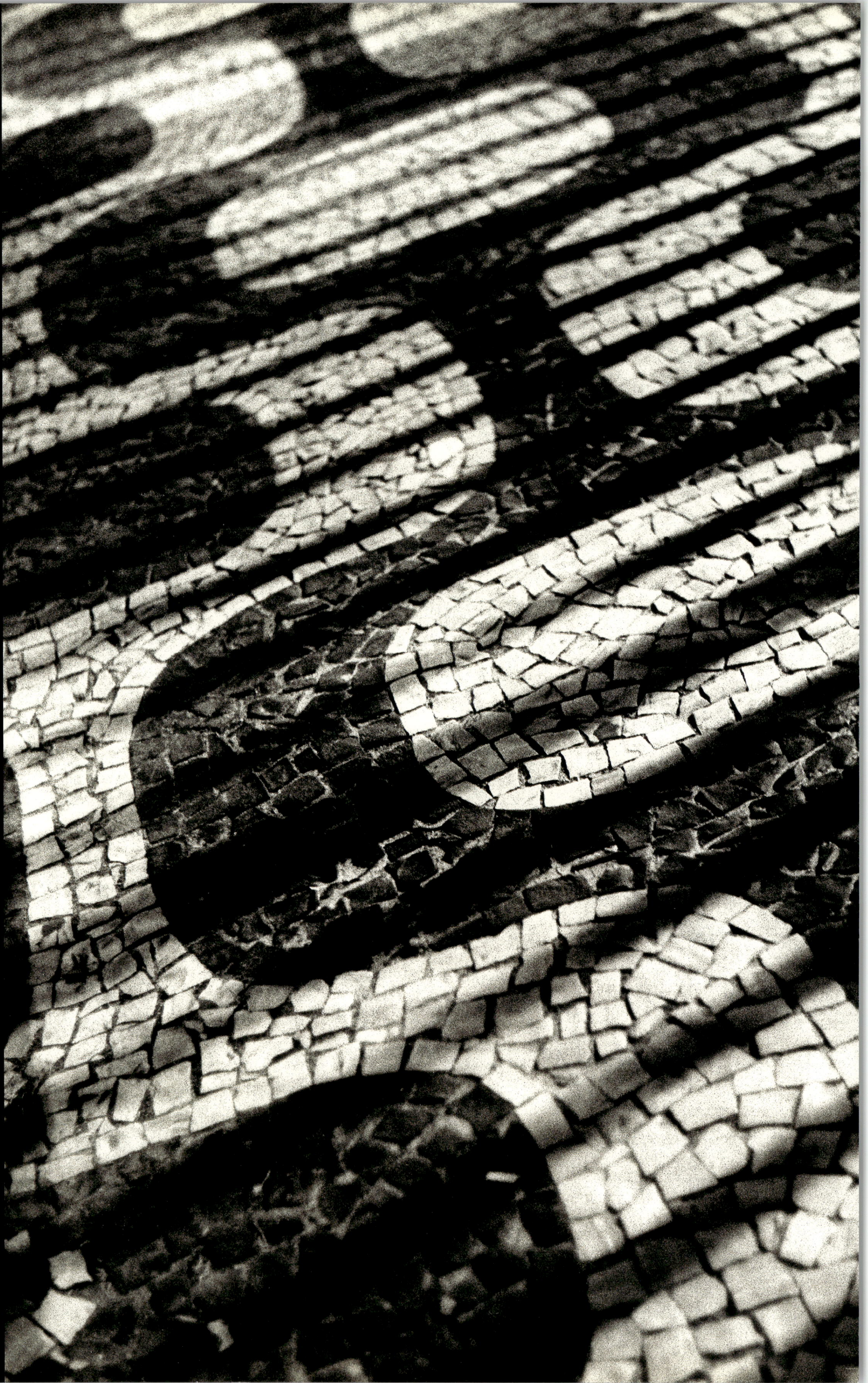

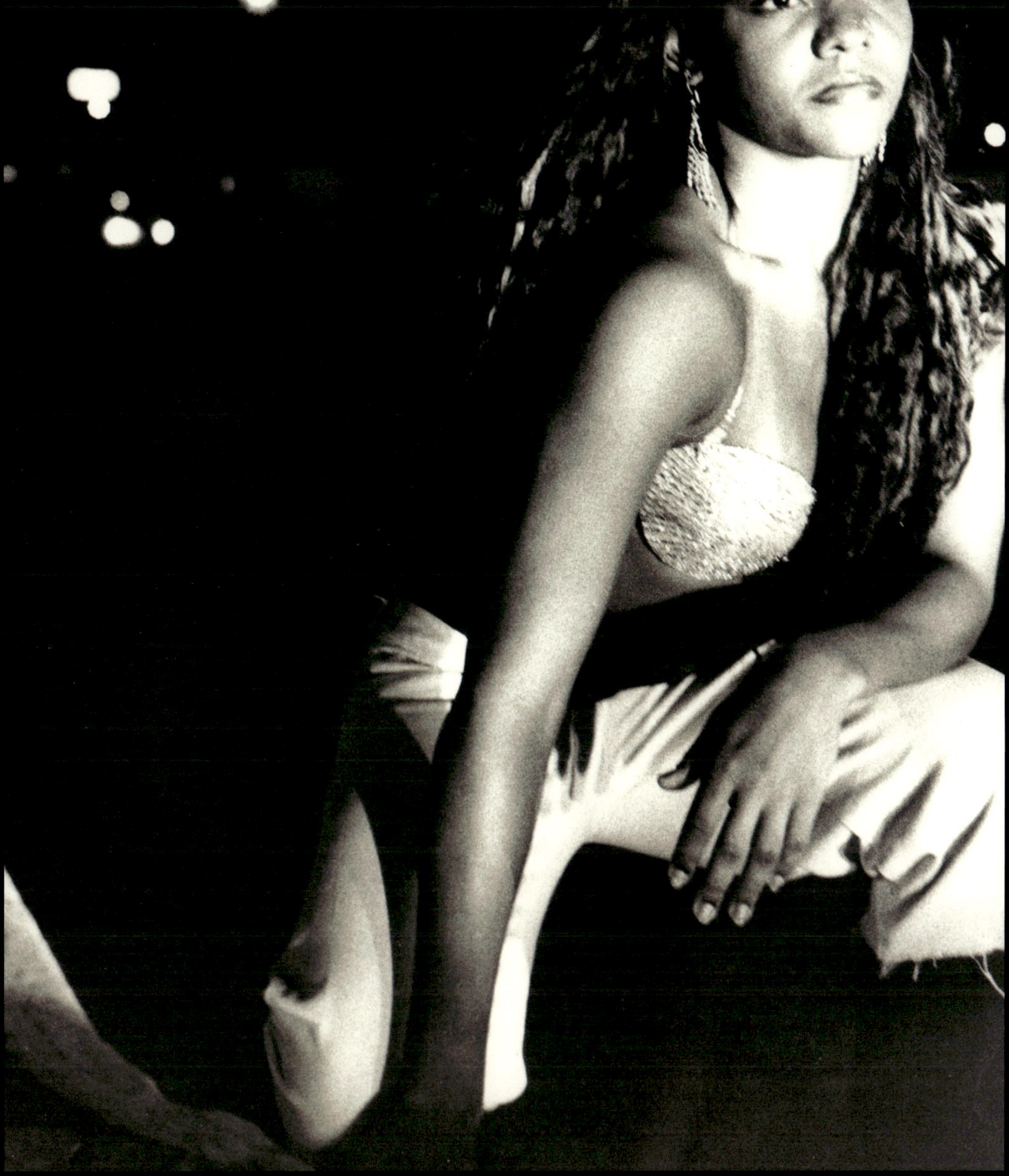

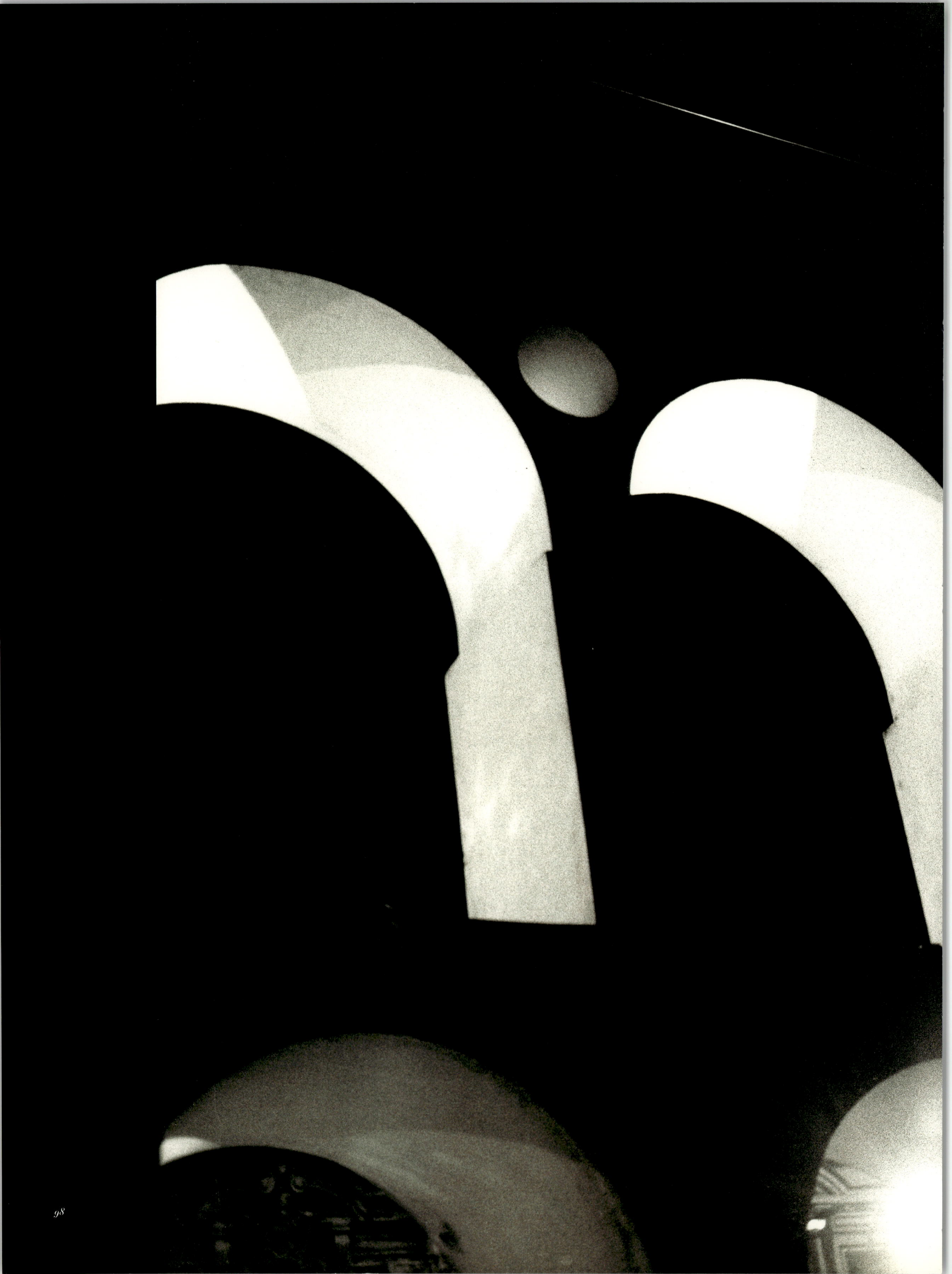

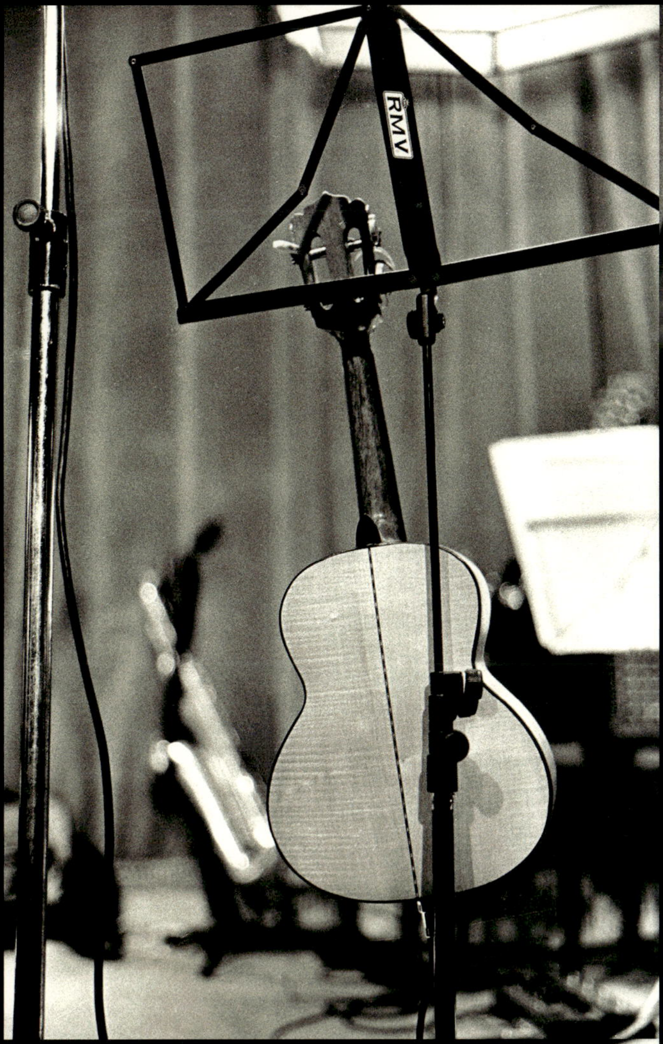
RMV

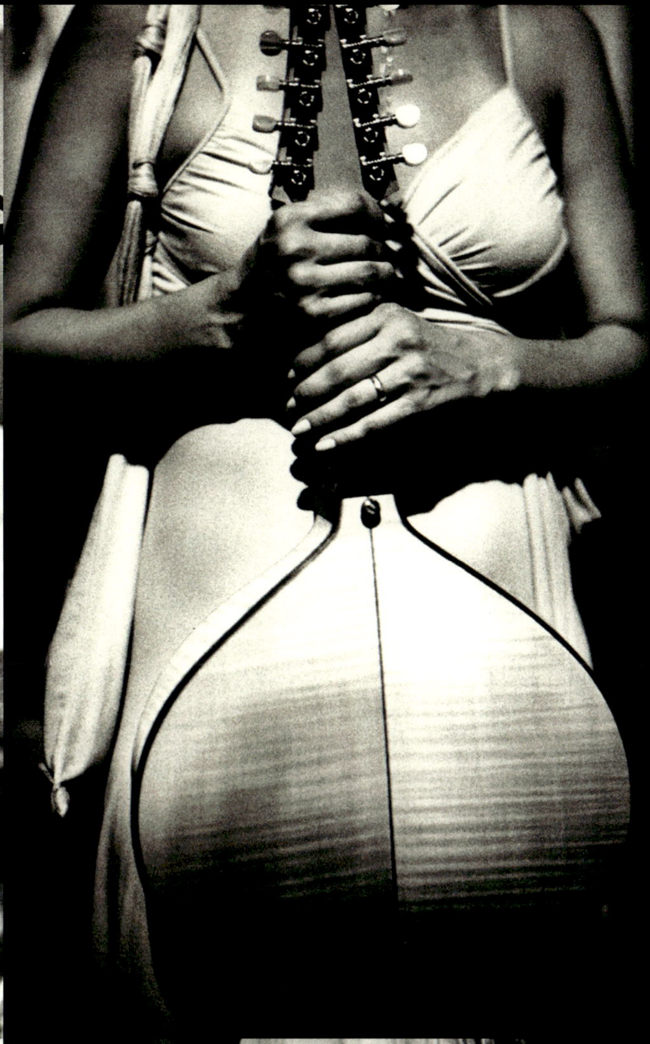

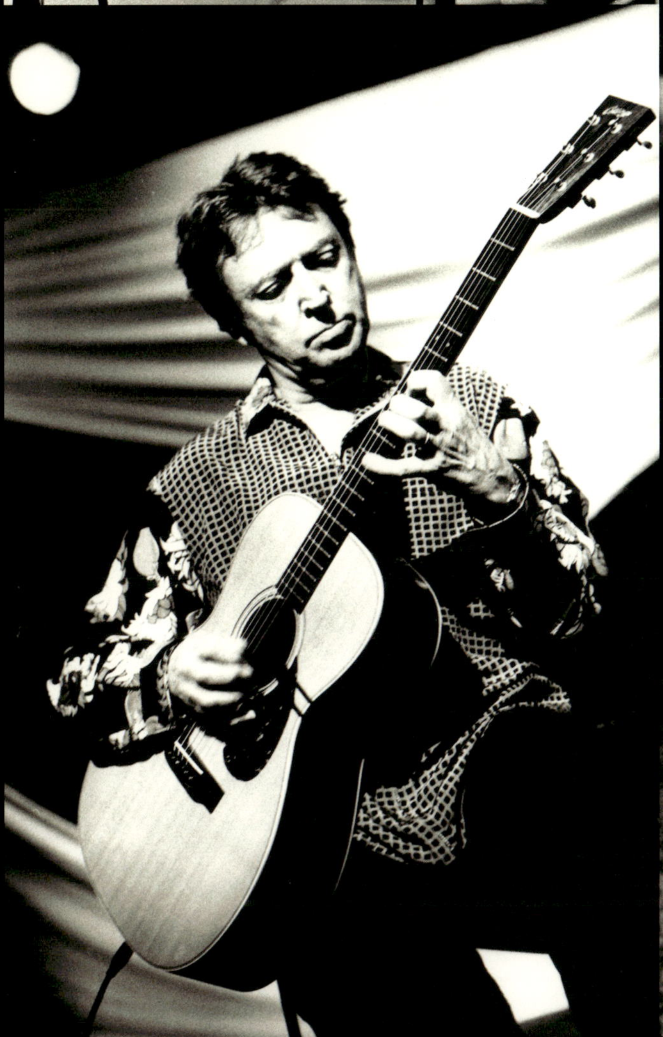

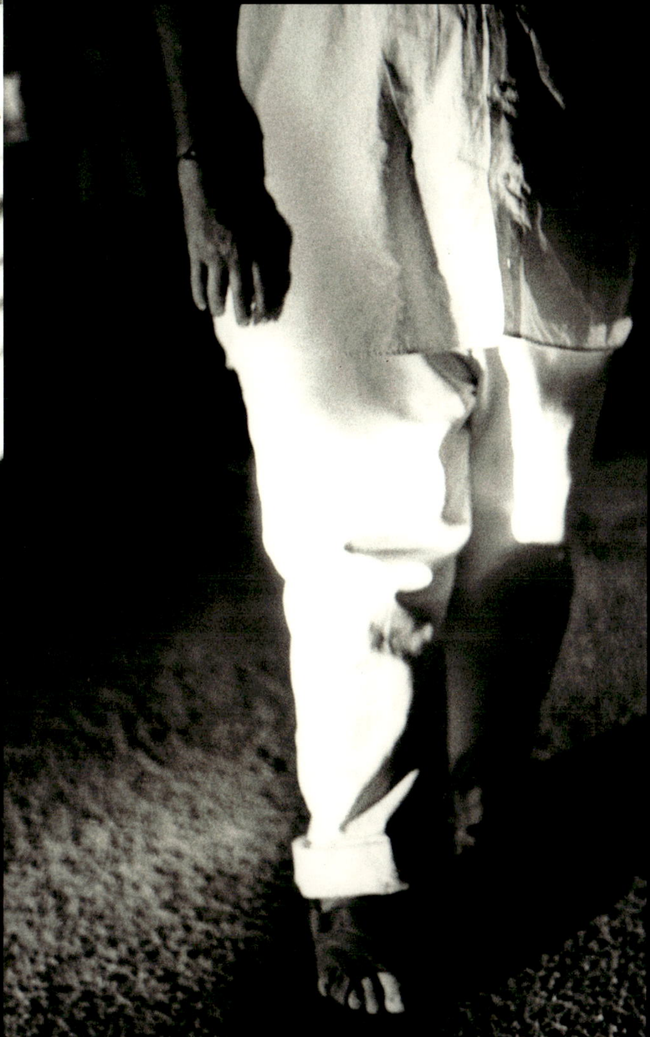

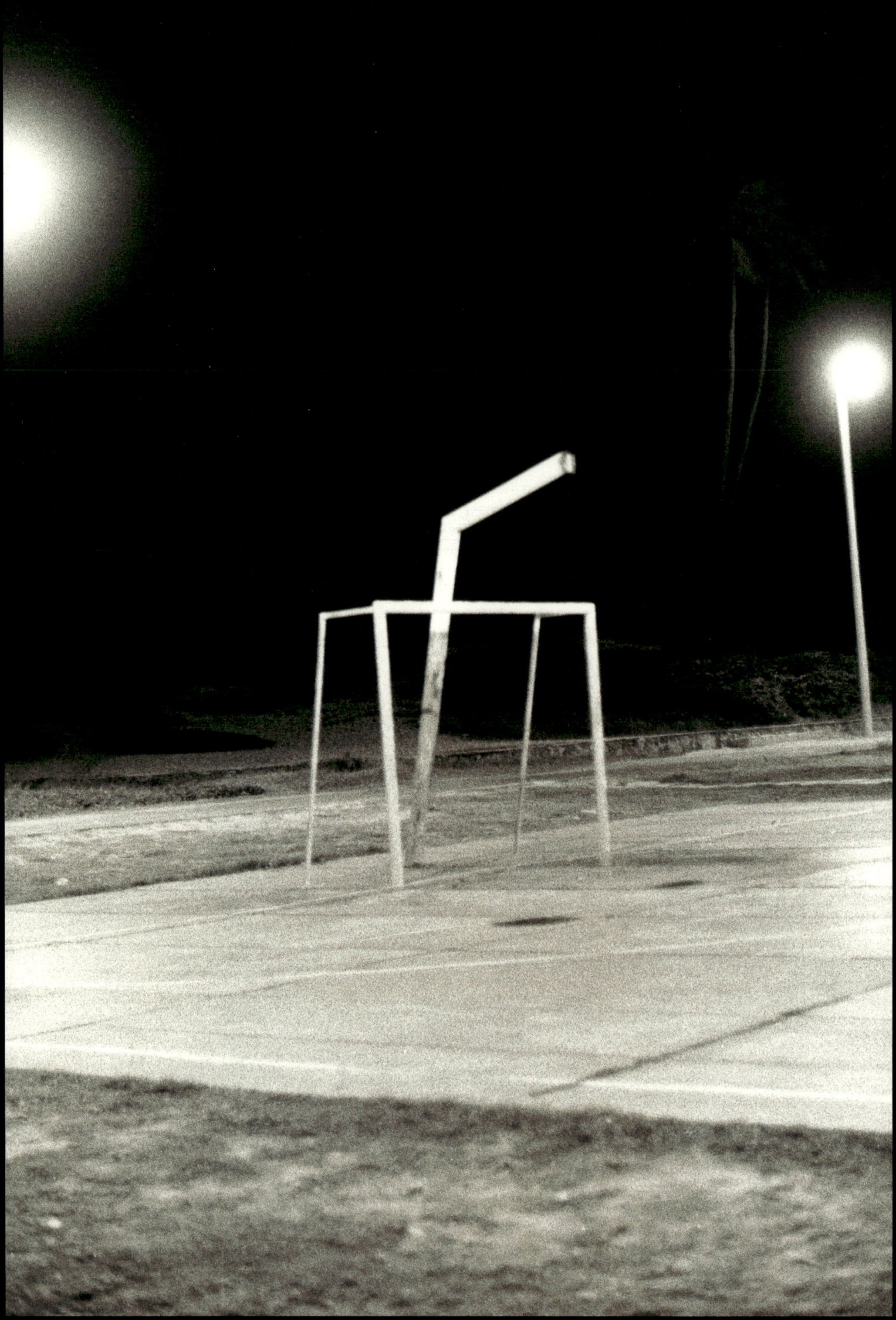

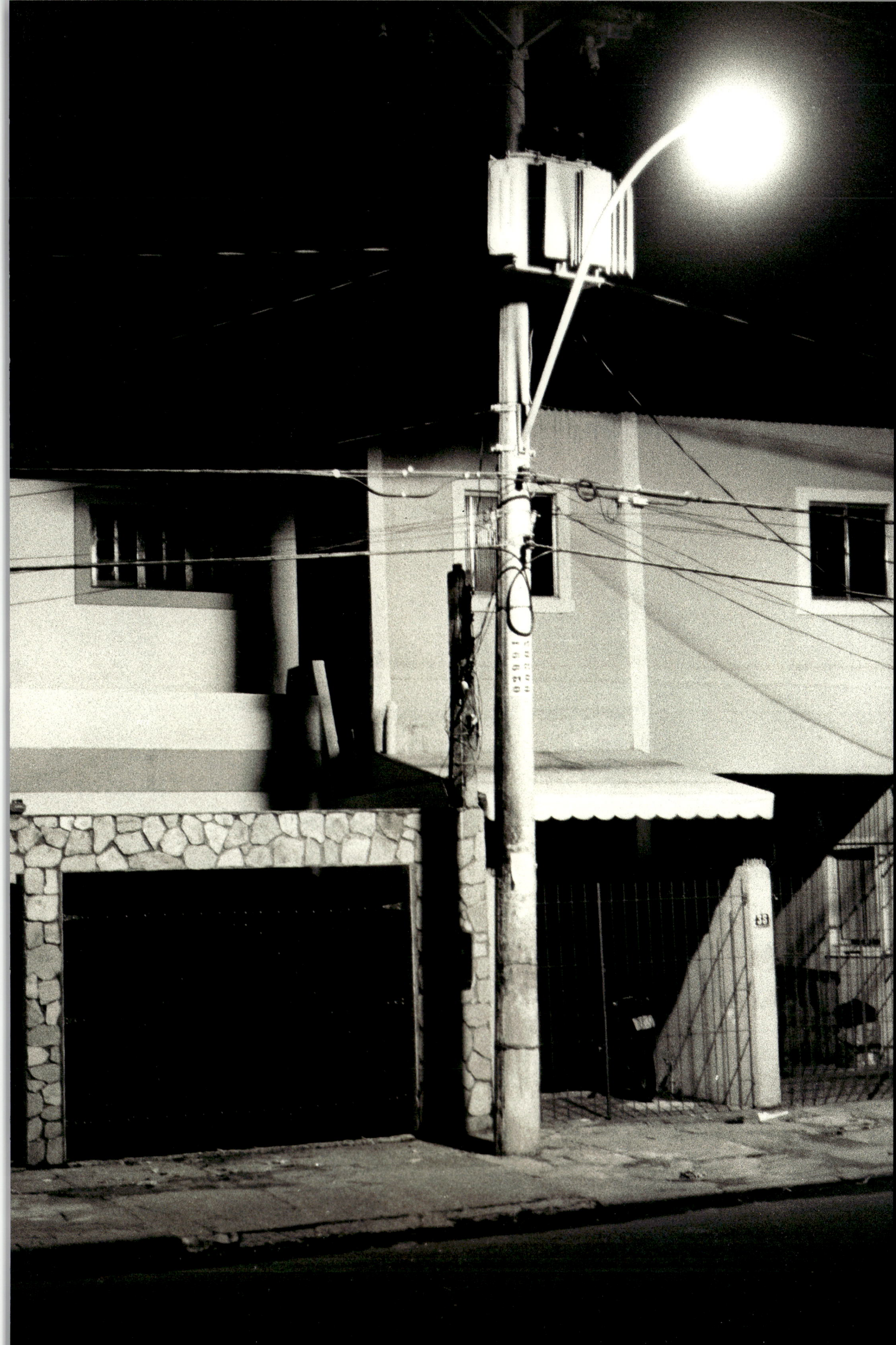

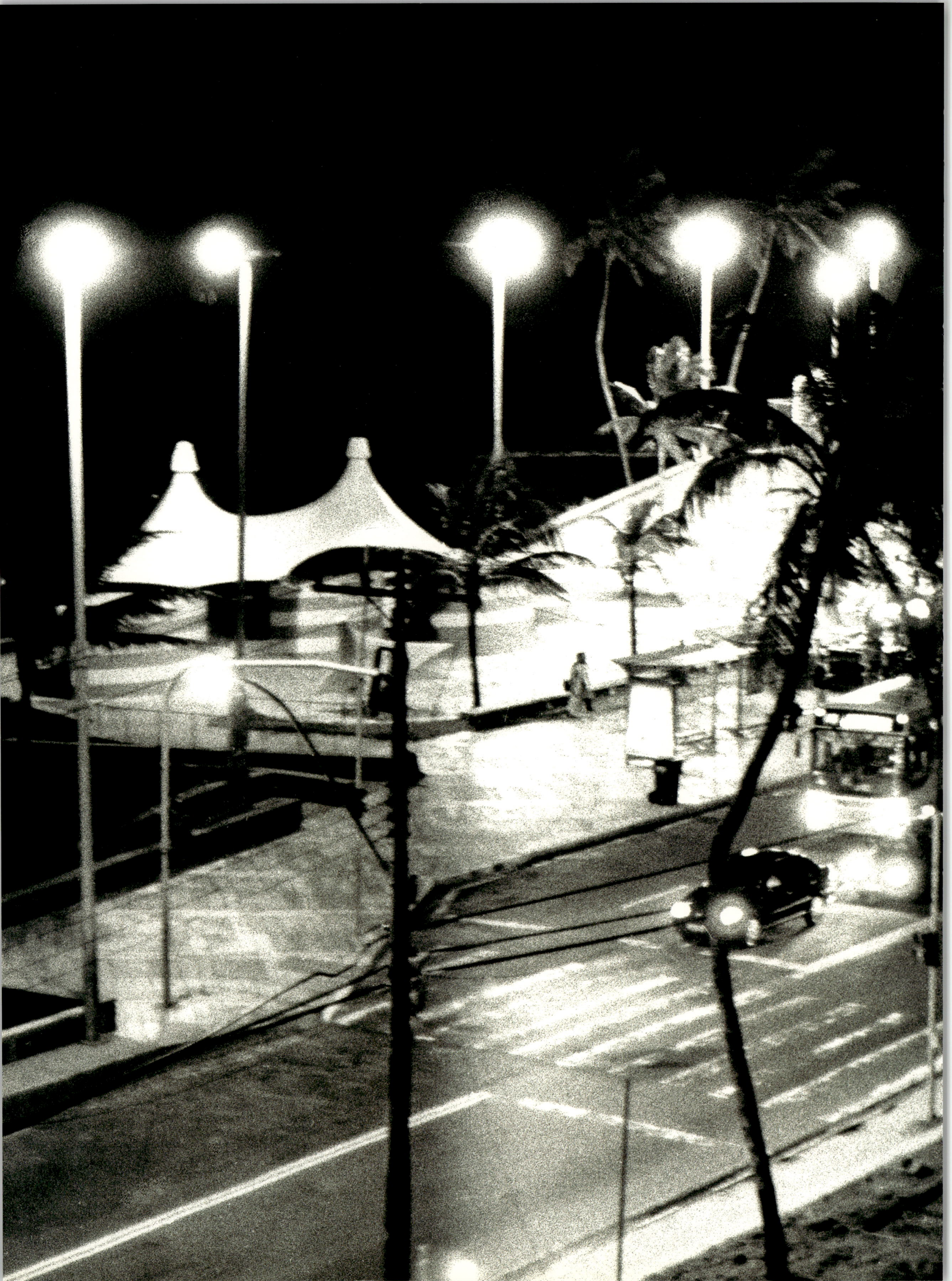

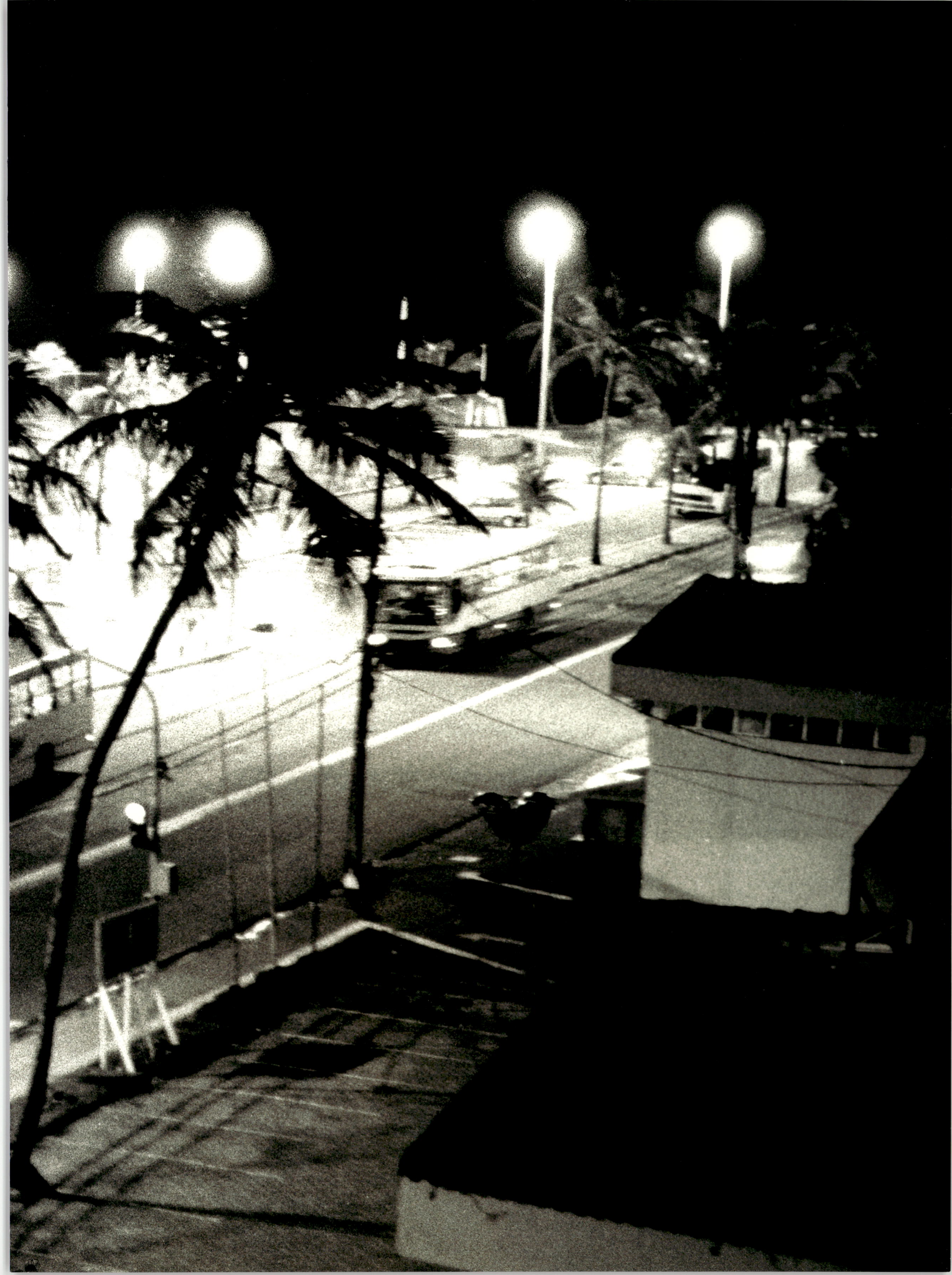

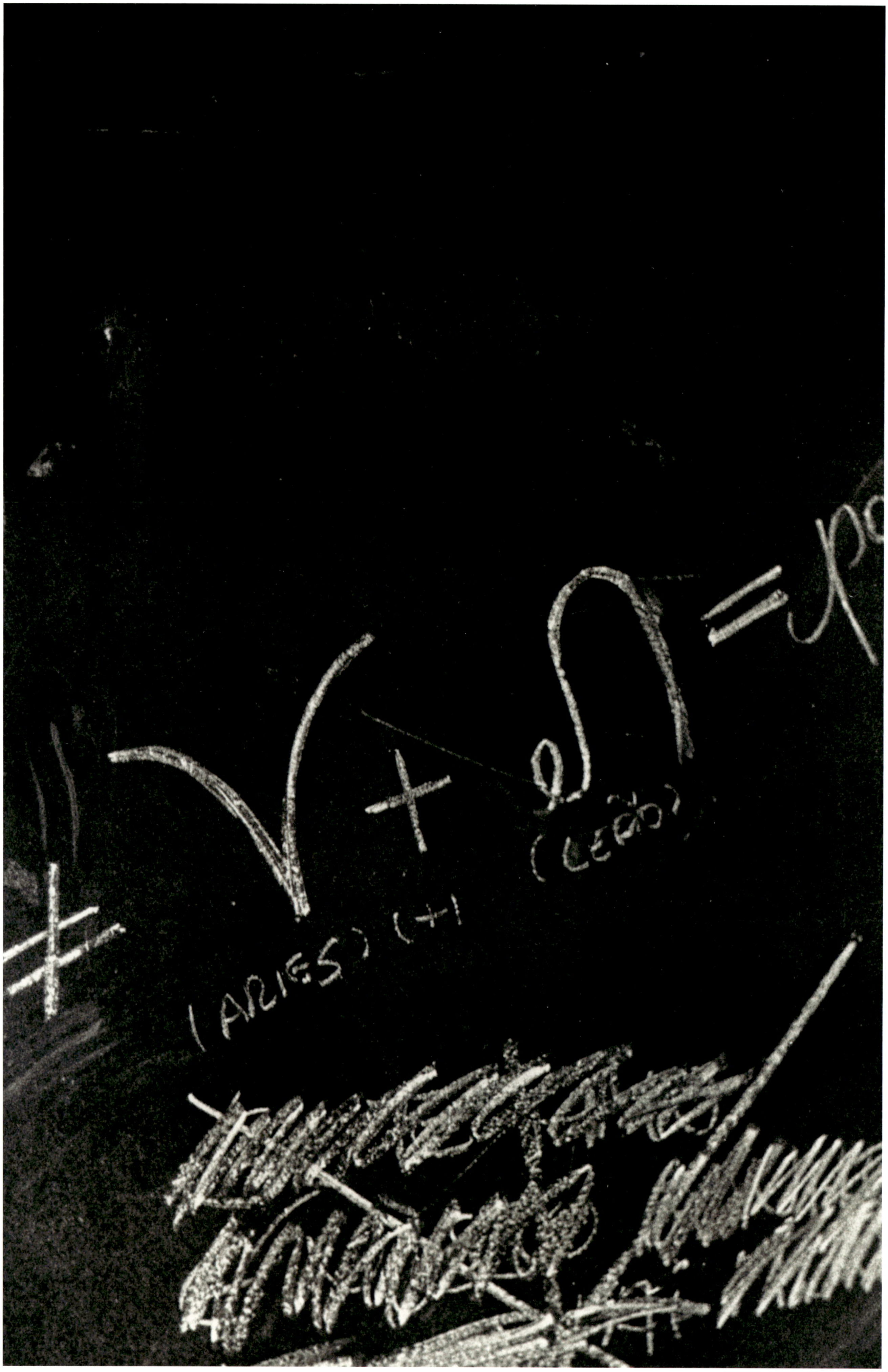
(ARIES) (+

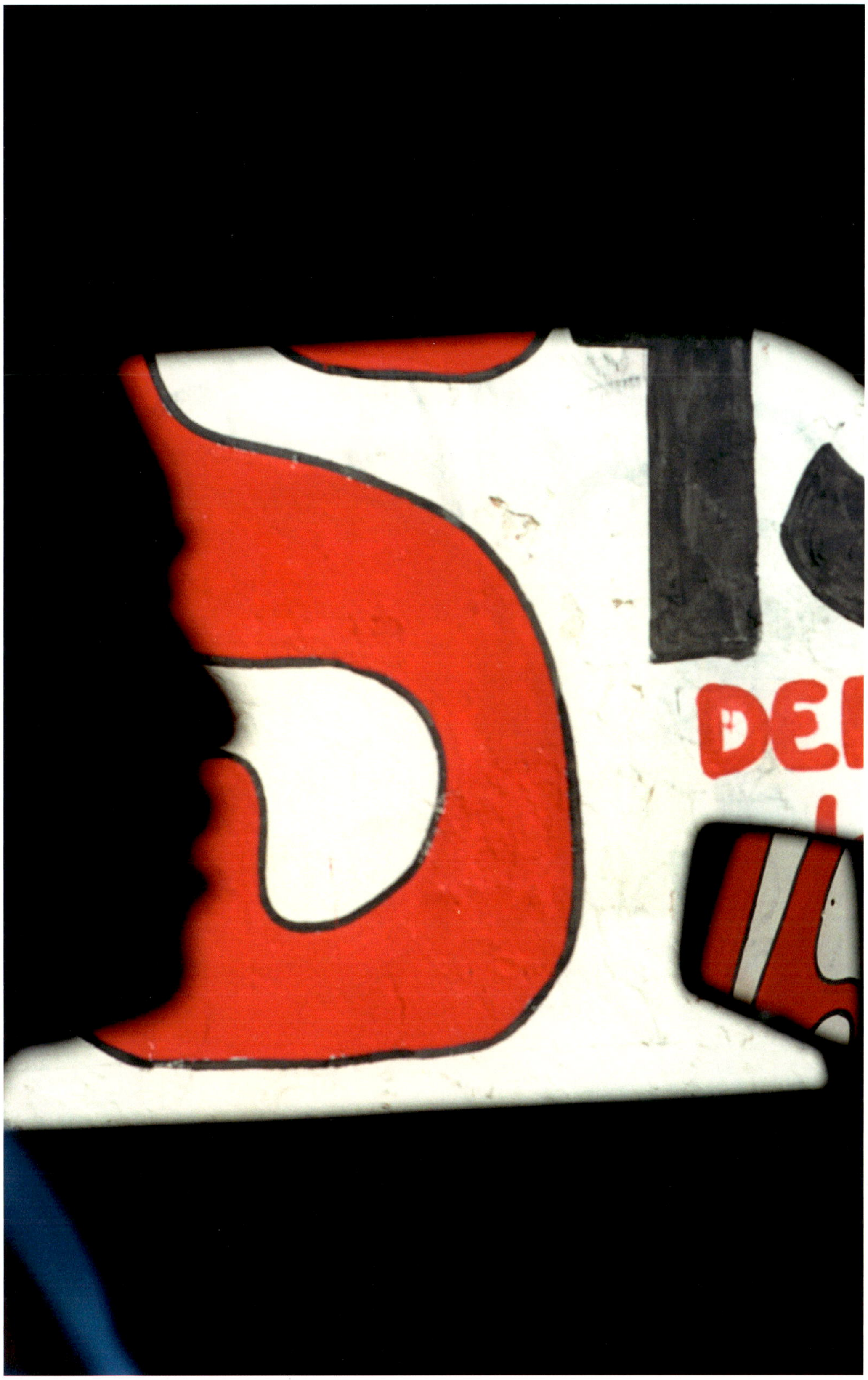
DE

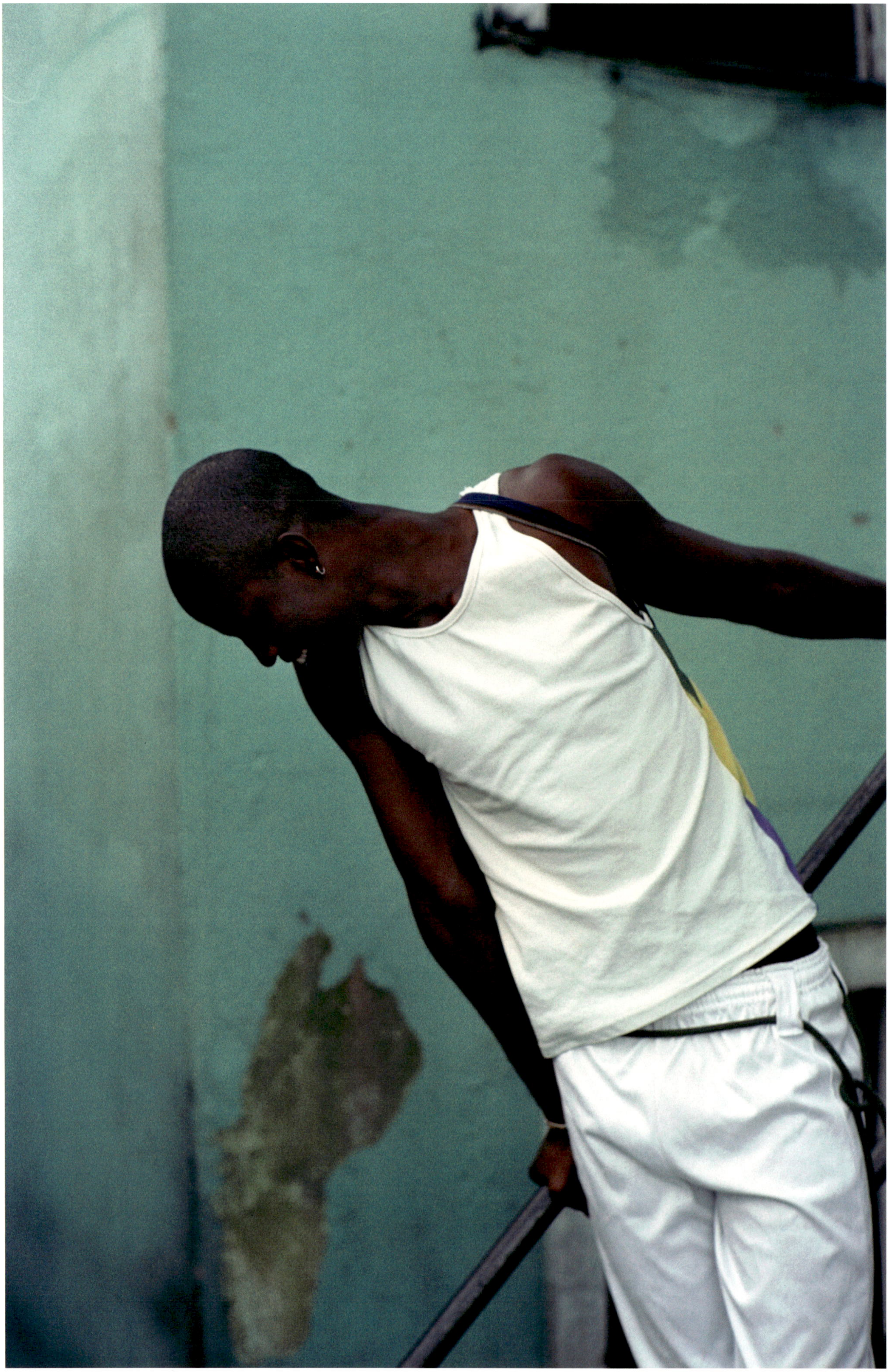

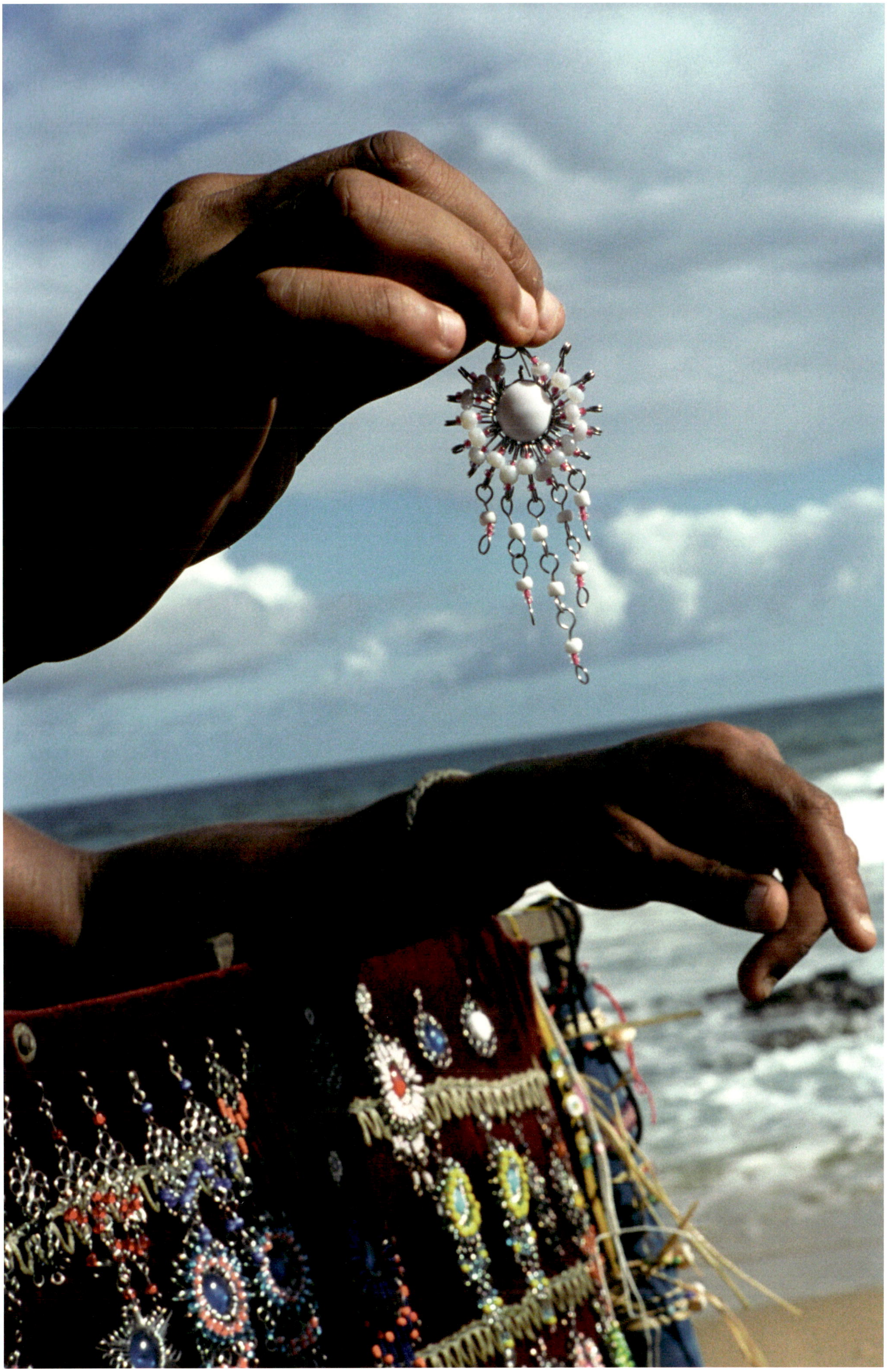

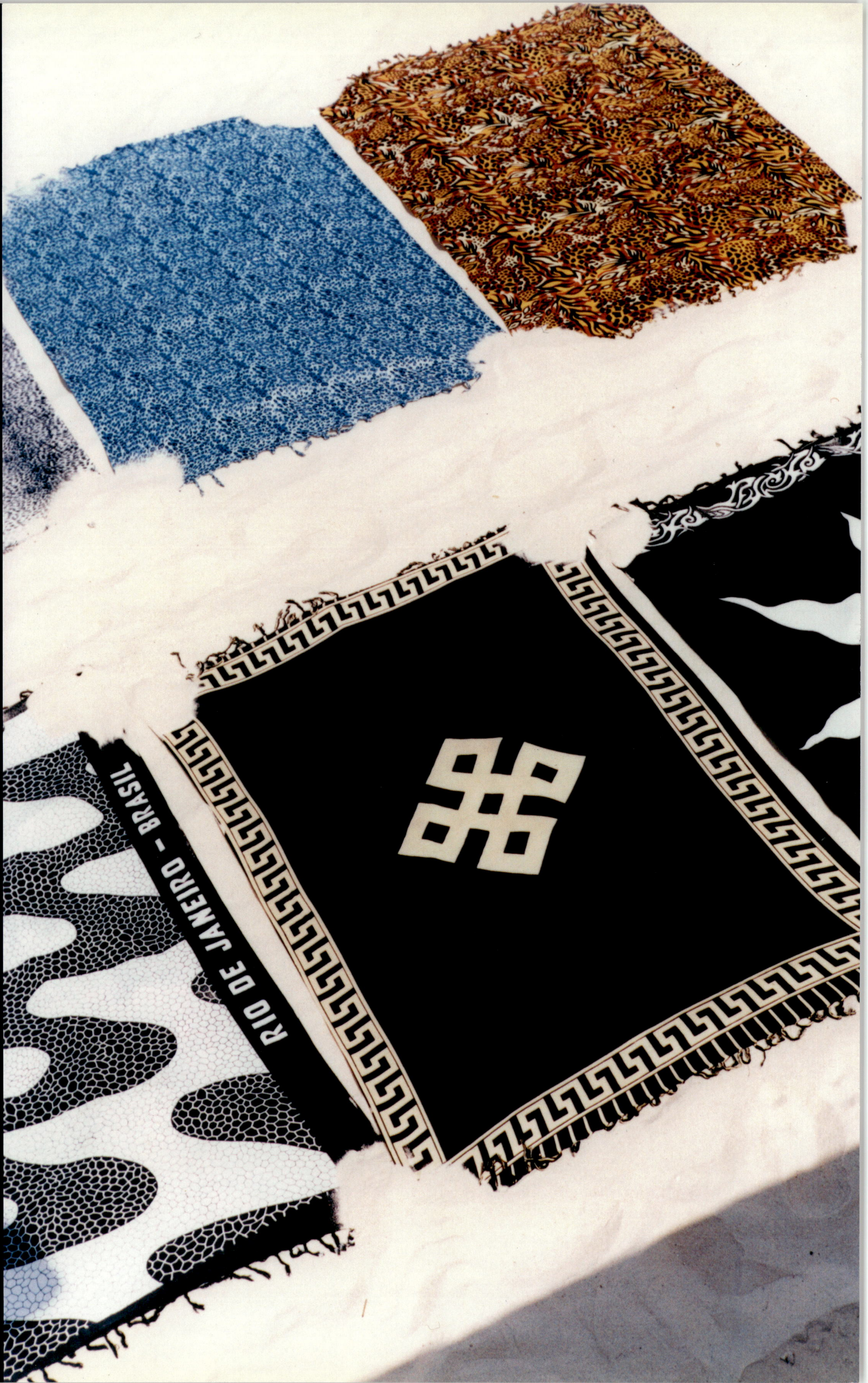
RIO DE JANEIRO – BRASIL

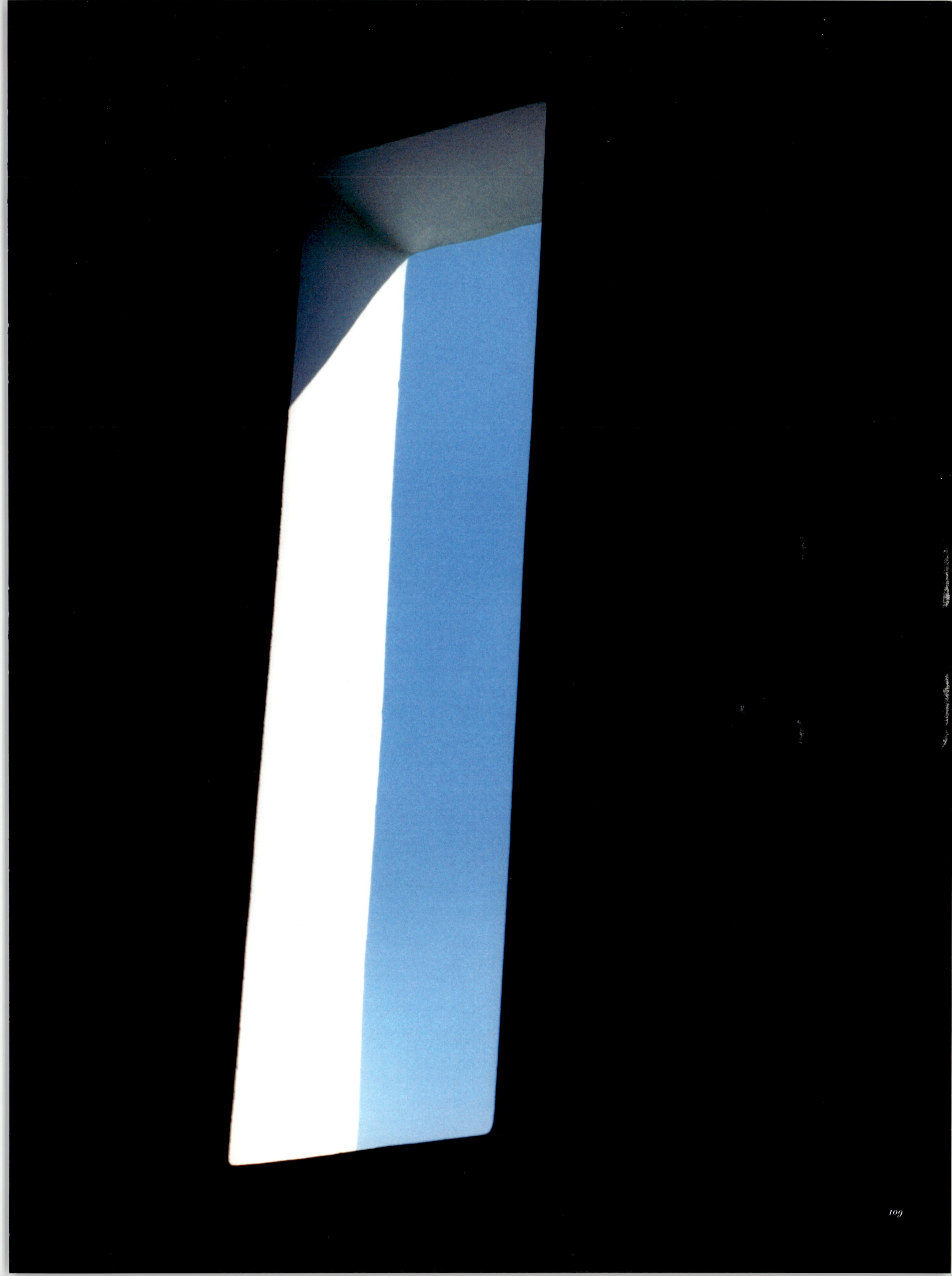

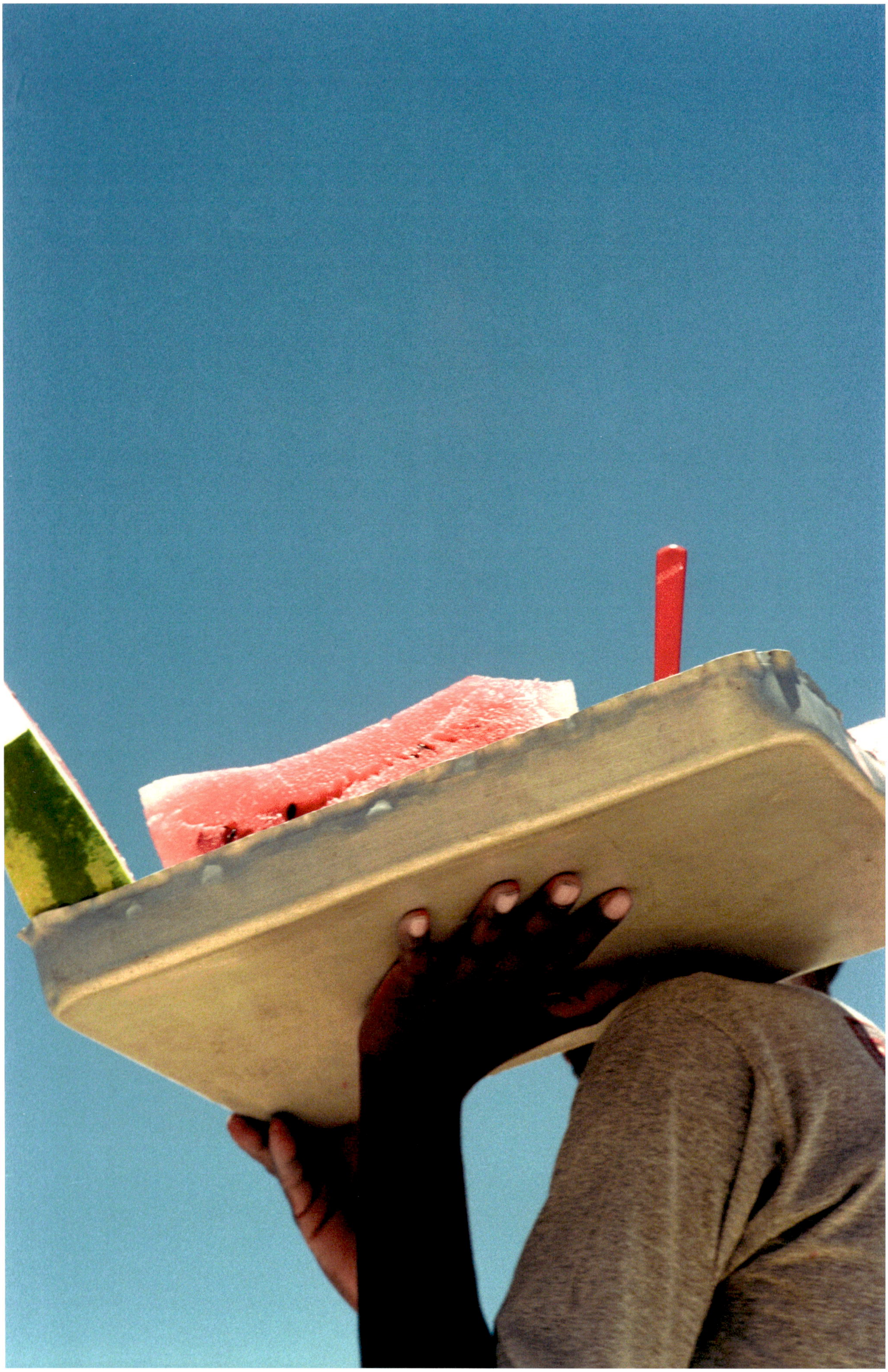

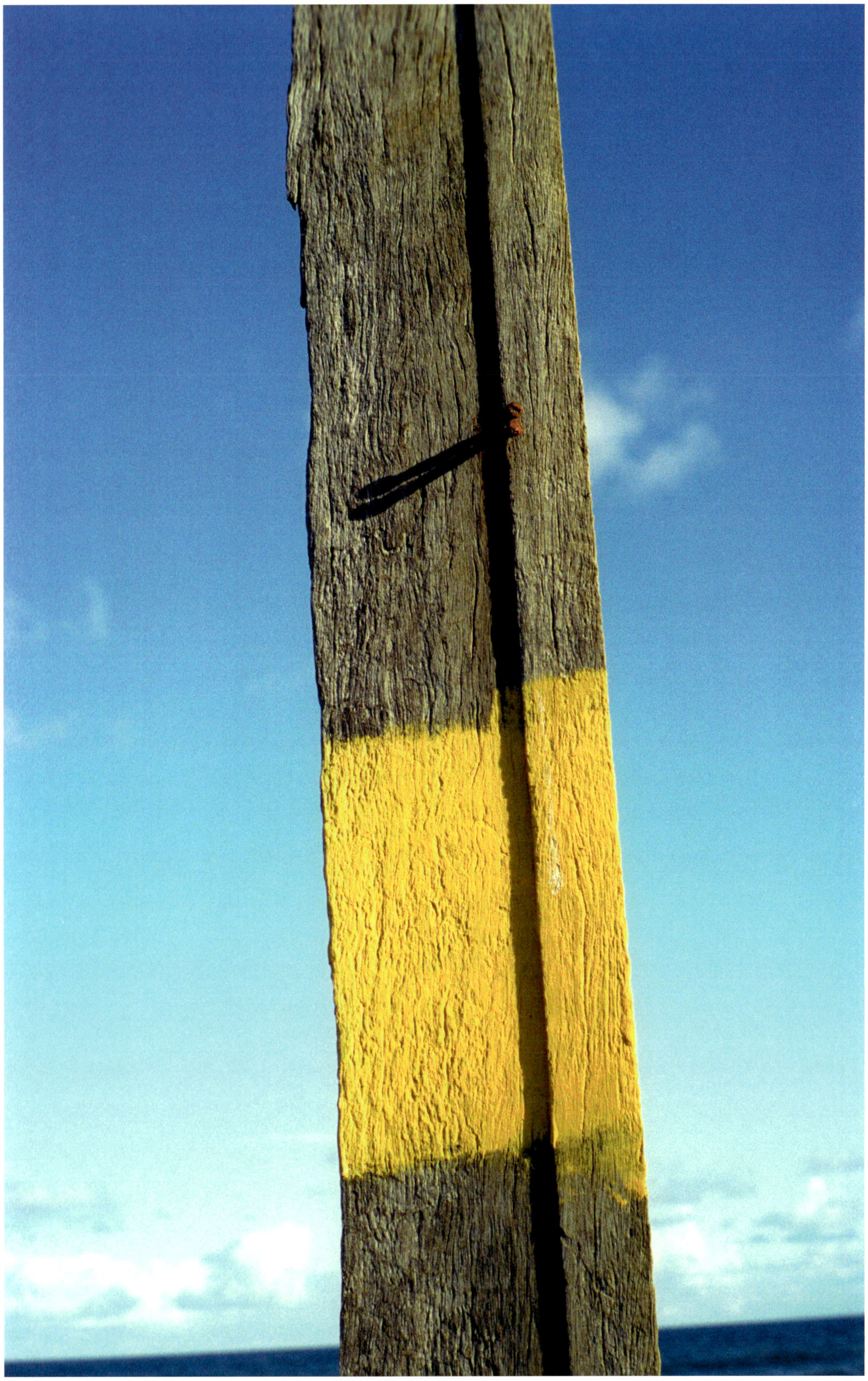

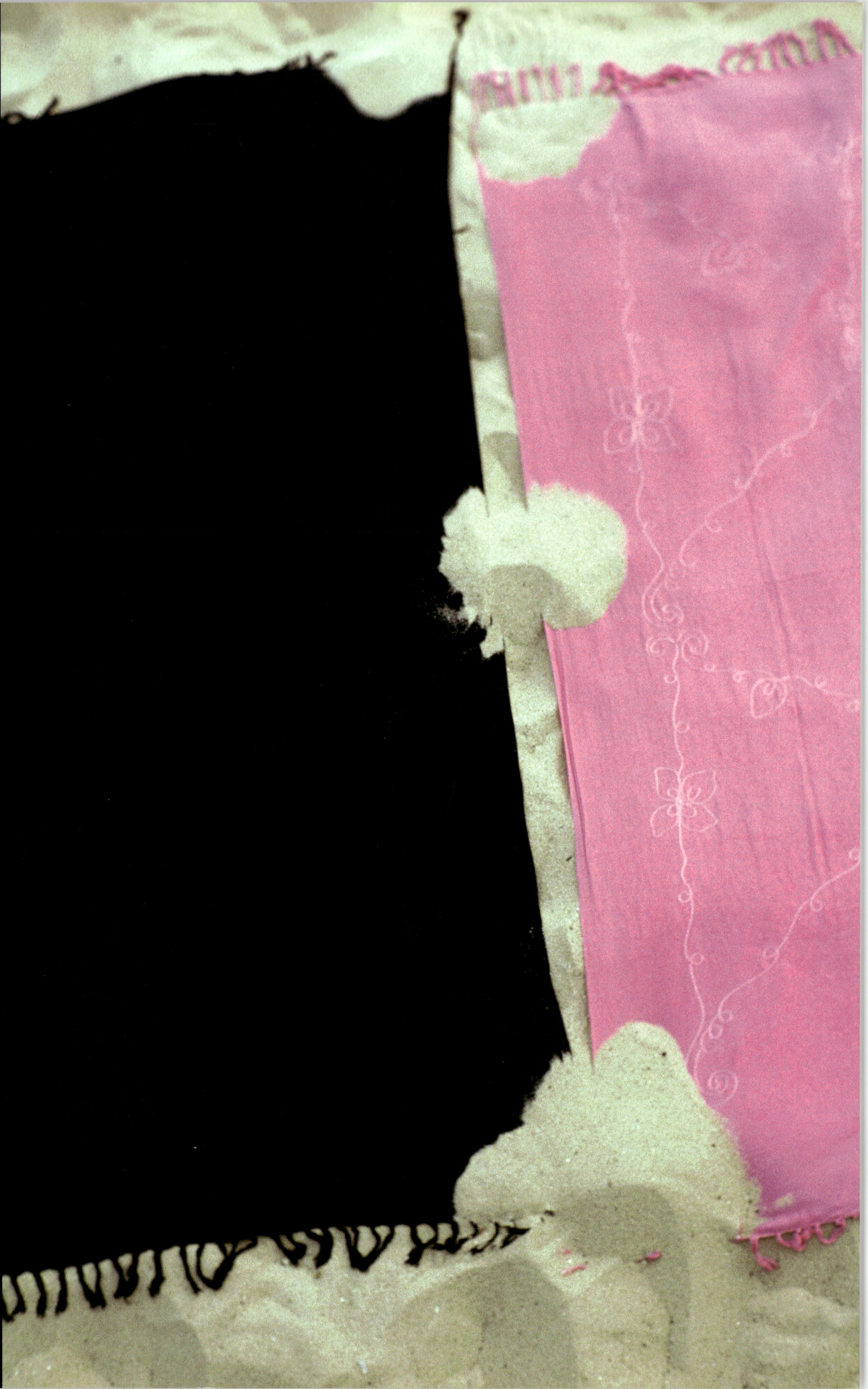

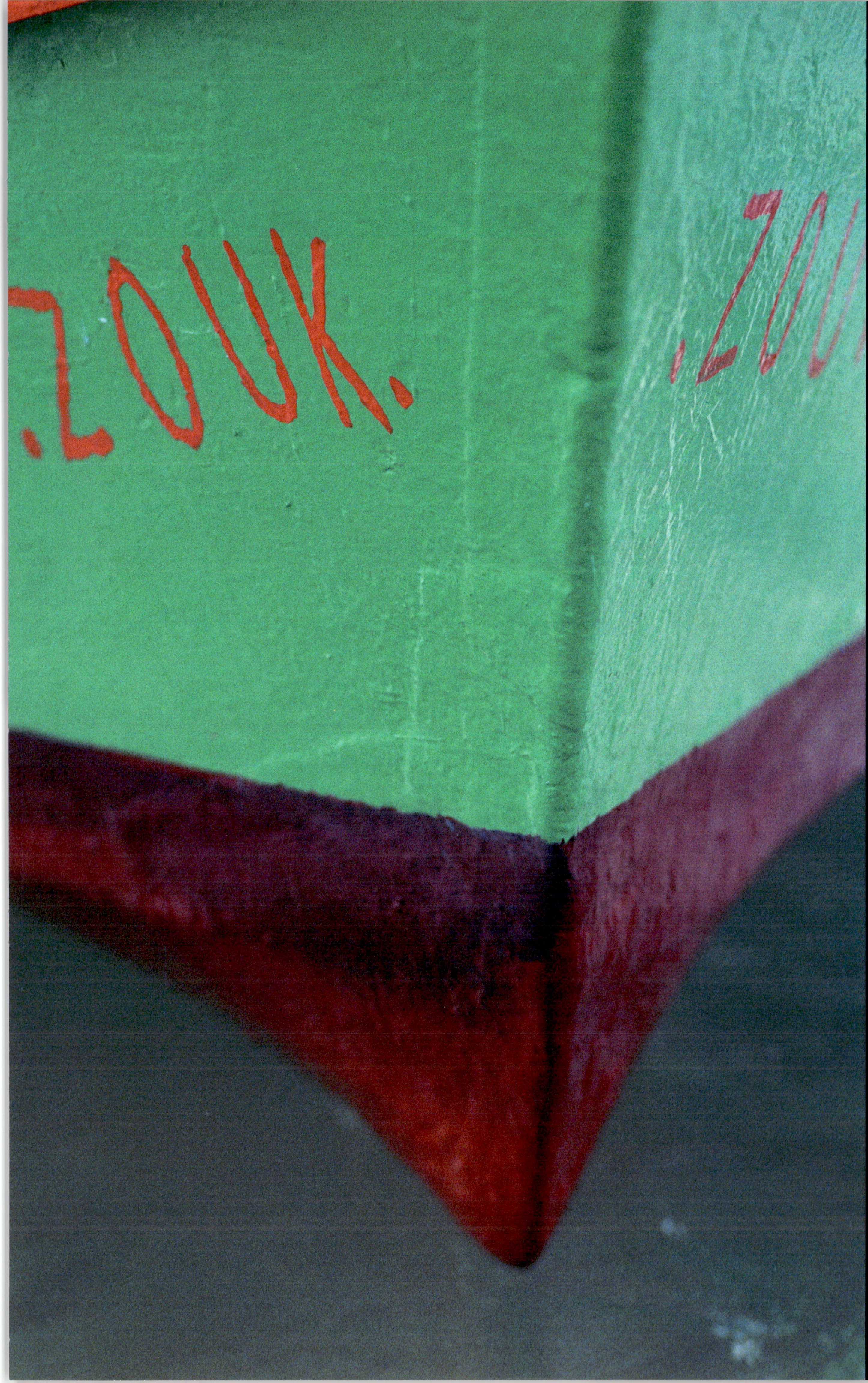
.ZOUK.

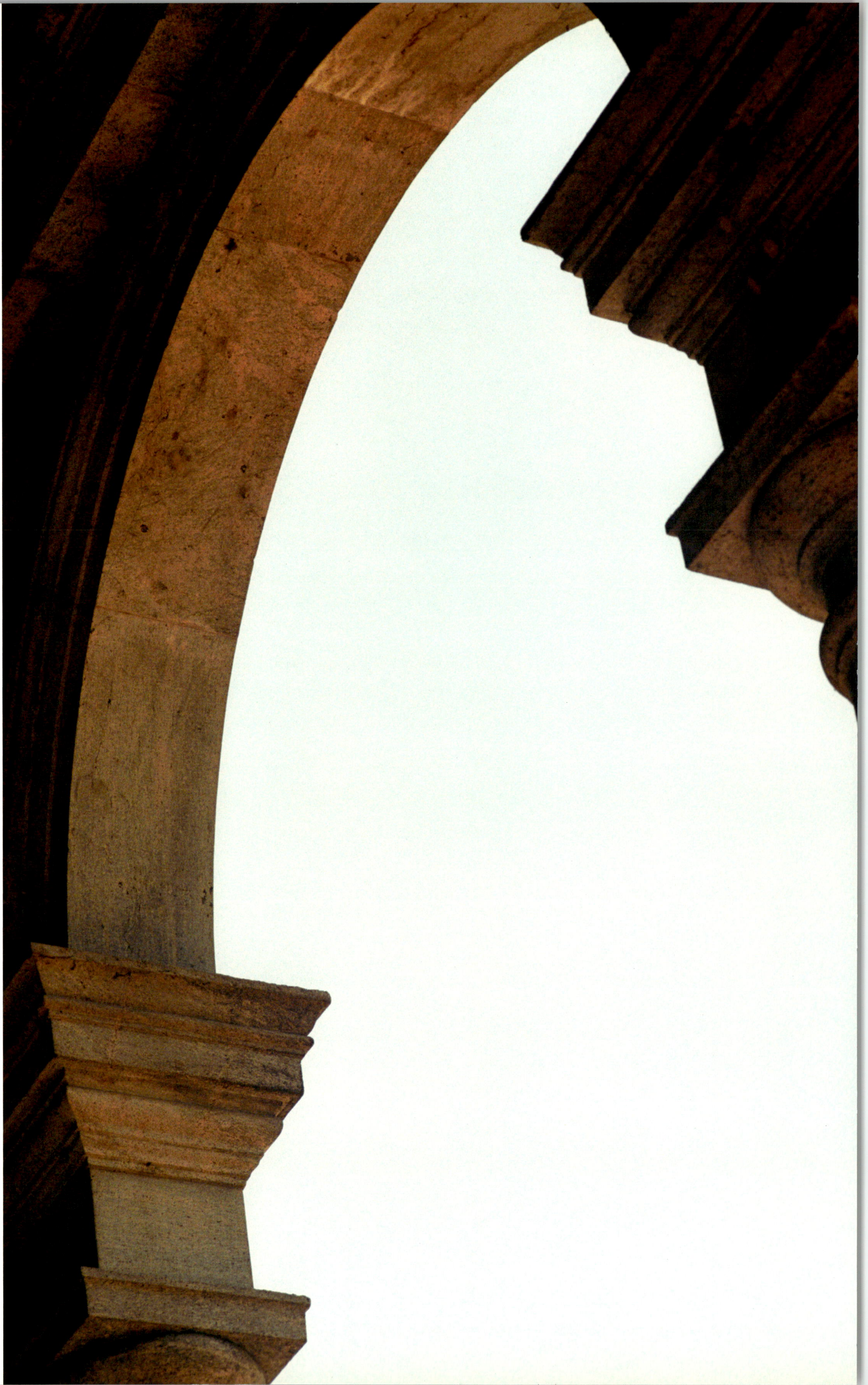

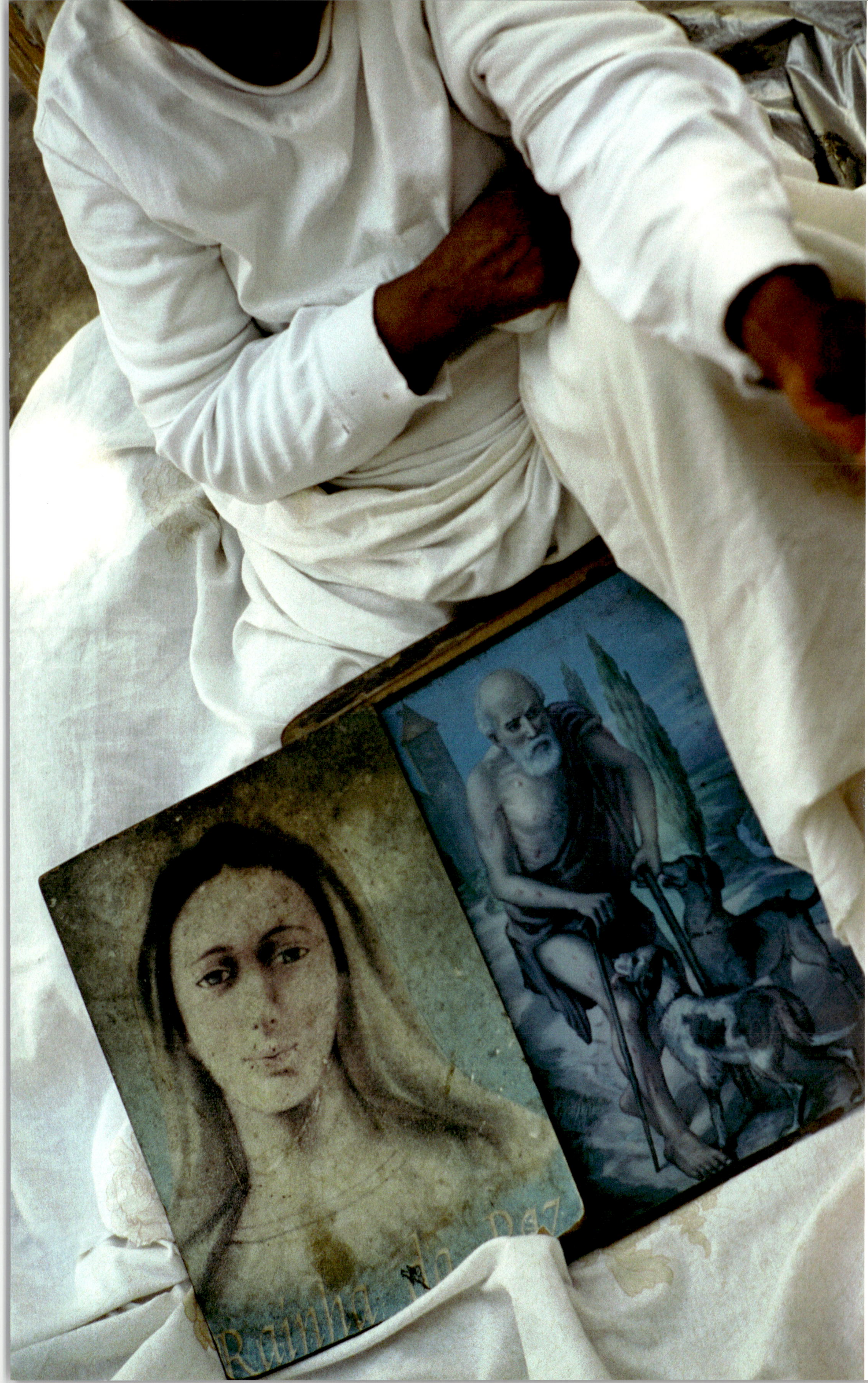
Rainha

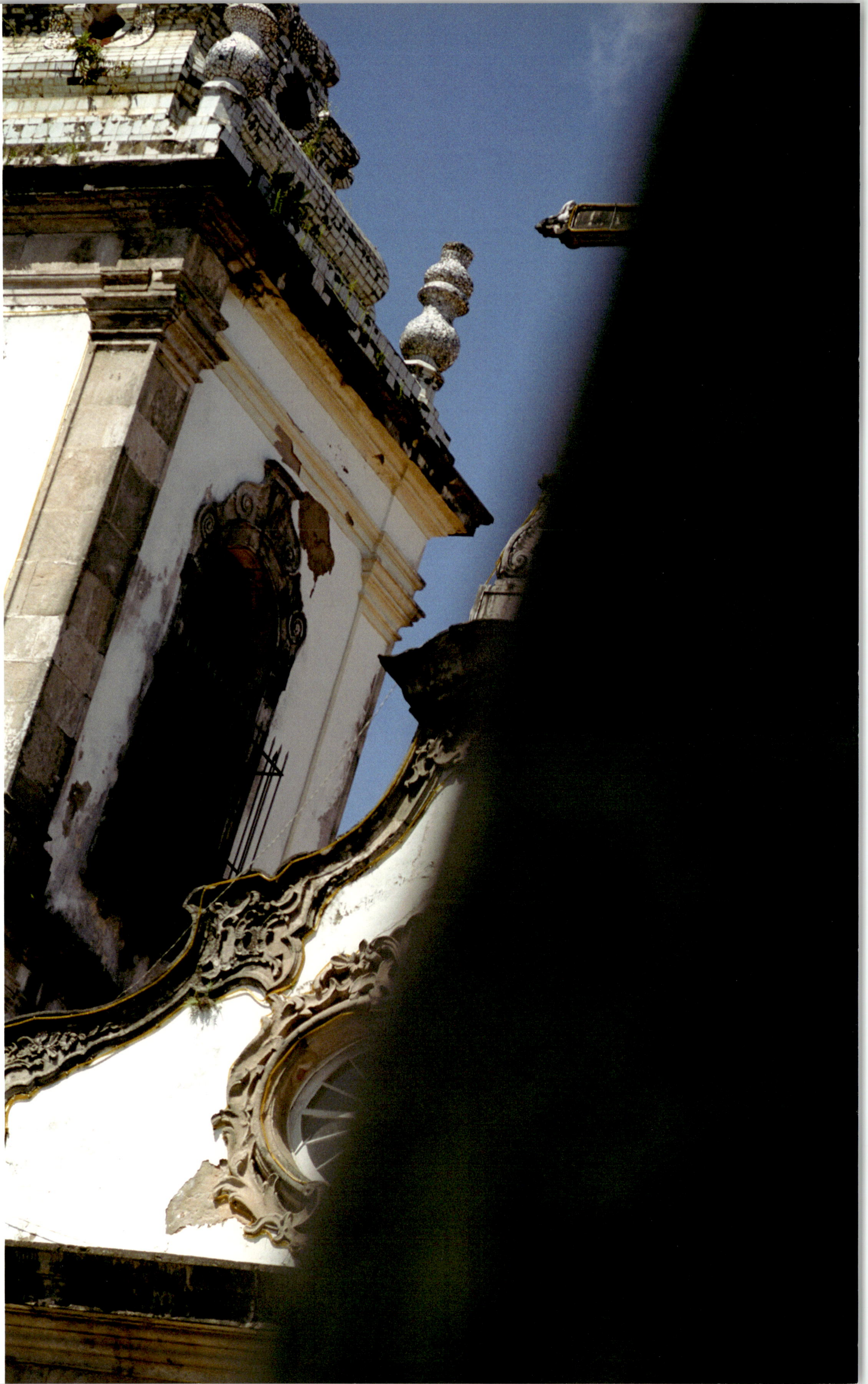

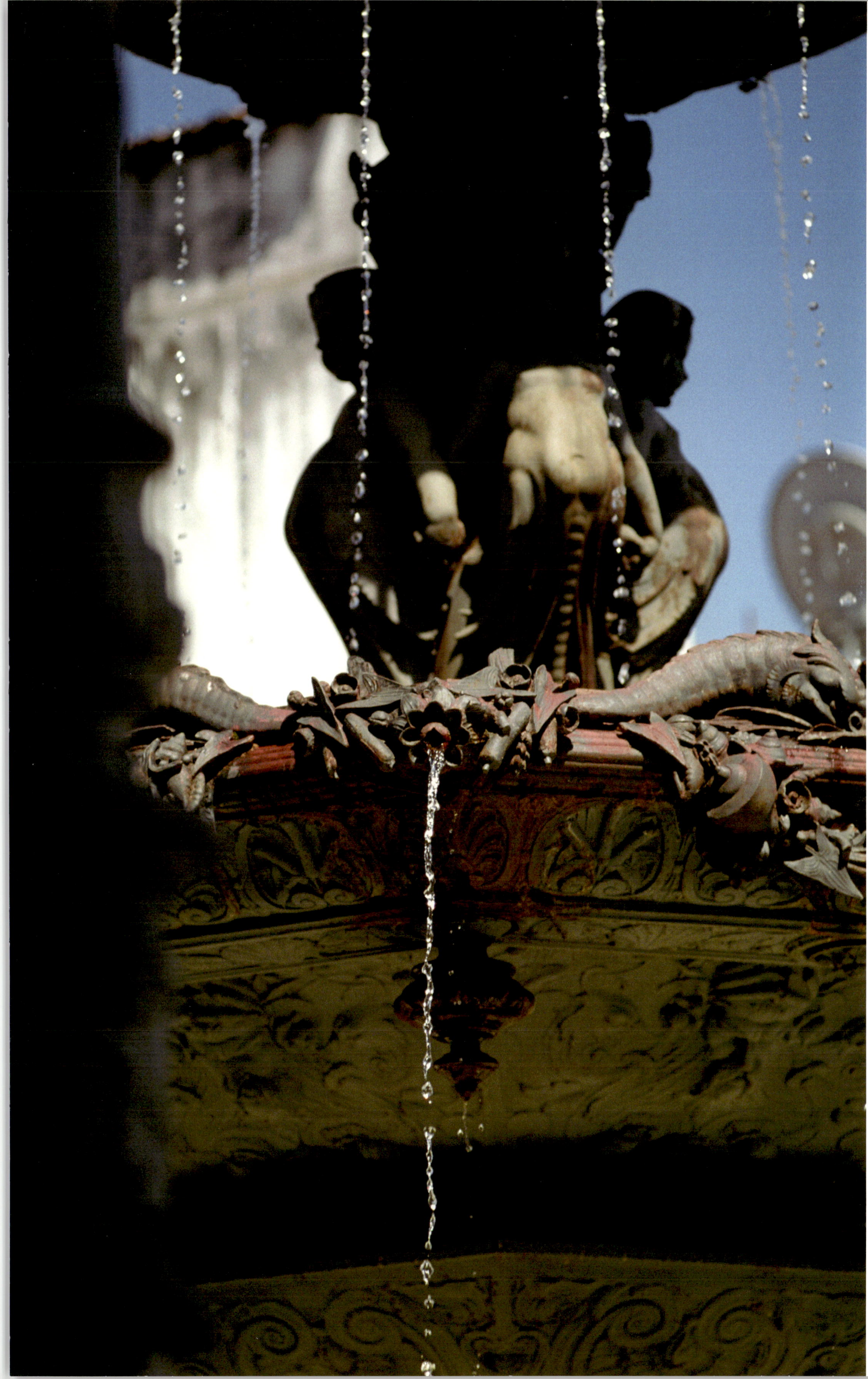

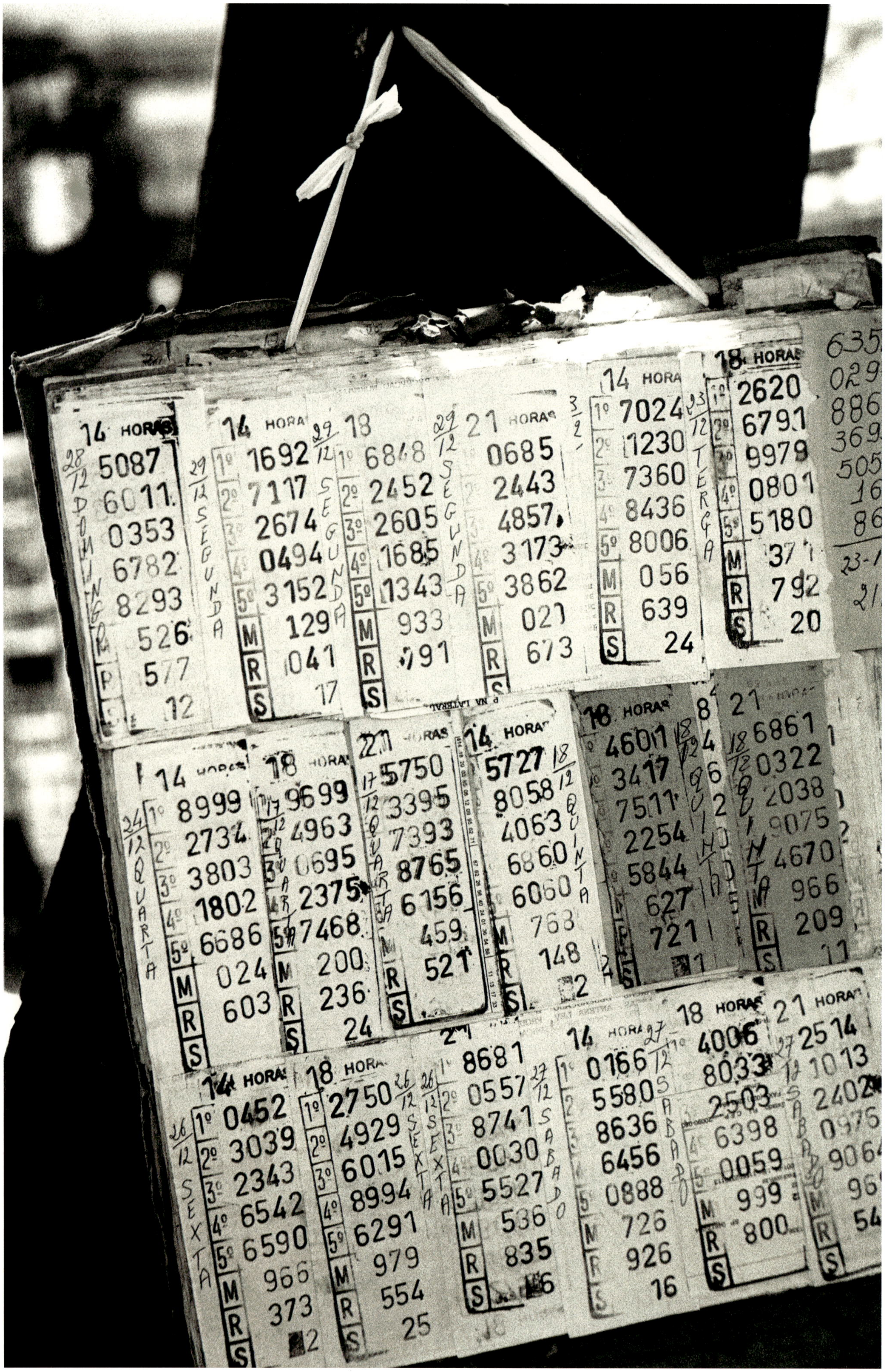
14 HORAS 28/12 DOMINGO 5087 6011 0353 6782 8293 526 577 12
14 HORAS 29/12 SEGUNDA 1692 7117 2674 0494 3152 129 041 17
18 29/12 SEGUNDA 6848 2452 2605 1685 1343 933 791
21 HORAS 29/12 SEGUNDA 0685 2443 4857 3173 3862 021 673
14 HORAS 30/12 TERÇA 7024 1230 7360 8436 8006 056 639 24
18 HORAS 2620 6791 9979 0801 5180 792 20
14 HORAS 24/12 QUARTA 8999 2734 3803 1802 6686 024 603
18 HORAS 9699 4963 0695 2375 7468 200 236 24
21 HORAS 5750 3395 7393 8765 6156 459 521
14 HORAS 5727 18/12 QUINTA 8058 4063 6860 6060 763 148
18 HORAS 4601 3417 7511 2254 5844 627 721
21 18/12 6861 0322 2038 9075 4670 966 209
14 HORAS 26/12 SEXTA 0452 3039 2343 6542 6590 966 373
18 HORAS 2750 26/12 SEXTA 4929 6015 8994 6291 979 554 25
8681 27/12 SABADO 0557 8741 0030 5527 536 835
14 HORAS 0166 5580 8636 6456 0888 726 926 16
18 HORAS 4006 8033 2503 6398 0059 999 800
21 HORAS 2514 1013

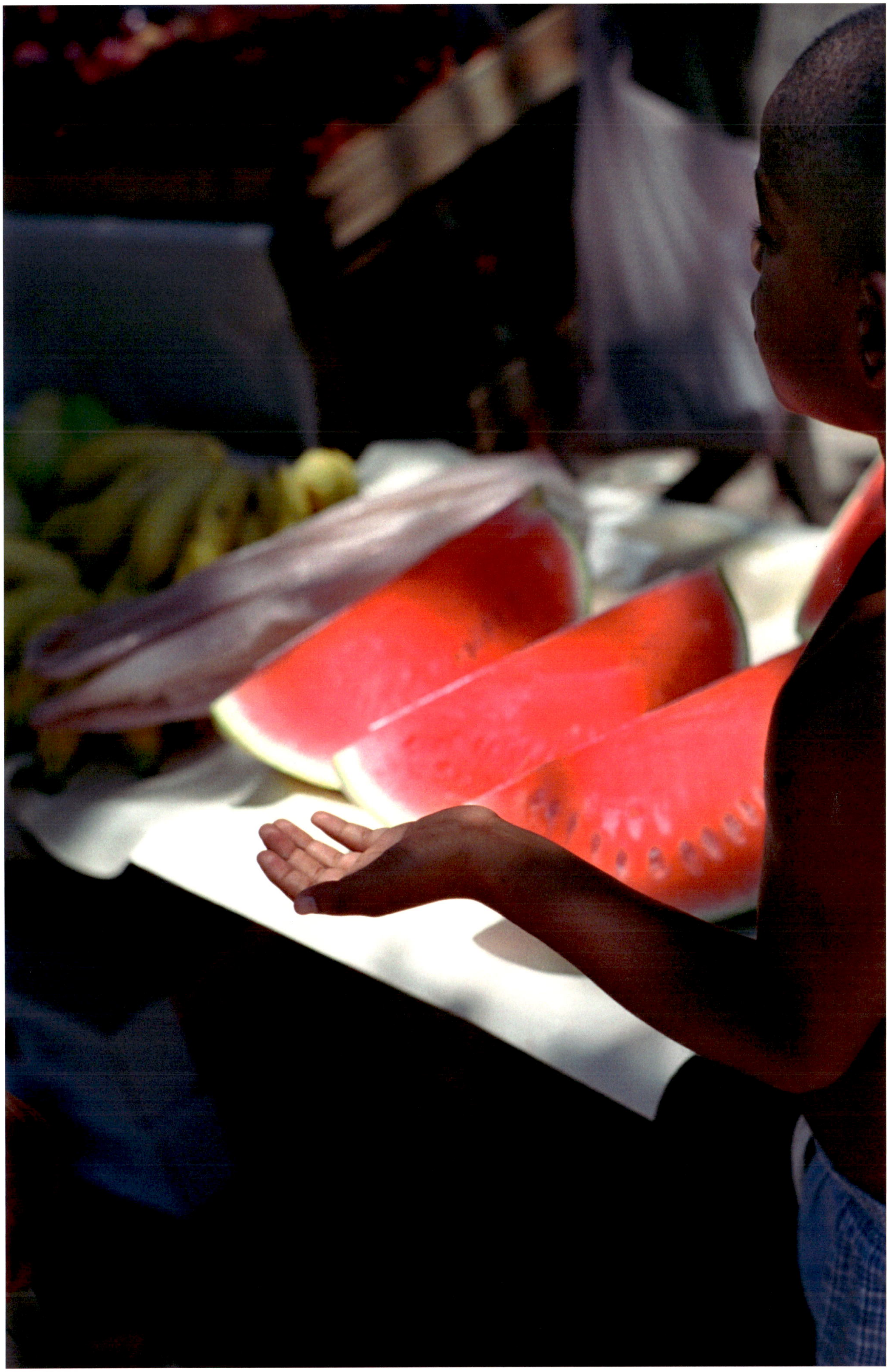

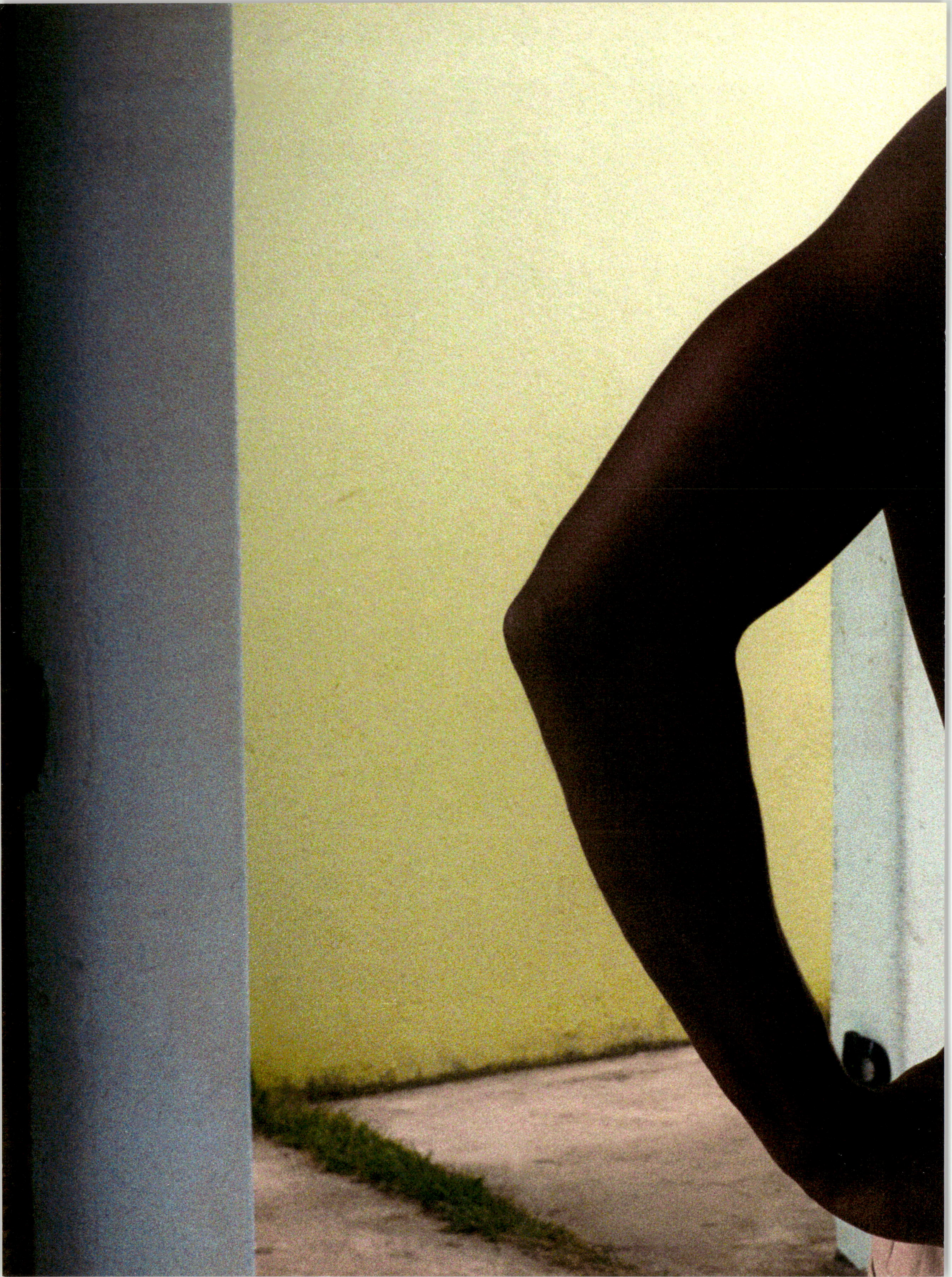

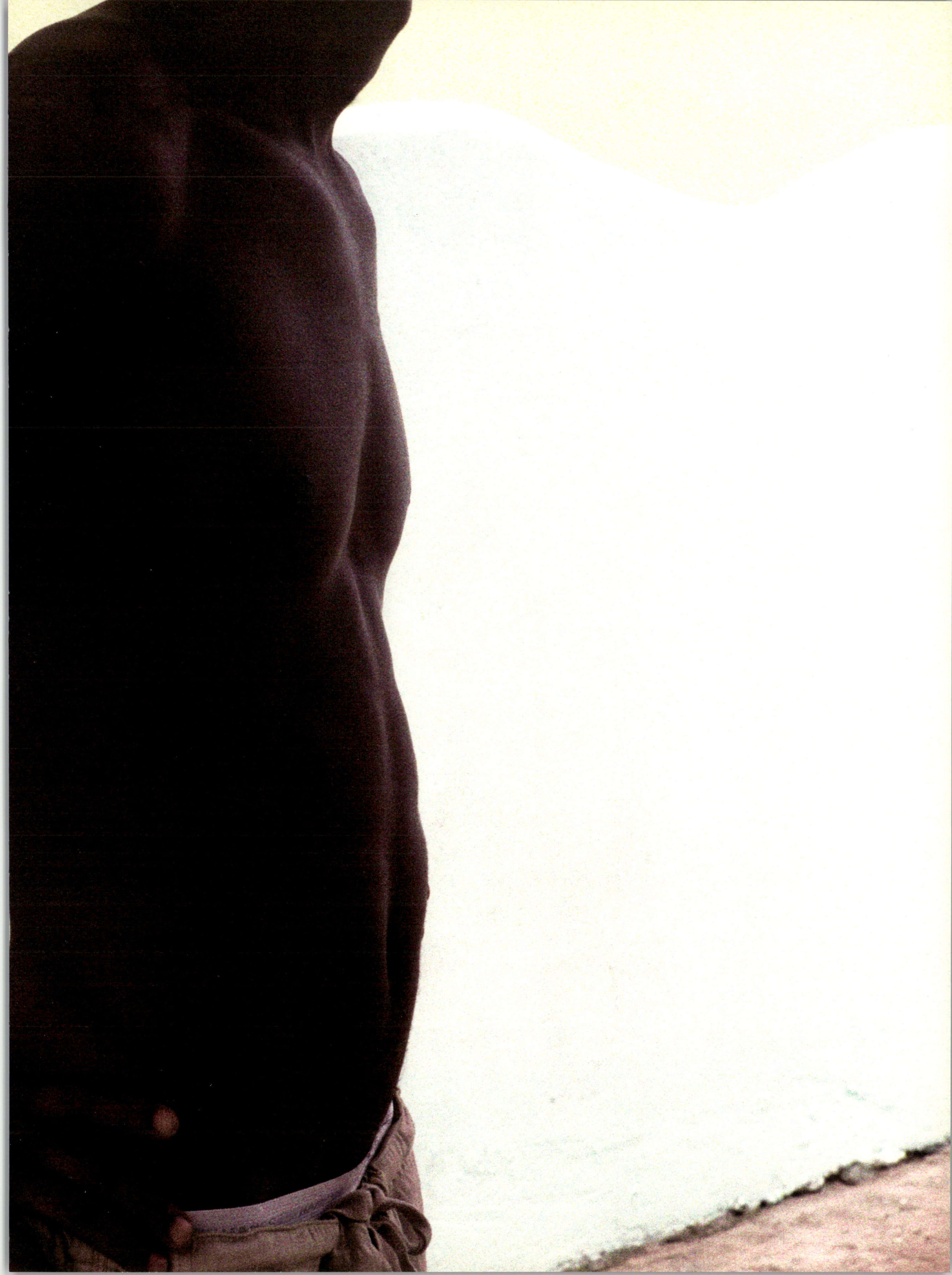

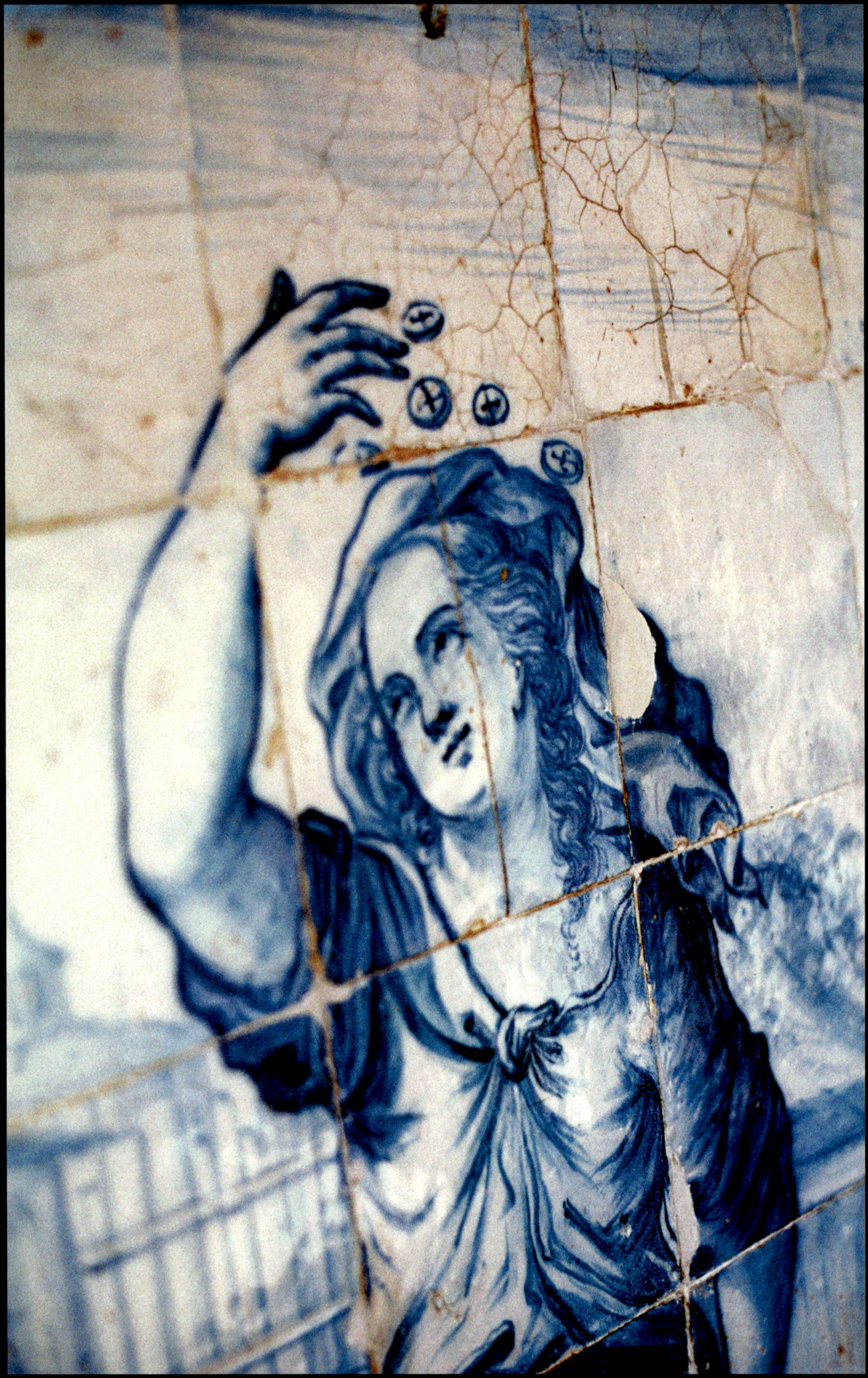

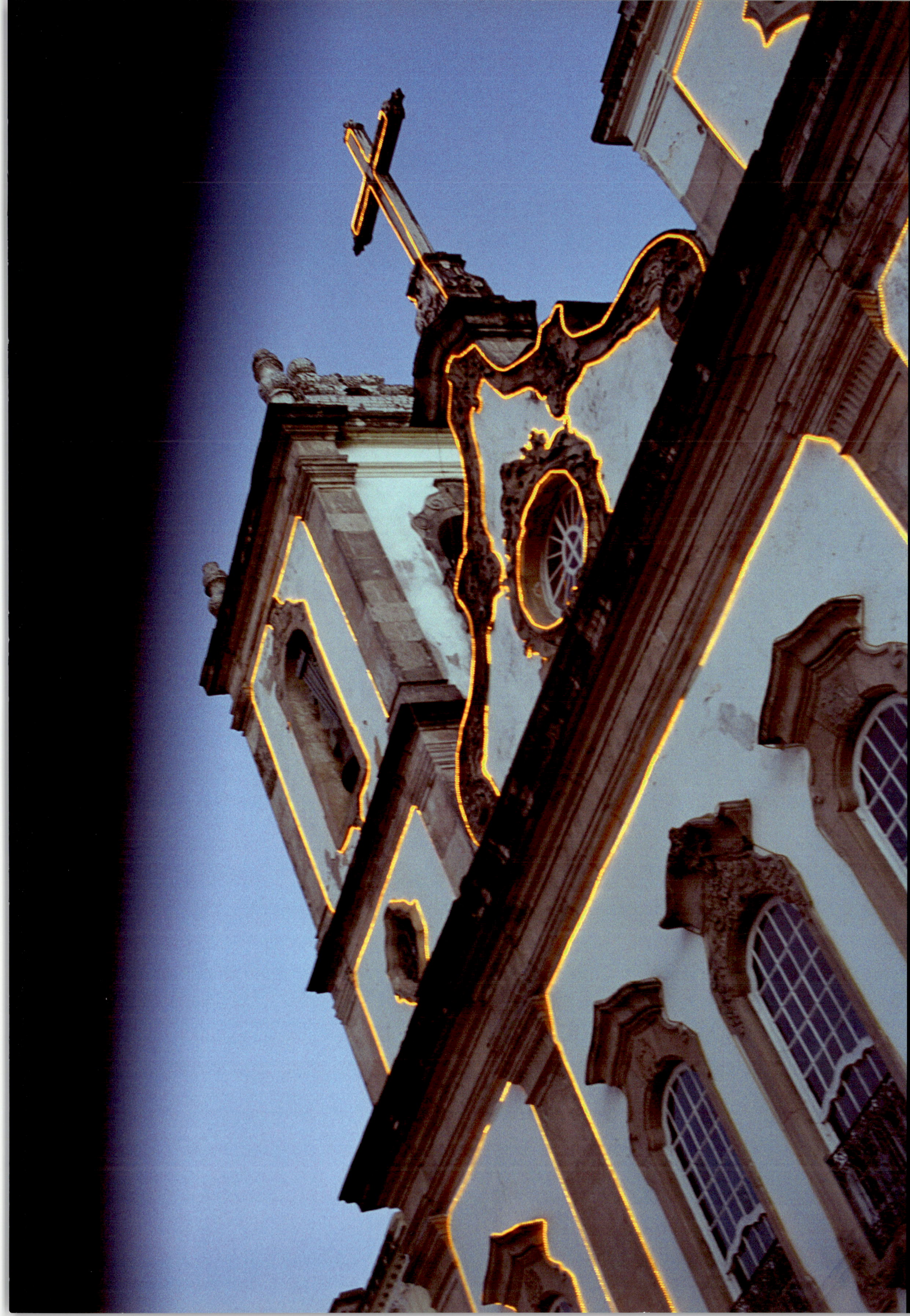

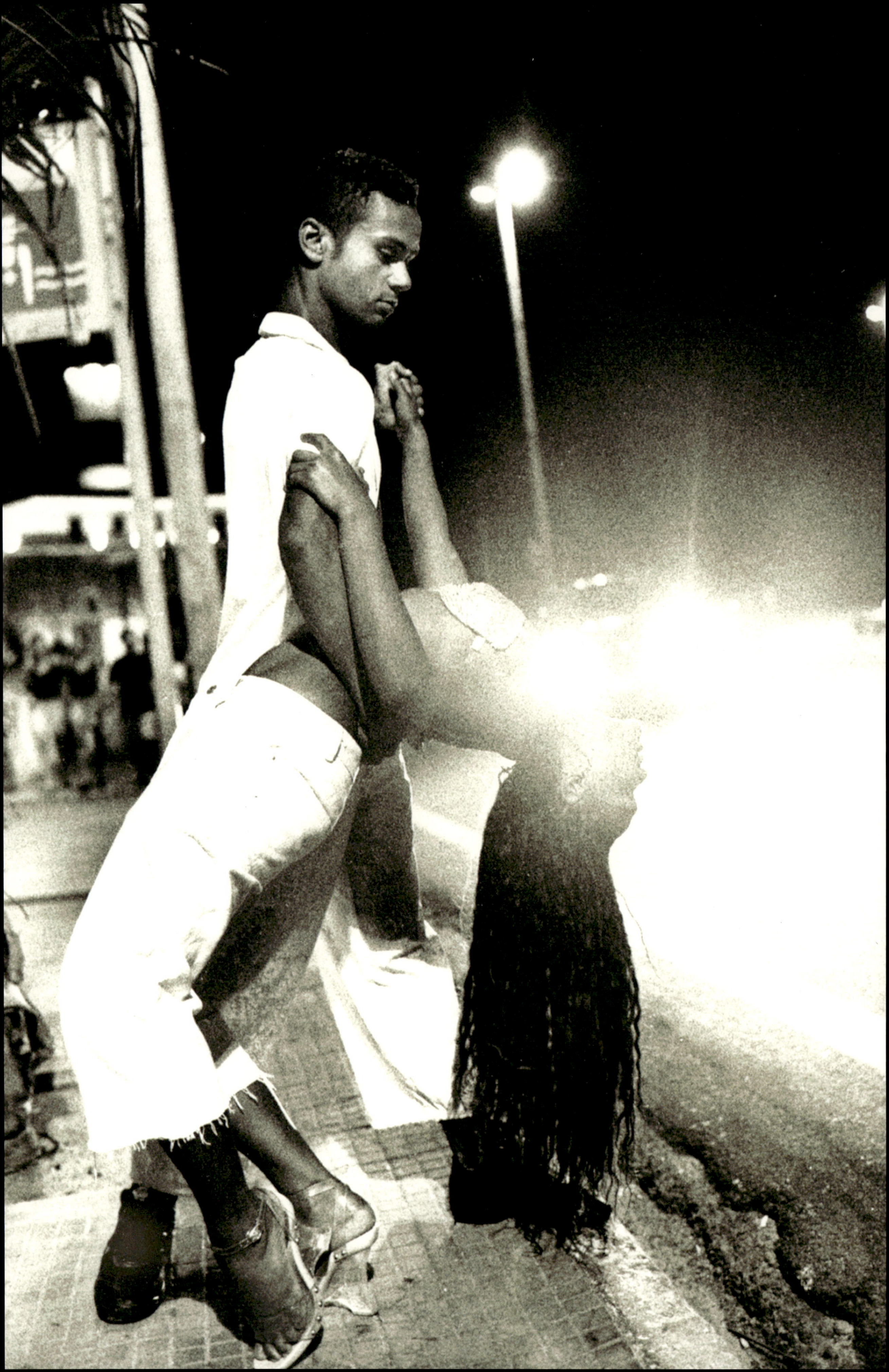

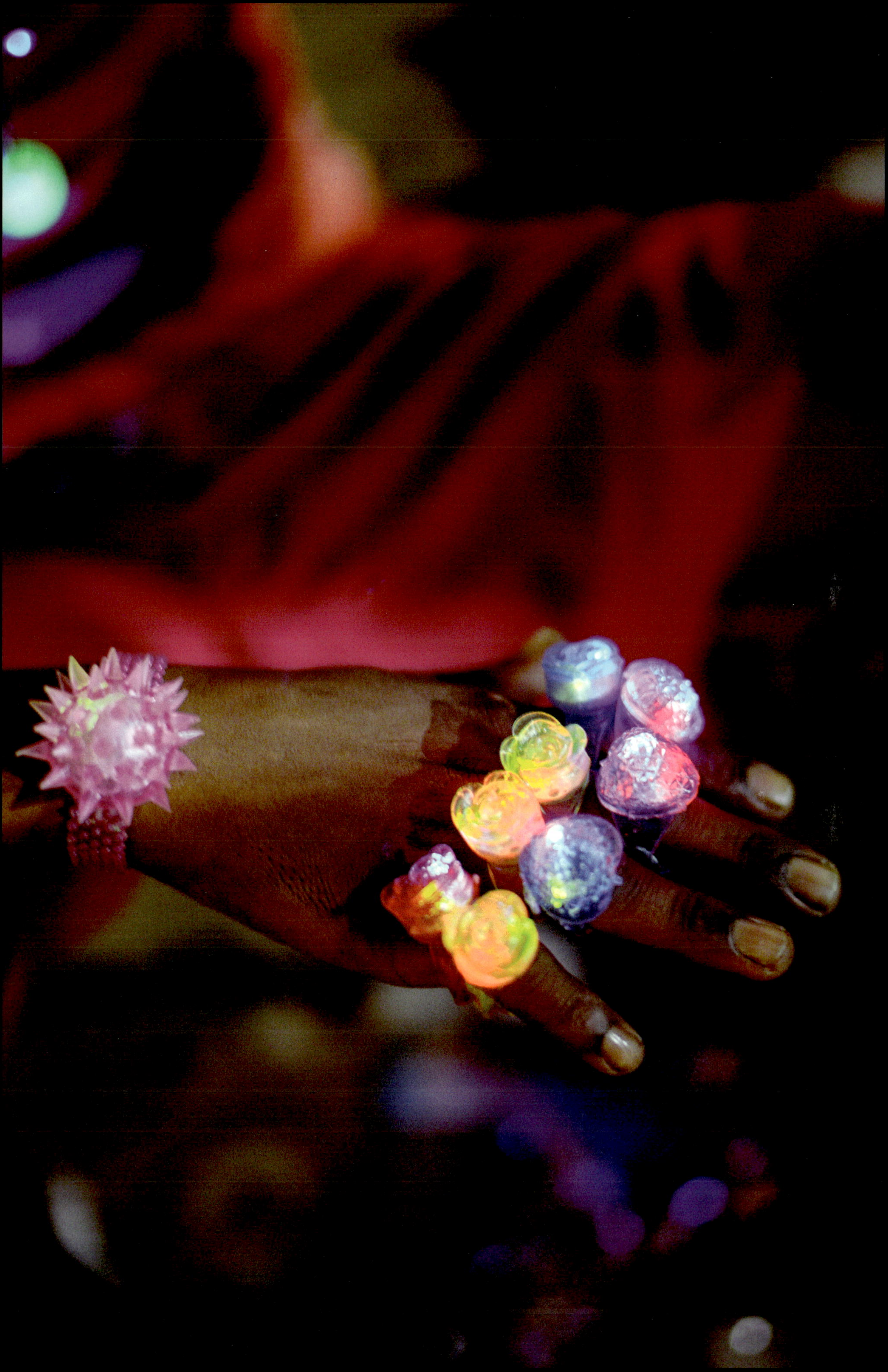

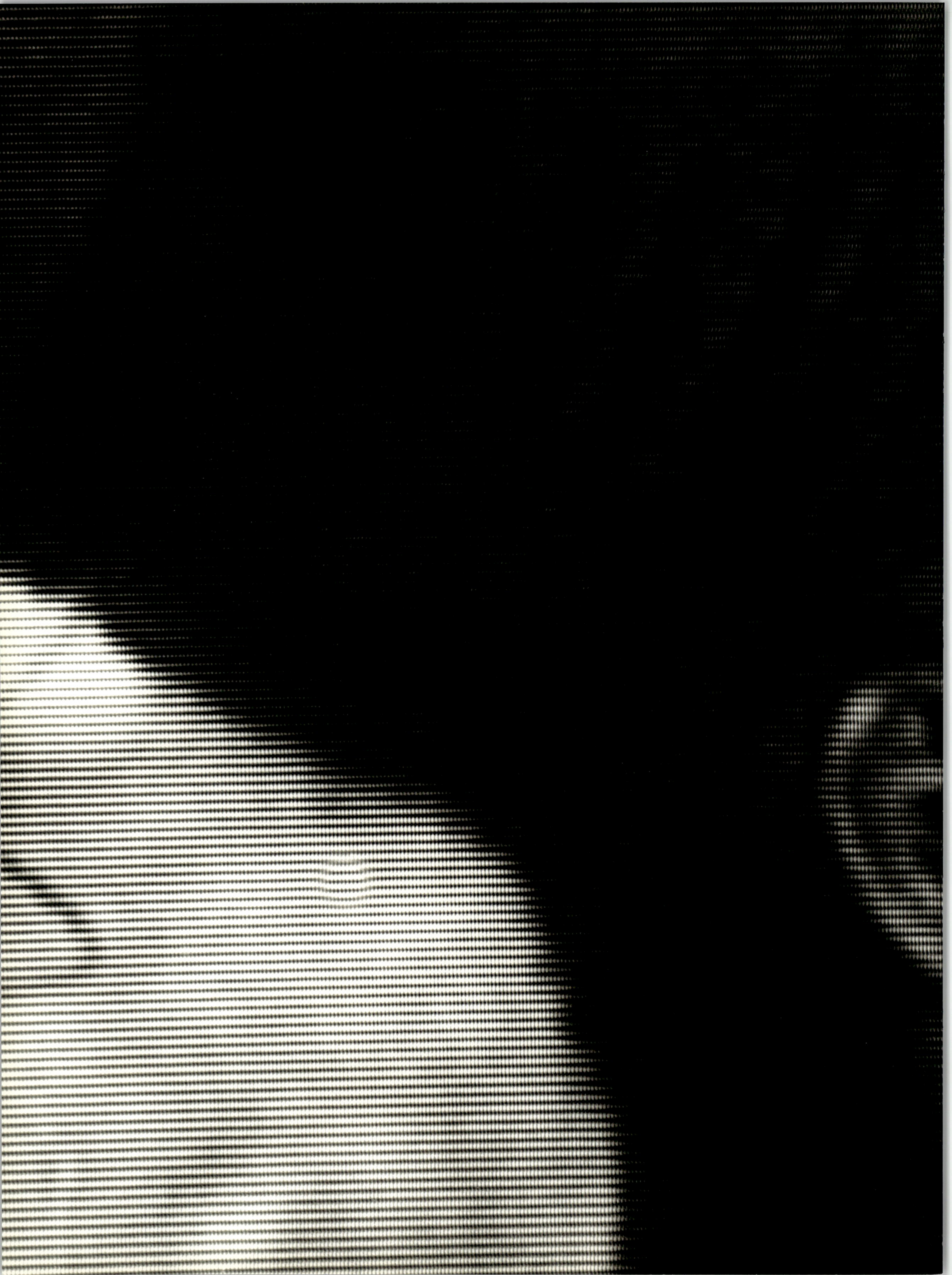

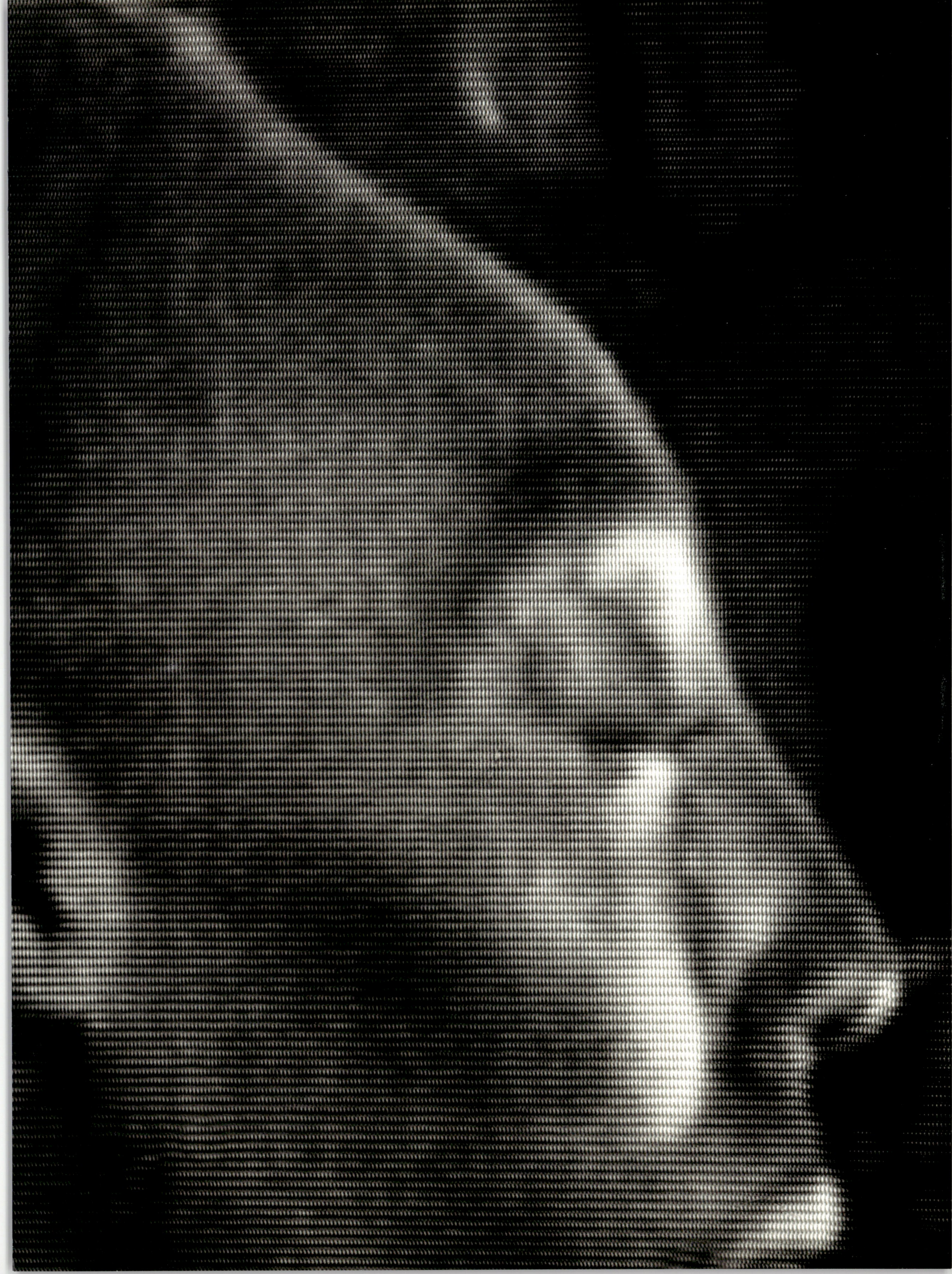

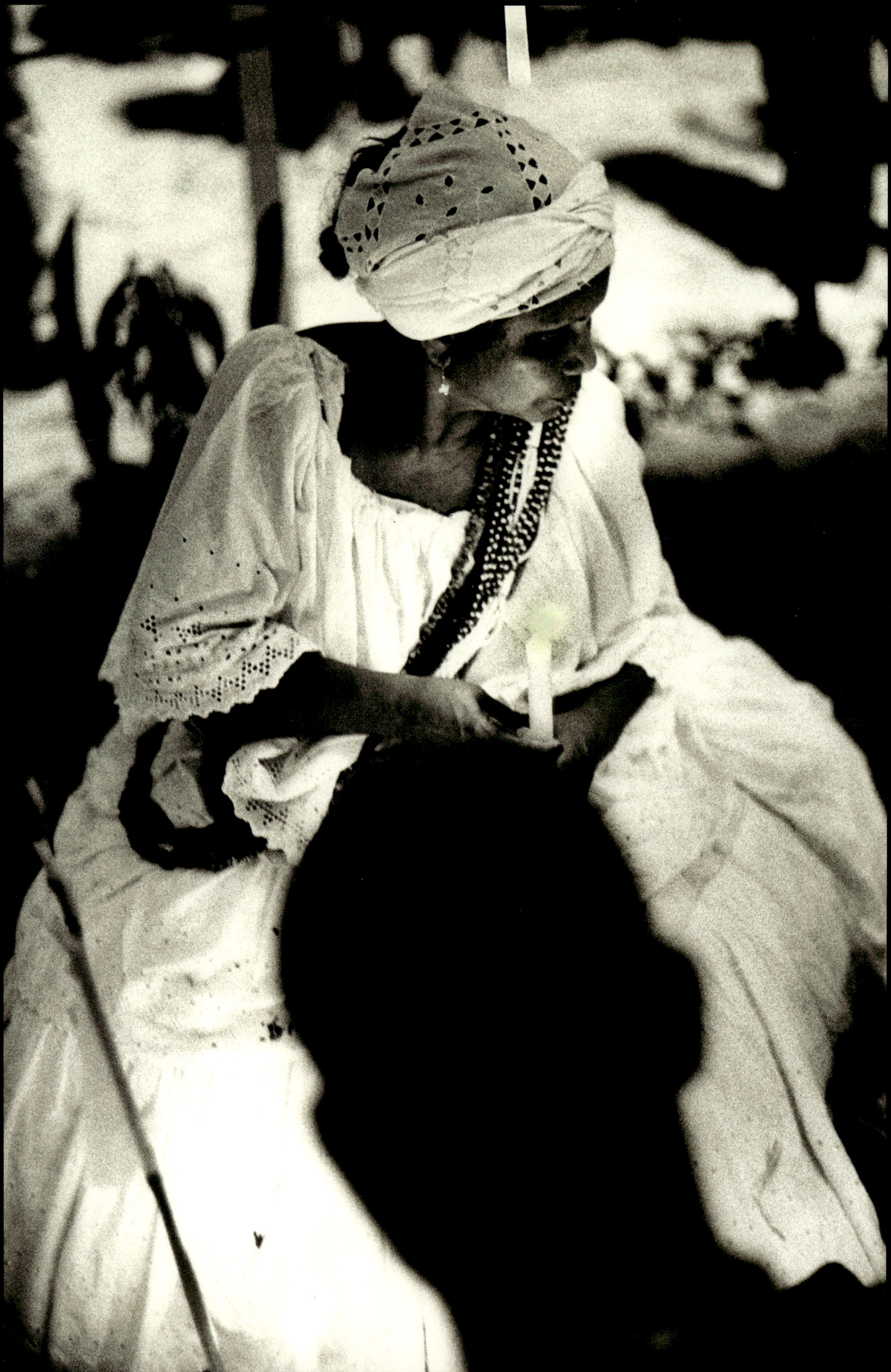

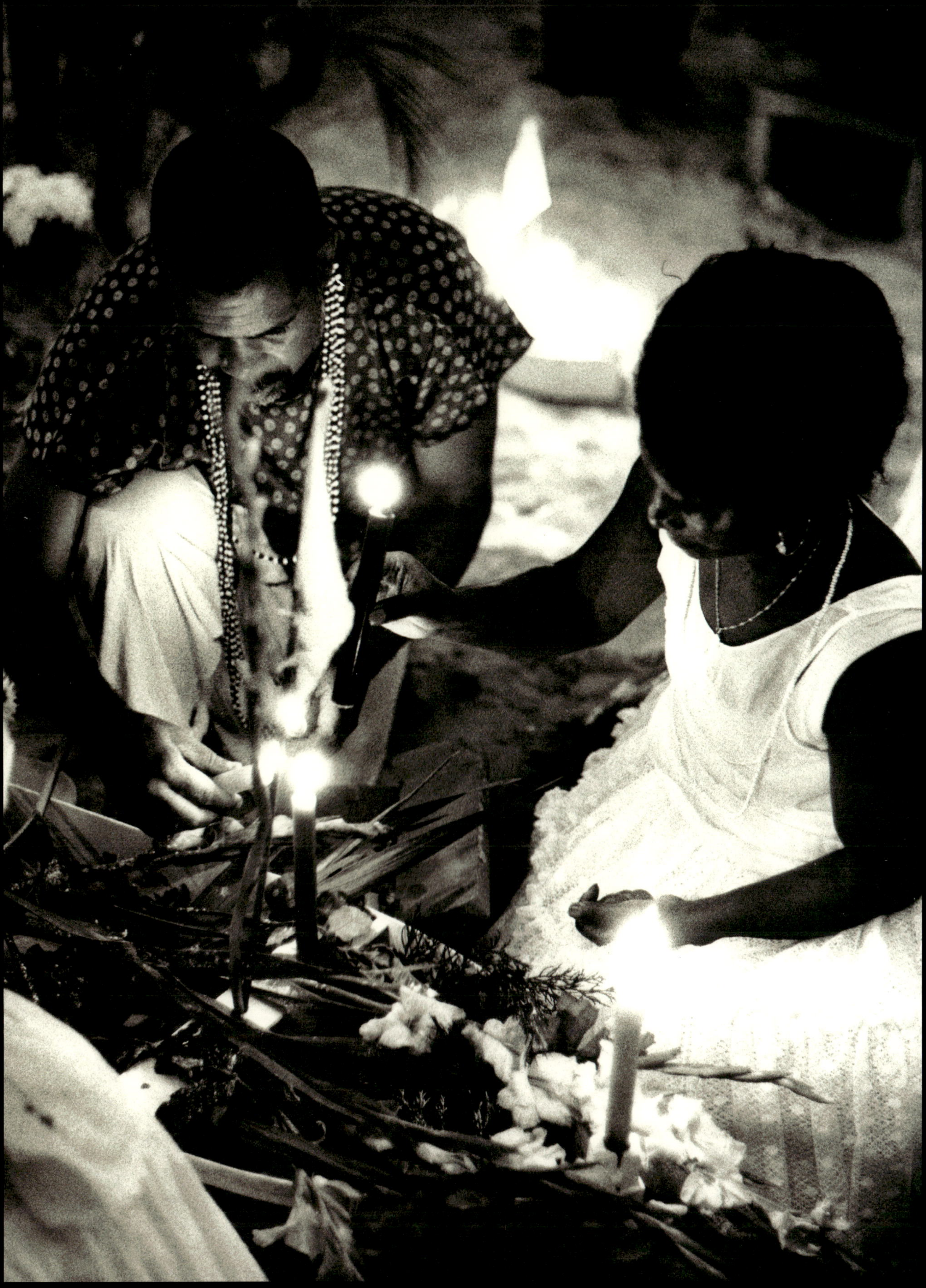

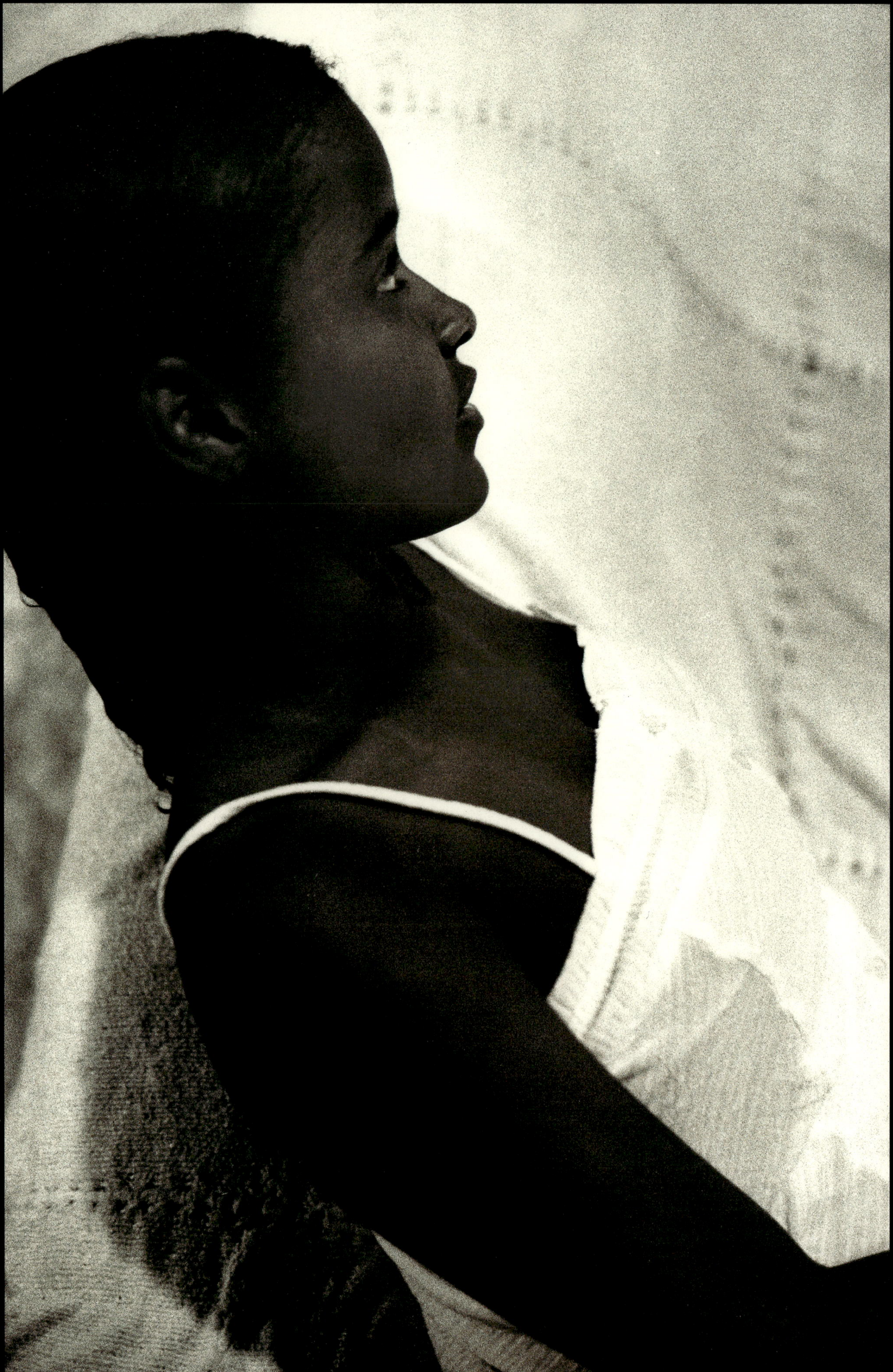

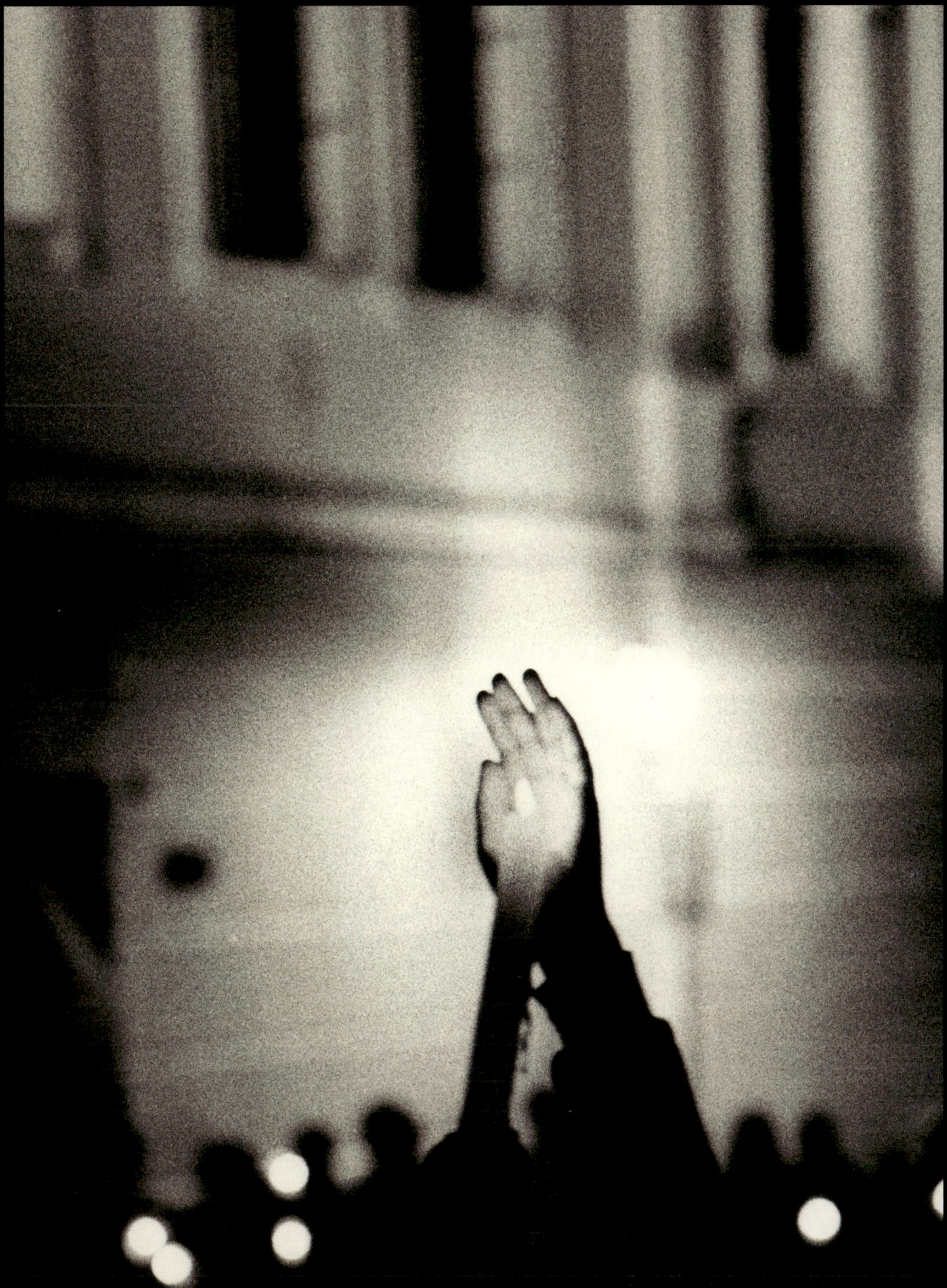

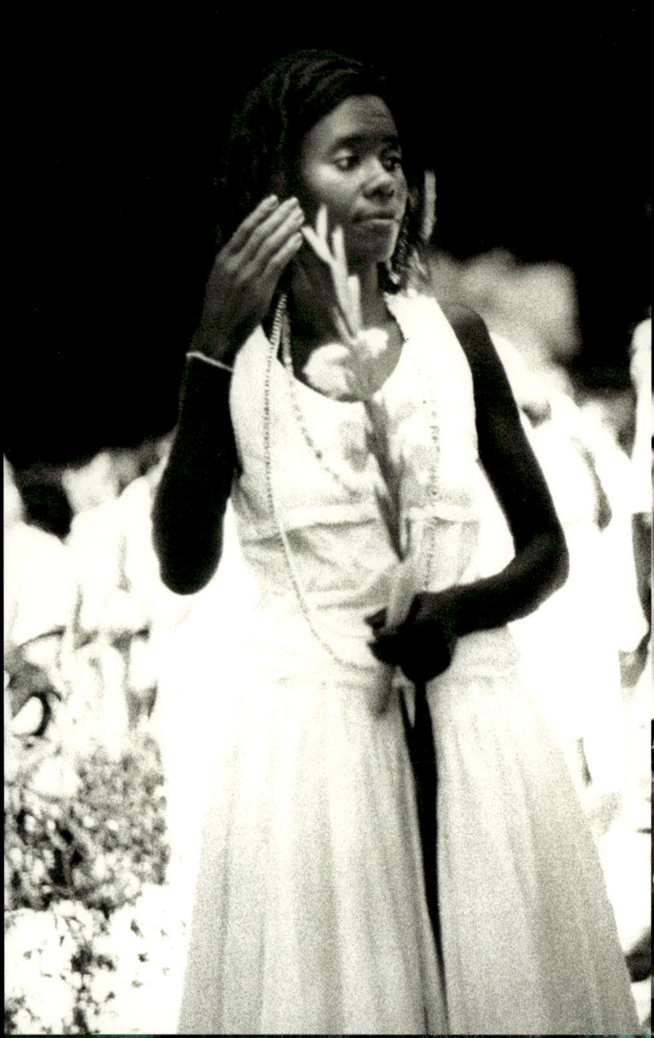

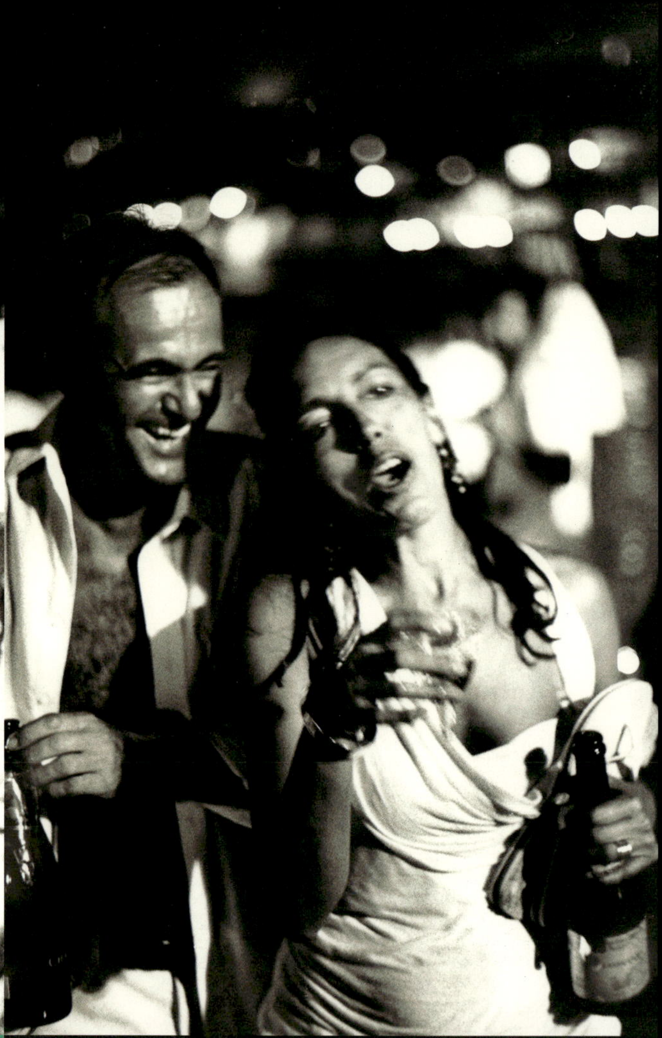

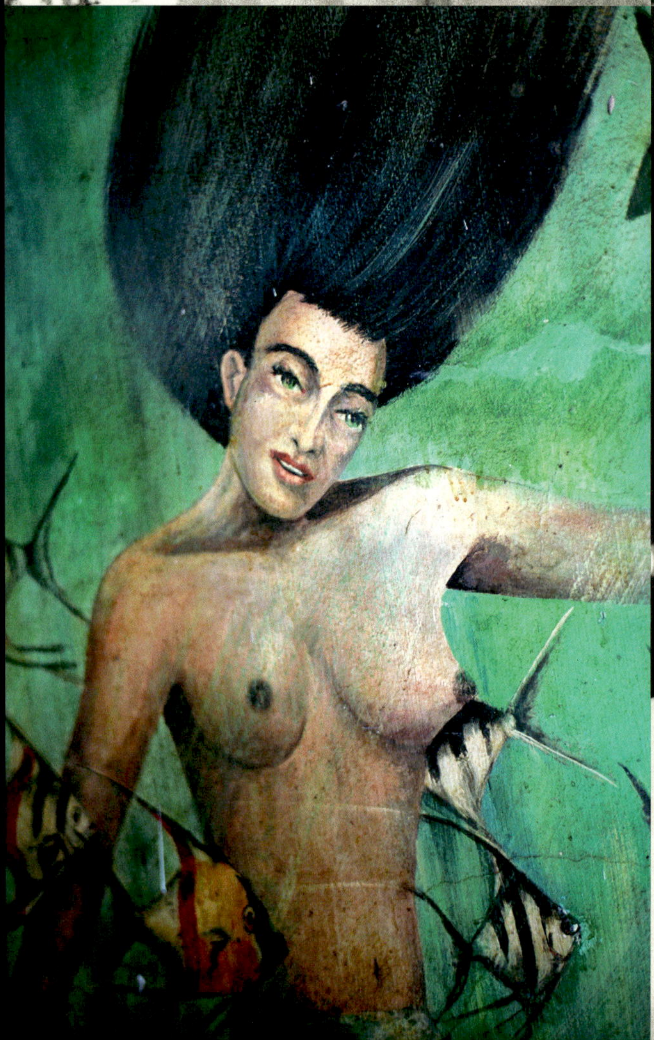

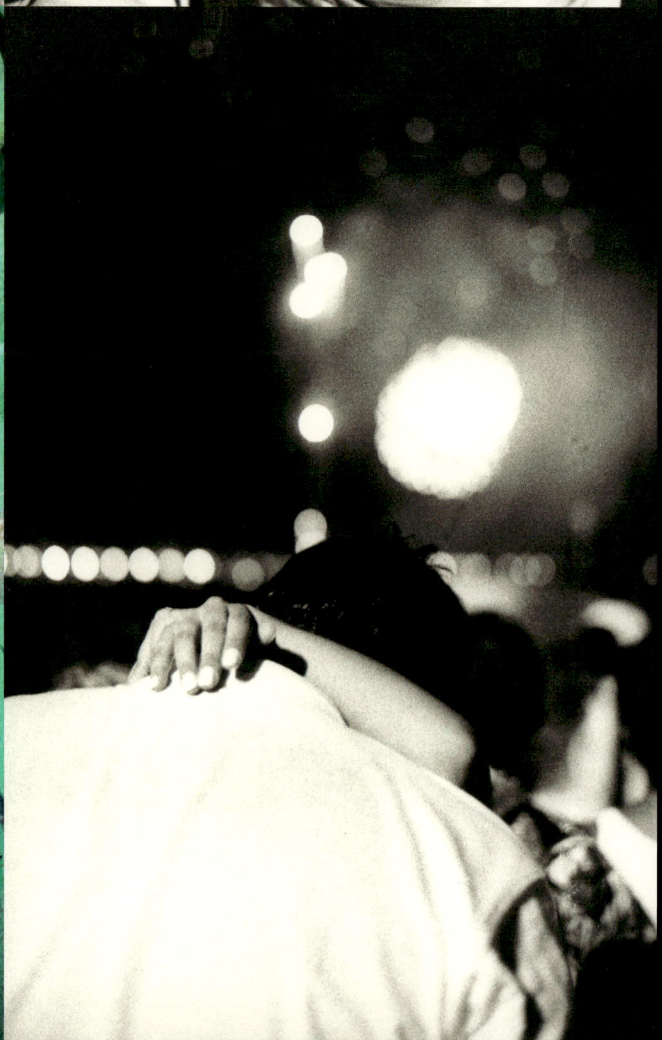

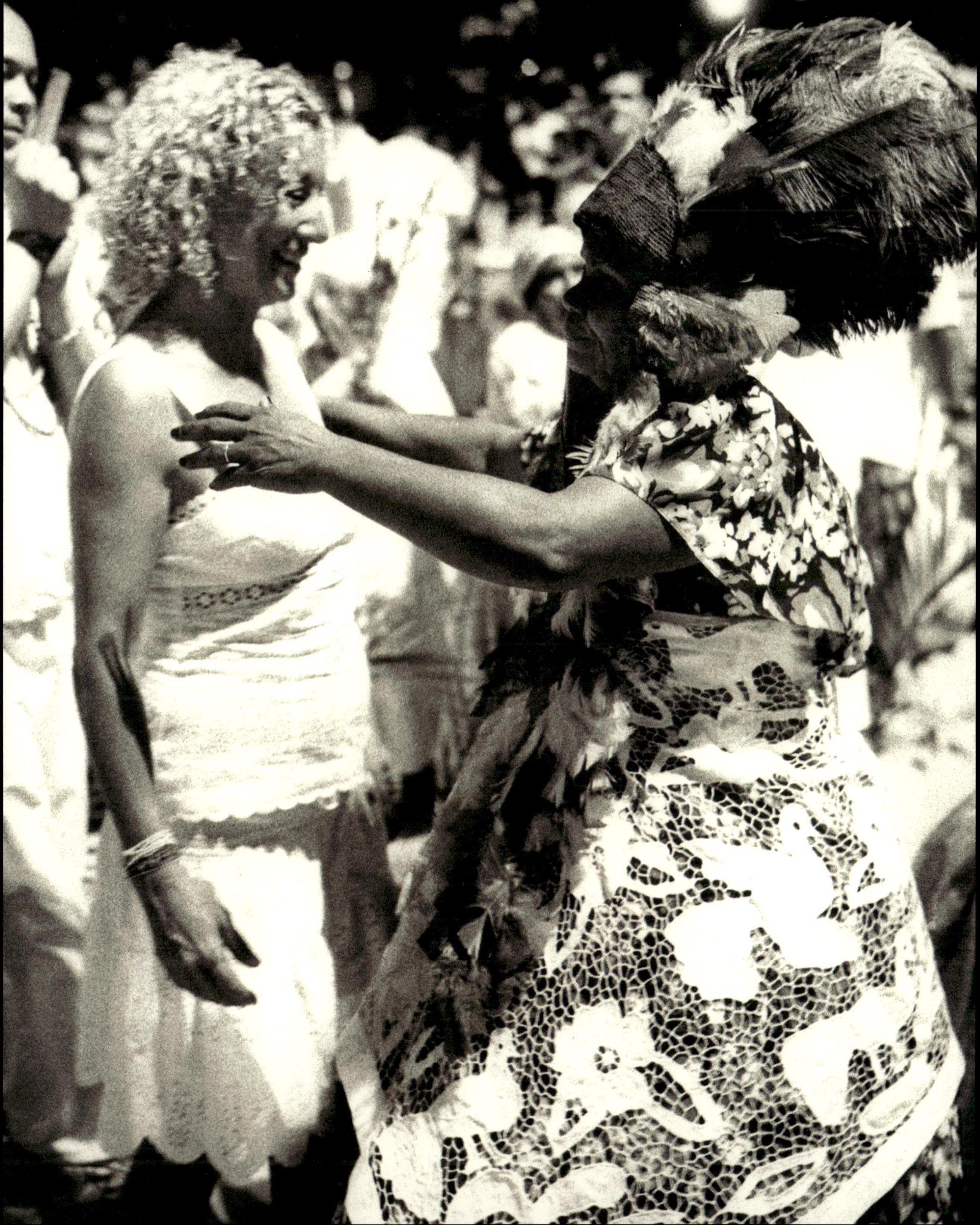

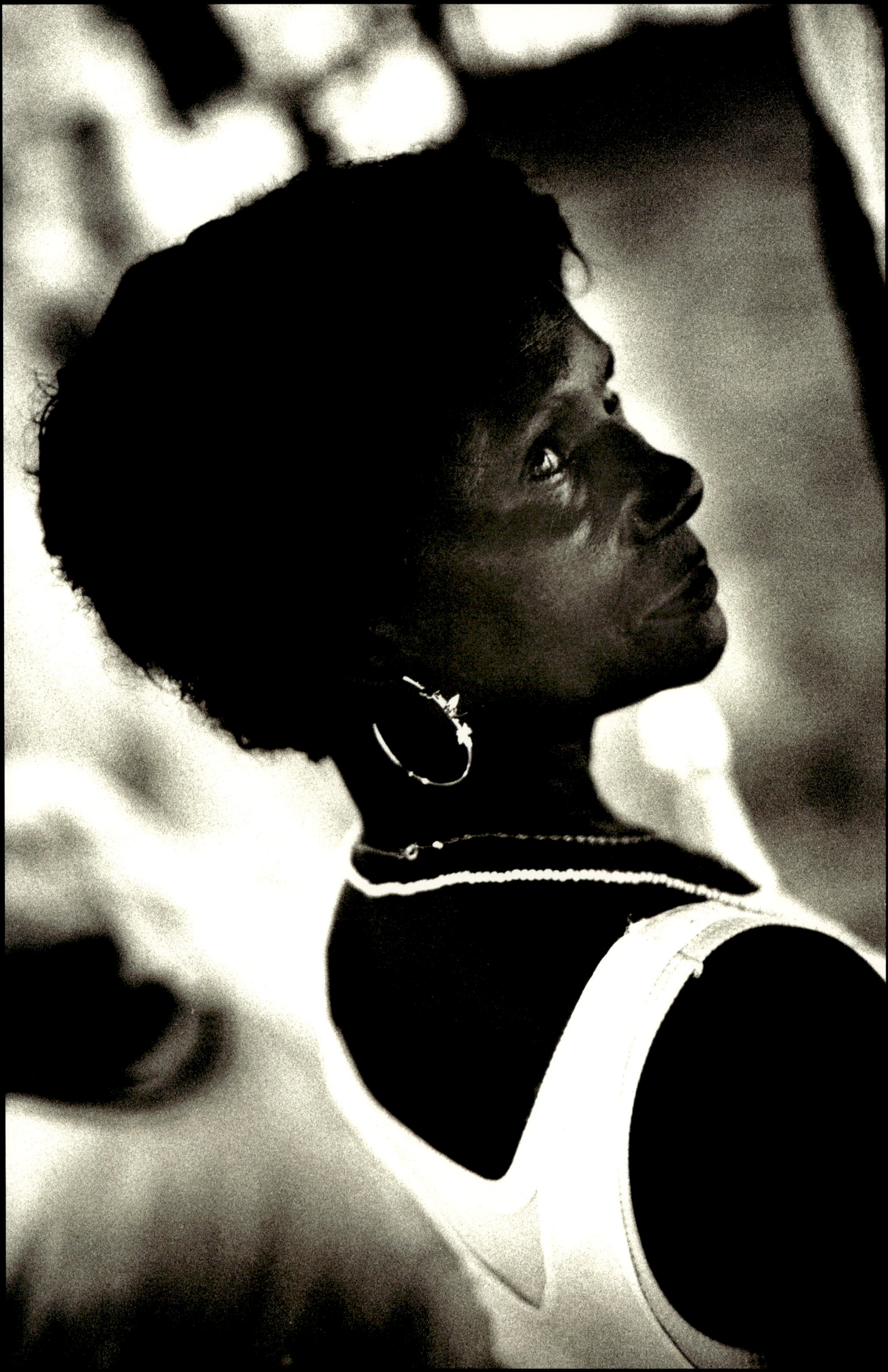

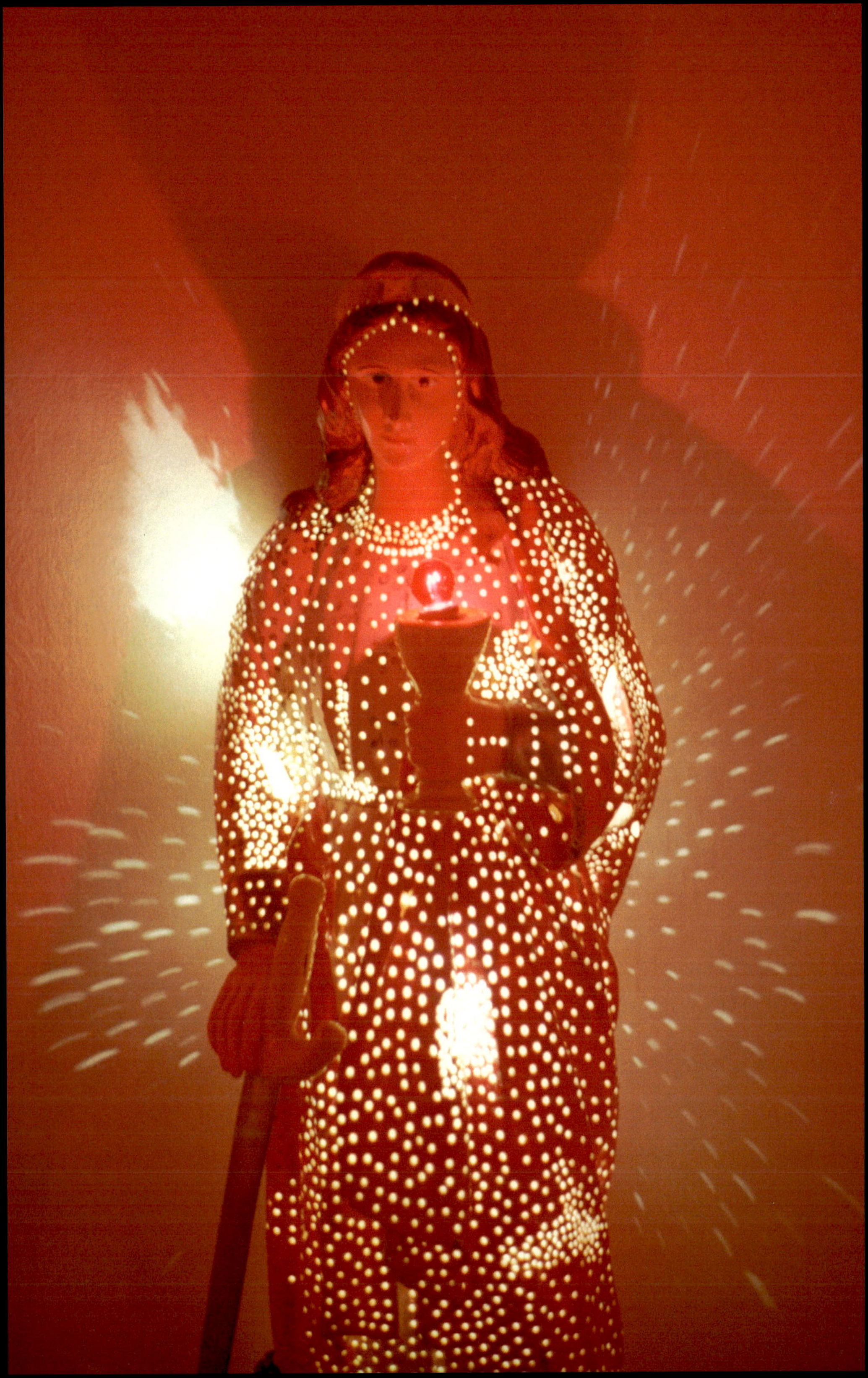

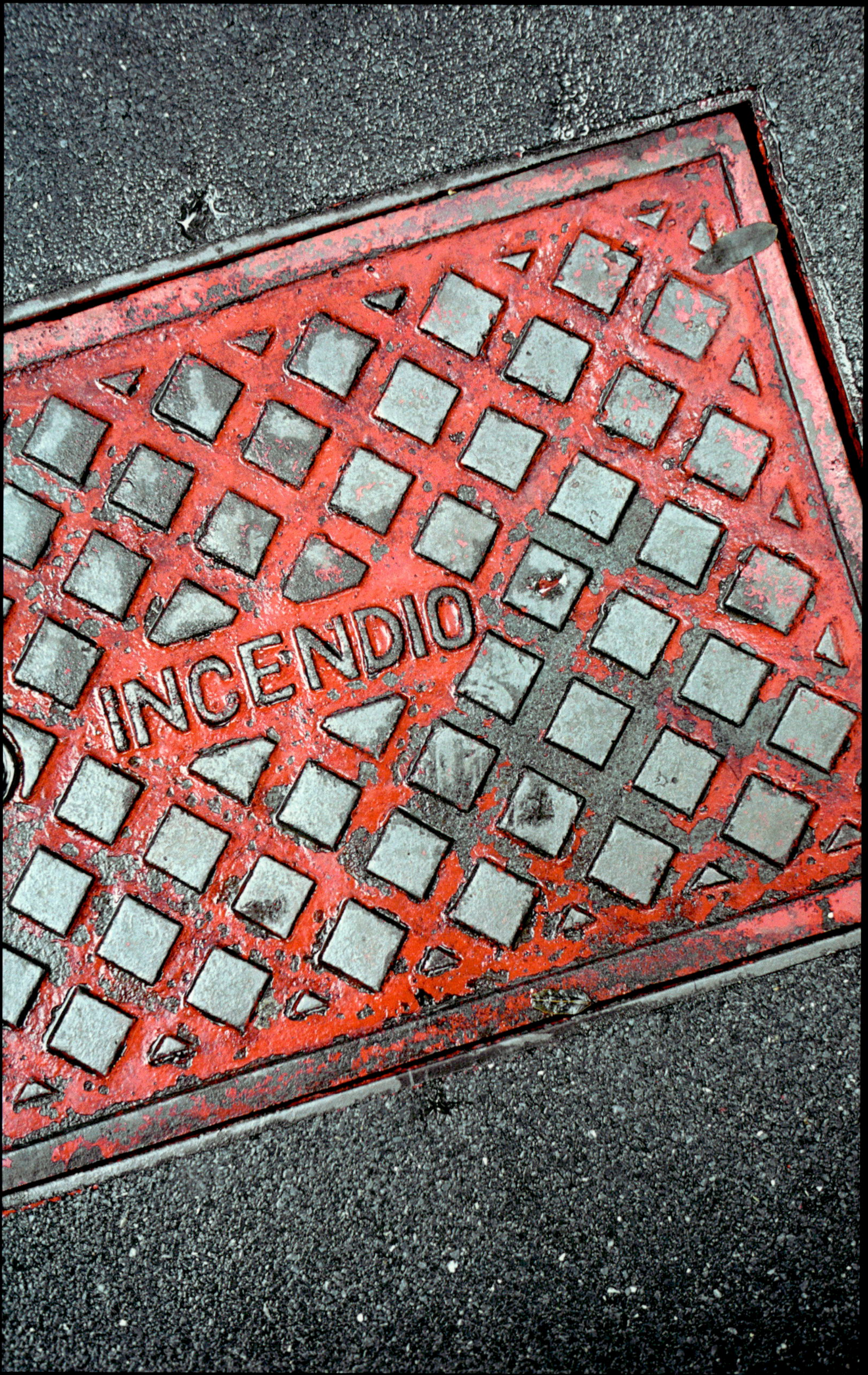
INCENDIO

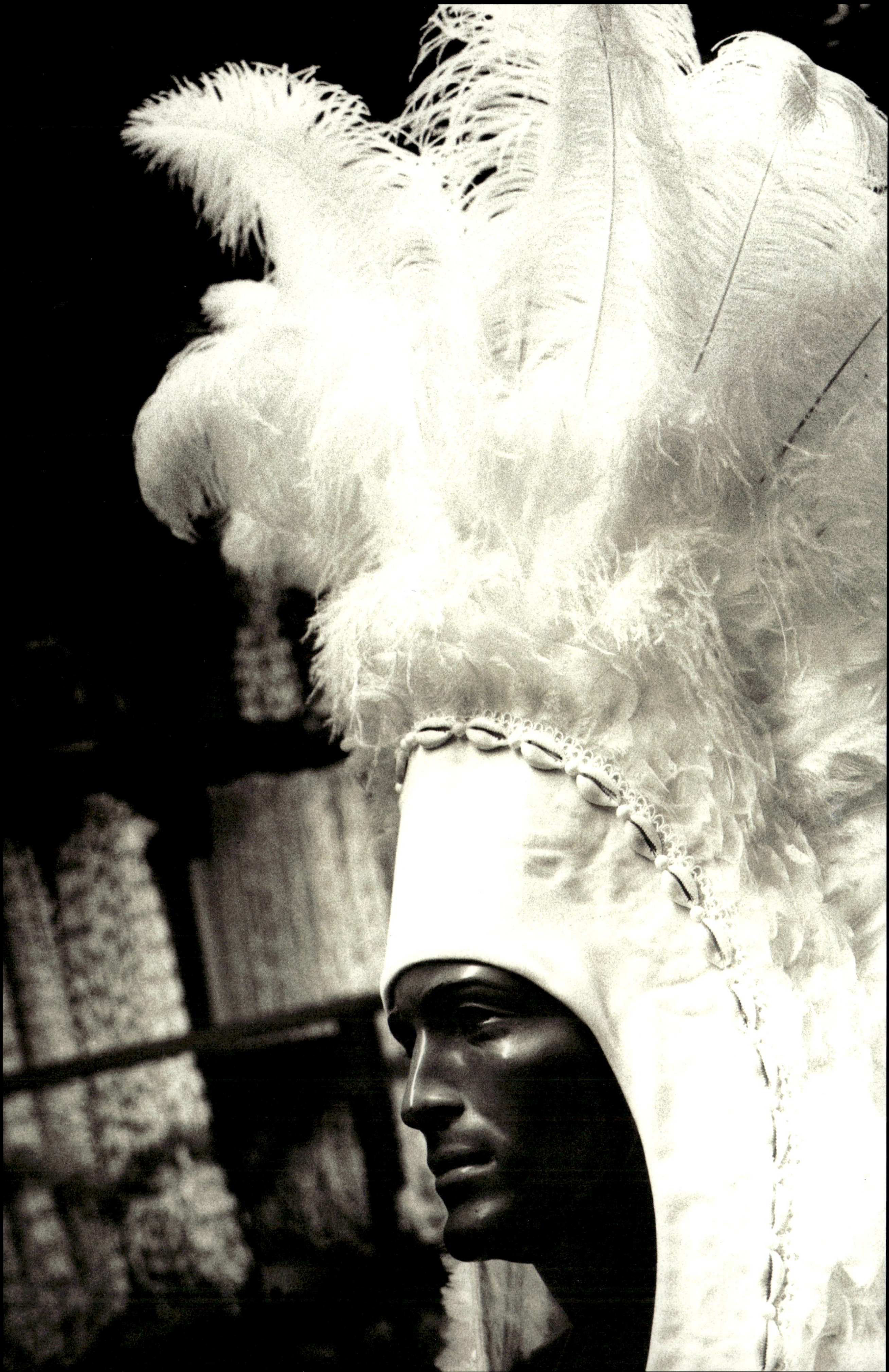

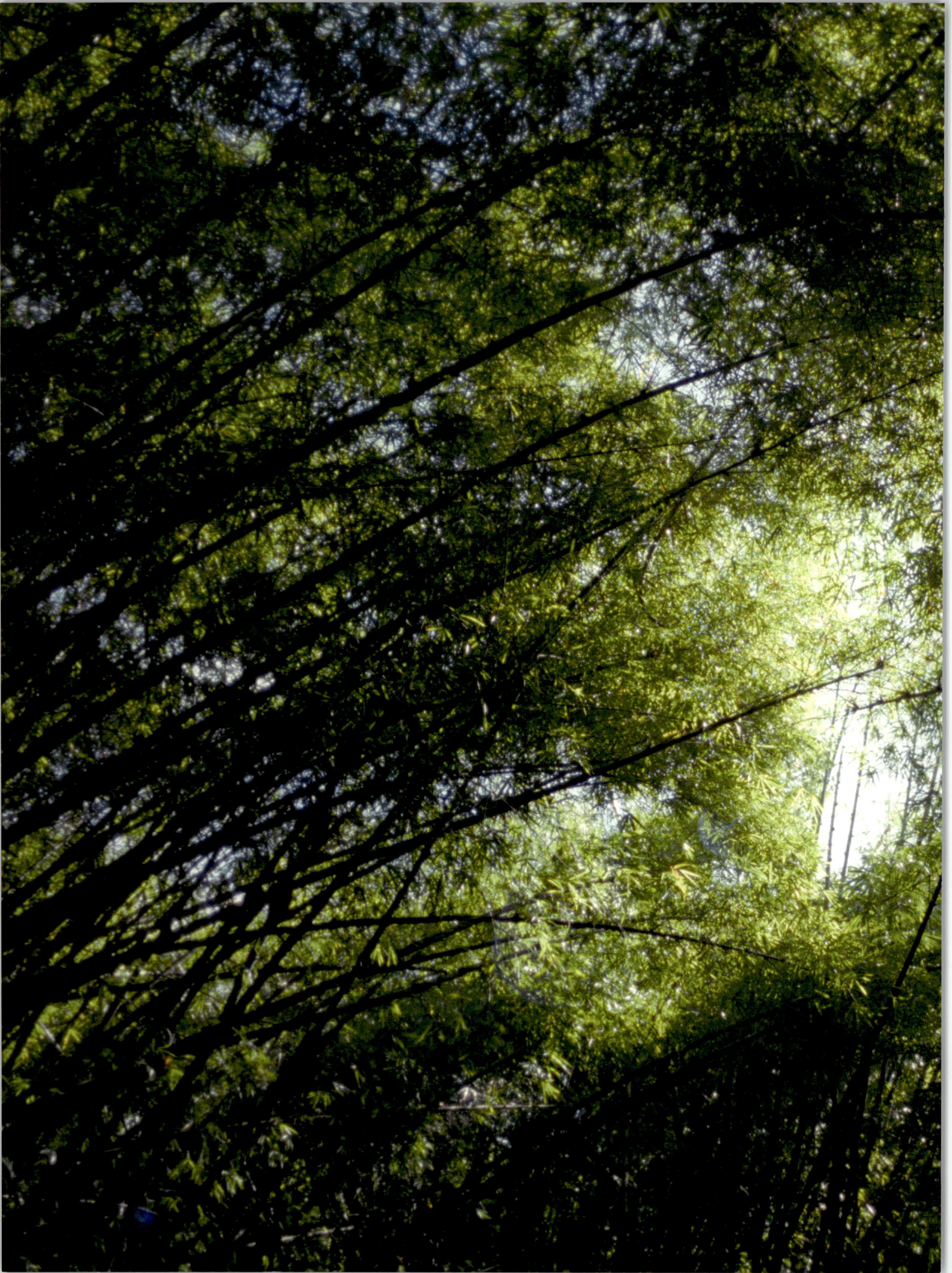

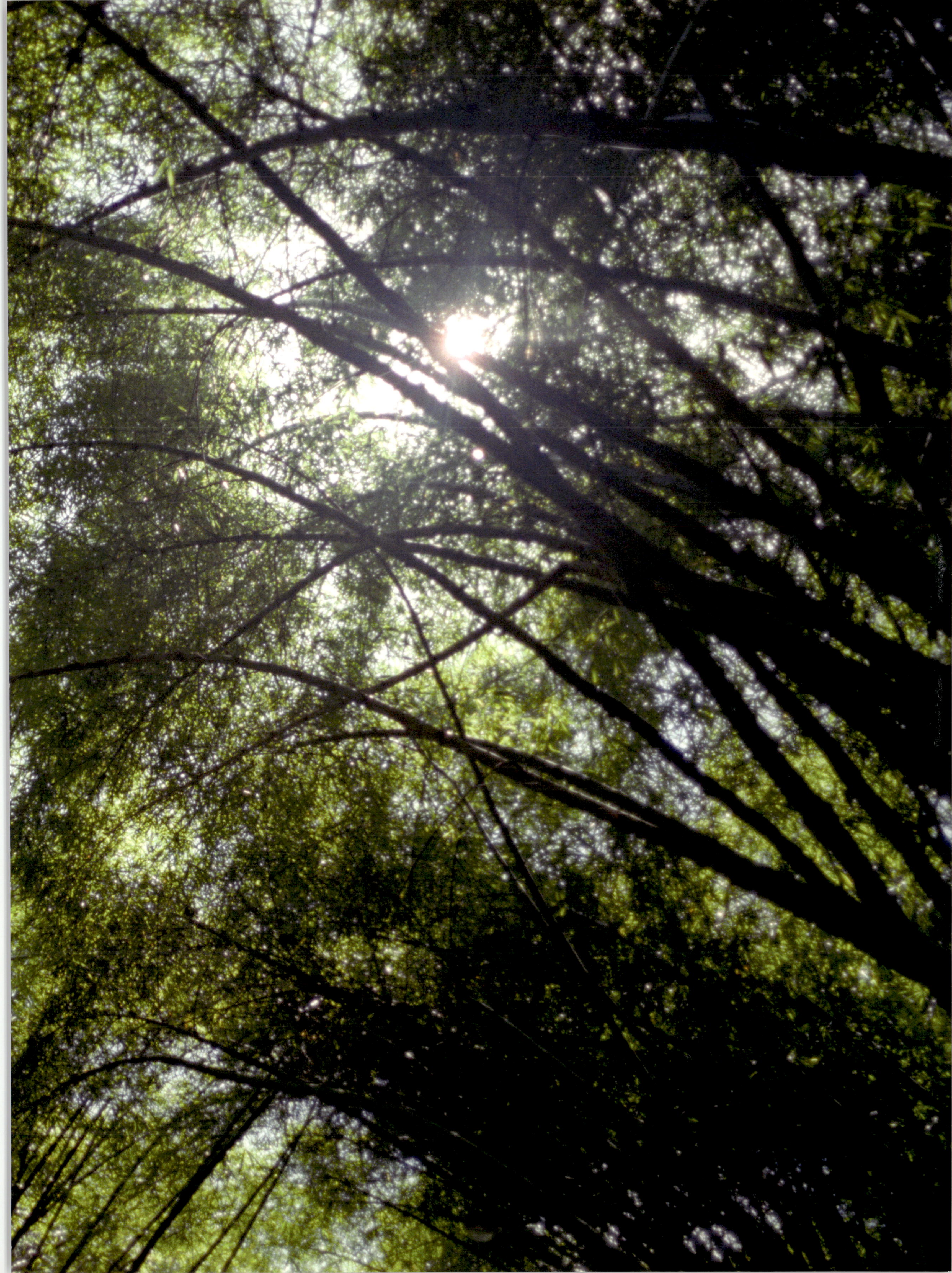

"I've never been to Black Africa", I told her. "Yes you have, she replied, you've been to Salvador". There is some truth to that. Bahia is just across the water from Benin, the place in Africa where the slave trade began....
It is not a pleasant thought but nonetheless one that remains in the foreground of one's thoughts. The people here are the descendants of the earliest waves imported at a time when the world was less entire as it is now. If the term "melting pot" applies anywhere it is here. The peoplel are among the most beautiful in Brazil and one delicate hued mulatta told me that there are over 300 words for the color of one's skin . That makes my sense to my eyes as I look around me and I see what humanity does in the New World atmosphere . Slavador is considered to be the more tranquil part of Brazil, a place to relax and enjoy the sea breeze and cocoa water. There is a languid quality to the day regardless of the season. One tends to walk a bit more calmly from here to there and back.

The only exception to this rule may be perhaps the cycle of the hours....In Salvador it goes from day to night in a few moments. The mocqueca boils....the music starts.

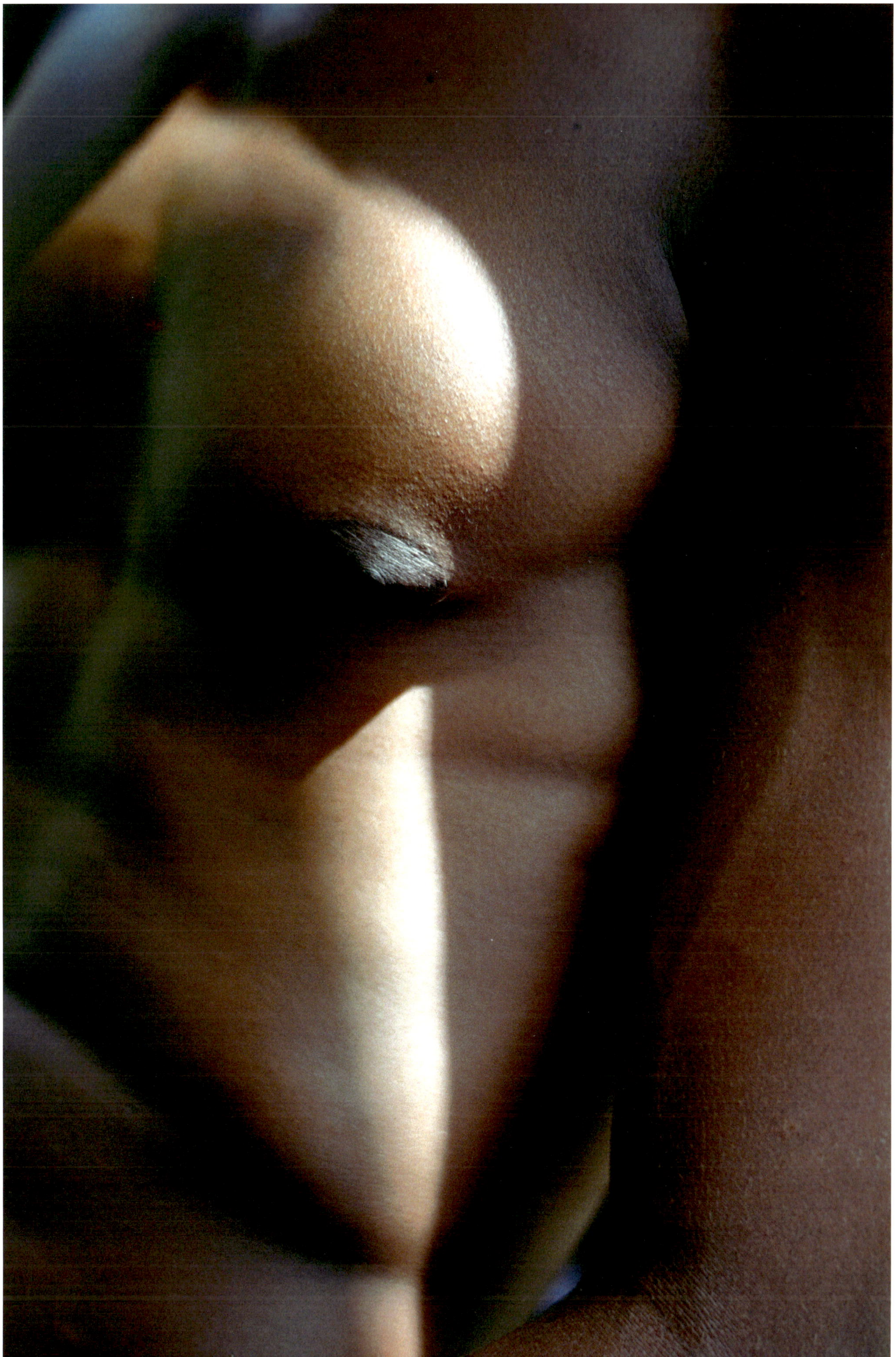

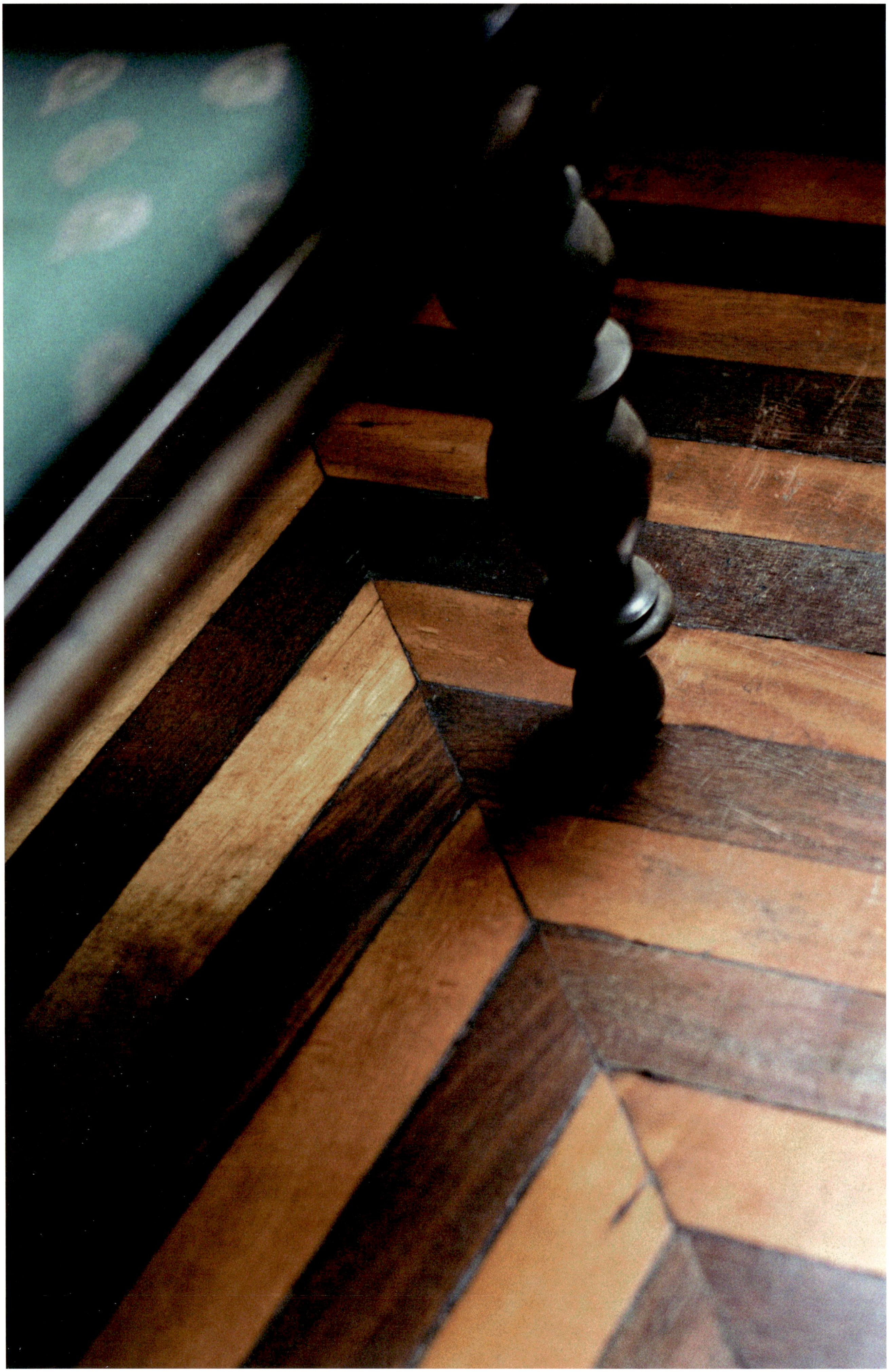

"Non sono mai stato in Africa", le dissi. "E invece sì, rispose, sei stato nel Salvador". C'è qualcosa di vero in questo. Bahia è proprio oltre l'acqua di fronte al Benin, dove in Africa ebbe inizio la tratta degli schiavi...
Non è un pensiero piacevole, e tuttavia è uno di quelli che rimangono al centro di tutti i pensieri. La gente di qui discende dai primi schiavi, importati in un tempo in cui il mondo non costituiva ancora un'unità come oggi. Se il termine "melting pot" si addice ad un qualche luogo, quel luogo è questo. La gente è tra la più bella del Brasile e una delicata mulatta dal colore intenso mi parlò dell'esistenza di almeno 300 termini per definire il colore della pelle. Ciò restituisce significato alla percezione dei miei occhi, mentre mi guardo intorno e vedo ciò che fa l'umanità nell'atmosfera del Nuovo Mondo. Il Salvador è considerato la parte più tranquilla del Brasile, un posto in cui rilassarsi e godere della brezza marina e dell'acqua di cocco. Un tratto di indolenza caratterizza le giornate a prescindere dalla stagione. Si tende a camminare in modo più rilassato, da un punto, ad un altro, e poi indietro.

L'unica eccezione alla regola è forse l'avvicendarsi delle ore. In Salvador si passa dal giorno alla notte in pochi istanti. La mocqueca bolle, la musica inizia.

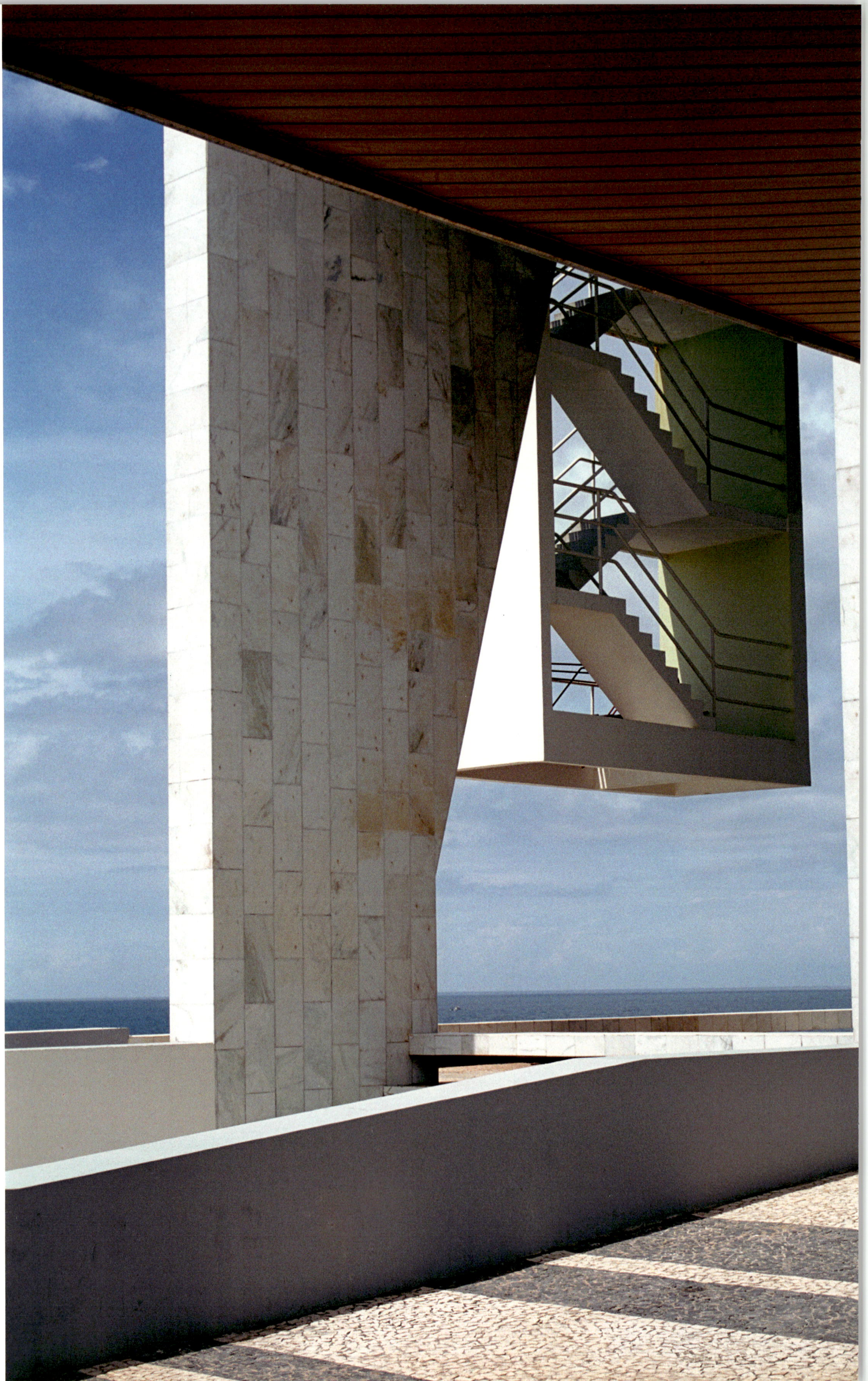

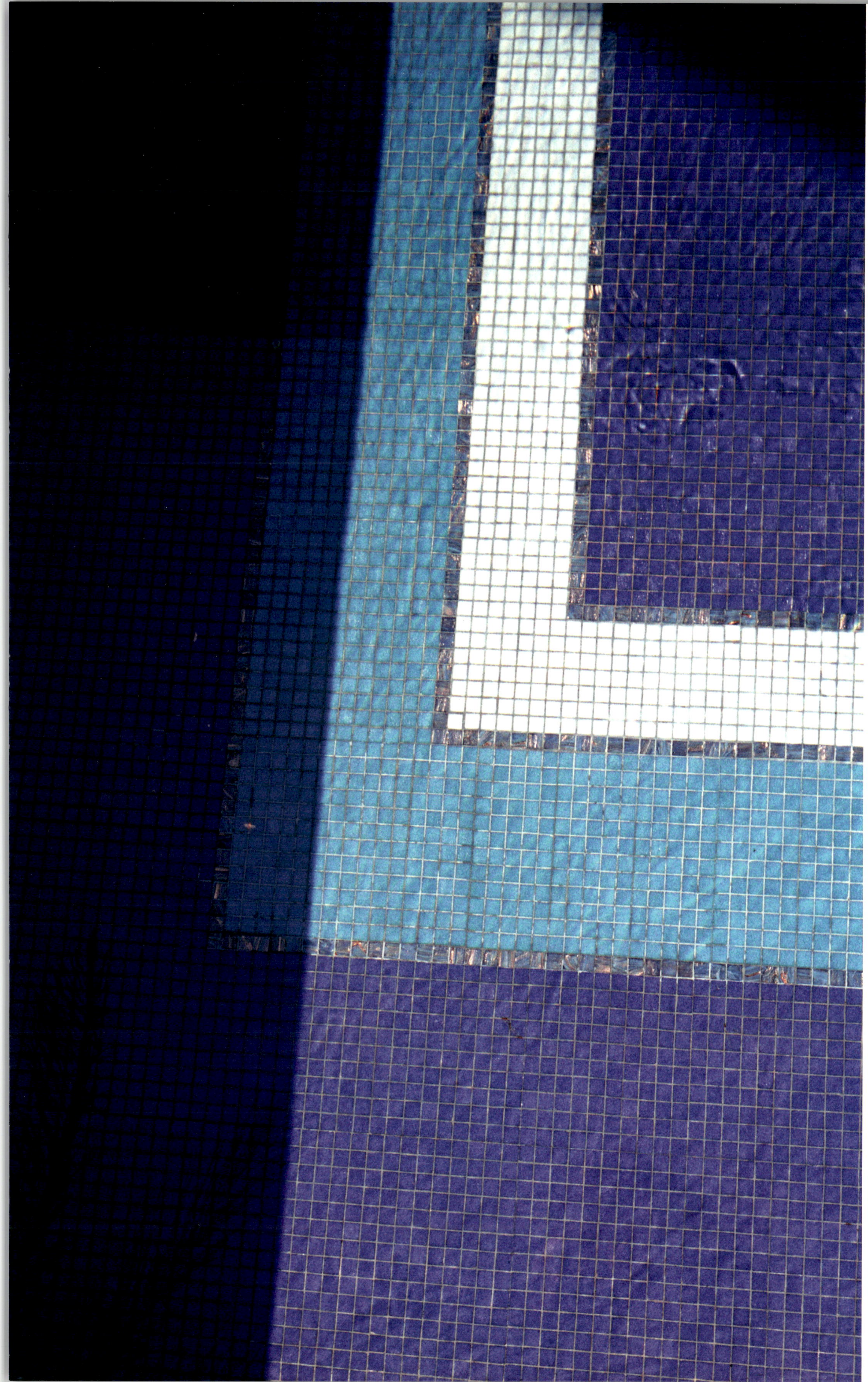

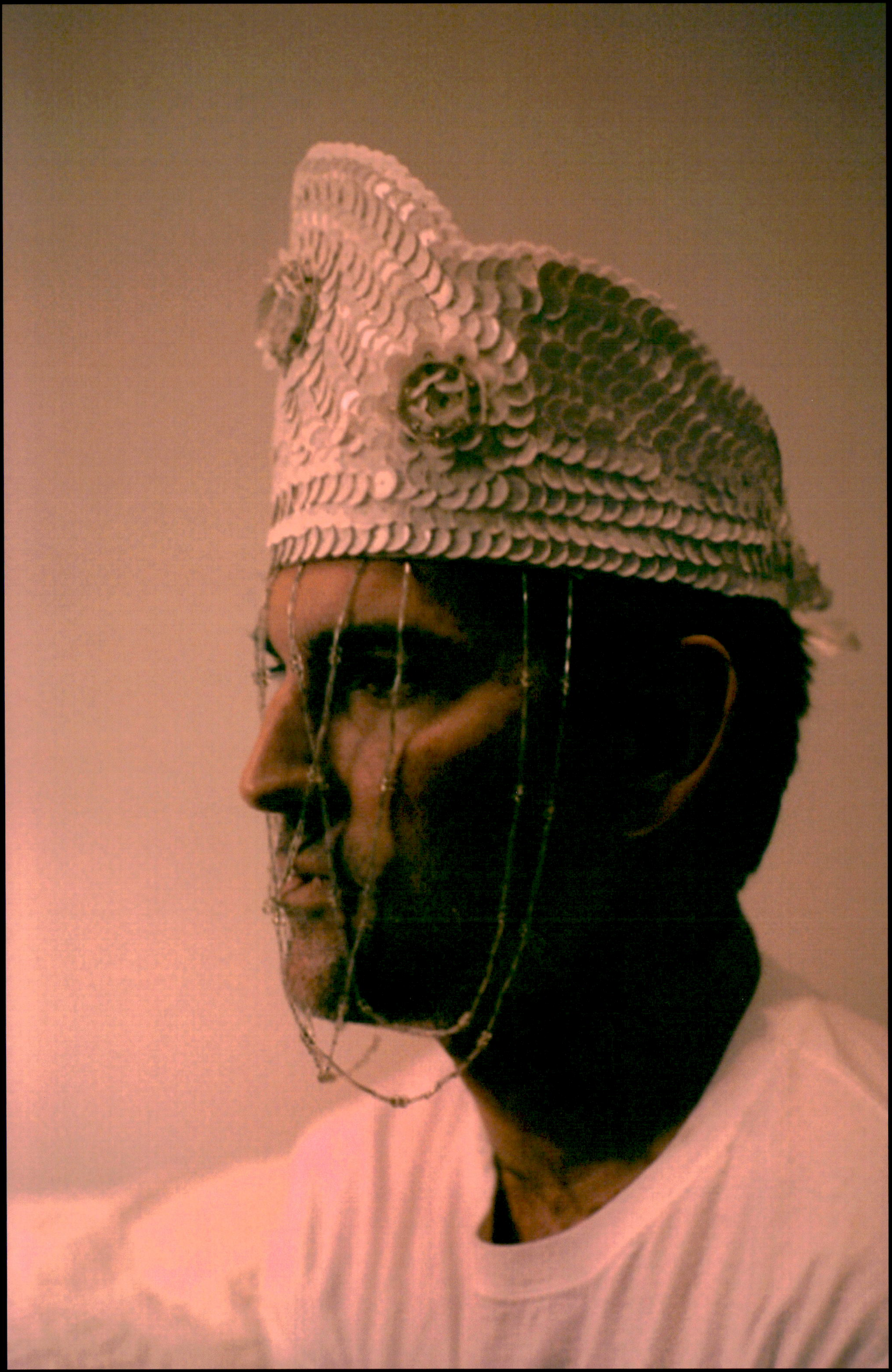

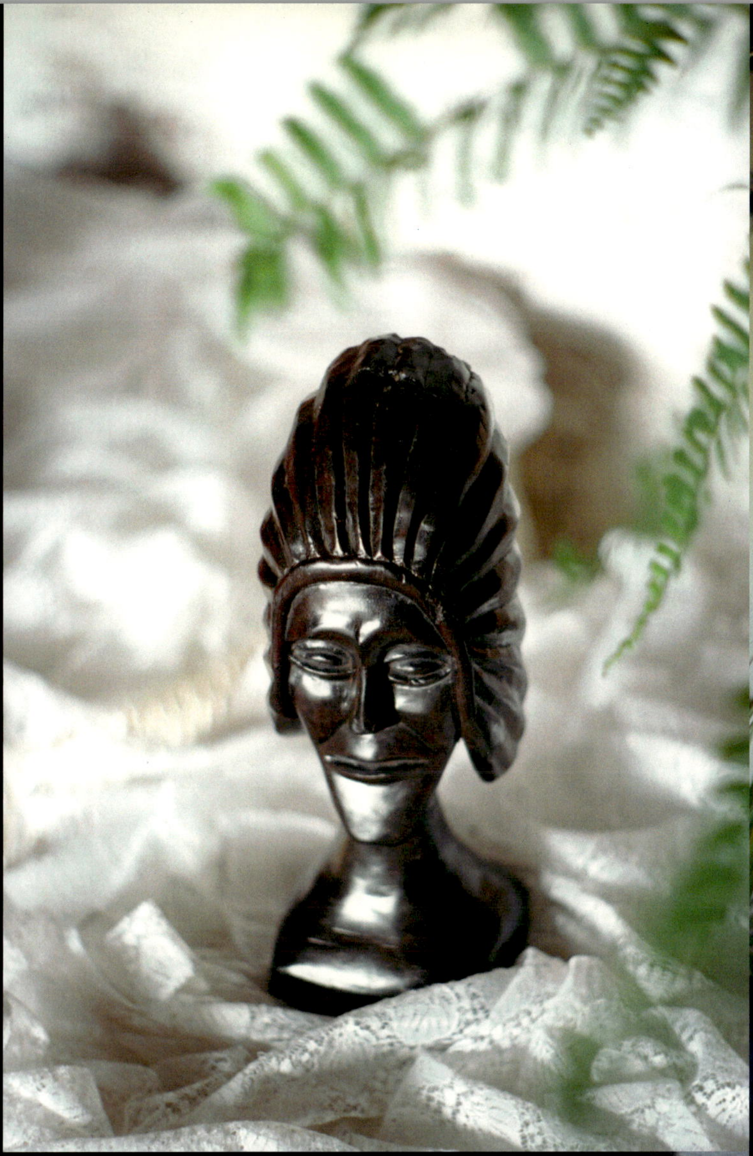
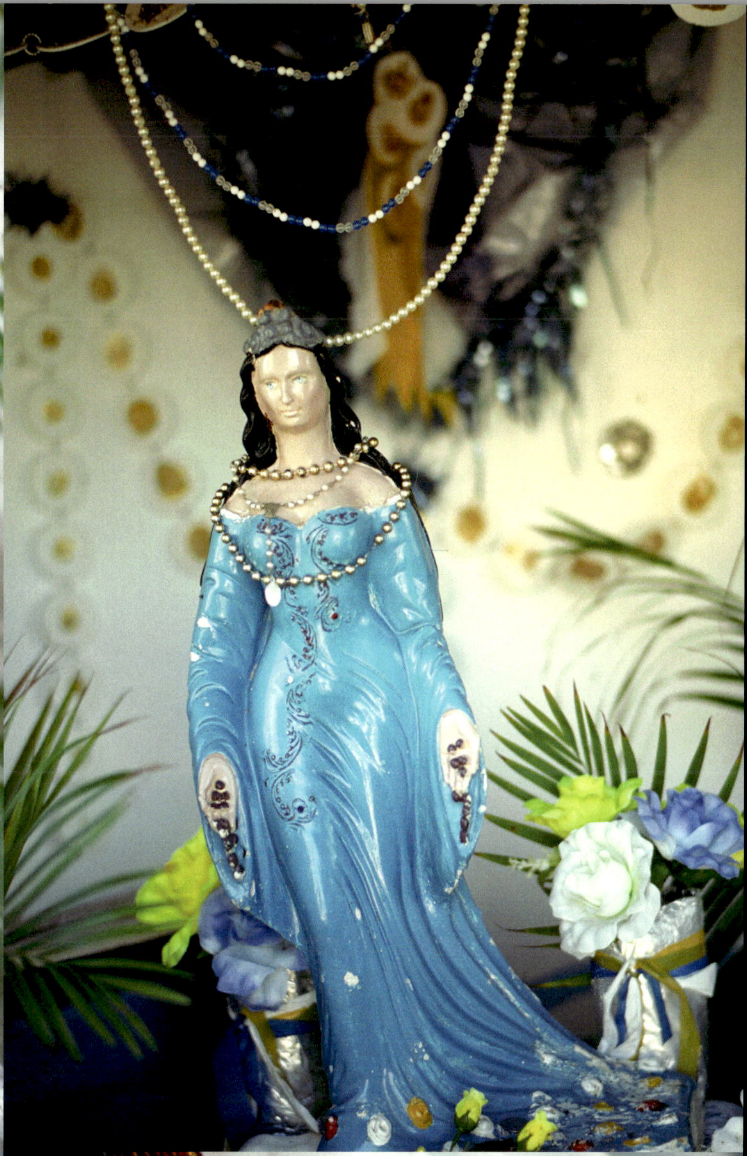
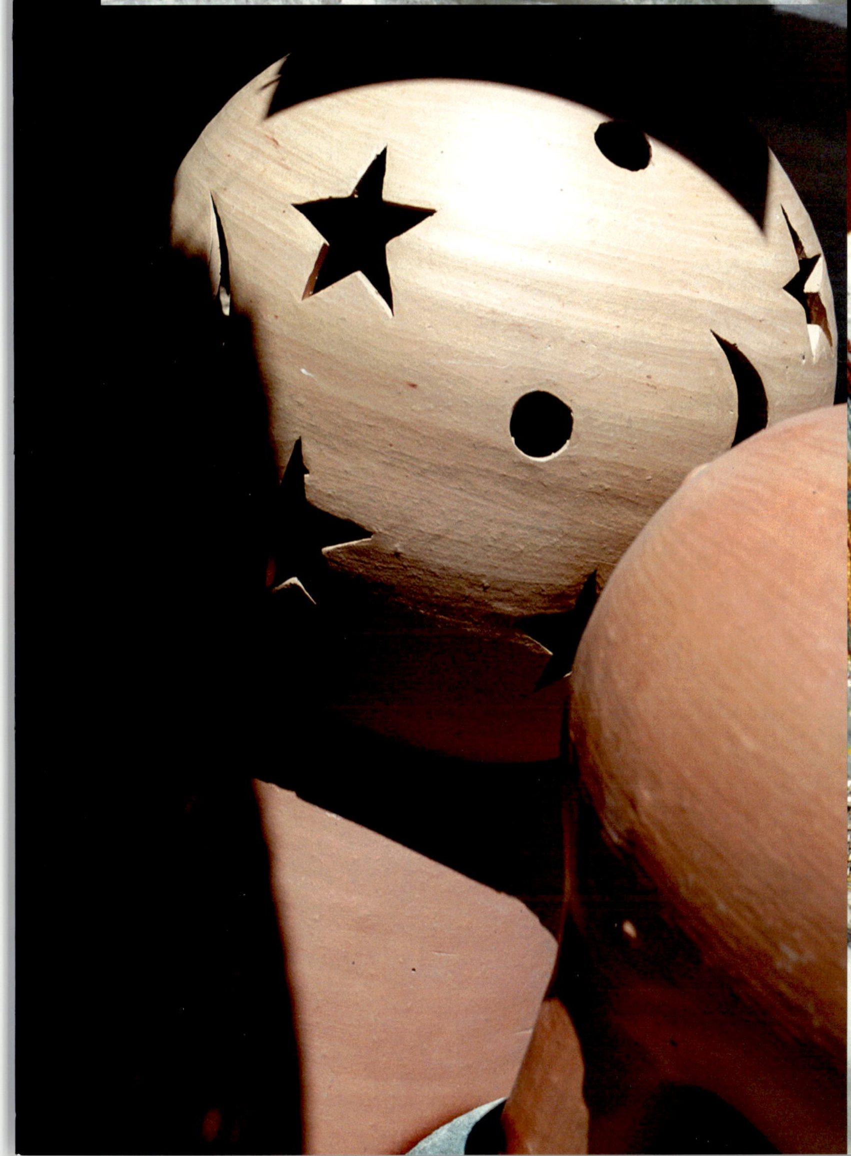
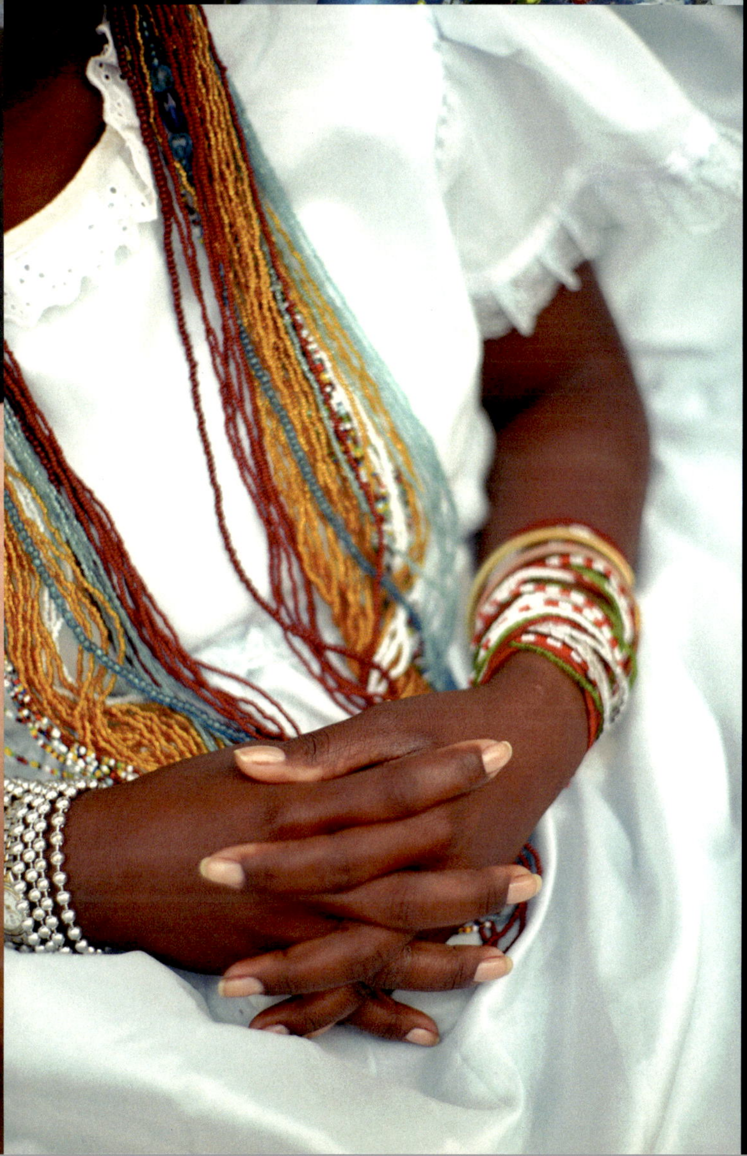

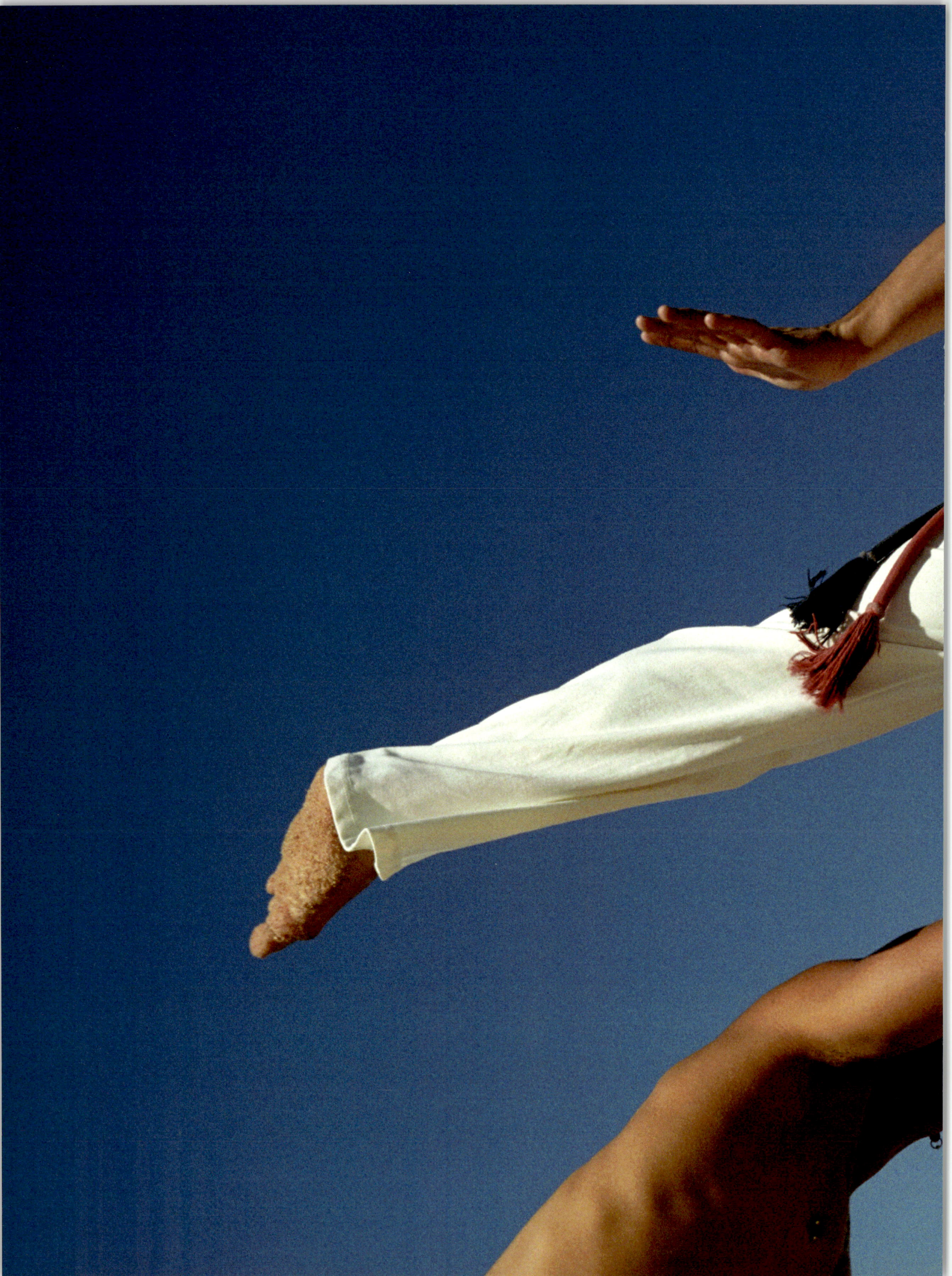

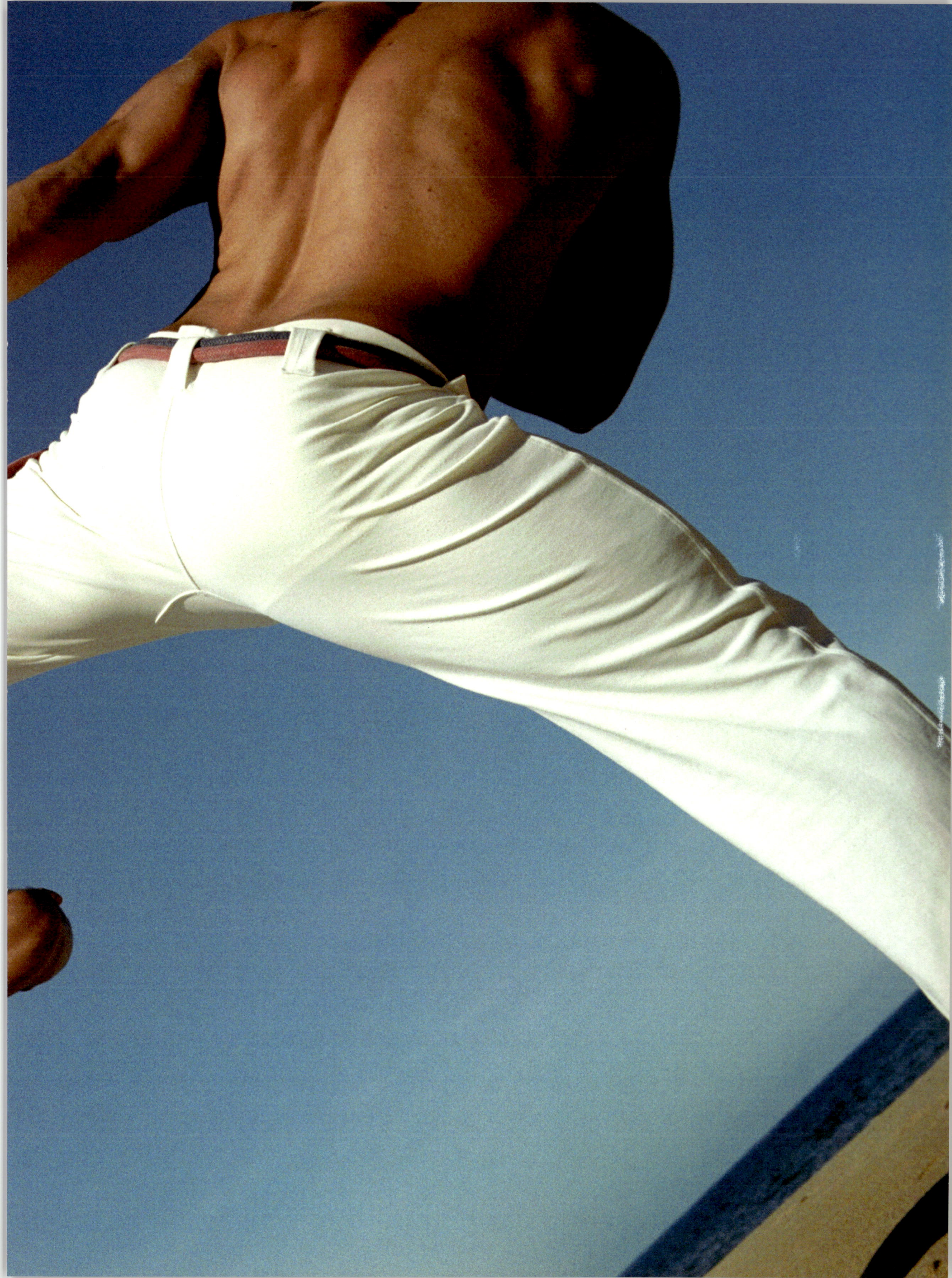

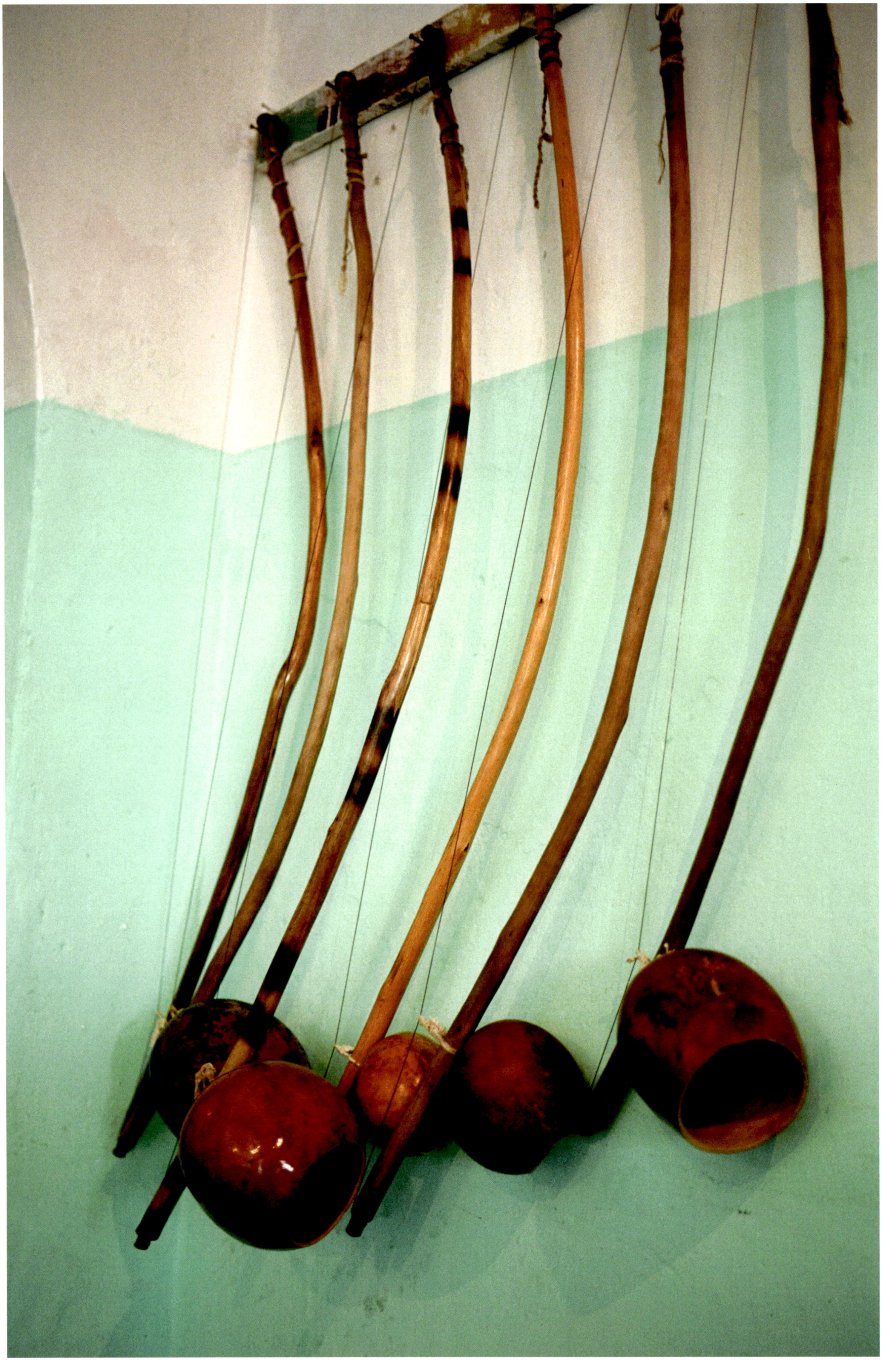

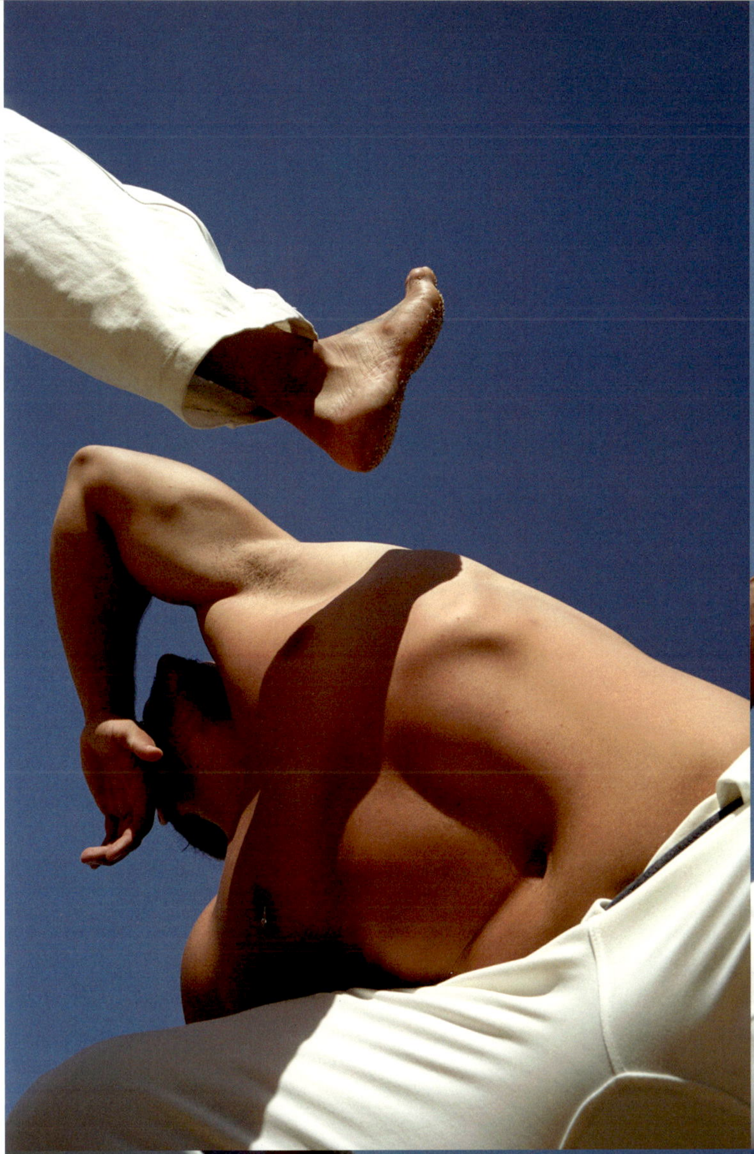
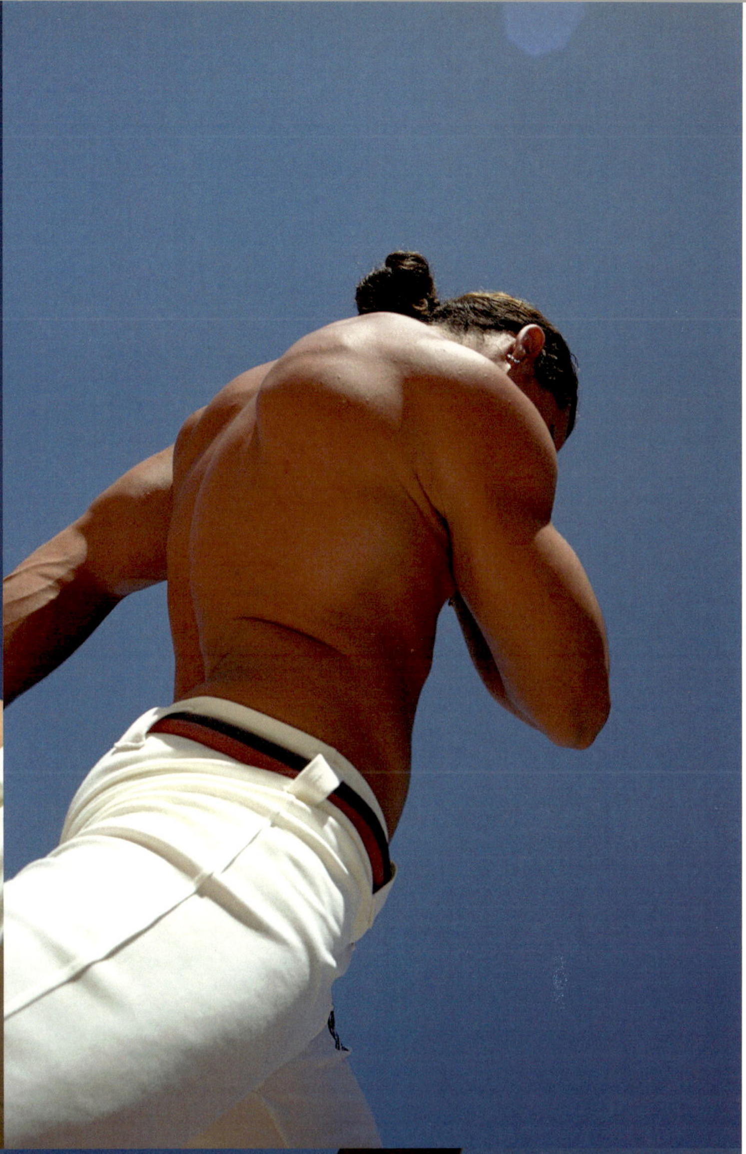
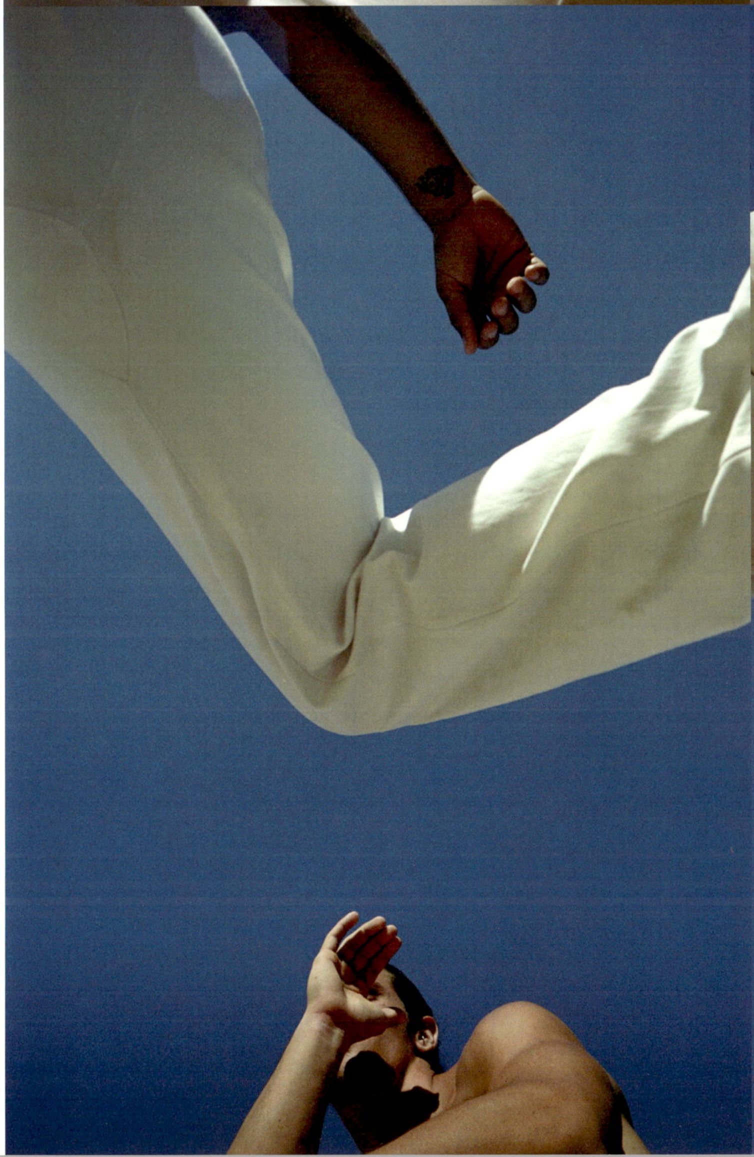
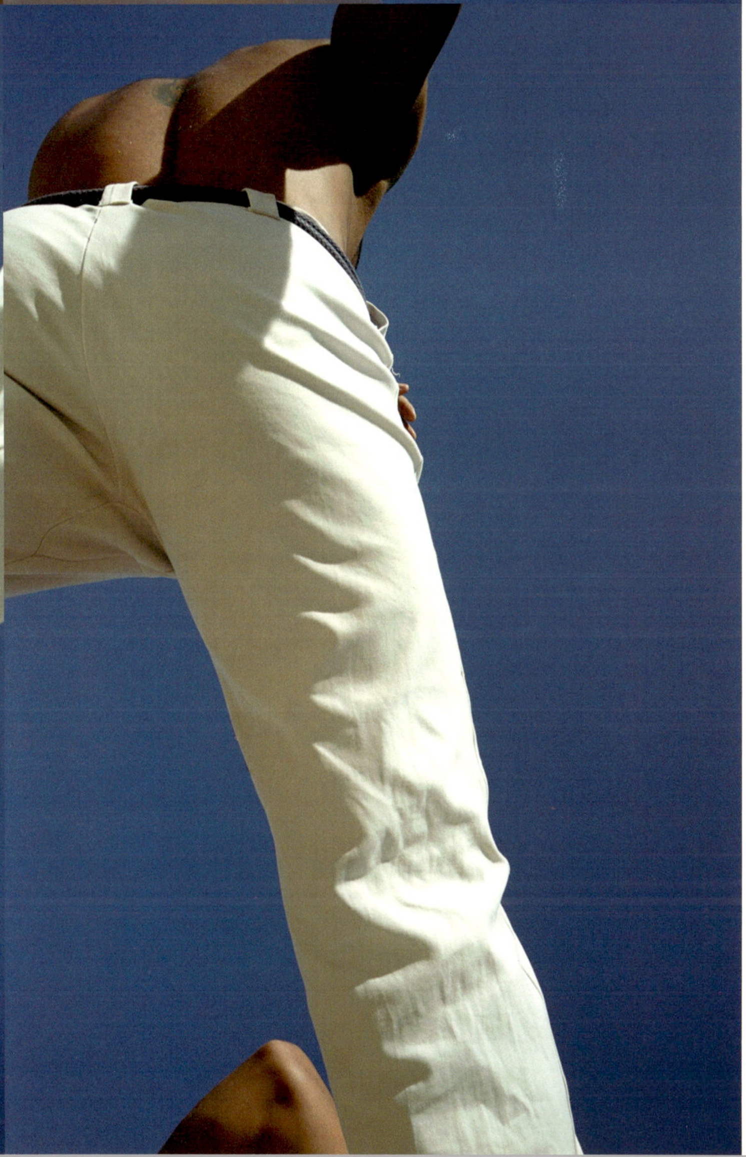

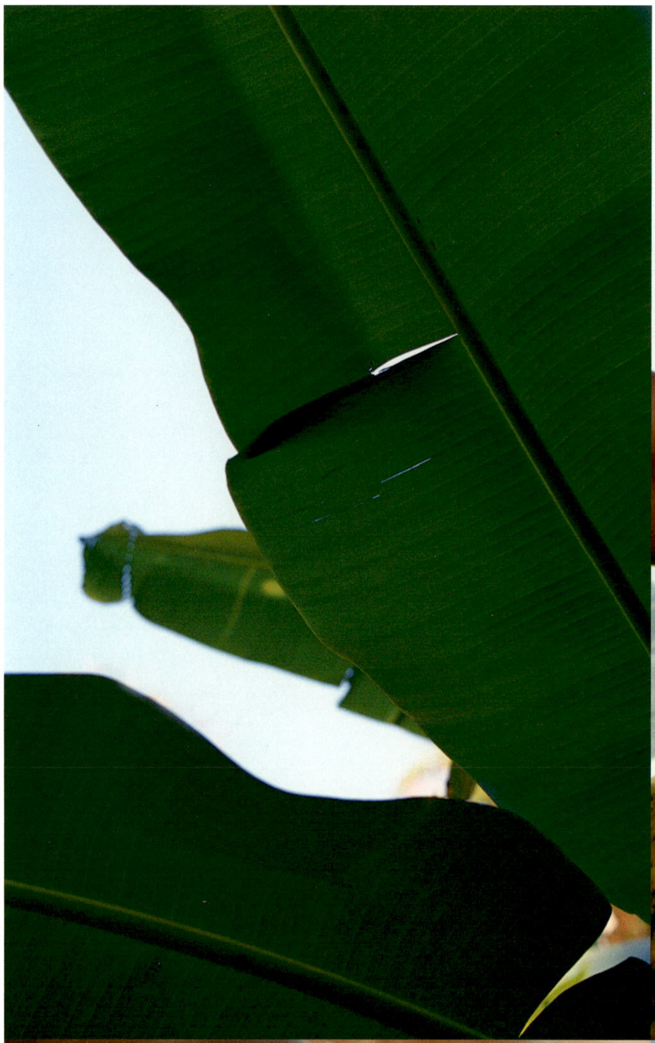

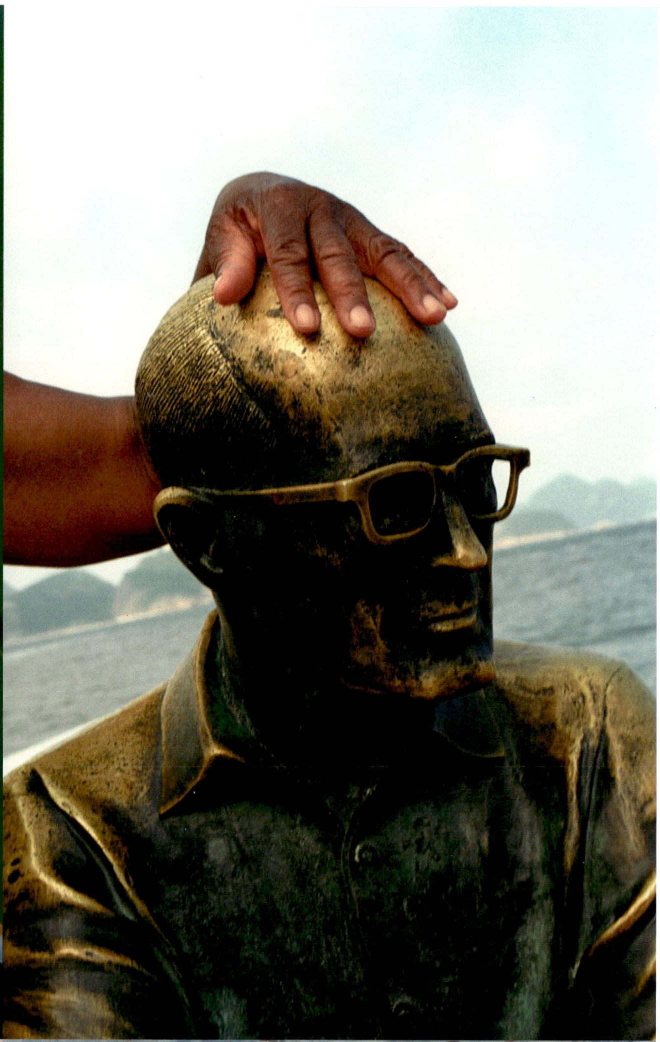

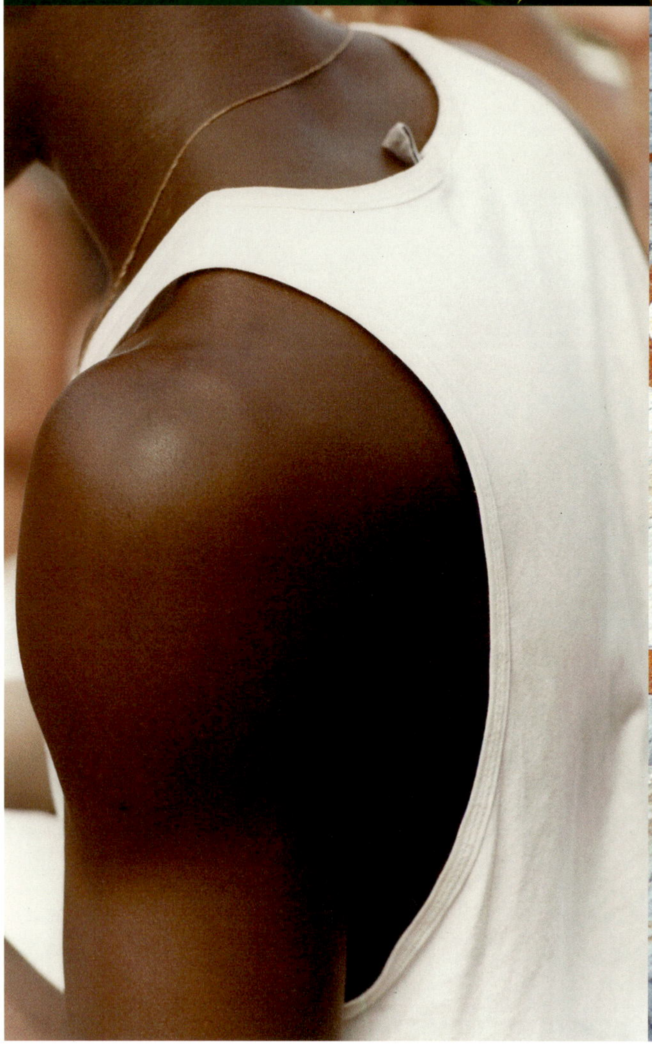

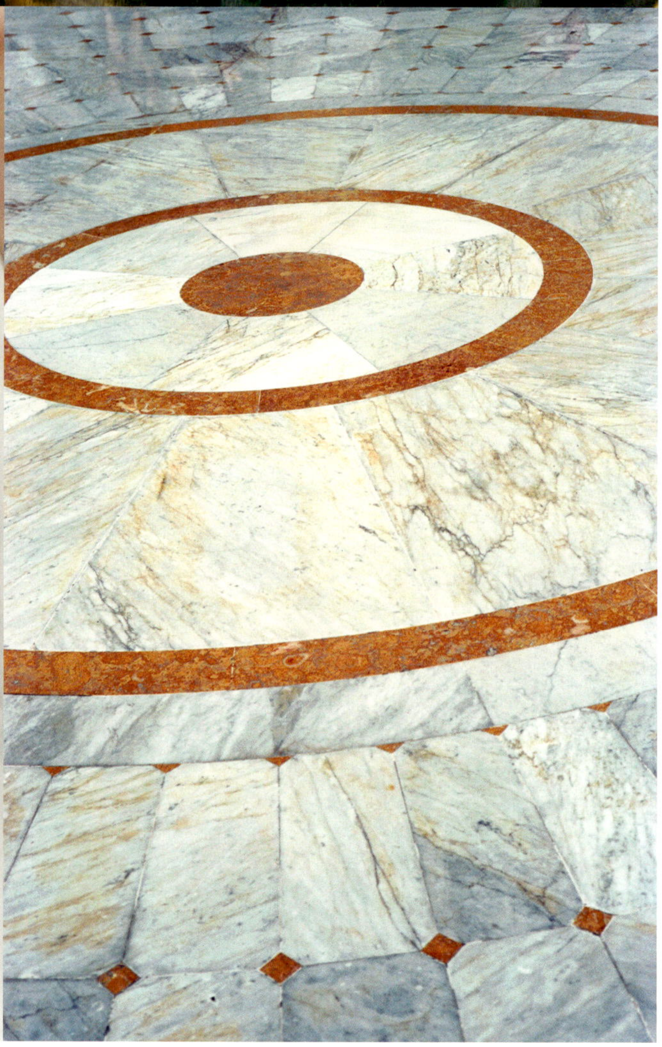

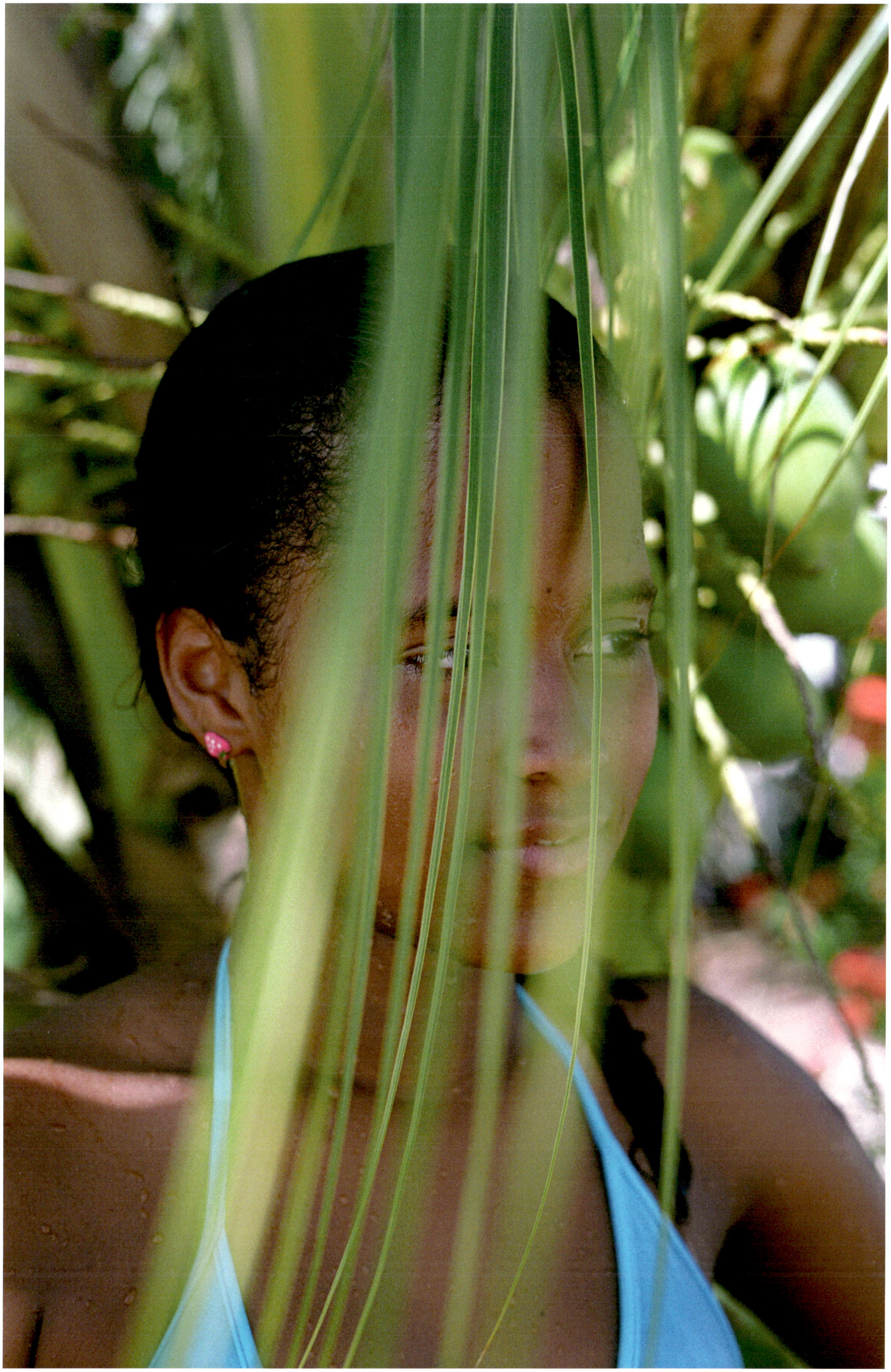

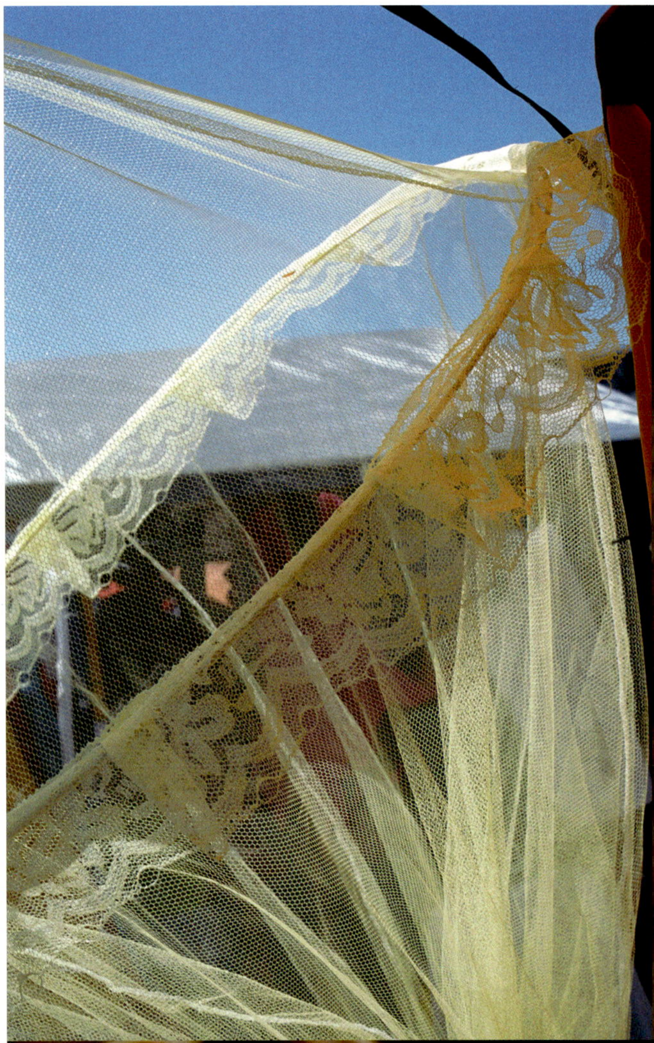
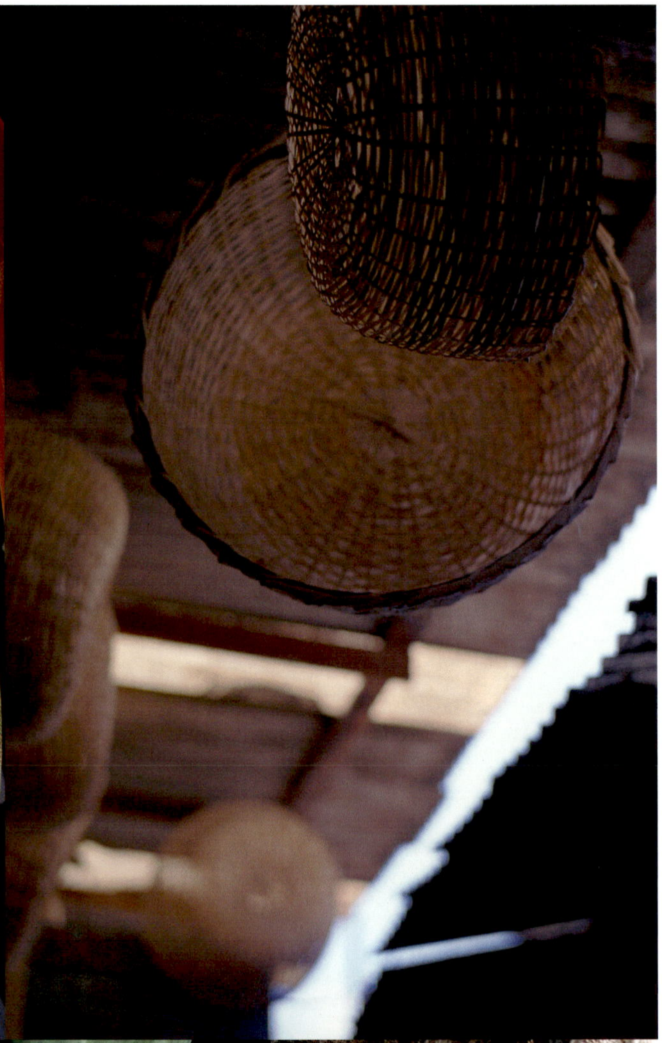
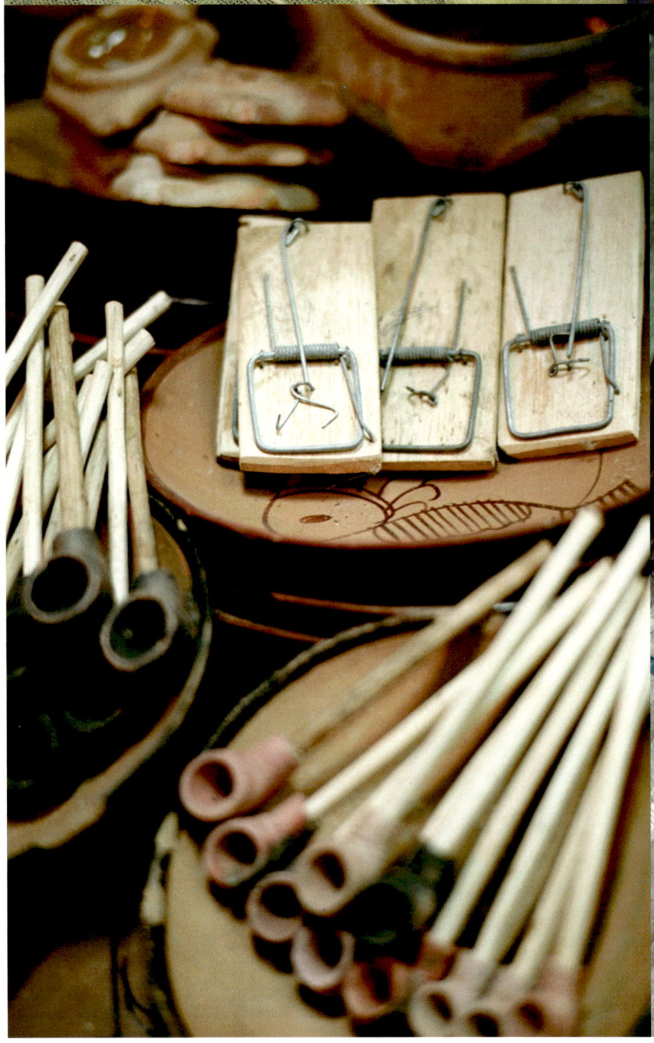
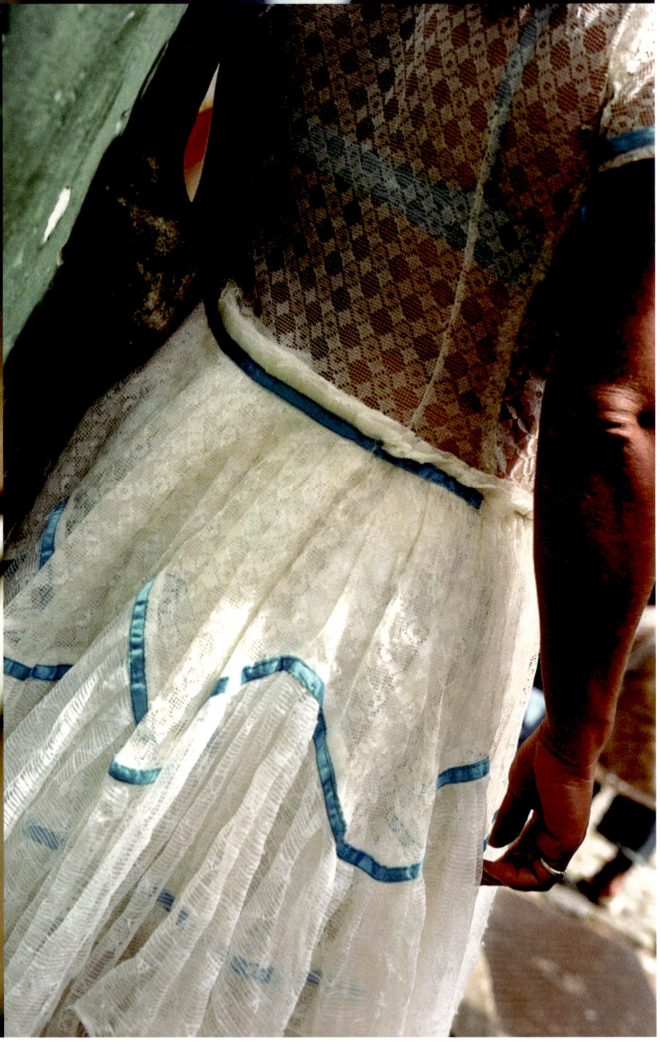

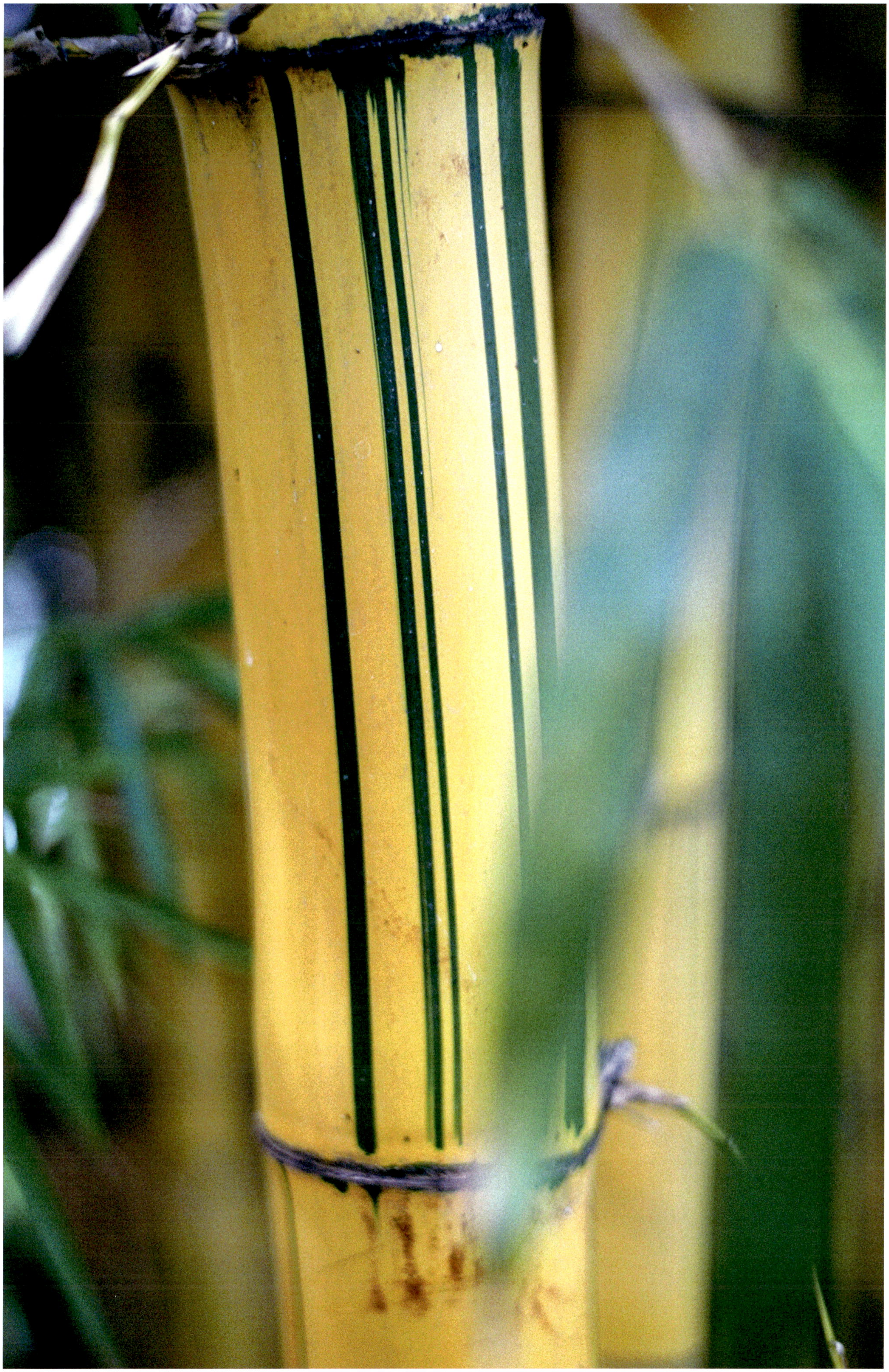

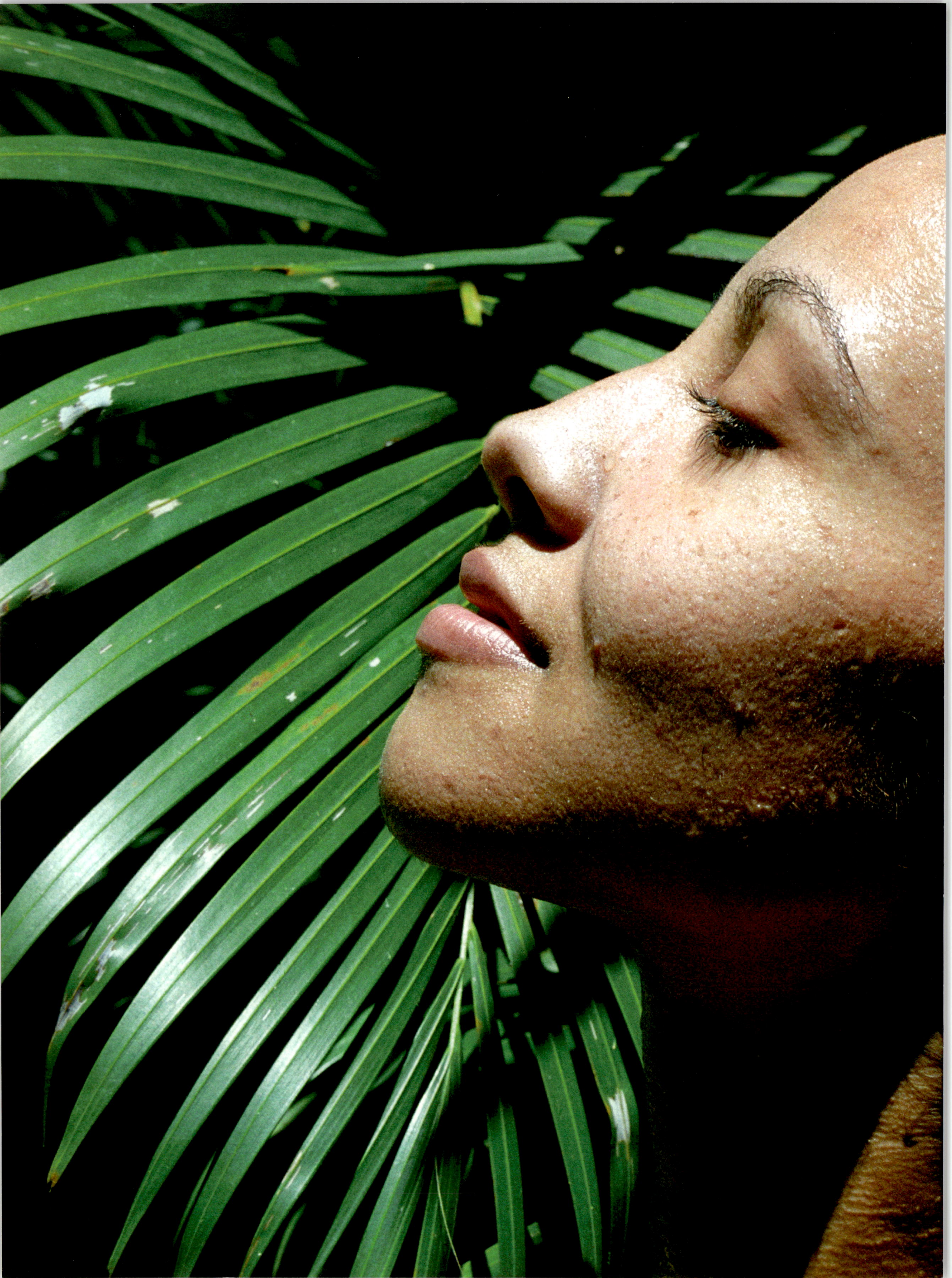

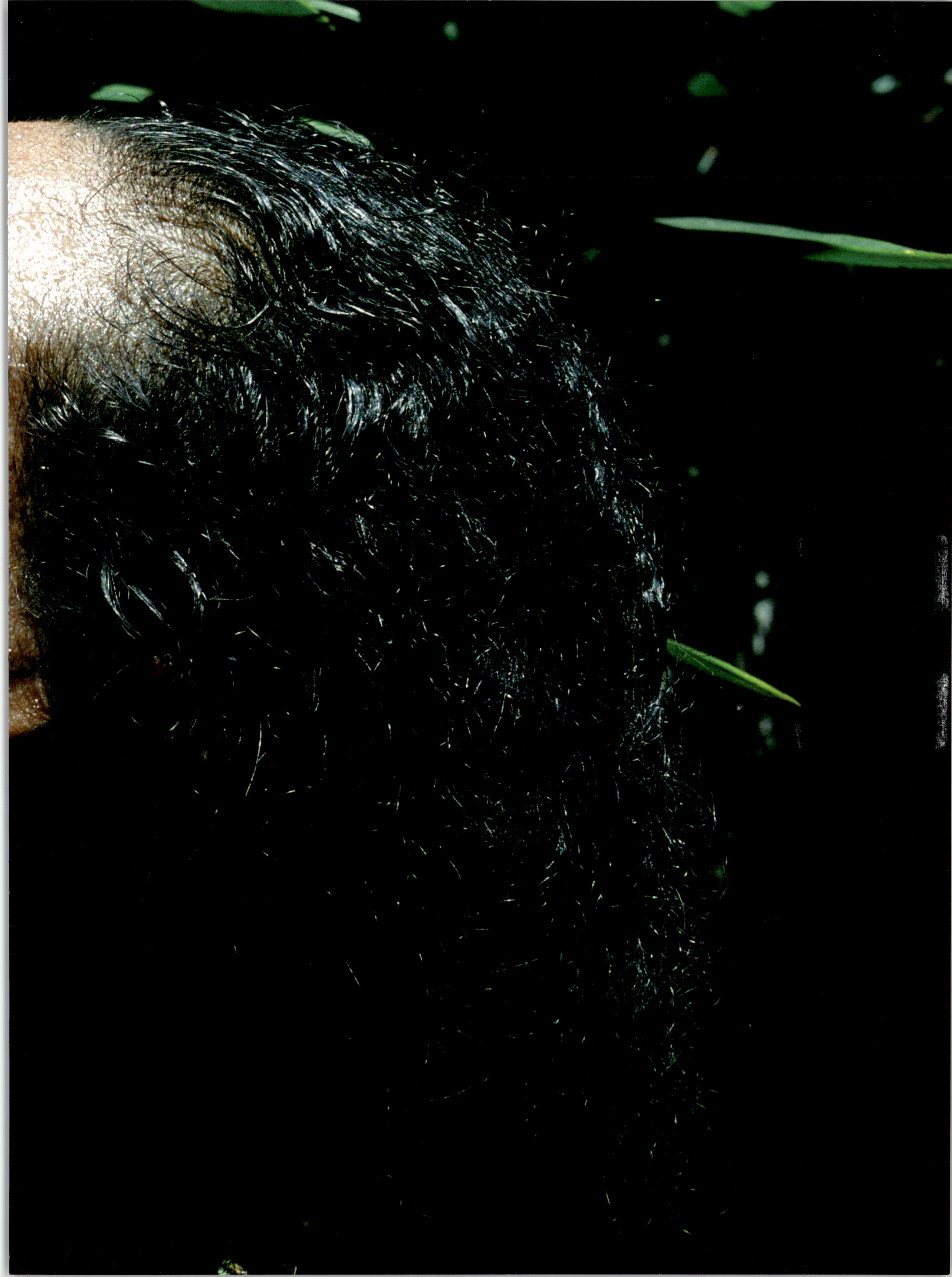

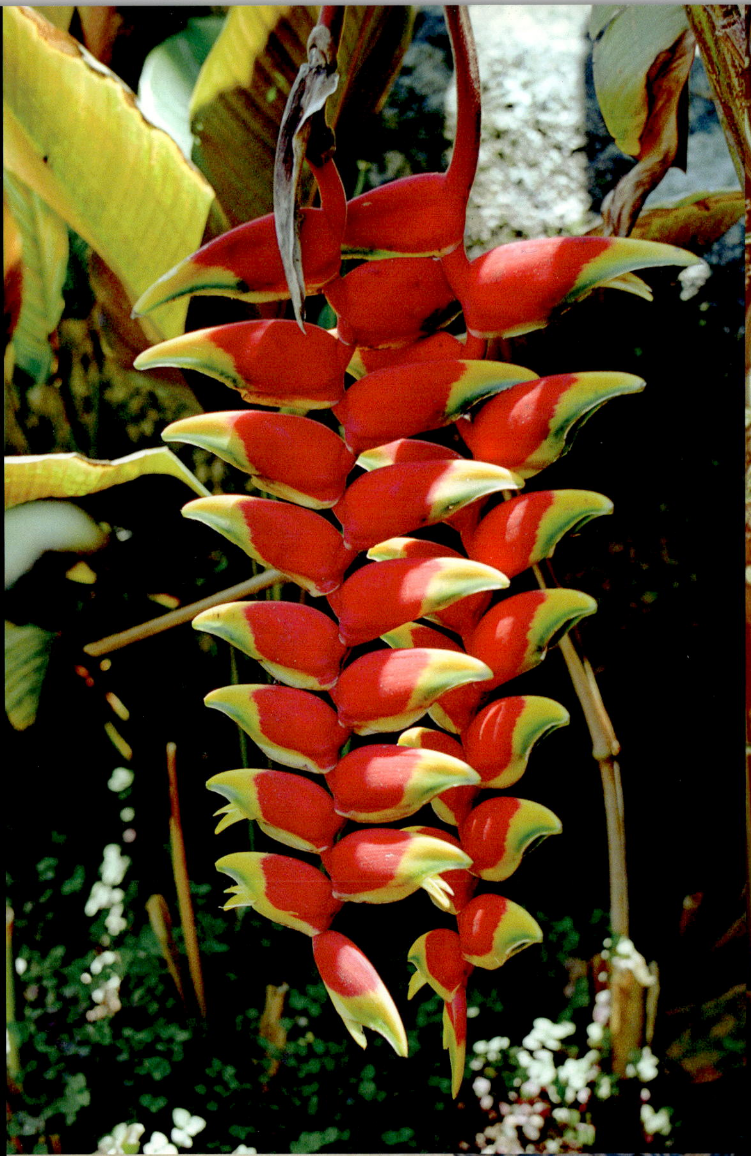
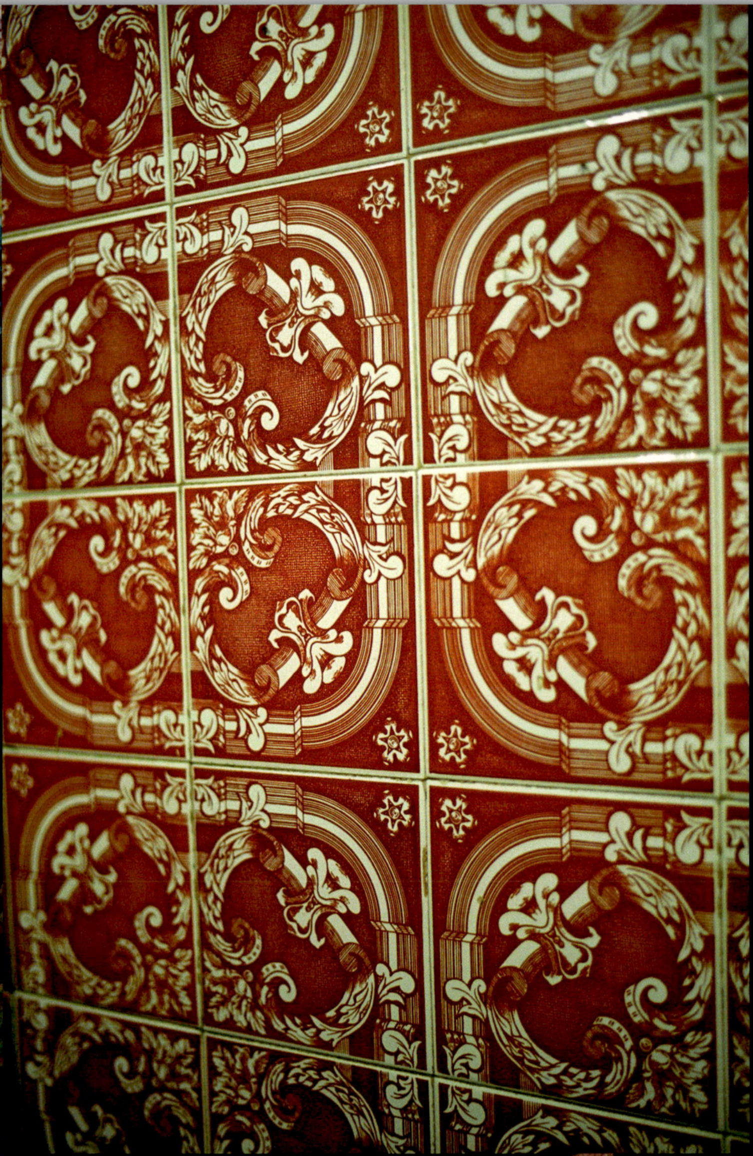
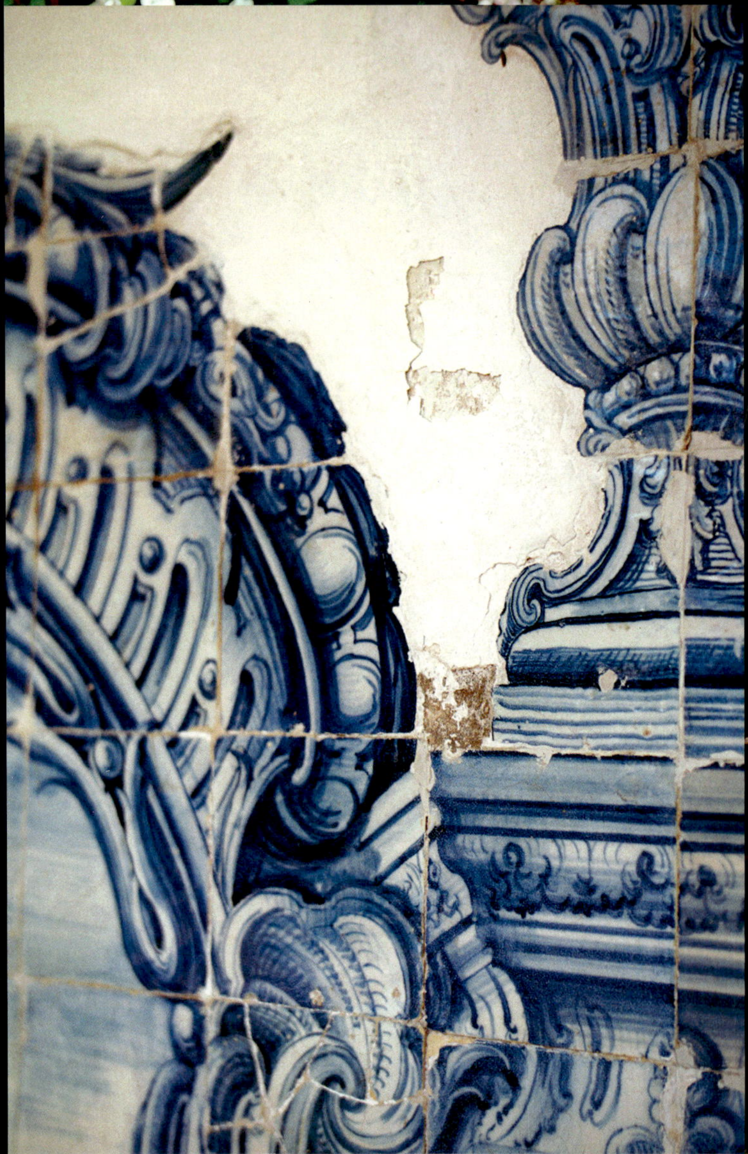
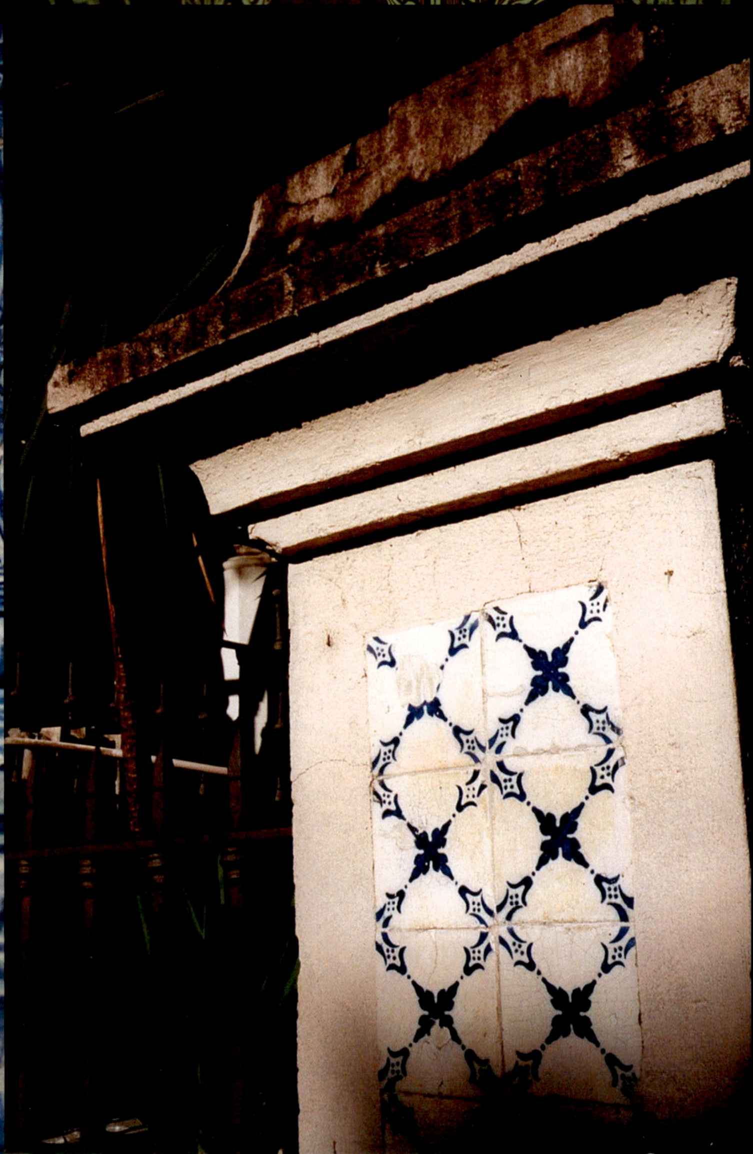

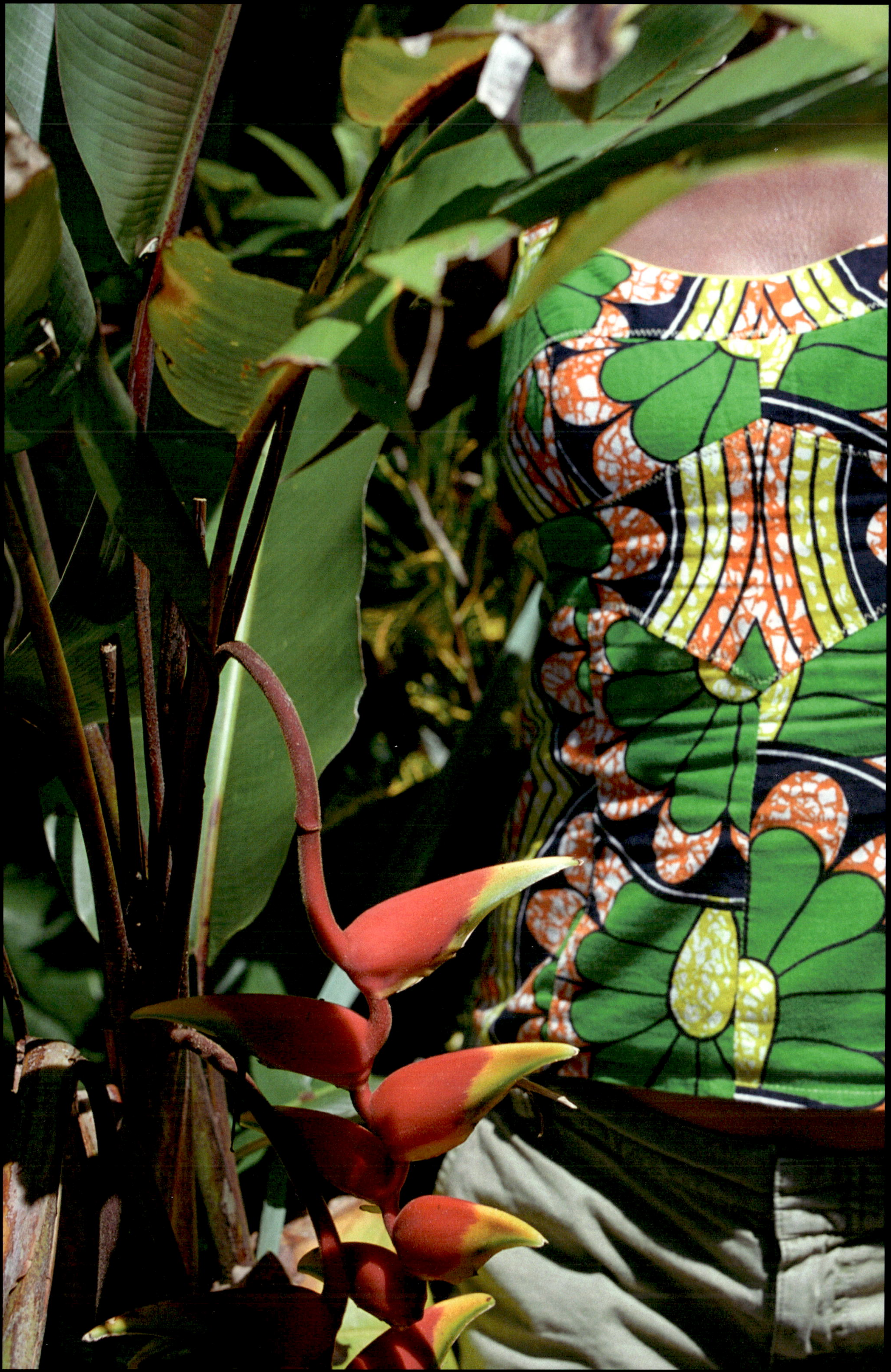

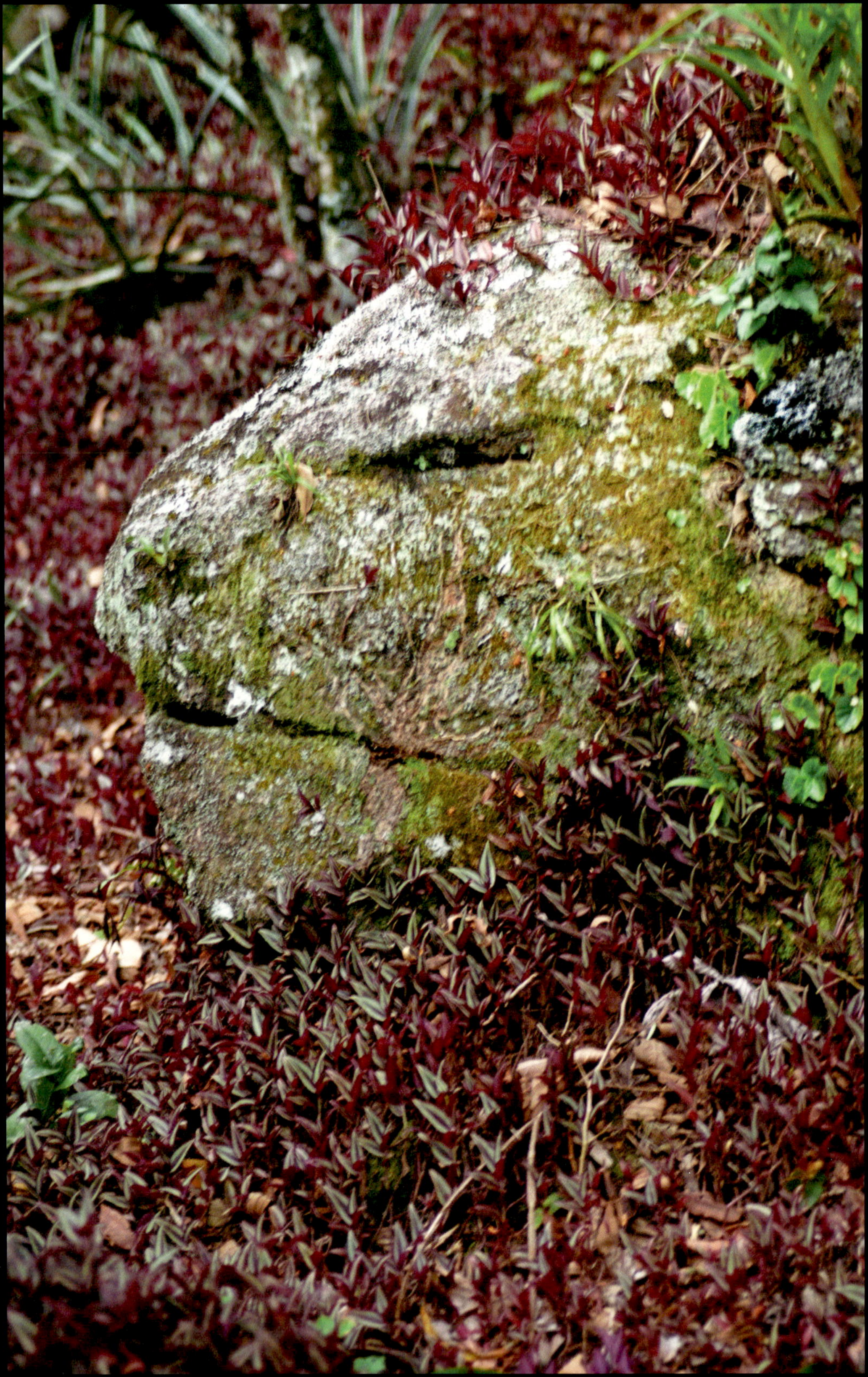

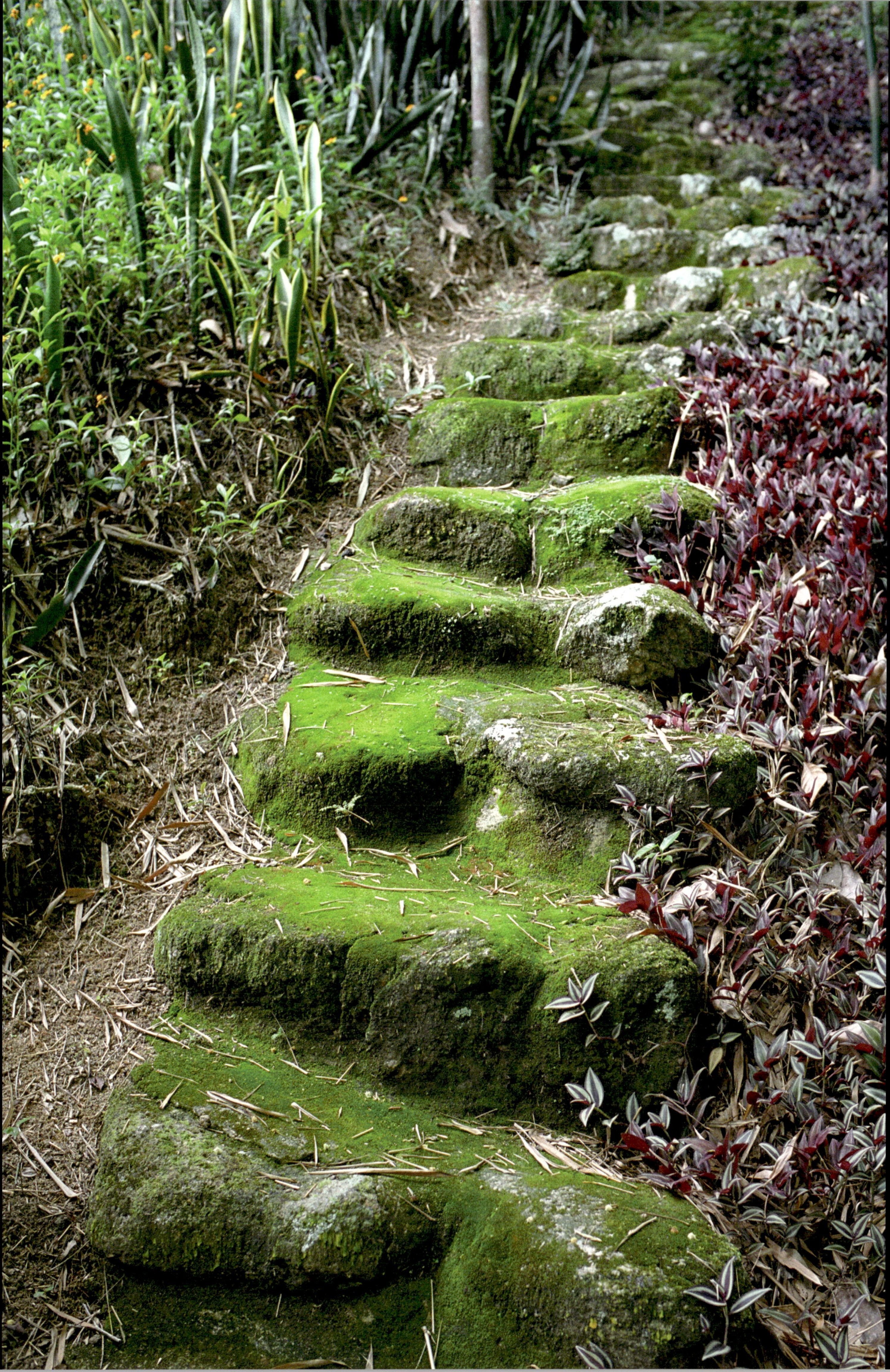

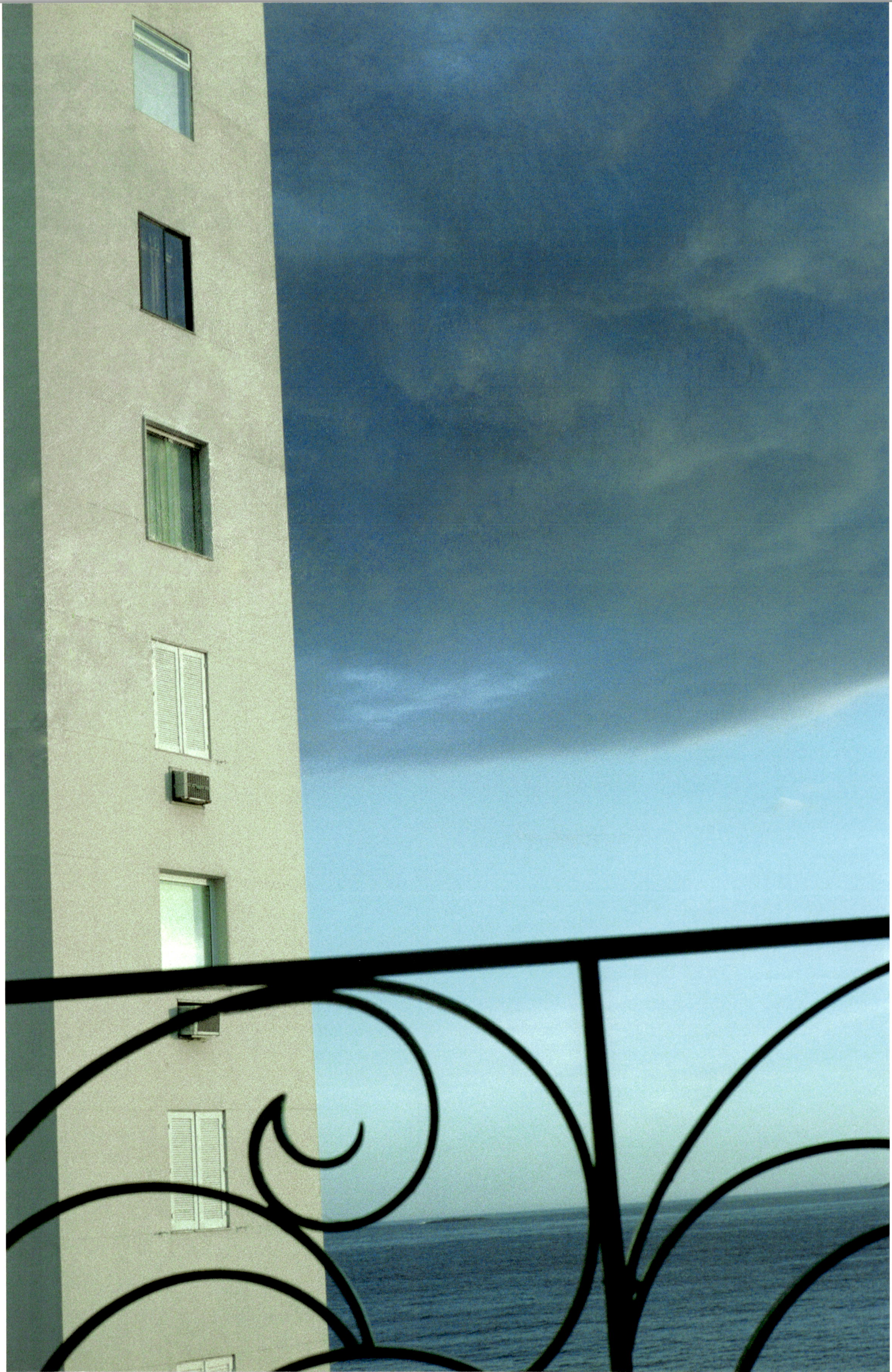

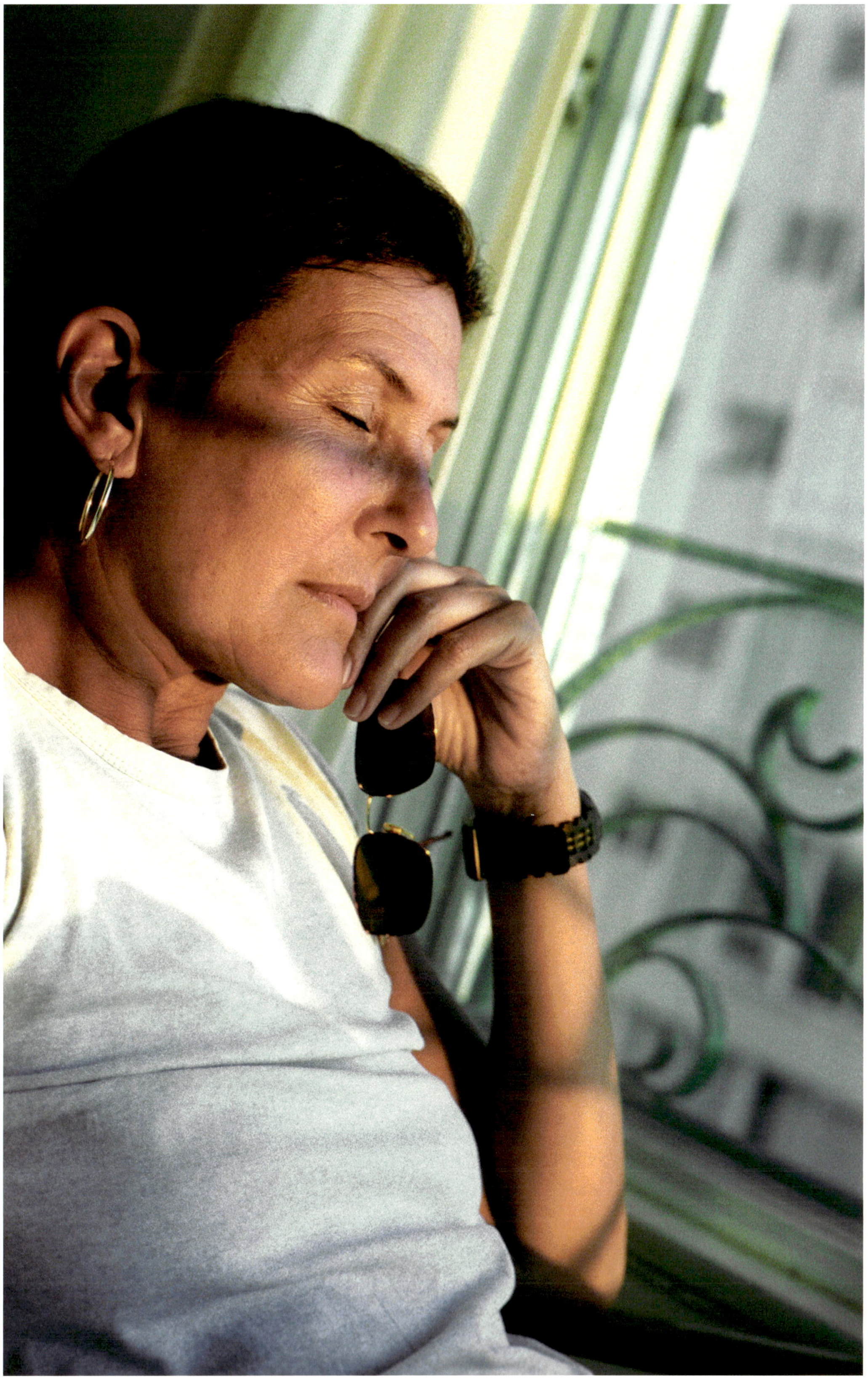

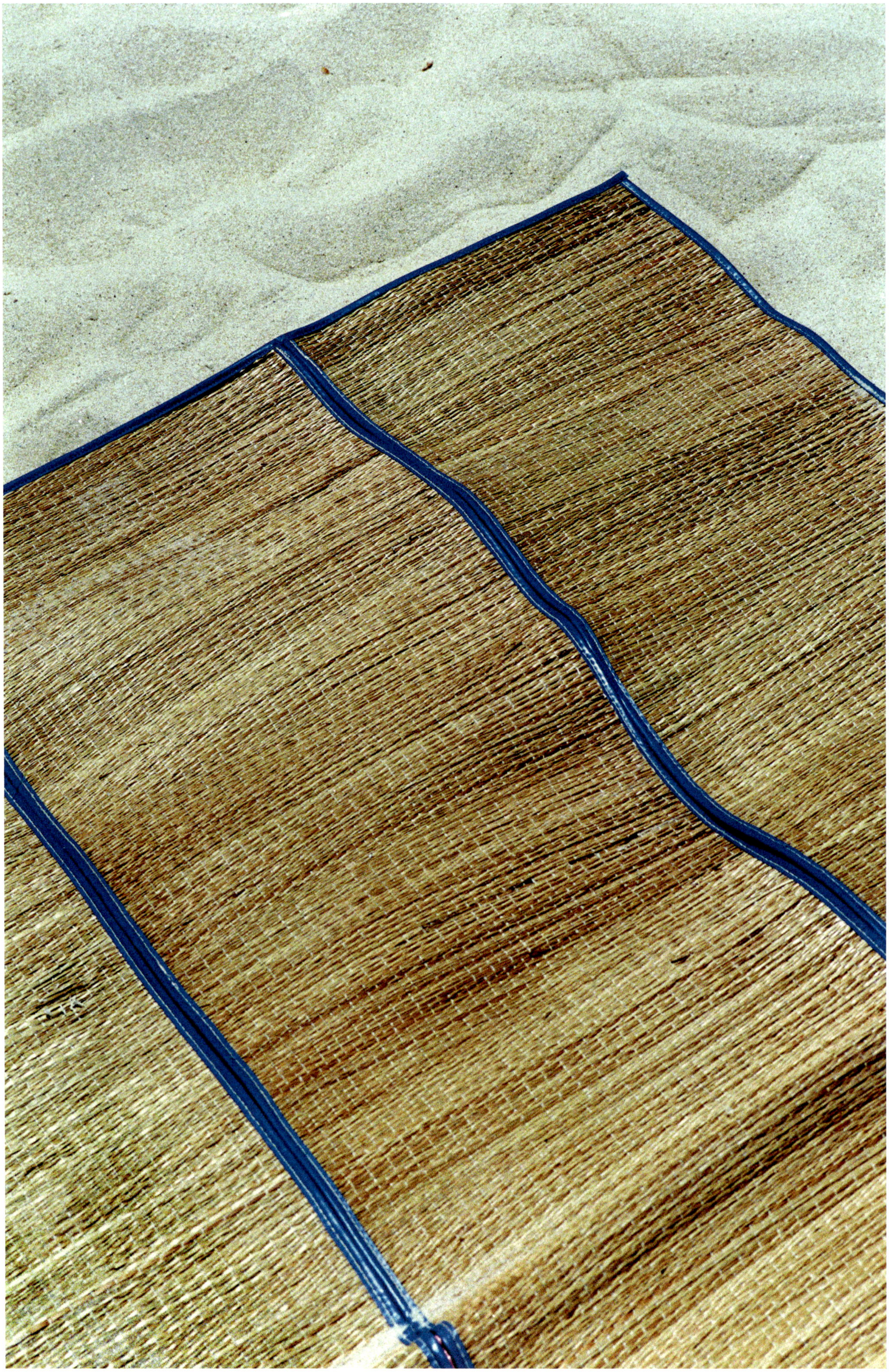

Mameluke

I am a leopard's dark spot
black on black and the snake
and the fish who will eat you

I am the fat man
400 years old
and the almond sweet girl
and the whore and the smell

I shall be the dance,
the point where the string plucks
the edge of the skin,
the night and the fear

I'll be mocqueca and plam heart
blood on the napkin to wipe the wine,
salt and sand for your tenderest part

Let me be a waiter or a dumb bodyguard
or maybe an evil hole in the highway
The night is my wife,
an old taxi or a dying horse

Don't lick those tears
Bathe your tongue in coco-bolo water sex

I love the breeze that inhales my destiny
in and out of the hardest wood in the forrest

I am the end of an un-written poem,
a yet born rhythm

It's only natural that the homeless and the landless
have no place to march
They bathe alone empty handed
hungry for less freedom from nothing

RALPH GIBSON

Born / Nato	January 16th, 1939, Los Angeles, California
Studio	13 -17 Laight Street, New York, N.Y., 10013
WEB SITE	www.ralphgibson.com
CONTACT	lustrum@pipeline.com

Awards / Onoreficenze

2002	Decorated Commandeur de l'Ordre des Arts et des Lettres, France
2000	Silver Plumb for Exellence, The Design Trust for Public Space, New York
1997	Honorary Doctor of Fine Arts, Ohio Wesleyan University
1994	Medal of the City of Arles, France
1991	Honorary Doctor of Fine Arts, University of Maryland
1989	Eastman Kodak Grant to photograph, *L'HISTOIRE DE FRANCE* "150 Years of Photography" Award, Photographic Society of Japan
1988	Leica Medal of Excellence Award
1986	Decorated, Officier de l'Ordre des Arts et des Lettres de France National Endowment for the Arts Fellowship
1985	John Simon Guggenheim Memorial Fellowship
1977	D.A.A.D., West Berlin, Germany C.A.P.S., New York State Council of the Arts
1975	National Endowment for the Arts Fellowship
1973	National Endowment for the Arts Fellowship

Books by the Artist / Pubblicazioni

2005	*BRAZIL,* Damiani, Bologna *PIEMONTE,* Agarttharte, Torino *REFRACTIONS,* Ed. Steidl,Gottingen, Maison Européene de la Photographie, Paris
2004	*LIGHT STRINGS,* Chronicle Books, San Francisco
2001	*EX LIBRIS,* powerHouse Books, New York
1999	*DEUS EX MACHINA,* Taschen, Cologne
1998	*COURANT CONTINU,* Marval, Paris *OVERTONES,* Ed. Stemmle,AG, Zurich *ERIC FISCHL: SCULPTURE,* Gagosian Gallery, New York
1996	*LICHT JAHRE,* Ed. Stemmle.AG, Zurich
1995	*INFANTA,* Takarajima, New York and Tokyo *PHARAONIC LIGHT,* Guild Hall, Southhampton, New York
1994	*THE SPIRIT OF BURGUNDY,* Aperture, New York *L'AIRE DE BOURGOGNE,* Altinea, Paris *TROPICAL DRIFT,* The Murray and Isabella Rayburn Foundation, New York
1993	*WOMEN,* Boca Raton Museum of Art
1992	*BOOKWORKS,* Ed. Galerie Antoine Candau, Paris
1991	*L'HISTOIRE DE FRANCE,* Aperture, New York; Paris-Audiovisuel, France
1990	*APROPOS DE MARY JANE,* Cahiers des Images, France *CHIAROSCURO,* Ed. Marval, Paris
1988	*LES CAHIERS DE LA PHOTOGRAPHIE #22,* Contrajour, Paris Navarin, France *ARCHIVE 24, RALPH GIBSON : EARLY WORK,* Center for Creative Photography, Arizona
1987	*TROPISM,* Aperture, New York; Alinari, Florence
1986	*L'ANONYME,* Aperture, New York; Contrejour, Paris

1983	*SYNTAX*, Lustrum Press, New York
1975	*DAYS AT SEA*, Lustrum Press, New York
1973	*DEJA VU*, Lustrum Press, New York
1970	*THE SOMNAMBULIST*, Lustrum Press, New York
1968	*THE HAWK*, Bobbs-Merrill, New York
1967	*THE STRIP* Roger Kennedy Graphics, Los Angeles
1966	*A.C.L.U. Appointment Calendar*, Los Angeles

Selected One-Man Exhibitions / Mostre Personali Selezionate

2005	The Castello di Rivoli, Turin, Italy
2004	The Norton Museum of Art, Palm Beach, Florida The Ross Museum, Ohio Wesleyan University, Delaware, OH
2003	Moscow House of Photography, Russia
2002	Galerie LWS , Paris France
2001	Center for Creative Photogtpahy, University of Arizona, Tucson Kerava Art Museum, Kereva,Finland
1999	Maison Européenne de la Photographie, Paris, France
1998	Museum für Kunst Modern, Frankfurt a.M., Germany Greenville County Museum of Art, Greenville. S.C. Narodni Muzei Zadar, Croatia
1997	High Museum of Art, Atlanta, Georgia Albin O. Kuhn Library, University of Maryland,Baltimore, Spalova Gallery, Prague, Czechoslovakia
1996	Whitney Museum of American Art, New York City Leo Castelli, New York City Frankfurter Kunstverein, Germany
1995	Tampa Museum of Art, Florida Guild Hall Museum, East Hampton, New York

Selected Public Collections / Mostre Collettive Selezionate

Whitney Museum of American Art, New York
Metropolitan Museum of Art, New York
Museum of Modern Art, New York
The Guggenheim Museum of Art, New York
High Museum of Art, Atlanta
Maison Europeénne de la Photographie, Paris, France
Castello di Rivoli, Turin, Italy
Bibliotheque National, Paris
National Gallery of Ottawa
Pasadena Art Museum, California
International Museum of Photography at George Eastman House, Rochester, New York
Visual Studies Workshop, Rochester, New York
Seattle Art Museum, Volunteer Park, Washington
Fogg Art Museum, Boston
Center for Creative Photography, Tuscon, Arizona

Australian National Gallery, Canberra, Australia
Smithsonian Institution, Washington, D.C.
National Gallery of Victoria, Australia
The Clevland Museum of Art, Ohio
Dallas Museum of Art, Texas
John Simon Guggenheim Memorial Foundation
Museum of Fine Arts, Houston, Texas
Musee Reattu, Arles, France
San Francisco Museum of Modern Art, California
Virginia Museum of Fine Art, Richmond, Virginia
Museum fur Kunst und Gewerbe, Hamburg, West Germany
Stedelijk Museum, Amsterdam
Museum Ludwig, Cologne, Germany
The Rupertinum, Salzburg, Austria
New Orleans Museum of Art, Louisiana
Fotografiska Museet, Stockholm
Atkins Museum of Fine Art, Kansas City, Missouri
Israel Museum, Tel Aviv
Jerusalem Museum, Israel
The Microsoft Collection, Seattle, Washington
Fashion Institute of Technology, New York
Ruttenberg Arts Foundation, Chicago
Chase Manhattan Bank, New York
Santa Barbara Museum of Art, California
John & Mable Ringling Museum, Sarasota, Florida
J.B. Speed Museum, Louisville, Kentucky
The Jewish Musuem, New York CIty
The National Museum of Modern Art, Tokyo
Yokohama Museum, Japan
Readers Digest, New York
Willkie, Farr and Gallagher, New York
Boca Raton Museum of Art, Florida
Los Angeles County Museum of Art,
Museo Fratelli Alinari, Florence
Museum of Fine Arts, Saint Petersburg, Florida
Metropolitan Museum of Art, Tokyo
The Cleveland Museum of Art, Ohio
Expo Photo Museum, Osaka, Japan
Musee de la Photographie, Charleroi,Belgium
Akron Art Museum, Ohio
The Art Institute of Chicago
H.F. Johnson Museum, Cornell University, Ithaca, New York
The Minneapolis Institute of Art, Minnesota
The Norton Museum of Art, Palm Beach, Florida
Fundacion Cultural televisa, Mexico
Atkins Museum of Fine Arts, Kansas City, Missouri
The Saint Louis Art Museum, Saint Louis, Missouri
Hood Museum, Dartmouth, Hanover, New Hampshire
Library of Congress, Washington, D.C.
American Friends of Jerusalem Museum, Israel
New Orleans Museum of Art, Lousiana
The Arts Club of Chicago
Galleria Civica di Modena, Italy
The Museum of Modern Art, Mexico City
The Brooklyn Museum of Art, New York
The Cooper Union, New York
The Museum of Fine Arts, Boston

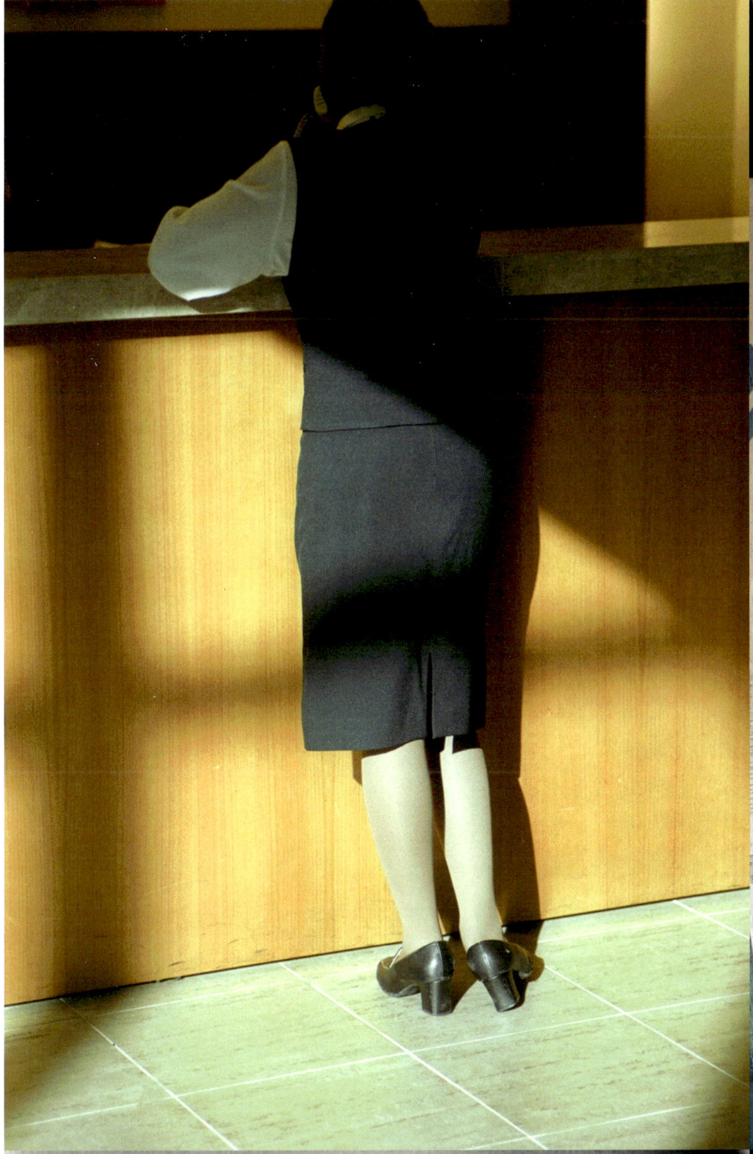
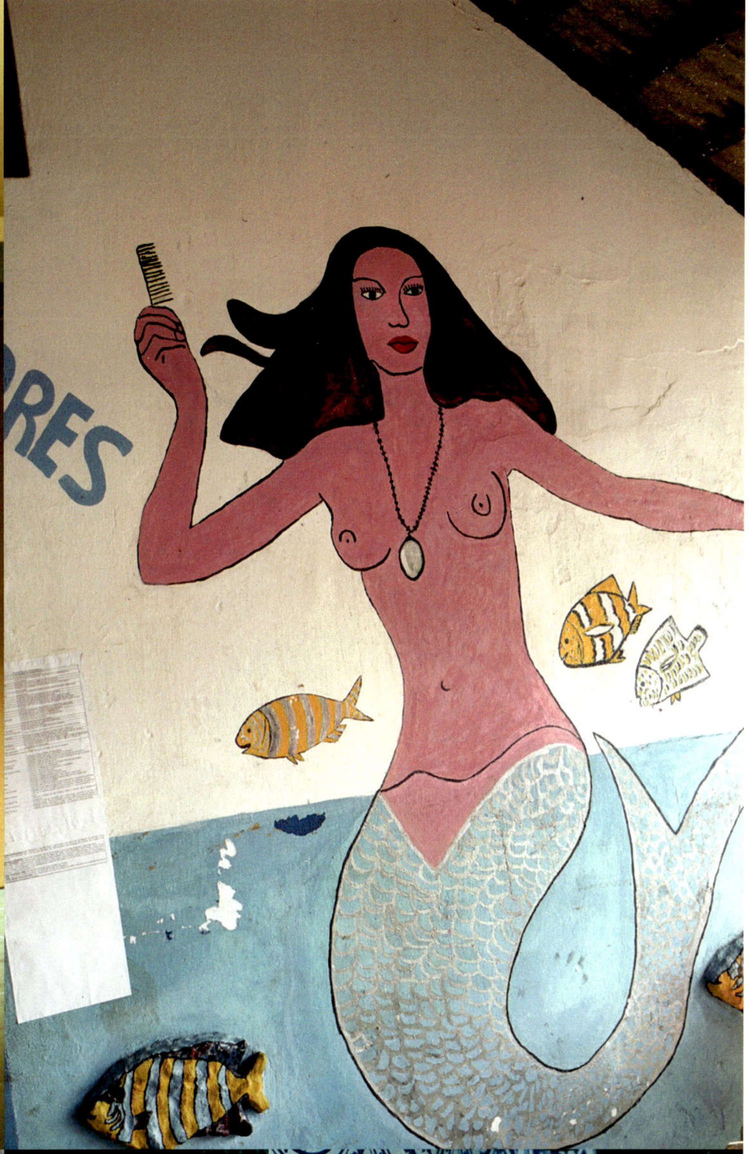
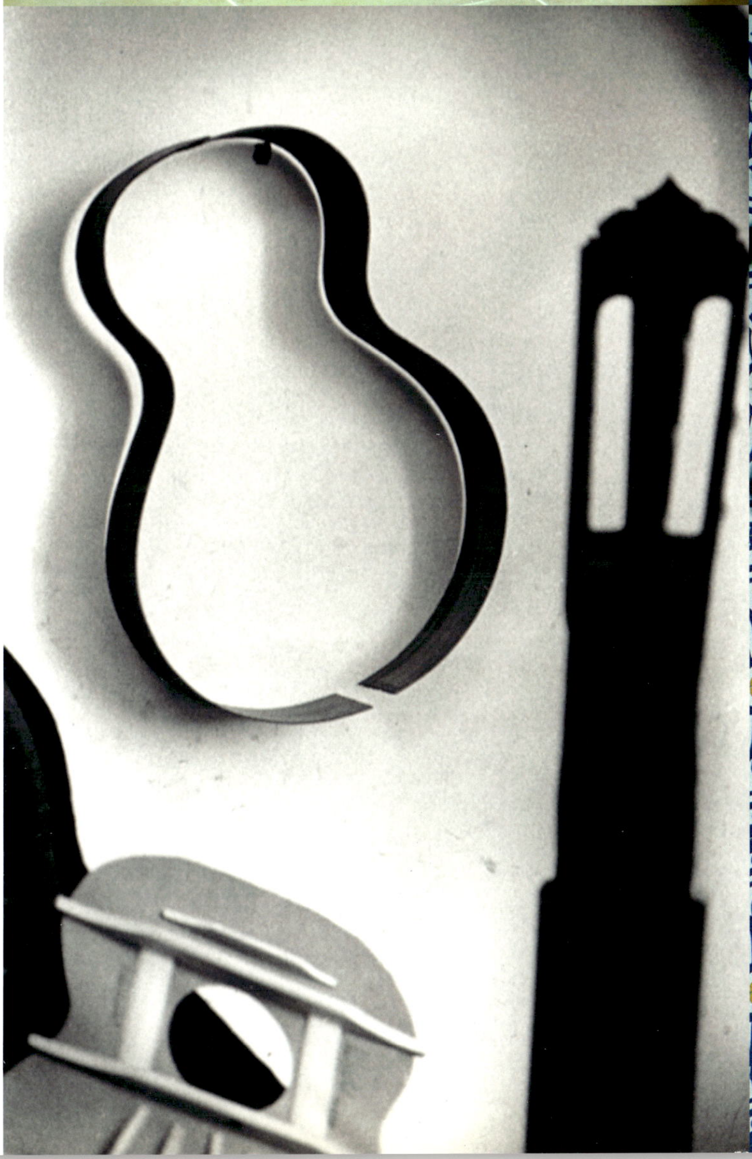
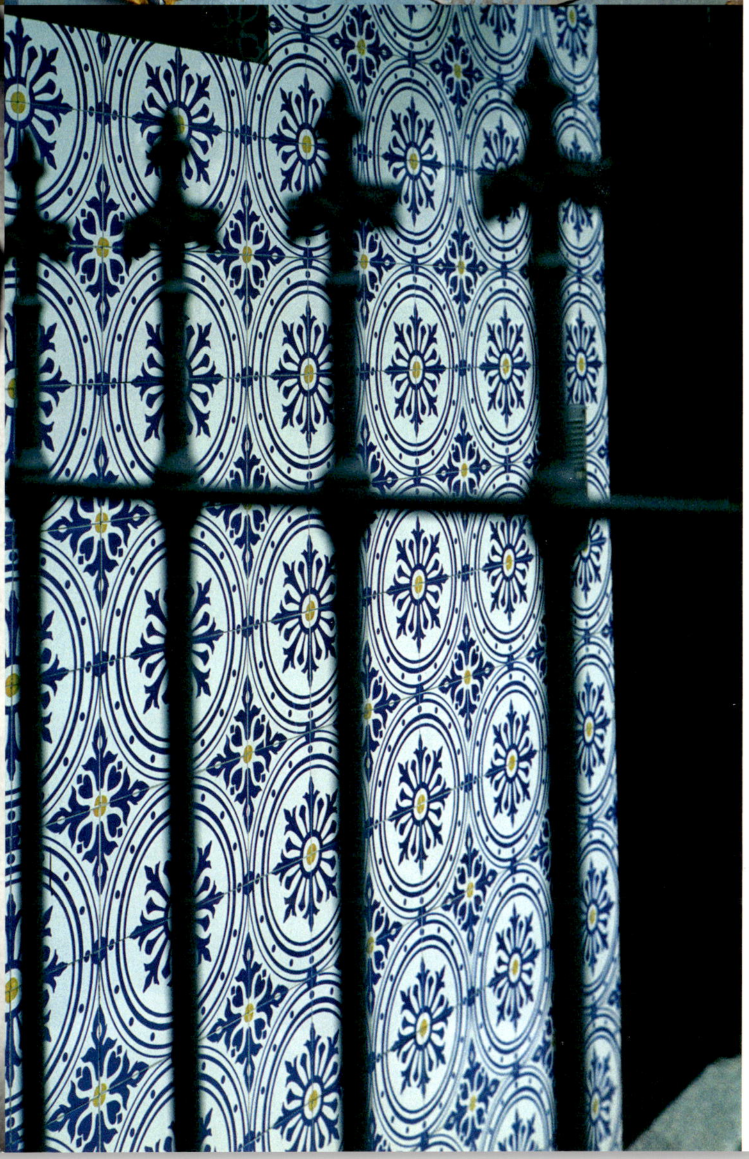

I wish to thank the many friends and associates who have helped realize this project. My intital inspiration comes from Mary Jane Marcasiano who lit the flame of desire to understand this wonderful country. Nessia Leonzini is the woman who is most Brazilian of all and she showed me what that means. Luiz Marinho of Leica Brasil made every effort to open the land and its customs. Caleb Cain Marcus prepared the the final scans and files. The architect Paolo Cermasi introduced me to the superb group at Damiani and I am certainly honored by this collaboration.

Obrigado a tudo...

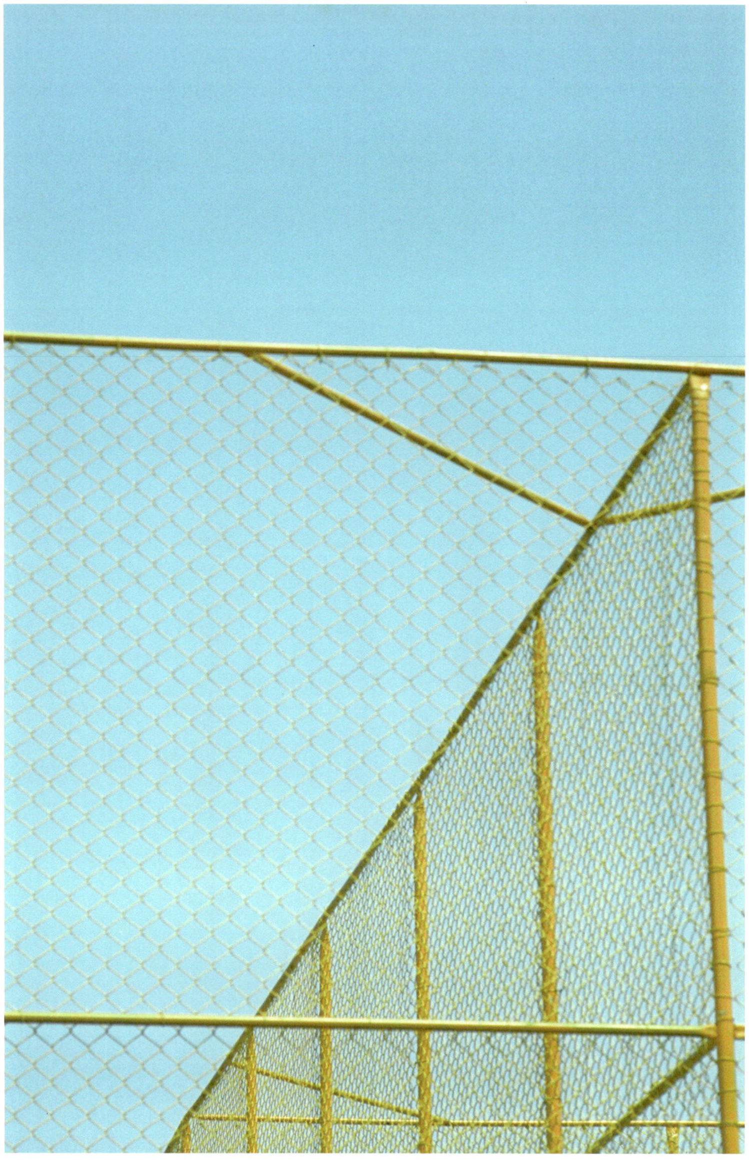

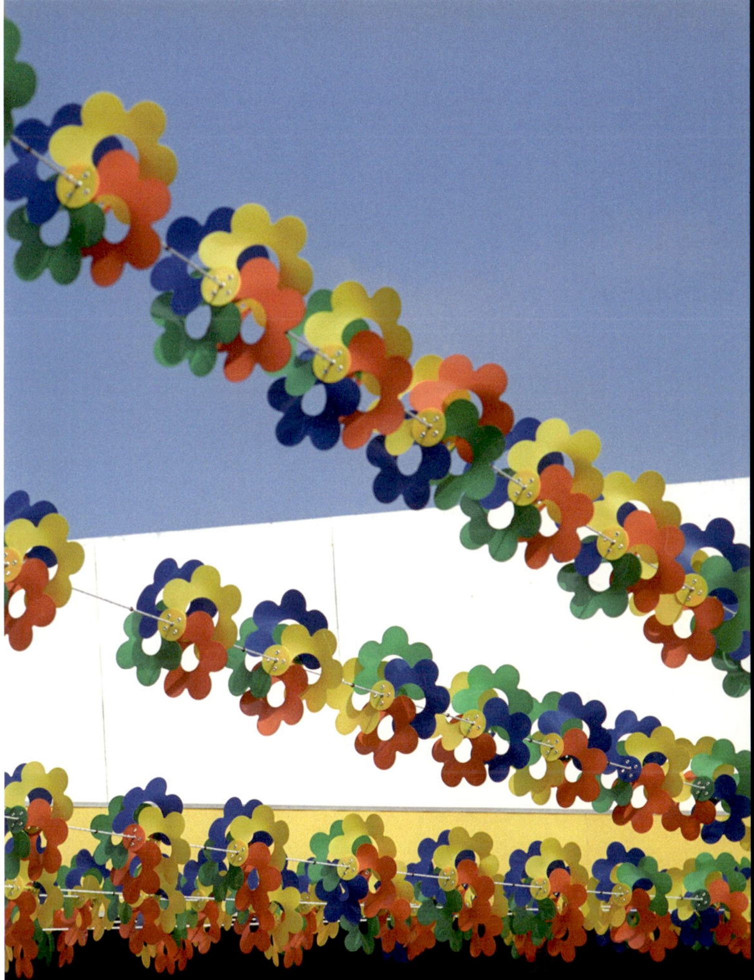
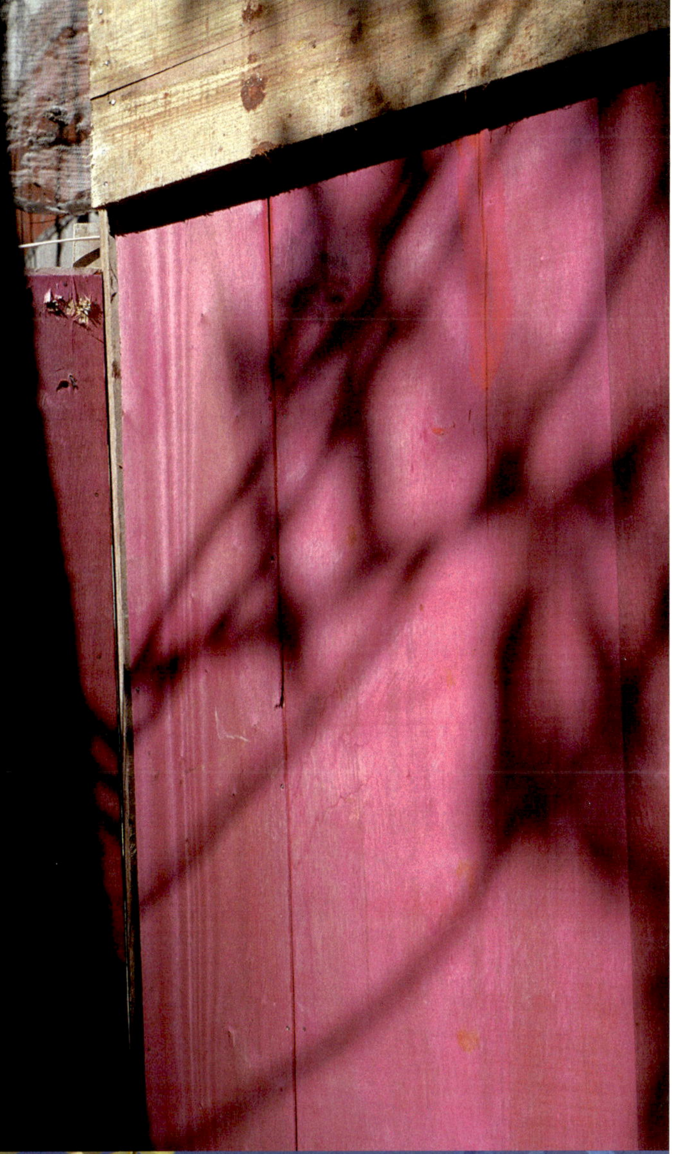
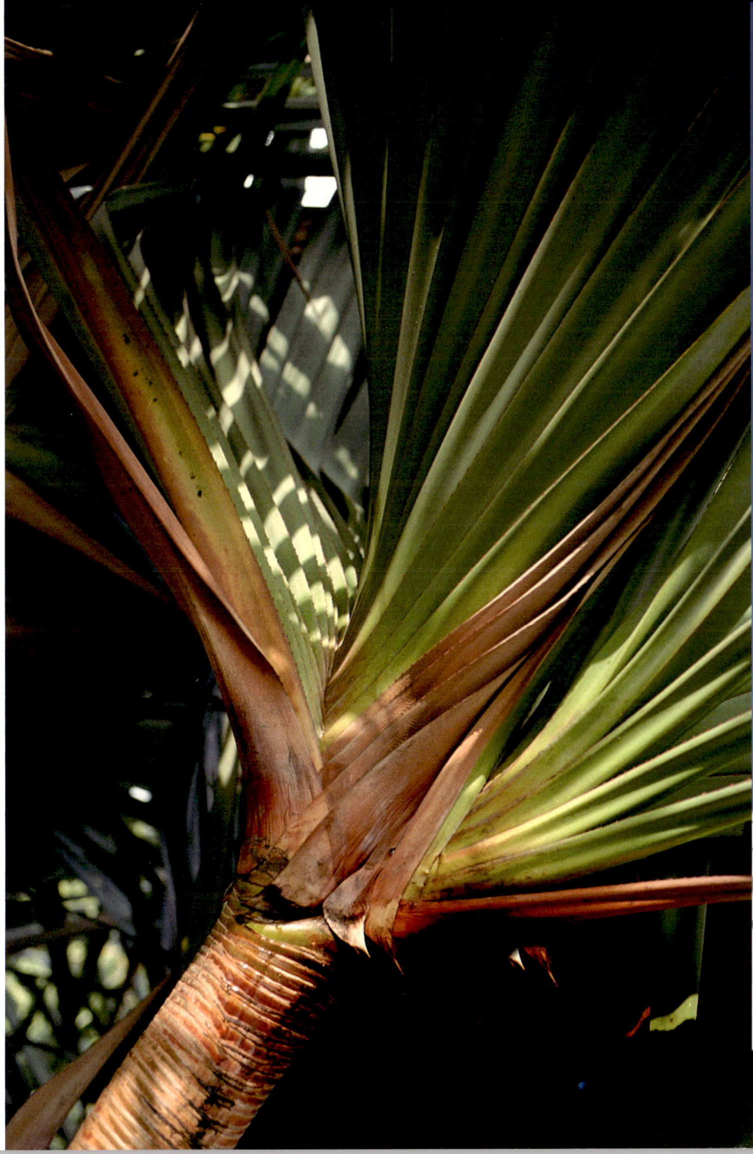
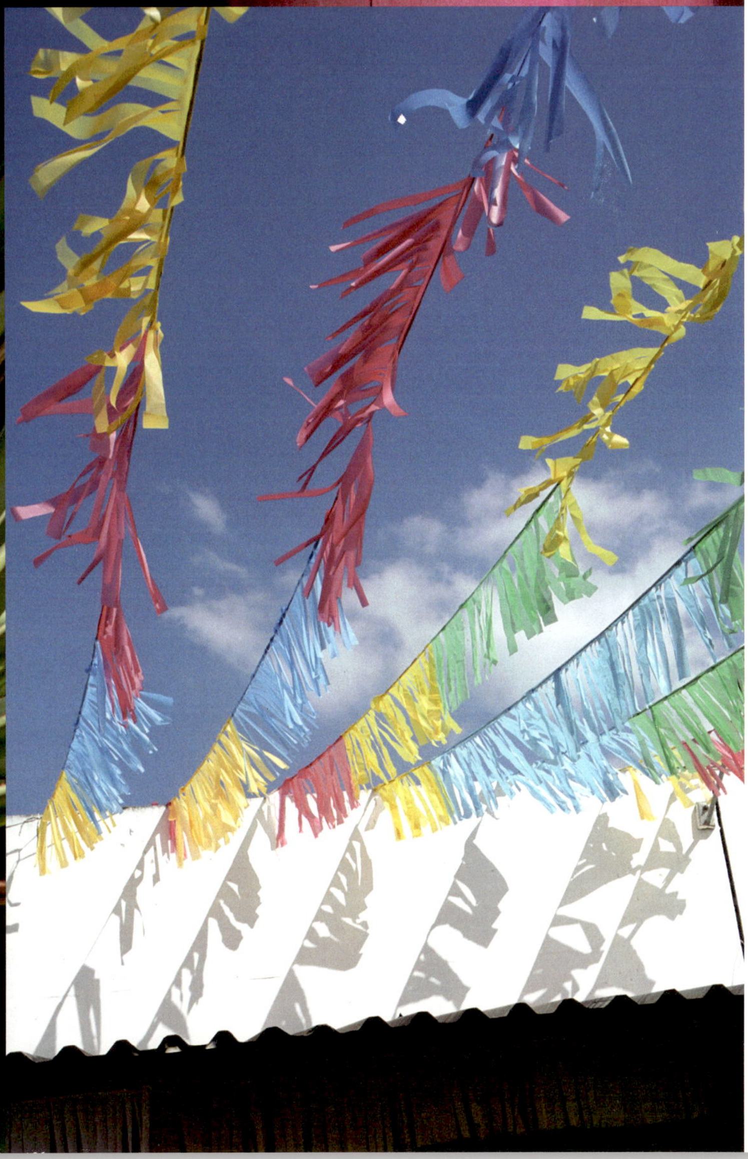

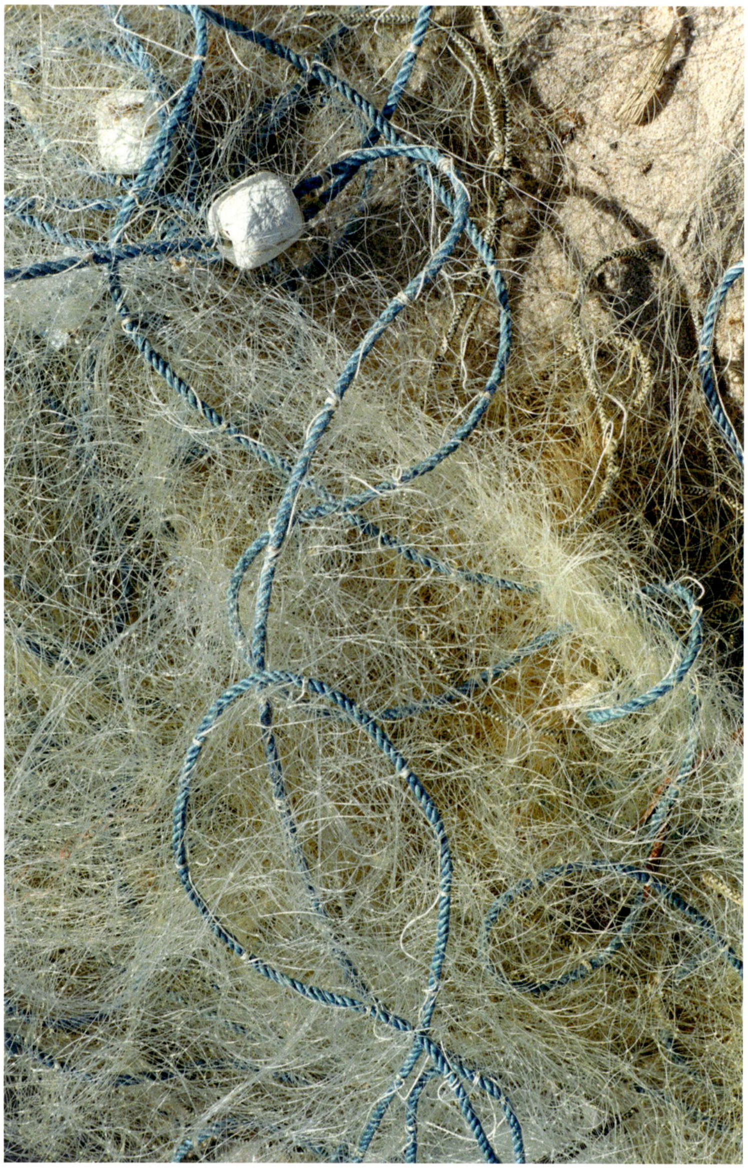

Printed in Italy, July 2005 by

Grafiche Damiani
www.grafichedamiani.it

Fondata nel 1961, IMA è oggi riconosciuta a livello mondiale come "Major Technology Provider" di sistemi di Processing & Packaging per l'industria Farmaceutica ed Alimentare nel segmento Tea & Coffee.

Founded in 1961, today IMA is renown world-wide as a Major Technology Provider of Processing & Packaging systems for the Pharmaceutical and Tea & Coffee segment of Food industries.

IMA
INDUSTRIA
MACCHINE
AUTOMATICHE

TEA, COFFEE & BEVERAGE DIVISION

IMA S.p.A.
Via Emilia, 428/442 - 40064 Ozzano Emilia (BO), Italy - Phone +39 051 6514111 - Fax +39 051 6514080 - mktg.tea@ima.it - www.ima.it